Earl Warren:
The Judge
Who Changed America

Books by Jack Harrison Pollack

Earl Warren: The Judge Who Changed America (1979)
Dr. Sam: An American Tragedy (1972)
Croiset, the Clairvoyant (1964)

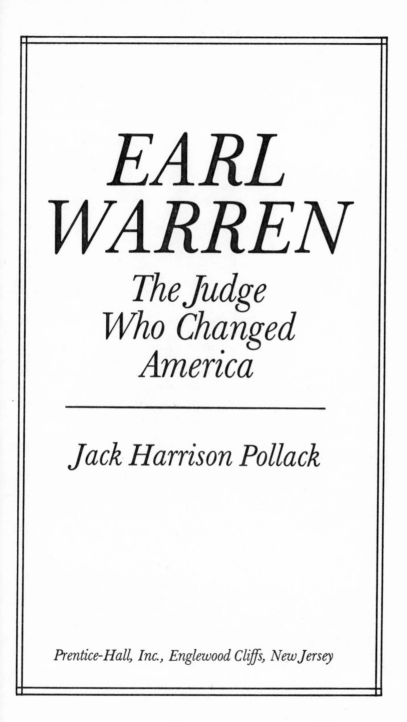

EARL WARREN

The Judge Who Changed America

Jack Harrison Pollack

Prentice-Hall, Inc., Englewood Cliffs, New Jersey

The author wishes to express his thanks for permission to quote from the works listed below:

American Bar Association Journal. Article by Earl Warren in issue of July 1973. Reprinted by permission.

Harvard Law Review. Cox, "Chief Justice Earl Warren," 83 *Harv. L. Rev.* 1, 3 (1969). Copyright © 1969 by the Harvard Law Review Association. Reprinted by permission.

Hastings Constitutional Law Quarterly. Excerpts by Robert J. Hoerner and Ralph J. Moore, Jr., from "Chief Justice Earl Warren: A Tribute," Winter 1975, Vol. 2 no. 1. Reprinted by permission.

New Republic. Article by Carey McWilliams in issue of October 18, 1943. Reprinted by permission.

Stanford Law Review. Spring 1978. Excerpt by Robert A Kagen, Bliss Cartwright, Lawrence M. Friedman and Stanton Wheeler. Reprinted by permission.

University of California Law Review. Article by Albert C. Wollenberg. Copyright © 1970, California Law Review, Inc. Reprinted by permission.

Inside U.S.A., by John Gunther (1947). Harper & Row, Publishers, Inc. Reprinted by permission.

Book Design: Joan Ann Jacobus
Art Director: Hal Siegel

Earl Warren: The Judge Who Changed America
by Jack Harrison Pollack
Copyright © 1979 by Jack Harrison Pollack

Printed in the United States of America
Prentice-Hall International, Inc., London/Prentice-Hall of Australia, Pty. Ltd., Sydney/ Prentice-Hall of Canada, Ltd., Toronto/Prentice-Hall of India Private Ltd., New Delhi/Prentice-Hall of Japan, Inc., Tokyo/Prentice-Hall of Southeast Asia Pte. Ltd., Singapore/Whitehall Books Limited, Wellington, New Zealand
10 9 8 7 6 5 4 3 2

Library of Congress Cataloging in Publication Data
Pollack, Jack Harrison.
    Earl Warren, the judge who changed America.
    Bibliography: p.
    Includes index.
    1. Warren, Earl, 1891–1974.   2. Judges—
United States—Biography.   I. Title.
KF8745.W3P64   347'.73'2634 [B]   78-24234
ISBN 0-13-222315-5

For
Margit, Queena & Joe

Prologue

*T*his is not an "official" or "authorized" biography; nor, despite all my efforts to be objective, is it a nonpartisan one. The truly objective biographer is perhaps yet to be born.

I have wanted to write this book for more than twenty years. Whenever I spoke to Earl Warren about it, he smiled and changed the subject. Yet once, when I showed him 117 pages of a first draft during his Chief Justiceship, Warren was cooperative and graciously made detailed handwritten corrections. In the end, I decided to delay the work, sensing that I needed to put more temporal and psychological distance between my subject and myself. After all, he lived three dominant professional lives: as a California governor, Supreme Court Chief Justice and Warren Commission chairman. In each, he was both praised for his independence and damned for his decisions.

I am glad that I waited. The passage of time has given me a deeper appreciation of *who* Warren really was and *what* he has meant to this nation. Even now, though, I do not claim to understand him fully. Nor do his incomplete, posthumously published memoirs illuminate him entirely. Some of the seemingly paradoxical and surprising aspects of his character and behavior that were so apparent during his lifetime remain no less cryptic today.

But I trust that this effort will enable both those who revered and those who reviled him to understand the man better.

Earl Warren, fourteenth Chief Justice of the United States (1953–69), has influenced our lives and those of our children possibly as much as any public figure during the past generation.

Not all of his countrymen agreed with his rulings on the Supreme Court center seat. For more than a decade, angry detractors demanded his impeachment—long before that call swirled about the head of former President Nixon (whom Warren detested for twenty-nine years). To many critics, Warren seemed to be forsaking the Republic for the blacks, desegregationists, criminals, Communists, aliens, atheists, free speechers, pornographers and other "enemies" of conservative, law-abiding, God-fearing White America.

Alabama Governor George Wallace once proclaimed: "Earl Warren doesn't have enough brains to try a chicken thief in my home county!" A millionaire Texas cattleman said: "He shoulda stayed in California as governor where they're all crazy anyhow!" No less than the eminent Judge Learned Hand, who long sat on the U.S. Court of Appeals in New York, privately referred to Chief Justice Warren as "that Swedish socialist sonofabitch!"

Moreover, many Americans who shared Warren's judicial philosophy criticized him for his role in the Warren Commission Report on President John F. Kennedy's assassination—probably the most disputed document of our era. Millions of words and dollars have been spent trying to disprove it. The report has been denounced by countless individuals throughout the world who never heard of the Warren Court.

In sharp contrast, a growing number of admirers claim that posterity will extol the late-blooming Warren for helping to rejuvenate the Bill of Rights and attempting to make the United States a more equitable land for the black schoolchild, the disenfranchised city and suburban voter, the penniless prisoner, the naturalized citizen—indeed, for all of us. In seeking to modernize the Constitution's noble yet vague language into a living document, this erstwhile upholder of the Establishment firmly championed the accused against the accusers, the governed against the governors, the underprivileged against the overprivileged. Warren himself in his final year privately claimed, "Everything that I ever did in my life that was worthwhile I caught hell for."

Three former Democratic Presidents of the United States—Truman, Kennedy and Johnson—enthusiastically hailed Republican Warren during their lifetimes. On the other hand, Republican

President Eisenhower grew increasingly disenchanted with the man whom he had appointed to lead the High Court, and Nixon had found him a thorn long before becoming Chief Executive. Today, in the Carter Era, some say that he subverted the Constitution and created an "Imperial Court," but enthusiasts insist that he already has proved to be a giant in American history.

Although millions of words have been written about him, Earl Warren remains, nonetheless, a comparatively unknown American. Who was this homespun man who—for good or ill—helped to change the face of America?

Contents

PART I

Chapter One

The Warren Paradox

In 1947 John Gunther, in his best-seller *Inside USA*, wrote:

> *Earl Warren . . . will never set the world on fire or even make it smoke; he has the limitations of all Americans of his type with little intellectual background, little genuine depth or coherent political philosophy; a man who has probably never bothered with an abstract thought twice in his life . . . no more a statesman in the European sense than Typhoid Mary is Einstein . . .*

Today, these remarks seem at best unperceptive. Yet three decades ago, most political observers would have tended to agree with Gunther's assessment of California Governor Warren. They probably would have continued to do so even in September 1953, when Warren was appointed to head the Supreme Court of the United States. For little that Warren had said or done in public until then seemed to indicate what he was soon to become.

To many, this constitutes the central mystery—the "paradox"—of Earl Warren. Was he, as has been suggested, one of those rare historical examples of a mediocrity almost magically transformed into a great man by the pressure of moral responsibility? Or had Warren always possessed hidden qualities of greatness to which his observers had been unaccountably blind? Was it Warren who changed—or merely our understanding of him?

The truth most likely lies somewhere in between. Indeed, one of the most fascinating aspects of Earl Warren's life is the way it reveals not only how a man ascends to greatness but also how contemporary pundits perceived—or failed to perceive—that ascent.

In terms of how Warren's contemporaries perceived him, it is ironic to remember that even up until 1955 he was persistently typecast as presidential timber. For a considerable time, Americans had sensed this potentiality in Warren almost to the exclusion of any other. No one ever had envisioned him as an ambassador or even a senator, let alone a judge. Certainly his important gubernatorial position in California—and hence, nationwide—politics contributed to this perception. There was something about his persona and the way he seemed to view himself that suggested he was ideally meant to occupy the highest office in government. As Anthony Lewis, then the Supreme Court correspondent for *The New York Times,* put it, Warren was "a man born to act, not to muse, and very likely a man born to govern." Was his mind more executive than judicial? Were his talents more administrative than legal? Was he better equipped to be Chief Executive than Chief Justice? Was he The President Who Never Was?

Certainly he possessed all the physical assets, mannerisms and instincts necessary for the highest success in politics. A six-foot, 215-pound chunk of man, with guileless blue eyes and an open expression, he wore wide-lapeled, double-breasted suits bought off the rack and usually blue in color, with maroon ties and overlarge silver cuff links. His total appearance was as avuncular, stolid and reassuring as any image ever devised by Norman Rockwell.

With his muscular handshake and contagious smile, Warren would invariably greet anyone who seemed a potential voter with a hearty "How are ya? Glad to see ya." If his sixth sense told him that the person was someone whose name he should have remembered, he would immediately follow with "How's the family?" The answer generally provided the necessary clue, for Warren had a well-cultivated politician's memory.

He was more good-humored than witty. (As his friend Adlai Stevenson sadly learned, wit is not always a political asset.) Yet Warren was capable of rising genially to an occasion. Once in 1949, Ronald Reagan recalls, Governor Warren was the scheduled speaker of honor at a banquet in a Los Angeles hotel. Because the earlier speakers had been so verbose, Warren was not introduced until nearly midnight. He began by saying, "I am delighted to have been invited to have come here yesterday to speak today." Hardly memorable, but appropriate and, like most things the political Warren said, well-received.

Prior to 1953, many left-of-center critics sneered at Warren as a "square," an "archetypical Boy Scout," "another Herbert Hoover." Nonetheless, he was what the majority of California voters wanted. Enormously popular, he was that key state's only three-term (1942–53), scandal-free governor, presiding over the era of its greatest growth. This, in turn, inevitably made him a force in presidential politics.

That Warren, at one important period of his life, would have wanted to be President there can be little doubt. "Any man," he told me in 1951 in his gubernatorial office in Sacramento, "is a cynical fathead if he belittles the Presidency by saying he would refuse the nomination when nobody's offering it to him." But there is a vast difference between accepting a nomination and winning it. For all his aspiration and ability, Warren seems not to have been temperamentally disposed to that obsessive, single-minded pursuit of victory that tends to be the hallmark of a successful presidential candidate. Still, he came remarkably close.

Franklin Roosevelt was among the first to recognize Warren's potential for winning a Republican presidential nomination. The canny FDR had observed and been impressed by the size and style of Warren's first upset California gubernatorial victory in 1942. But the two men were destined never to challenge one another directly. In 1944, New York Governor Thomas E. Dewey emerged as the Republican presidential nominee and Governor Warren declined to be his running mate. Even more significant than his distaste for Dewey was Warren's realistic decision that Commander-in-Chief Roosevelt was unbeatable in wartime America, even for a fourth term. Instead, Warren kept a low profile, contenting himself with being the Republican convention's temporary chairman and keynote speaker. Neither then nor later was the cautious Californian desirous of engaging in uphill fights for election—a characteristic that later would mislead many into believing that he likewise would be loath to take unpopular stands.

In 1948 the political situation was different. It seemed highly probable that Dewey would defeat President Harry S. Truman.

Hence, despite Warren's misgivings about Dewey, he reluctantly acceded to GOP pressure to be the New York governor's running mate. But by the time Dewey's overconfident campaign was in its final stages, Warren already had concluded that he had gone astray. He was less surprised than most by Truman's "Election Day Miracle" and certainly less personally disappointed than many of his Republican cohorts. "If I had been elected Vice President," he told me years later, "I suppose I'd have been just another minor cog in the Establishment." Ironically, it was always Truman's view that had the Republican ticket been reversed, with Warren the presidential nominee, the Republicans might well have won.

Unlike 1944 and 1948, 1952 was the year that Warren truly wanted the Republican presidential nomination. If Richard Nixon, the junior senator from California, had not deviously deserted him for Eisenhower, or if Senator Taft had succeeded in deadlocking the embattled convention forces, Warren might well have been the party's compromise choice. But these are large "ifs." In any event, the Warren candidacy never really took off, and Eisenhower and Nixon won the prizes. Yet Warren's brief dark-horse campaign—in which he was never overinsistent about his candidacy—contained some novel and possibly significant features. For example, then Senator Margaret Chase Smith, from Maine and one of Senator Joseph McCarthy's bitterest foes, later recalled that Warren publicly stated that he would be happy to have her as his running mate. In the America of 1952, that pledge required courage on more than one count—another latent clue of the Warren-to-be.

In keeping with the tentative way that Warren had pursued the presidential nomination, he came closest to achieving it when he least wanted it! Yet his demonstrated vote-getting potential worried the ambitious new Vice President. Nixon, accordingly, badgered Eisenhower to find a suitable appointment for Governor Warren which would effectively separate him from his electoral constituency. The ideal solution presented itself in September 1953, when a vacancy arose on the Supreme Court after Chief Justice Fred Vinson suddenly died. Warren, who already had decided not to seek a fourth term as governor, was offered the prized seat and, to Nixon's delight, accepted.

Yet the matter did not quite end there. In early 1955, a year and a half after Warren had ascended to the Court, considerable doubt was voiced over Eisenhower's desire to seek reelection. In the spring air along the Potomac, the political birds again began to warble their song of Warren-for-President. Victory-hungry Republicans argued that should Ike not run again, Warren this time would not be able to remove himself from the presidential sweepstakes. He could, they hopefully believed, be "drafted."

On April 13, a Gallup Poll reported that if Eisenhower declined to seek a second term, Warren was the Number One choice among Republican and Independent voters to succeed him (he led Nixon three to one). Yet the next day, the sixty-four-year-old Chief Justice released a statement which dashed the hopes of his supporters. It said, in part: "When I accepted [the position of Chief Justice] it was with the fixed intention of leaving politics permanently for the service of the Court. That is still my purpose. It is irrevocable." And when someone predicted that, come Inauguration Day, 1957, it would be Warren standing on the Capitol steps, he just grinned and said, "Sure, swearing in the President."

On this point he remained firm, turning aside with easygoing inflexibility the blandishments of those who sought to persuade him to change his mind. Over tea at New York's Idlewild Airport in July 1955, just before his departure for a trip to Scandinavia, he answered my urgings that he reconsider running for President with a smile and the comment, "Why on earth should I want to run to save the country from my friend Adlai Stevenson?" The idealistic if naïve Stevenson wistfully remarked to Agnes Meyer, wife of the *Washington Post* publisher and close friend to both himself and Warren, that he would prefer to run against the Chief Justice than Nixon in 1956 because then whoever won, at least the republic would be secure.

But other Democrats were more fearful. *New York Times* columnist James Reston reported in November 1955 that a possible Warren candidacy "terrifies them." Alabama Senator John Sparkman, the 1952 vice presidential nominee, conceded: "I think Chief Justice Warren would offer the stiffest competition." Georgia Senator Richard B. Russell, who nine years later would serve on the Warren Commission, flatly predicted in October that Warren definitely would be the Republican nominee and needled him for having visited that summer "several European countries with large minority populations in the United States."

Still, Warren's refusal to permit himself to be considered for the presidency in 1955 was in no way an act of necessity: William

Howard Taft was both President and Chief Justice. Nor is there anything that formally prohibits a sitting Supreme Court Justice from seeking high political office, and many have done so. Indeed, our very first Chief Justice, John Jay, resigned from the Court to run for (and become) governor of New York, doubtless in the hope that this would put him in line for a presidential nomination. Associate Justice John McLean, known as "The Politician on the Supreme Court," constantly had his eye on the White House, offering himself as a presidential candidate four times between 1832 and 1856. Chief Justice Salmon Chase attempted to run for President in 1868 and 1872. Justice Charles Evans Hughes actually won the Republican nomination and narrowly missed defeating Woodrow Wilson in 1916. And but for the opposition of Democratic Party Chairman Robert S. Hannegan, Franklin Roosevelt probably would have chosen Justice William O. Douglas as his running mate in 1944, thus assuring that Douglas, rather than Harry Truman, would have been our thirty-third President.

Yet perhaps Warren found the example of Chief Justice Morrison R. Waite more compelling. A year after having been appointed to the Court by President Grant, Waite was urged to run for the presidency by his nephew, a Connecticut congressman. In reply he wrote:

> *In these days of politico-judicial questions, it is dangerous to have a judge who thinks beyond the judicial in his personal ambitions. The Court is now looked upon as the sheet-anchor. Will it be if its Chief Justice is placed in the political whirlpool? The office has come down to me covered with honor. When I accepted it, my duty was not to make it a stepping stone to something else, but to preserve its purity and make my own name as honorable, if possible, as my predecessors'.*

A more mundane explanation of Warren's refusal to be considered might, of course, simply be the fact that there had never been any reason to assume that Eisenhower would *not* run again. But all that changed on September 24, 1955, when the President suffered his first heart attack. Overnight, the Warren-for-President boom resounded again, and the polls reaffirmed that not only was he the strongest potential Republican candidate after Eisenhower, but also that Warren could defeat any likely Democratic nominee by at least 6 percent of the popular vote.

Two Supreme Court Justices privately told friends in the Senate that they believed their Chief would agree to run for the presidency if Ike definitely asked him to do so. But failing that, and even without any further signs from Warren, most experienced observers in both parties confidently believed that if Eisenhower were to step down, become incapacitated or die, a draft-Warren movement would inevitably erupt at the nominating convention in August. And it might have been difficult for Warren to resist such a spontaneous draft as a matter of patriotic duty, particularly if, as some proposed, he were offered Milton Eisenhower, the President's brother, as a running mate. It would likewise have been difficult for him to decline, for more personal reasons, if he thought that the alternative would be the nomination of Nixon (whose most vocal supporter now was Dewey).

Warren's distrust of Nixon was long-standing and ill-disguised. Since both men came from the same state, there could be no question of a Warren-Nixon ticket, if only because constitutionally this was open to question. Moreover, Warren's feelings were so intense that he might have been prompted to act to prevent Nixon's being on *any* ticket. In January 1956, Oscar Jahnsen, a thirty-year Warren aide, told me, "Earl will run for President rather than see Nixon in the White House. He indicated this to me very clearly at Christmas." Nixon's popularity at this time, though, as he candidly admitted in his 1962 book, *Six Crises*, was not such that he entertained very high hopes of being offered the nomination.

Indeed, the question of who would get the nomination still lay largely in Eisenhower's hands. Even if he did not run, his political prestige was so enormous that he could virtually compel the party to accept his choice. Although it would have been unthinkable later, in 1956 Eisenhower might very well have chosen Warren. Nixon, in *Six Crises,* describes a conversation with the ailing President in which Eisenhower expressed disappointment that Warren had been so outspoken in refusing to be a candidate. "I don't see why he couldn't just have said nothing," Eisenhower complained, adding that Warren owed it to the party to keep himself available. Despite Warren's role in the previous year's desegregation decision, Ike still seemingly perceived him as a decent man, essentially one like

himself: middle-of-the-road, conscientious, affable, basically conciliatory, yet capable of being tough in the face of outrage. In a word,
safe.

Many were convinced that the President would eventually ask
Warren to run. However, as Eisenhower's strength returned, his
thoughts increasingly veered away from the designation of a successor and toward the expectation of his own candidacy. Significantly, Eisenhower's press secretary, James C. Hagerty, noted in his
diary on December 15, 1955, that the President had remarked:
"Earl is one of the fellows who needs time to make decisions and his
present spot is the best possible spot for him."

A little over a month later, at a White House news conference,
the President vaguely remarked that, in his opinion, it was not
seemly for Chief Justices to be too much involved in politics. When
asked if this meant that he would be opposed to a Warren candidacy, the President replied, in one of those masterpieces of confusion for which he was justly famous: "Opposed? For goodness
sake! I appointed him as Chief Justice of the United States and there
is no office in the world that I respect more. Of course, I admire and
respect and have a deep affection for Mr. Warren. What I did—I was
trying to say—he made a statement in which he argued for the
complete separation of the judiciary and politics, and I was supporting him in his views. Now, there are many ways in which he *could*
be a candidate, and if he were, he would have no opposition from
me."

Newsmen, skilled at extracting meaning from Ike's circuitous
prose, interpreted this as an ominous portent for a Warren candidacy. In less than a month though, the President announced his
intention to run again, and Warren's career as a national politician at
last had ended.

Two years later, it was revived momentarily when Walter
Reuther, head of the United Automobile Workers Union, who
dreaded a 1960 Nixon candidacy, suggested in an October 1958
television interview that labor would be happy to support a Warren
presidential bid. Immediately, eager-beaver backers of Nelson
Rockefeller, a would-be GOP nominee, got into the Warren act by
proclaiming that the New York governor would be delighted to
accept the Chief Justice as a running mate. But the now truly
embarrassed Warren, who was having his own difficulties with
President Eisenhower at the time, did not take seriously this armchair speculation—nor did anyone else.

Would he have been a good President? Probably. He would have been a wise Mr. Honest, and not in the sanctimonious manner of Jimmy Carter. He had a broader, less partisan vision than Ford; he was more principled than Nixon; less devious and arrogant than Johnson; more experienced and mature than Kennedy; more of an activist than Eisenhower; less impulsive than Truman.

By the same token, he may also have lacked some of the virtues indigenous to each of these men. Certainly Warren had his flaws. Even his partisans conceded that he was not a man who acted swiftly. Deliberate and methodical, he was fond of quoting Lincoln: "I'm a slow walker, but I never walk backward." Yet he would almost certainly have been a strong leader. Once convinced that he understood what course of action was "right," he was dogged and utterly courageous in pursuing it—a quality to which his entire career as Chief Justice bears witness. His easygoing manner masked a strong resolve. He saw the Oval Office as a place of leadership, as exemplified by both Roosevelts, not one of mere stewardship, as treated by an Eisenhower or a Taft.

Retired Justice William O. Douglas wrote me in May 1977: "I think Earl Warren would have made an excellent President. He might have been both President and Chief Justice. Taft filled both seats and Warren was an abler man than Taft . . . He [Warren] and I talked about it in later years and I always mentioned that he should have been President. All he would do is smile. What his real sentiments were I don't know."

Earlier, Justice Hugo L. Black, according to the *Richmond News Leader,* opined: "The smartest thing these reactionaries ever did from their point of view was to shunt the Chief off onto this Court. Not that he has not been great here. But the Chief could have gone all the way. He's one of the greatest vote-getters ever. What a President he would have made. They could never have gotten him out—anti-third term statute and all—until he was ready to go."

Banning E. (Bert) Whittington, the Supreme Court's press officer during Warren's sixteen-year tenure, recently said: "If Eisenhower had *really* asked Warren to resign to run for President, I think he would have considered it his patriotic duty to do so, just as Lyndon Johnson persuaded him to accept the Warren Commission chairmanship. Warren would have made a great President, too. His ability to identify with all types of people would have given him a truly broad view of the office. He was as comfortable with secretaries, gardeners, barbers and elevator operators as with Presidents and

Justices. The Chief Justice's human antennae enabled him to see quickly the big important issues."

These views are at variance with John Gunther's final summation of Warren in 1947: "... quite possibly, and with luck, [he] could make a tolerable president of the United States."

But another detractor, Carey McWilliams, retired editor of *The Nation* and a Warren-watcher for more than three decades, now concedes: "Warren would have been a greater President than Chief Justice. All the political skills that he brought to the Supreme Court, including the handling of the Justices of such diverse viewpoints with such finesse, would have served him and the nation well in the White House. He was a great politician on the Court."

But to theorize from the vantage point of the late 1970s about Warren's qualifications for the presidency during the 1950s is superficial. We can now say that he probably would have made a good President if we already believe that he was a great Chief Justice. Yet no such easy knowledge was available in 1955 or earlier. Then, the dominant perception of Warren was simply that of a popular, conservative, middle-of-the-road politician whose philosophy seemed to be expressed primarily through the medium of clichés and whose aspirations were hardly distinguishable from those of any other high-level political office-seeker.

This, of course, is the heart of the Warren paradox. Eisenhower had appointed him to the Chief Justiceship largely because the President believed him to be a high-level mediocrity. Everything about Warren seemed to indicate that his role on the Court would be that of an unimaginative moderate-conservative conformist. His loyalty to the President and the Republican party, together with his politician's instinct for trying to be all things to all men, would surely prevent him from doing anything likely to cause problems for the Administration. Moreover, the composition of the Court itself would tend to hold him in line. Only two of his eight fellow Justices were avowed liberals; three were moderates (like Warren, Eisenhower must have assumed), and three were strongly conservative.

In the beginning, Warren's Court performance conformed perfectly to the general expectation: He voted with the conservatives and showed a marked inclination to be tough on criminals, Communists and aliens. Then, with the desegregation decision of May 1954, the astonishing reversal began. Liberals and conservatives alike were stunned; the embarrassed President was enraged. Gentle, soft-spoken Earl Warren was not only beginning to behave like a "radical-activist liberal," but was doing so with such apparent disregard for the social and political consequences of his actions that he was throwing the nation into turmoil.

There is, of course, nothing extraordinary about a man becoming more liberal as he grows older, although this is not the usual sequence. But Warren's liberalism—if, indeed, that is the proper word—had a unique quality. It was in no sense doctrinaire, and occasionally even seemed at variance with some of his private inclinations. Nor was it all-inclusive: On a number of issues, such as obscenity, Warren's positions continued to be either obscure or downright conservative. However, in confronting those problems about which he cared the most, he demonstrated a single-minded intensity of commitment which his admirers found thrillingly courageous and his enemies, reckless and obtuse.

As Chief Justice, Warren changed American profoundly—more, probably, than he would have if he had been President.

I once made the mistake of writing in a draft for a magazine profile of Warren that "the Supreme Court has always been the dream of lawyer Earl Warren's career." Warren struck out the sentence. It simply wasn't true, he said. Far from dreaming of the Court, he had never even considered it. If anything, he had dreamed of being President. Only when the Court appointment was offered to him did he apparently realize that it was something he wanted—wanted enough to sacrifice most of his political ambitions for, just as Nixon had hoped he would.

The two decisions, first to accept the Supreme Court appointment and, later, to disavow the Warren-for-President movement must have posed deep dilemmas for Earl Warren. What passed through his mind as he pondered the Chief Justiceship? Did it suddenly occur to him that on the High Court he might find his true vocation, or was it merely the best available option for a three-term governor who did not want to risk running for a fourth term? Was the Court merely a place to mark time while planning his next political moves, or did he sense that his acceptance would be a commitment to something deeper?

Similarly, in 1955, when Warren wrote that he would not leave the Court "under any conditions or circumstances," was he confirming his commitment, or was he simply making the conventional political noises of a presidential aspirant reluctant to have his candidacy peak too soon? Only a clear Eisenhower endorsement could have persuaded Warren to run in 1956, most observers agree. Yet it is entirely possible that by that time not even President Eisenhower could have made him change his mind.

The simple answers to these questions would help unravel the paradox of Earl Warren. Was he a truly great man or merely a conspicuous one? Did he bring greatness to his time or was it the time that conferred greatness upon him? Were his early observers deceived by equating his lack of eloquence and charisma with an absence of imagination and dedication? What turned this skilled politician into what many regard as a judicial statesman?

The Warren paradox may be rooted in his nurturing. California, which cradled this unpredictable—even inscrutable—figure, is a monstrously large state of great paradoxes itself: the redwoods of the cool north stand in contrast to the palm trees in the southern desert; cosmopolitan, well-groomed, foggy San Francisco and provincial, casual, sunny-smoggy Los Angeles are diametrically different worlds. It is unlikely that such a contradictory character and enigmatic phenomenon as Earl Warren could have come out of any other state which produced both an Upton Sinclair yesterday and a Howard Jarvis today.

As a rule, leaders are more accurately assessed by their deeds than by their personalities. The exception is the moral leader; and that, for good or ill, is what Warren ultimately became. Thus, in order to judge Earl Warren we must first try to know him, try to unearth in the record of a seemingly unremarkable man who lived a remarkable life the insights and foreshadowing that will enable us to understand his unique significance.

PART II

Chapter Two

The Early Years 1891–1932

*T*he fourteenth Chief Justice of the United States was christened simply Earl Warren, though newspapers later gave him a fictitious middle initial of *C* or *J*. "My parents were too poor to afford the luxury of a middle name," he once joked.

The man whom fellow politicians would often call "the Stubborn Swede" sprang from sturdy Scandinavian immigrant stock. His family name was originally Varran, but it was anglicized by his paternal uncle, a carpenter, in 1865 when Iowa farm neighbors had difficulty pronouncing the *V*. Perhaps his Viking genes may in part explain Earl Warren's future venturesome spirit.

Both of his parents were born in Scandinavia and were brought as young children to America, where their families settled in the Middle West; the New World seemed to offer greater reward to their farming skills than their rigorous native landscape had. Earl's father, Erik Methias (Matt) Varran, was born in Haugesund, a small village near Stavanger, Norway, an important seaport and fishing center. His mother, Chrystal (née Christine—a name that she never liked) Hernlund, came from Halsingland, a rural, mountainous province on the coast, two hundred miles north of Stockholm, boasting great forests, rivers and paper mills.

A tall, sinewy man with a curled barbershop moustache, Methias Warren had been brought to tiny Eagle Grove, Iowa, shortly after the Civil War. When he was four his mother died, and three years later he moved in with a neighboring family, toiling on their meager farm in exchange for his room and board. Though heavy farm duties prevented him from studying beyond the seventh grade of a one-room prairie elementary school, he did manage to attend it faithfully during winters when the rich Iowa soil was locked in by snow.

In their teens, Methias and his brother, Ole, two years older, left Iowa to roam the Middle West. At first the youths toiled in the fields but later they sought factory work. Within a few years Methias and his brother were destitute in Chicago, desperately searching for employment while trying to survive in an unheated, flea-infested room. Ole developed tuberculosis. The young men had no money for food, much less for a doctor, medicines or a hospital. Methias tried to nurse Ole himself, but on Christmas Eve his brother, exhausted by malnutrition, died in his arms. For the rest of his life Methias was convinced that if his brother could have afforded medical care that fate could have been averted. Many times afterward he said to his only son: "Earl, don't ever let yourself be caught broke."

Methias drifted to Minneapolis, where he finally secured a factory job. There, he met Chrystal Hernlund, whose own Swedish immigrant family had moved there from Chicago after all their belongings had been destroyed in the great fire of 1871. Chrystal was a quiet, pretty girl of eighteen with tightly drawn brown curls and small forehead bangs. She and Methias were married and a year later, in 1887, their first child, Ethel, was born.

Because of his own delicate health and the memory of his brother's death in the cold Chicago room, Methias Warren decided to move his family to the warm climate of Southern California. Their first stop was San Diego. Unable to find the mechanic's job that he sought, he moved a hundred and twenty miles north to Los Angeles, then a city of 50,000 persons. There, Methias was hired by the Southern Pacific Railroad as a repairman at a salary of seventy dollars a month.

The Warrens rented an unpretentious frame cottage with five small rooms at 457 Turner Street, near the railroad depot where Methias worked. Happily, their new home on this dingy, unpaved street had a white picket fence, some trees and a yard where Chrystal

Warren planted flowers. Nearby was the Mexican settlement on historic Olivera Street, the City of the Angels' oldest thoroughfare, where tolerance and tamales prevailed.

It was at the Turner Street house, with a midwife's assistance, that Methias and Chrystal Warren's only other child was born, on March 19, 1891—a blond, blue-eyed, healthy male of unrecorded weight whom they named Earl. The name means "Chief" or "Nobleman" in Anglo-Saxon.

That year a new Los Angeles law had been passed requiring that all newborn children be issued birth certificates. However, the midwife who recorded the birth of the newest Warren child was something less than a legal scholar. She recorded Earl simply as an unnamed male born of "Warn, M." and "F. Warn." Sixty years later, when the Governor of California applied for his first passport, he was obliged to file a correcting affidavit—accompanied by his sister Ethel's corroboration—finally setting the record straight in the Los Angeles Bureau of Vital Statistics.

Methias and Chrystal Warren deliberately spoke only English to their children. Father Warren was determined that his two children should secure the education that he lacked, reasoning that knowledge was power in this new land of opportunity. When Earl was three, Methias moved his family into a rented bungalow on Ann Street, just across from a school. Earl, of course, was too young to attend, but his seven-year-old sister occasionally brought him along with her, and the teacher permitted the tow-haired preschooler to sit quietly in the back of the classroom and listen. By that time his father had already taught him to memorize the names of the forty-four states and their capitals.

Matt Warren, as he was now called by fellow workers, had joined a union, together with most of the Southern Pacific employees, after paying his dollar initiation fee. It was the American Railway Union, founded by Eugene V. Debs in 1893, forty years before the nation's first great (all-white) industrial union, the Congress of Industrial Organizations (CIO) was launched. It included *all* railway workers from trackwalkers to skilled car repairmen such as Methias now had become. Railway management flatly refused to bargain with or even recognize this industrial union, preferring to deal with old craft unions they could control, such as the Brotherhood of Locomotive Firemen from which Debs had resigned as national secretary. The fiery Debs called a nationwide railroad strike in 1894, for recognition and better working conditions. Methias joined the strike, not out of profound labor or Socialist convictions, but simply because of loyalty to his fellow workers. The bitter strike lasted three months.

One morning, four-year-old Earl, who was playing outside his home, observed a group of angry strikers dragging a straw-stuffed effigy of the railroad manager through the street. They strung it up, hung it by the neck and tied it to the top of the flagpole while making a large bonfire in the schoolyard. The small boy ran into the house in terror. His mother comforted him in her arms—so goes a fond family story—explaining that it was merely a big straw doll, not a human being. Yet the memory of this simulated lynching disturbed the sensitive mind of the youngster who, decades later, would himself become the object of would-be lynchers. The boy who grew up to prefer reason to violence later told me: "This childhood incident always made me hate mob action."

The nationwide strike was eventually crushed by federal troops ordered by President Grover Cleveland, with the U.S. Supreme Court in 1895 upholding the government's right to use such force in interstate commerce. Debs was imprisoned for six months, becoming a martyr for his principles. Methias Warren and other strikers not only lost their jobs but were promptly blacklisted by the Southern Pacific and most other large Los Angeles area employers. Since there were at that time no union strike benefits or unemployment insurance, Matt was compelled to leave his family temporarily to work for the competitive Santa Fe Railroad at odd jobs in the burning Mojave Desert. A frugal man, he was able to send home most of his earnings. When he heard that the Southern Pacific was moving its repair yards from northern Tulare down to Bakersfield, a hot, dusty, lawless frontier town 110 miles north of Los Angeles in the San Joaquin Valley, and had an urgent need for skilled car repairmen, he rushed there immediately. Desperate, the company removed his name from the blacklist and rehired him.

When Earl was five, his father decided to move the family into a row house in Sumner, a tiny railroad village two miles from Bakersfield. There, Methias rented a bungalow in the dusty railroad section near the yards.

When the God-fearing Methodist Warrens moved to Bakersfield in 1896, the wide-open town was a hub for railroaders, miners, oil workers, construction laborers and picturesque Basque sheep-herders from the adjoining hills, but was more famous—or in-famous—as the Western citadel for an armed horde of luck-seeking gamblers, saloon keepers, promoters, pimps and prostitutes. At the turn of the century, the Bakersfield area had a population of 7,000, with an estimated 500 of them prostitutes. The town smelled of horses, whiskey and desert dust, and its predominant sounds were the jingle of spurs, cries of coyotes and throaty ballads of dance-hall girls singing for their favorite males of the moment as the piano players rolled up their sleeve guards and boisterously pounded away. One Bakersfield story has it that when a British visitor asked a ranch attendant, "May I speak with your master?" the man snarled, "The sonofabitch hasn't been born yet!"

The future Chief Justice of the United States was somehow able to adjust simultaneously to this tough, brawling outside world and to the gentler, more highly principled one of his family, in which telling a lie was a major crime. Puritanical Methias Warren shunned the other Bakersfield world. He neither gambled nor smoked, and he did not drink or permit alcohol in his home.

Yet Bakersfield accommodated both worlds, and this frontier tolerance did not escape Methias Warren's son. People of widely divergent ethnic backgrounds, occupations and moral stances, he observed, *could* live together harmoniously. A person's present and future counted for more than his past. These were the important lessons that an impressionable boy learned out of school.

In 1897, six-year-old Earl, his hair still in ringlets, entered the one-room Washington School, where some of his fellow pupils were full-grown, belligerent sixteen-year-olds who often threatened to thrash the principal. As an adult, Warren vividly recalled those days of frequent educational use of rulers on knuckles and straps on posteriors to preserve discipline. But he himself, undersized and somewhat frail, was seldom unruly. He was a natural left-hander, but a strict teacher tied his left hand behind him and compelled him to write with his right hand. This then-fashionable but dubious child-educating practice apparently instilled no psychological scars upon Earl Warren who later moved politically from right to left. For the rest of his life, he ambidextrously wrote with his right hand but did everything else with his left.

His favorite principal, Leo G. Pauley, blended a soft voice with a hard left uppercut. Pauley, who, in his mid-nineties, saw his most famous pupil appointed Chief Justice, recollected at the time: "Earl was just an average student. He was neither a leader nor a follower, just a docile pupil. There was no special promise of a brilliant career." Earl's third-grade teacher, Mrs. Millie Munsey, confirmed that he was no outstanding scholar. But she wrote President Eisenhower a half century later that his appointee had been a "truthful, upstanding and right-minded boy."

Because he was one of the smallest boys in his class, Earl tried to avoid becoming embroiled in the frequent fist fights during recess and after school. Sometimes, though, he was goaded into a scrap. To his amazement, he often won. When Earl arrived home with bruises and tattered clothes, Methias invariably spanked him for fighting instead of concentrating upon his school studies.

"My father wasn't exactly a failure at handling the birch rod," he smilingly remembered. "Sometimes it took a darn good beating to get results from me." The adult law enforcer, who practiced other methods of disciplining his own children, concluded, "If a boy isn't made to obey the laws when he is young, he won't obey the laws of his country when he is older."

One Sunday in April 1903, twelve-year-old Earl rode his burro, Jack, into downtown Bakersfield because he had heard that a gunfight was raging between two trapped bandits who were terrorizing the town. The sheriff of Kern County was William Tibbett, father of six-year-old Lawrence Tibbett, the future opera baritone. Lawrence's uncle, Jeff Packard, was Bakersfield city marshal. Young Earl arrived just in time to learn that both peace officers had been shot to death, along with one of the desperadoes. The other outlaw, said to be a deadly rifleman, had been captured and hustled off to jail. When the wide-eyed boy heard of this captured bandit's fearsome marksmanship, he was suddenly reminded of a sharp-shooting stranger who had befriended him at a turkey shoot several weeks earlier. The man had bagged a turkey with nearly every shot and then had charitably tossed a large white wild turkey to Earl, saying, "Here, kid, take this one home." Could this possibly be the same man who now had fatally shot Sheriff Tibbett and Marshal Packard? Earl eagerly attended the trial of this outlaw rifleman, who did indeed turn out to be the rifle-toting stranger of the turkey shoot.

After this, Earl, now at the Kern County Union High School,

began to stop off at the County Courthouse on his way home to listen to other trials. Railroaders and cowboys had been his early childhood heroes. Now he had begun to admire the criminal lawyers, as he heard them plead for their clients and tried to understand the fine points of their arguments. It was probably during this period that he decided he would like to become a lawyer. "At one time he thought of becoming a doctor," Ethel later recollected. "He thought a doctor could help people. He always wanted to do good in the world. But once he made up his mind to be a lawyer, he never changed it."

The curious boy in knee pants, who enjoyed reading history and Horatio Alger, likewise occasionally visited Bakersfield's gambling houses to gaze at the gold stacks on the table. He tried his luck a few times and always lost, but he won the goodwill of friendly dealers and croupiers. During dull afternoons, they showed him how they used their loaded dice and marked cards. The boy who grew up to become an uncompromising law enforcer never forgot this tutelage, nor the sad sight of workers losing their weekly wages at the gambling tables.

Still, there was a considerably less seamy side to his Bakersfield boyhood. In his backyard, Earl ministered to the rabbits, chickens, dog and eagle which he kept as pets. He rode his burro into the nearby hills, hunted, fished and swam—recreations he continued to pursue throughout his life.

In grammar school and high school, Earl worked at a variety of jobs. During the summer he chopped and delivered ice, earning twenty-five cents a day and a daily free cake of ice for the Warren icebox. All year round he arose at 6:30 A.M. to deliver Hearst's morning Los Angeles *Herald* to his customers, and after school he maintained a second paper route, delivering the afternoon Bakersfield *Californian* on a pony and cart. The year he was twelve, Earl worked in a bakery, drove a mule-drawn grocery wagon and distributed circus handbills.

In high school, Earl worked part-time as a freight hustler, farmhand and railway mechanic's helper. But the job that he relished most came during the summer of his fifteenth year, when he toiled as a Southern Pacific "call boy." He worked twelve hours daily, six days a week, for twenty-two cents an hour, checking the train schedule lists and rounding up the crews in East Bakersfield before the trains were to depart. On his bicycle he tracked down the engineers, firemen and brakemen wherever they happened to be: in dilapidated furnished rooms; in saloons; in the middle of games at the poker, crap and blackjack tables; and even abed in the brothels of Bakersfield's red-light district, Jap Alley.

Of all his jobs, the only one Earl Warren failed at was as door-to-door salesman. As a teenager he tried peddling leather-bound sets of *The Life of McKinley* during the presidency of colorful Theodore Roosevelt. "I was too shy and couldn't talk to people," he admitted years later. "When my own father refused to be persuaded by my sales talk, I decided that I was in the wrong job."

Methias and Chrystal Warren owned a large black-horned hand-crank phonograph on which they played Caruso and Sousa records, and were determined that their two children should learn to appreciate music.

Toward this goal, they purchased a piano for Ethel and a clarinet for Earl, who took lessons twice a week. As a fifteen-year-old high-school junior, Earl became so proficient that he began playing for an honorarium in the town band and became a charter member of Bakersfield Local 263 of the American Federation of Musicians. The young Warren's professional status prevented him from playing in the amateur high-school orchestra, which offered no stipend. Nevertheless, he recalled years later, "I got invited around because of my clarinet playing. It wasn't that my playing was so good. It was just that the union needed members."

At the union's 55th Annual Convention in Santa Barbara, California, in June 1952, President James C. Petrillo introduced host Governor Warren as a "great liberal Republican of our time, a member of the musicians' union and a clarinet player." The smiling recipient of this encomium replied that he wished to amend the introduction to read: "a *former* clarinet player." The union kept him on its rolls as an honorary member for many years, but in 1964 the former clarinet player's half-century-old performing past caught up with him. Without comment, to avoid any possible conflict of interest, the Chief Justice of the United States quietly disqualified himself in an American Federation of Musicians case being argued before the Supreme Court. None of the other Justices knew why.

During his seventeenth summer, Earl was also a brakeman on a freight train out of Bakersfield. This put him in touch with laboring conditions, and with people who were injured in rail accidents.

24

Justice Douglas later joked, "This gave Hugo Black and me one extra vote on many of those cases."

Earl was neither a girl-chaser nor an athlete, even though he managed to make the baseball team in his senior year. He was short, skinny, and could not, even had he the time or inclination, compete in sports with his huskier classmates. "Probably the reason that I am such a baseball and football fan," he told me decades later, "is because I was never much of a player myself. I played very little at my Kern County Union High School. My parents were anything but sports-minded. My mother especially opposed my playing football because she was afraid I would get hurt." (A not unreasonable fear in the wild early days of football, when injuries were so frequent and serious that several universities, including the University of California and Stanford, were shortly to abolish the sport from their campuses.)

But if Methias and Chrystal thought of sport as a potentially dangerous frivolity, they were relentless in their pursuit of intellectual and moral uplift. Inevitably, Methias was a fancier of Chautauqua lectures. "My father loved visiting Chautauqua speakers," Warren recalled. "They were big entertainment in small towns before radio, movies and television."

One day when Earl was still in high school, Methias took him to hear a memorable Bakersfield lecture by Dr. Russell H. Conwell, the well-known minister and founder of Philadelphia's Temple University. The dynamic Conwell was delivering his famed "Acres of Diamonds" speech, whose theme was that there is no need to search the world for riches when they exist in your own backyard. As an example, Conwell told of a wealthy Persian who had heard from a stranger of vast riches in diamonds to be found in a far-off land. The fortune-seeker sold his land, left his family and circled the globe seeking this treasure, only to wind up destitute. After his death, a stranger dug the land behind his home, which he had sold for naught, and there lay the richest diamond treasure on earth.

Corny? Earl Warren never thought so. Reminiscing one day in 1954, he said, "Of all the lectures that I heard in my youth this one made the greatest impression upon me. The little town where we lived did not appear to offer too many advantages. It was located in an area covered largely by sagebrush and populated mainly by jackrabbits. But my father assured me that Dr. Conwell's story about

'Acres of Diamonds' applied to our little town as well as to the largest and most beautiful cities in America, and that people who were always thinking of fortune-hunting in the other parts of the world were actually overlooking golden opportunities at home. He kept this picture before me through all the years I was growing into manhood. That little town is now the center of a population of a hundred and fifty thousand. Many who left there in search of oil and gold in Alaska, Mexico and other distant places returned at a later date empty-handed, only to find that those who had remained had not only struck oil at home but, by harnessing mountain water and irrigating the parched land, had profitably made a veritable Garden of Eden out of the desert."

Methias Warren practiced this "Acres of Diamonds" philosophy himself. He worked his way up to become a master car repairman, and finally foreman, overseeing Southern Pacific wrecking crews, carpenters and steam fitters. From his savings, he began to build houses which he then rented to other workers. "I tried to help my father with the plumbing and electrical work," recollected his son. "But frankly, I wasn't much help. I was never mechanically inclined as he was."

Knowledge-hungry Methias was lovingly remembered by his son sitting beside the family's pot-bellied coal stove poring over his International Correspondence Courses in mechanics and engineering. Next to health, education was the most important thing in the world to this Norwegian immigrant who was becoming a prosperous small property owner. He nurtured lofty dreams for his only son—far more ambitious than those the easygoing boy ever entertained for himself.

The day before commencement, however, Earl Warren and two other senior boys were expelled from high school for allegedly going on a hayride the night before. Defendant Warren's version of this expulsion, given at a sixty-fifth reunion of the dwindling class in 1973 in Bakersfield, was that he and two classmates, after rehearsing for the traditional senior class play until past midnight, missed the last streetcar home and had to walk the long distance. The following morning, the sleepy youths all arrived at school an hour late for the graduation rehearsal.

"The principal thought that we had conspired to be late," reported the retired jurist, who later suspected that his civil liberties had been infringed. "We insisted that we had not. He didn't believe us and expelled all three of us. Of course, we couldn't act in the play that night."

An emergency session of the distraught local board of education was held early that evening. The three thespians were reinstated and the show went on—late, of course. But the performance did not go unrecognized in the annals of world drama. In the May 28, 1908, issue of the Bakersfield *Californian,* a review of a farce entitled *What Became of Parker?* included this somewhat less than fervid acclaim: "The character of Fred Parker was played by Earl Warren and his scenes with Miss Campbell were well acted."

Earl's relaxed attitude did not escape his classmates. The will of the June 1908 senior class of Kern County Union High School recorded this statement taken voluntarily but not under oath: "I, Earl Warren, will to Lorraine K. Stoner my ability to slide through, doing as little work as possible."

The boy with an "ability to slide through" was unenthusiastic about continuing his education. But Methias Warren insisted, assuring the boy that he would undertake the entire expense of college. Although highly frugal toward himself, he refused to take any of his son's earnings, saying, "Put it in the bank, so you'll never go broke. You'll need it for a start in life. Get in the habit of saving, Earl, even though it's only fifty cents a week. The first thousand dollars are the hardest."

In late August 1908, an awkward, bespectacled young man in a wide-lapeled blue serge suit with starched detachable white collar arrived at the University of California's bustling Berkeley campus. As far as Earl Warren knew, he was the first person from Bakersfield's "railroad section" to attend college. However, with $800 saved from his miscellaneous high-school jobs, he felt confident, and he immediately liked the northern California area—which was fortunate, since he was to spend the next forty-five years there.

Living away from home for the first time, he happily found what he called "a new freedom." Although Methias would have preferred that his son become a mining engineer, Earl matriculated as a pre-law student, selecting political science as his major. For want of any other burning ambition, he had vaguely decided to become a trial lawyer, like those he had observed in Bakersfield. "I thought that I might have made a pretty good railroader," he joked years later, "but my father saw that I was a failure and had no choice but to make a lawyer out of me."

The gangling seventeen-year-old had now sprouted to five feet, eleven inches but still weighed only 129 pounds. During his first year at Berkeley, however, he gained nearly thirty pounds, mostly by munching hot dogs at the Dog Man's snack bar and wolfing the potato samples and five-cent beers at the free lunch tables of hospitable bars.

But more important than any changes in his appearance were the changes Berkeley was fashioning in his personality. He was beginning to outgrow his youthful environment—both the rough-and-ready Bakersfield world and the austere, rigidly moral world of the Warren household. The Berkeley-San Francisco-Oakland area offered a brand-new universe of social possibilities. And young Warren soon discovered in himself a talent for graceful conviviality which made it relatively easy for him to sample a new spectrum of life-styles. Many of his classmates came from prosperous and comparatively sophisticated upper-middle-class families. Visiting their elegant homes, he learned social graces undreamed of in Bakersfield. At firsthand he observed the curious social mores of self-proclaimed intellectual circles, although he was far from being an intellectual himself. He entered into the boisterous, exhilarating off-campus life of the popular undergraduate taverns such as Pop Kessler's (where he recited Kipling's *Barrack Room Ballads*), and experienced the camaraderie of fraternity life at Sigma Phi, where he lived. Finally, on the streets of San Francisco itself, he glimpsed the remoter world of commerce and power that would determine the burgeoning twentieth century's destiny.

Merrily playing Joe College, he began to affect the then-fashionable brightly colored vest, and ostentatiously puffed a corn-cob pipe. To Methias' horror, he even took up cigarettes. He became active in extra-curricular activities, performed as first clari-netist in the college band, was named chairman of the Senior Hop Reception Committee and of the Senior Banquet Committee. All in all, it was a time of discovery—of himself and others. "I was no scholar," he remembered. "I never had a real craving for knowledge. No professor or book had any profound influence on me. The greatest thing I got out of college was companionship. It was probably more important than anything I ever learned in my classes."

One college friendship that may have had a far-reaching influence on the future Chief Justice was with Walter Arthur Gordon, an outstanding black University of California athlete. Their many afternoons boxing in the college gymnasium began a lifelong friendship. (Gordon charitably remembers his former sparring partner as "rugged.") The son of an Atlanta janitor and grandson of a Confederate slave, Gordon later became a Berkeley police officer and for fourteen years headed the Alameda County branch of the National Association for the Advancement of Colored People. In 1945 he was appointed chairman of the California Adult Authority by Governor Warren; in 1955, Chief Justice Warren swore him in as Governor of the Virgin Islands; and in 1958 welcomed Gordon as federal district judge.

Happy as he was in his carefree collegiate world, Warren was nevertheless often homesick for his family. Methias sent him free railroad passes so that he could make the 291-mile trip home during vacations, long weekends and summer months. Because of his father's loathing of idleness, Earl worked during summers in the Southern Pacific shops and, more interesting to him, as a substitute cub reporter covering court trials for the Bakersfield *Californian* during a staff member's vacation.

Methias' prodding would always send him back to school determined—at least for a while—to work harder at his studies. His grades were consistently good in political science, history and English, but trigonometry, Greek and science gave him difficulty. Teachers and classmates remember the future public figure as an "average" undergraduate, a man in the middle, whose goal was primarily to get by, not to excel.

But an eloquent speech that he heard by a famed visiting political figure seems to have been a little-known turning point in his life. As a wide-eyed visitor in the Sacramento Senate gallery, he heard fifty-seven-year-old Senator Robert Marion ("Fighting Bob") La Follette, Sr., pour out his heart from the floor of the chamber, and in those moments found his first political hero.

The young political science major knew that as Republican governor of Wisconsin from 1901 to 1906, La Follette had pushed through a direct primary law, tax-reform legislation, railroad-rate control and other liberal measures known as the "Wisconsin Idea." As United States senator from 1906 until his death in 1925, he spearheaded countless battles against political dictators, industrial Goliaths, war measures and what he deemed dubious peace treaties. He championed federal railroad regulation of Methias Warren's Southern Pacific and other railways which controlled many state legislatures. His growing band of enemies attempted to have him expelled from the Senate, but by then his popularity had become too great for them to hope to succeed. In 1924, when he ran for President on the Progressive Party ticket, La Follette polled nearly 5,000,000 votes, largely in protest against the candidacies of Republican Calvin Coolidge and Democrat John W. Davis.

Though failing to include this important fact in his own unfinished memoirs, Earl Warren never ceased to admire the courageous Republican during the next sixty-two years of his life. Of all the men Warren later met in public life, only a few, such as California Governor Hiram Johnson, did he ever consider to be in La Follette's league. Certainly Warren was always his own man, and it would be oversimplification to attribute the later courageous acts in his own career to La Follette's influence; still, one cannot help noting how, in later life, Warren, perhaps subconsciously, tended to link the example of La Follette to his own home-grown idealism and progressive pragmatism.

An illuminating instance occurred in June 1955, when Warren delayed a holiday trip to Sweden to be the speaker of honor in Madison, Wisconsin, at a celebration honoring the hundredth anniversary of La Follette's birth. Approximately one year earlier, the Warren Court had handed down the epochal school desegregation decision. Simultaneously, Senator Joseph McCarthy (who, ironically, had defeated "Young Bob" La Follette in the 1946 Republican primary) had moved toward the end of his notorious career following the Army-McCarthy Hearings. To the audience and assembled members of the State Historical Society in Madison, headed by Dr. Clifford L. Lord (later president of Hofstra University), Warren said:

> *I know the pressures that Bob La Follette found it necessary to resist and overcome in order to give our democratic process the broad base it must have to serve its purpose . . . [He was] . . . one*

of the last of our log cabin statesmen to turn the searchlight upon our social problems and grind out with mortar and pestle the answers to them. And he suffered the same treatment that courageous men of vision in all ages have suffered. He was called a radical, a disrupter, a socialist, a subverter, and perhaps the only reason he was not called a Communist was because the term had not then been popularized as a term of opprobrium . . . Bob La Follette was a dissenter—a dissenter in the finest sense of the word. He did not dissent through mere obstinacy. He dissented in righteous indignation when he thought the objectives of our Government were being subverted . . . How important it is that we keep alive this type of dissent in America! . . . We must test all of our public actions by dissent. The majority does not always discover the right answer until it is so tested.

The links that connect the eloquent Chief Justice of 1955 and the callow undergraduate of 1912 may seem tenuous. But they are there, nonetheless, and the spirit of Bob La Follette in some mysterious way is one of them.

In June 1912, Warren was awarded his Bachelor of Letters degree, and in September was enrolled in the first class of the University of California's newly opened law school at Berkeley. Here his personality began to exhibit, if not changes, then some unexpected new facets. He began to work harder at his studies. At the same time, he began to reveal surprising truculence toward his teachers. He was convinced that the law school curriculum, which emphasized casework instruction, was far too theoretical. Over the objections of his dean, William Carey Jones, Earl insisted on taking an after-school job clerking in a Berkeley law office where, he felt, he could learn practical law. Dean Jones warned him that because he neither contributed enough to classroom discussions, nor spent enough time in the library, he might not graduate.

The boy from rough-and-tumble Bakersfield was not easily crushed by such a threat. He acknowledged the deficiency, but then calmly inquired, "Is that absolutely necessary for graduation?"

"No," hedged the dean.

"Well, then," Earl said confidently, "I have every intention of passing all my exams and graduating."

There was a painful pause as each appraised the other.

Finally, Warren rhetorically asked, "Dean, isn't law supposed to be a *living* thing and not just a textbook-library abstraction?"

The dean grimaced but kept silent. He may have been chagrined, but he was also impressed. Thereafter, in his own constitutional law course, he made a point of never calling upon the quietly rebellious youth to recite in class. The fair-minded dean passed him solely on the basis of the excellence of his written work.

On May 14, 1914, Earl Warren received his degree from the University of California Law School as a Doctor of Jurisprudence. He was nearer the bottom than the top of his class, and he did not make the *Law Review* staff or win any other coveted honors. He had a C average (called a 3 then) and was certainly not voted Lawyer Most Likely to Succeed. Presumably neither he nor anyone else ever thought then that one day he would preside over the highest court in the land, or that Boalt Hall would later proudly exhibit a bust and oil painting of him or have both an Earl Warren Hall and Earl Warren Legal Center; or that Bancroft Library would start an Earl Warren Oral History Project in 1969; or that he would receive an honorary LL.D. degree at Berkeley in 1954; or that he would win the Clark Kerr Award in 1972; or that an Earl Warren Chair in Public Law would be established at Berkeley in 1975; or that the University of California at San Diego would open an Earl Warren College in 1978.

When dedicating the Earl Warren Legal Center in 1969, the retired Chief Justice quipped, "You don't have to be a great success in law school to have a building named after you."

Warren was admitted to the California State Bar in May 1914. Though his law-school thesis had been on "The Personal Liability of Corporation Directors in the State of California," corporate law did not really interest Methias Warren's son as a life pursuit. But he lacked the financial resources to strike out on his own as a criminal lawyer in Alameda County, and none of the established Alameda law firms wanted to hire him. So he reluctantly decided to look for a job across the bay in San Francisco. To his surprise, he was soon offered a job in the small legal department of the Associated Oil Company.

At fifty dollars a month, the oil company junior lawyer earned barely enough money to cover his lunches, cigarettes and carfare from his Oakland furnished room. In his cramped office space, his duties were mainly clerical, checking contracts, reading leases, maintaining legal records and preparing occasional briefs. They provided him no opportunity for the courtroom experience that he wanted so intensely. Convinced after a year that this oil company position would yield no legal gushers for him, he quit, not sorry likewise to be leaving his boss, an irritable old man who embarrassed him before clients by ordering him out to buy cigars.

He found a job in a private law firm across the bay in his preferred Oakland, Alameda's county seat. The firm was Robinson and Robinson and its senior partner was Judge E. C. Robinson. Here again, though, he was assigned to routine chores and was never given an opportunity to argue in court. His happiest activities were social in nature, centering mostly around his duties as president of the new Young Lawyers Club of Alameda, which goaded the inert county bar association (it had held no meetings in six years) into giving young lawyers a voice and holding regular annual meetings. But after a year and a half of working longer hours, for the same salary at what he came to consider another dead-end job, he decided that if he was ever going to secure any trial experience he must open his own law office. "I wanted to become a successful trial lawyer and this now seemed the only way to begin," he recollected.

At a series of lunches with two fellow Boalt Hall classmates, they carefully blocked out plans for the three of them to open their own law office. They had just found inexpensive office space in downtown Oakland which they planned to rent when the drums of World War I rolled away their plans.

The United States declared war against Germany on Good Friday, April 6, 1917. Since young soldiers would now clearly be more useful than young lawyers, the twenty-six-year-old Warren temporarily shelved his dreams and immediately applied for a commission at the newly opened Army Officers' Training Corps office in San Francisco. The Army rejected Warren's application on physical grounds, but advised him that he could reapply in two months.

He began a daily exercise program to build himself up and on his second try, he was accepted. During his physical examination, however, army doctors discovered that he had hemorrhoids. Informed that this ailment must be remedied before he could be accepted, that afternoon he entered an Oakland hospital for what he supposed would be a minor operation and a two-day hospital stay.

But complications developed. He caught ether pneumonia on the operating table and was hospitalized for nearly a month. When he was released, the OTC program was closed. Selective Service was now law.

Warren did not wait for his draft number to be called. In August 1917, he enlisted as an infantry private. Shipped to Camp Lewis, Washington, near Tacoma, he was assigned to Company I, 363rd Infantry of the 91st Division. After a month of basic training, he was made a first sergeant in a unit of 250 men and found that he enjoyed this first experience in supervising large groups of people.

At Camp Lewis as at college, he made many lifelong friendships. Among his closest Army buddies was Leo Carillo, the Mexican-American actor, who was descended from California settlers. Carillo, later known in movies as "The Cisco Kid," remembered his sergeant as a "big man mentally and physically, a great hulking, strong, sturdy soldier without any pettiness." Though Carillo was a Democrat, he later worked on Republican candidate Warren's campaigns.

In January 1918, five months after arriving at Camp Lewis, Sergeant Warren was finally admitted to the officers' training program. He was shipped to Camp Lee in Petersburg, Virginia, where he was commissioned a Second Lieutenant in May 1918 and, as he later recalled, saw more Confederate than American flags flying. He was assigned to train troops for overseas duty in thirty days, though he later insisted that most left camp unprepared. The unbelligerent Warren was himself assigned to Camp Lee's rigorous Bayonet School to prepare for imminent combat action. Warren and one other bayonet student were the only ones not hospitalized after this exhausting training.

Second Lieutenant Warren, now a bayonet expert, fully expected to be transferred overseas immediately as a replacement for the American officers then being killed in the fierce battles raging in France and Belgium. Instead, the Army, with inexplicable logic, shipped him to Camp MacArthur in Waco, Texas, to teach at the Central Infantry Officers' Training School. Part of this transfer involved his being promoted to First Lieutenant, but shortly after donning his new silver bar, almost as he was unpacking, the Armistice was signed on November 11, 1918. The war had ended without Lieutenant Warren having fired a shot at the enemy. The following month he was discharged at age twenty-seven.

By Christmas 1918, he was back in Bakersfield, spending the holidays with his family. His entire fortune consisted of the sixty dollars he had received as mustering-out pay, and he spent half of it on Christmas presents. But he was too proud to admit his poverty to Methias, who had forewarned him never to be "caught broke." His old suits no longer fit him and he was infuriated at the price of new clothes. "I remember the shock of then being asked sixteen dollars for a new shirt," he later mused. The demobilized veteran wore his Army uniform for a protracted period, not out of patriotism but out of sartorial necessity.

While Warren was pondering how best to resume his legal career, chance, family ties and friendship took over, temporarily deflecting him from his path.

His sister, Ethel, and her husband, Vernon Plank, a Southern Pacific Railroad storekeeper, invited him to live with them in their rented Oakland home until he decided what he wanted to do. He accepted their offer. One morning, on an Oakland street, he encountered Leon Gray, a pre-war friend in the Robinson law firm, who had recently been elected to the state legislature in Sacramento.

Gray suggested that while Earl was making up his mind what he really wanted to do, he should take a job as Gray's legal assistant during the session in Sacramento. The pay would be only five dollars a day, but Warren, being single, could live on that.

It seemed a splendid opportunity to shed his now-faded khaki uniform and don the civilian clothes he would wear for the next fifty-five years.

In Sacramento, he met another new assemblyman, Charles Kasch, who had been his fraternity brother in Berkeley. Kasch and Gray soon jointly promoted Warren to an even better job which happened to be vacant: clerk of the Judiciary Committee in the Assembly at a whopping seven dollars a day. This was to be the young lawyer's first taste of professional politics and he found that he loved it. His political education was also enhanced by the fact that he shared a room with Gray in the Old Hotel Sequoia near the capitol, which was a hangout for politicians, lawyers, lobbyists and assorted visiting firemen. Many took a liking to young Warren, and he began accumulating valuable other contacts.

One of his new friends, Frank Anderson, an Oakland assemblyman, was extremely sympathetic to young Warren's ambition to secure trial experience in practical law. The best way to get this,

Anderson advised him, would be by working on the staff of Ezra DeCoto, the Alameda County district attorney, whose office handled numerous criminal and civil cases.

Thus, when long-time District Attorney DeCoto came to Sacramento seeking funds to hire another deputy, Anderson and Gray suggested that the funds might be made available on condition that Warren would be the deputy.

DeCoto demurred. Warren was too inexperienced, and DeCoto already had his own nominee for the job.

Hearing of this impasse, Warren called upon DeCoto. "I would love to work in your office," he admitted. "But I want you to know that I have had no knowledge until now of the attempt to force my services upon you. Under these circumstances, I could not in good conscience accept the position at this time even if you offered it to me. I think it only fair that you go ahead and engage your own man that you wish."

District Attorney DeCoto was astounded by such candor from a political job-seeker. Gratefully, he thanked the young man and assured him that he would keep him in mind should any vacancies arise in his office.

When Warren informed his patrons of his conversation with DeCoto they chided him for being naïve, a political yokel, for not going along with the deal. But Warren had made no enemies by that action and, in fact, had gained respect on both sides. He believed that ultimately his patience would pay off.

When the legislative term ended in June 1919, he was invited to hang out his shingle, which he did for the first time, in Gray's Oakland law office in the Bank of Italy building. But before he could secure a single client, another political contact yielded results. Oakland's city attorney, C. L. Hagen, invited him to become a deputy city attorney at $200 a month, with the privilege of continuing his (nonexistent) law practice on the side.

He worked at this job for the better part of a year, and derived real pleasure from serving the public. Little wonder. Among other benefits, the working conditions were unusually pleasant for the twenty-eight-year-old City of Oakland assistant attorney. His office, on the top floor of the new, gleaming white Oakland City Hall, boasted a panoramic view of the thriving industrial area. Quietly and efficiently, Warren advised the older directors of Oakland's respective departments on the interpretation of city laws. He wrote briefs for them, and in so doing gained considerable insight into how a municipal body functioned. He finally even had an opportunity to appear in court, defending Oakland in a wide range of civil suits.

By now, private trial law had lost an advocate. The hardworking attorney was far too preoccupied with his city legal work to solicit any clients of his own. He concluded that government law work, while perhaps not as lucrative as successful private practice, nonetheless offered other rewards. Although not then fully aware of it, he was now unswervingly embarked upon a long career in politics and public service.

In due course, the DeCoto episode bore fruit. The Alameda County district attorney had been carefully observing Warren's legal actions in the Oakland city government office, and when one of DeCoto's junior deputies abruptly resigned, he offered the job to Warren. Despite its being a fifty-dollar cut in salary, the ambitious Warren instantly accepted. Experience, not a paycheck, was what he needed most if he were ever to secure his long-desired trial experience.

"I thought that I might work in the D.A.'s office for about a year and a half and then go into private practice to become a trial lawyer," he recalled. "So I ended up working there eighteen years."

He began on May 1, 1920, at the lowest rung of the official ladder. Swiftly he climbed it, thanks to his dedication and inexhaustible energy. He often worked until midnight, and on many weekends, in the dilapidated old Alameda County Courthouse.

"When Earl Warren first worked in my office," DeCoto fondly recounted before his death in 1948, "I would often ask him on a Saturday morning if he could pull together some legal background on one of our new cases. On Monday morning, I would almost always have on my desk his memorandum explaining all the law involved." Whenever one of DeCoto's other deputies was absent, he would ask: "Who the hell knows anything about this case?" The answer invariably was: "Warren." Soon he was propelled into court appearances as a prosecutor. It was what he had always wanted. Warren was now a trial lawyer—but in public rather than private practice. However, he soon found a new private interest.

One Sunday morning in April 1921, Warren was invited by a young married couple to a breakfast swimming party of twenty guests at the

Piedmont Baths in Oakland, a popular recreation center for young people. While standing by the poolside, he found himself captivated by the sight of a comely young girl leisurely practicing her stroke in the water. He quickly asked his hostess for an introduction, and at the ten o'clock breakfast sat beside the auburn-haired, blue-eyed young woman.

"I spotted him just as quickly as he spotted me," Nina Warren laughingly recollects, "so maybe there is such a thing as love at first sight. Actually, he took a big chance that day—all he could see of me was my head above the water." Outside the water, the rest of Nina Palmquist Meyers, a twenty-three-year-old Swedish-born widow, readily passed the young deputy district attorney's inspection. Unaffected, she put him at ease immediately. He swiftly admired her peach-skinned loveliness and shy, soft-spoken charm. Later, when he spoke with her, he admired her sympathetic spirit, practical intelligence, and courage in managing a specialty dress shop in order to raise her fatherless two-year-old son. He found her candor, warmth and sincerity completely disarming, and observed that her Swedish background, thoughts and outlook seemed to blend with his own.

She was born Nina Elisabeth Palmquist in Visby, the seaport capital of the isle of Gotland off Sweden. One of Europe's most picturesque cities, Visby is surrounded by the blue Baltic and a thirteenth-century wall. The gabled houses on its narrow cobblestone streets are covered with roses and ivy. A romantic, unspoiled island, it still boasts the ruins of eleven cathedrals and has resisted most of time's inroads while accommodating itself to others in its own way; thus, when automobiles came to Visby, residents on opposite sides of the narrow streets had to keep their window shutters closed at alternate hours of the day so that the cars could pass.

Nina's father, Dr. Niles Peter Palmquist, was a tall, slender, osteopath with a Van Dyke beard who also served as pastor of Visby's Immanual Baptist Church. Her mother, the former Hannah Elise Malmgren, Nina remembers as an angelic five-foot, 110-pound woman who bore five children eighteen months apart—Edward, Eva, James, Nina and Hannah, in that order.

Nina was brought to America as an infant. Like the Warrens, the Palmquist family had settled in rural Iowa before moving to

California. When Nina was three, her mother died of uremic poisoning in San Diego at the age of twenty-eight, while carrying her sixth child. At first, Nina and her brothers and sisters were cared for by a housekeeper. But later their father, anxious to flee the scene of his tragic loss, moved his family over five hundred miles north to Oakland.

Here, Niles Palmquist resumed his osteopathic practice and substituted on Sunday in the local pulpit when the regular pastor was away. In time, Niles met and married Swedish-born Sophia Albertina Rosenberg, who lovingly raised his children and helped keep the family together. Nina has warm memories of her step-mother.

In grammar school, classmates teased Nina by calling her "Neenie." An understanding teacher then began calling her "N-eye-nuh"—with the long *i*—which is how she and her friends have pronounced it ever since.

When Nina was thirteen, her father, then only fifty years old, suddenly died of tuberculosis. Dr. Palmquist left few resources, and now, instead of entering high school, it was necessary for Nina to get a job. Her older sister Eva, who was working for a small local plumbing firm, was offered a position in the Oakland office of the giant Crane Plumbing Company. Eva thereupon broke Nina into her old job answering the telephone and doing cashiering and bookkeeping. Evenings, she attended Heald's Business College, where she learned stenography and typing.

One day the Crane Company representative offered Nina a job working with her sister Eva in its Oakland office. Nina, in turn, broke her younger sister Hannah into her former job. But it wasn't long before all three Palmquist girls were employed by the Crane Company. The shrewd office manager justified his action on these grounds: "I like to hire three sisters. They're all talked out by the time they get to the office, so they don't engage in personal con-versation on company time like so many other girls do."

One morning Nina didn't follow her boss's conversation too well when she was transcribing his words from a new office dictating machine. It was one of the early dictaphones and she had consid-erable difficulty because, as the cylinder wore on, her boss's voice grew fainter. He had dictated a letter into the machine explaining to the home office how an important account had been lost. "We must have been completely fooled," her employer had dictated. But on Miss Nina Palmquist's typed letter, it came out: "We must have been two sleepy fools!"

"He went home and told his wife that the new girl in the office had called him a sleepy fool!" this former secretary laughingly reported to the amused junior D.A. deputy.

In 1918, when she was twenty, Nina had married Grover Meyers, a promising musician. A year later, he died of tuberculosis, leaving her with their three-week-old son, James.

In those days there was no social security and little public concern for the rearing of fatherless children. Nina and her infant son moved in with her stepmother while she pondered what type of breadwinning job she would take to support all three of them.

One day when she was wheeling her baby carriage on the street, a woman neighbor who owned an exclusive women's specialty shop offered her a job, saying, "You haven't any merchandising experience, so you won't be worth a cent to me for months. But I'm willing to take a chance on you." This plain-talking woman proved to be a canny judge of character because, before long, the young widow was an outstanding success in her job. She had started in the office but was soon transferred to the floor to sell hosiery, lingerie and women's clothing. Evenings, Nina checked the books, making sure that everything came out to the exact penny. When the woman bought another shop, Nina became manager of the old one, and around the time she met Earl Warren had begun saving money from her $250-a-month salary to open her own store. Earl was then earning approximately the same amount.

Still, Nina was terribly unhappy every working day that she had to leave her young son with her stepmother. "It used to break my heart," she remembers, "when Jimmy would stand at the window and wave good-bye to me until I was out of sight."

Hardheaded Swedes both, neither Nina nor Earl were the sort to be carried away on the first wave of love's careless rapture. They worked too hard to see each other on weeknights, and Nina always spent Sunday with her son, Jimmy. Thus, the only time they had together was Saturday night, for which they had a standing date, generally to dine and attend a repertory theatre. It took them two years to become officially engaged.

Even then they delayed marriage for two additional years until Earl could get a promotion and a higher salary. Certainly there was no question of their delaying on the grounds of parental objection; Methias, in a private conversation with Earl, paid Nina the highest tribute of which he was capable: "She's the most efficient person I ever met."

While Earl and Nina were slowly but surely making their way to the altar, Earl's legal career was advancing along unexpected lines. When he had entered the Alameda County district attorney's office, a new era was dawning in America—the age of prohibition, lost innocence, wonderful nonsense and easy morals: the Roaring Twenties. Warren G. Harding, a handsome Ohio Republican U.S. Senator, whose affable exterior concealed a spineless interior, was soon to become President, pledging to return the country to "normalcy." But the scandals of his administration, uncovered after his sudden death in San Francisco in August 1923, reflected the nation's shabby morality. "The difference between George Washington and Warren Harding," went a contemporary wisecrack, "is that while Washington could not tell a lie, Harding could not tell a liar."

The crime and corruption of the times were augmented by the prohibition of alcohol, which had become law in 1919 under the Eighteenth Amendment. Junior Deputy District Attorney Warren, together with countless other Americans, smiled at this current jingle:

> *My mother works in the laundry,*
> *My father sells bootlegger gin,*
> *My sister lives in a whorehouse,*
> *My God! How the money rolls in!*

Prohibition spawned new types of crime, creating new problems in law enforcement. Bootleggers, rumrunners, smugglers and assorted gangsters, seeking to control the lucrative booze market, bribed police and judges. Prohibition enforcement officials proved ineffectual throughout the United States, including wide-open, live-and-let-live Alameda County. Scrupulously, Warren gave up his occasional drinking in public, reasoning, "How can I violate the law and take a drink on Saturday night and then prosecute bootleggers on Monday morning?"

Still, he did not hesitate to prosecute communists. In a 1921 case, he prosecuted four members of the Communist Labor Party for allegedly violating the California criminal syndicalism statute.

After a hung jury, Warren dropped the case on the grounds that Alameda County could not afford the expense of a retrial. One of the survivors, ninety-four-year-old James H. Dolsen, recollects, "Warren had no particular bias against us, even though he undoubtedly hoped to gain prestige by convicting us. Many years later, when I was prosecuted under a Pennsylvania state sedition law involving the Smith Act, I became the beneficiary of a liberal Warren Court ruling which I doubt would have happened under today's Burger Court.

To Deputy D. A. Warren during the 1920s, law enforcement now seemed a more challenging career than private trial work—or even the tempting, far more lucrative position as a trust officer now proffered him by a San Francisco bank. In 1923 Warren, who was gaining a reputation as a "take charge guy" in criminal prosecutions, was promoted to chief deputy by DeCoto. His salary was boosted to $5,000 a year and even more significantly, DeCoto named him legal counsel to the Alameda County Board of Supervisors, which gave him an inside view of all county operations.

Two years later DeCoto, who had been district attorney since 1916 and was weary of the office's growing demands in the field of criminal enforcement, was appointed to the State Railroad Commission by Republican Governor Friend W. Richardson. He resigned as district attorney. The county supervisers were obliged to appoint an interim successor until the 1926 election the following year.

By now Warren, who had worked in the office for five years, had ambitiously decided that he could invigorate it if he held the top spot. DeCoto probably had appointed him to the Board of Supervisors position to groom him as his successor. But county Republican boss Mike Kelly favored another deputy, Frank Shay.

Encountering Warren in the courthouse corridor one day, Kelly assured him that he had nothing against him personally. Speaking frankly, he said that he had promised the job to Frank Shay, who had supported his organization for many years. Shay, in his view, had earned the job politically; Warren had not.

Warren and Shay each had two sure votes on the five-man Board of Supervisors. A long-time board member, John F. Mullins, who had been elected by Mike Kelly's machine, would cast the decisive ballot. Mullins owed nothing to Warren and wanted nothing from him, but he had been tremendously impressed by the young man's public-spirited legal labors for the Board of Supervisors. Now, Johnny Mullins had decided to vote his conscience.

"To make sure that I didn't change my mind or have it changed for me by Mike Kelly," he recollected, "I went into Earl Warren's office and told him and everybody else that I was going to vote for him. I knew that it meant political suicide for me. But I loved Alameda County and thought that Warren could do better than anyone else in fighting all the crooks in it. I wanted him to come into office clean because I was confident that he would *stay* clean. He always behaved like a fellow who just came out of a church and not a poolroom."

Sure enough, the Kelly machine got its revenge. Mullins was defeated in the next election for the Board of Supervisors. Thereafter, Mullins sold insurance. In old age, his proudest possession was a photograph inscribed: "To John F. Mullins, the first sponsor, and for thirty years the most loyal supporter in public life of his friend, Earl Warren." Whenever the beneficiary of his selfless act had a free hour in Oakland, he unfailingly visited John Mullins in the tiny apartment where he lived, confined to a wheelchair with crippling arthritis. In 1970 Mullins died, happy in the realization that in renouncing his own career, he had helped launch that of another man who had exceeded his fondest expectations.

Earl Warren, at age thirty-four, was now one of the nation's youngest district attorneys, earning an annual salary of $7,000. With all deliberate speed, he celebrated by getting married—nine months later. Late blooming could be said to be a recurrent pattern in his life.

Nina Palmquist Meyers and Earl Warren were married on October 14, 1925 (the same date as the 35th birthday of unknown Major Dwight D. Eisenhower). The simple wedding ceremony took place in the First Baptist Church in Oakland at eleven o'clock on a typically foggy West Coast morning, with only the immediate families in attendance, and two Warren friends who crashed the services. It was such an unpretentious affair that no one remembered to take a wedding picture. The groom wore a navy blue suit. The bride remembers her outfit in more detail: a gray dress with royal blue velvet trim, matching large royal blue velvet hat with silver trim, gray shoes, gray stockings and a blue coat trimmed in gray fur. There were few wedding presents. The most extravagant was a sterling silver setting for twelve, given to them by Methias and

Chrystal Warren. The new District Attorney's staff gave them a tea set; an Oakland friend, a marble statue of a dancer.

That afternoon, in the groom's black Buick sedan, the bridal couple drove up the Pacific Coast to British Columbia on the new Redwood Highway for a two-week honeymoon. On their return to Oakland, they lived in a hotel for several months before moving into a rented five-room apartment which Nina cheerfully decorated with chintz curtains and comfortable furniture. Earl Warren legally adopted his bride's six-year-old son, Jimmy, thus beginning what was to become one of America's best-known families. During the next six and a half years, the Warrens were to have five other children.

Earl Warren had to run for re-election the following year, 1926. For the first time in his life, the politician-to-be was compelled to face the electorate. And it would be a tough fight. Boss Kelly wanted nothing more than to toss this upstart into San Francisco Bay. According to Warren, a $25,000 slush fund was collected to defeat him. To offset this, and to spark his campaign, he badly needed some dramatic public service campaign issue. He chose the bail bond racket.

It worked something like this: Whenever a defendant had to post bail, often for a relatively minor crime, his cash would be refused and he was informed that he must secure a bond from a bail bond company. This bail broker's runner was often right there in court, cynically paying off unscrupulous clerks, sheriffs, police and occasionally judges in cash before the very eyes of the hapless defendant, who was compelled to post his home, furniture or other valuable assets as collateral. Through a series of manipulated postponements, the exorbitant interest and service charges could be made to soar until a defendant's foreclosed home could be seized. Crooked officials likewise "lost" vital documents and maneuvered illogical dismissals. When a defendant jumped bail, the bond broker frequently schemed with cooperative officials to have the case set aside without forfeiting the bond.

District Attorney Warren summoned these predatory bail bond operators into his office and warned that he would indict them unless they immediately stopped these practices. The racketeers fought hard and threatened Warren, but he presented the grand jury and later the court with a cavalcade of witnesses and such a mass of incontrovertible evidence from hundreds of victims that he succeeded in smashing the bail bond ring. Brokers had to repay bail-forfeited bonds to the state and return seized properties to many victims. Moreover, they were forced to discontinue their usurious practices and charge merely the legal fees thereafter. Publisher Joseph Knowland's Oakland *Tribune,* which had been battling the Kelly machine, publicized this crusade, which helped Warren's campaign.

Nevertheless, Warren took nothing for granted but traveled all over Alameda County in his loner campaign, pumping hands and introducing himself.

More than three decades later, as Chief Justice, he laughingly recalled an incident from this 1926 campaign. At one town meeting, the story goes, Warren was invited to speak along with candidates for other offices. It was the custom to schedule the speakers in alphabetical order, which naturally put Warren way down on the list. As each speaker droned on, voters began drifting out of the hall. When candidate Warren was finally called upon, after midnight, only one person remained in the audience.

"Thank you very much for your patience in staying to the end to hear me," Warren said gratefully.

"My name's Zimmerman," the man replied, "I'm the last speaker on the program."

Warren refused to permit anyone on his D.A. staff to campaign for him. Even Nina was kept on the sidelines. He took her along on one trip and when voters asked her to speak, he jocularly interceded, "We have a strict rule in our family. I do all the speaking in public and Mrs. Warren does it all at home!"

To the surprise of most observers, Warren won overwhelmingly and was elected to a four-year term as district attorney. With this mandate, the onetime carefree college boy—now a maturing 35-year-old district attorney—zealously launched an all-out campaign against crime in Alameda County.

Quietly but vigorously, he prosecuted oil stock swindlers, unscrupulous health insurance promoters, school board embezzlers, cleaning and dyeing racketeers, fraudulent building and loan sharks, lawyers and stockbrokers who stole funds from estates entrusted to them, and assorted confidence artists. He indicted an aircraft manufacturer for making a defective wing on an airplane which killed a pilot on takeoff. He convicted dope peddlers, and reached into a sheriff's office to break up a slot machine and prostitution-protection ring. One lawbreaker, whose trail he had pursued relentlessly, waved a revolver in public, exclaiming, "This has two bullets in it—one for Warren and one for me." Warren responded by calmly carrying out the processes leading to his conviction.

When the Ku Klux Klan—perhaps seduced by the fact that Warren had joined nearly every other available fraternal organization—offered him membership, he sent the Klan's emissaries packing with the reply: "Your goals and methods are the antithesis of everything I believe in." When prominent local merchants asked him to "go easy" on brothel closings, Warren icily told them he was not prepared to discuss the matter further until they submitted their request in writing, signed—which, of course, he knew they never would do.

All in all, he had become a rather tough customer. "Honest, grim and relentless" is the way journalist Robert Sherrill described him. Others were less kind. "Humorless and prudish," Cary McWilliams of *The Nation* called him. "Warren can't understand anyone he can't indict," added a political opponent.

But one legal adversary, Willard W. Shea, the gifted longtime public defender of Alameda County who represented defendants unable to afford private attorneys, admitted, "Warren never brought people into court unless he could prove they were guilty. Nothing troubled him more than the possibility that he might be sending an innocent person to jail."

Warren and Shea had a gentlemen's agreement, Shea recalled. "I want to be fair with you, Willard," the D.A. had told the public defender. "If you are ever certain that we have indicted an innocent person, come see me and I'll show you my evidence. I don't want to pull anything on you as a surprise in court. If you're still convinced of your client's innocence after seeing our evidence, I'll drop the prosecution. We're both interested in fair play, aren't we?"

"I don't remember ever once winning a case against Warren," Shea later mused. But the highly principled public defender knew that the no less highly principled district attorney was seeking justice more than convictions.

Warren applied the same "reasonable doubt" rule to his staff. Oscar J. Jahnsen, his chief investigator in the district attorney's and later the governor's office, now reminisces, "His instructions to us were: 'Get the facts honestly and don't color them. If the facts are there, you can proceed. If they're not, we don't want them. Be fair, courteous and never go against your honest instincts.' "

On at least one occasion, Warren followed his own instincts when a man's fate was at stake. A black youth, accused of a series of rapes, was "identified" by two women victims. But because Warren had some misgivings over the defendant's guilt, he kept the case out of court while instructing an aide to investigate further. His caution was vindicated when another man later confessed to the crimes.

Thanks to such careful investigation, Warren's conviction rate was an astonishing 86 percent—far higher than that of San Francisco, Los Angeles and other areas in the state, a 1936 University of California study reported. Not one of the thousands of cases he prosecuted was ever reversed by a higher court. Nor did any court ever overrule his interpretations of the law. Not bad for a student who had not exactly overawed his law school professors.

The callow young man who had yearned to be a private trial lawyer had come a long way from his first court appearance a brief few years earlier. "I was then so tense" he recollected, "that on the streetcar ride down to the courthouse, I hoped the car would be wrecked so that I wouldn't have to appear in court." When he rose to offer a simple demurrer, his knees trembled and his mouth was so dry that he could hardly speak.

Now, however, he had developed a new courtroom confidence. When trying cases personally, he often swayed juries with his homey, even corny, illustrations. For example, in a murder trial where circumstantial evidence was crucial, he explained in terms as simple as those an elementary schoolteacher might use, what sort of evidence could be considered valid: "Suppose I arrive home to find my small son with his face full of jam, with jam smeared all over the shelf, dirty footprints on the floor leading to the cupboard where the jam jar was and a kitchen chair near the shelf where Mrs. Warren kept it. In spite of any denial by my son, it hardly needs verbal confirmation that *he* raided the jam jar. The observable evidence is there."

Thorough investigator that he was, however, the Chief—as Warren was now called by his aides—scrupulously refused to permit his staff to engage in such dubious practices as wiretapping. "Secret listening devices were absolutely forbidden by Earl Warren," reports one of his deputies, Arthur H. Sherry, now a Berkeley law professor. "You can get better and quicker confessions by intelligence and proper handling than by force or illegal activities. You don't break the law to enforce the law," he always told us.

Two decades before Congressman Richard Nixon and Senator Joseph McCarthy had discovered the Communist issue, District Attorney Warren was battling communism in Alameda County. As early as 1927, FBI agents—as well as military and naval intelligence officers—freely used Warren's extensive files. "In those days," he reminisced in retirement, "we discovered the difficulties of proving who were communists. The difficulties always have been great. But at least then we tried to use the processes of law for determining this rather than reckless accusations."

One Warren prosecution, under the state's criminal syndicalism law, was upheld by the U.S. Supreme Court in 1927 (*Whitney v. California*). But Justice Brandeis, in a stinging concurring opinion, passionately defended the constitutional protection of free press and speech—which deeply moved the future Chief Justice.

Seeking to coordinate the state's sprawling law-enforcement agencies, he became chairman of the State Board of Criminal Investigation. He also sparked a pioneer program at San Jose State College in which police officers taught the most modern methods to younger officers, an innovation which foreshadowed the present departments of criminology in many universities.

Former aides remember how he forbade them to do any outside legal work or accept any gifts including Christmas presents or Thanksgiving turkeys. His sharp lookout for even the appearance of impropriety extended to his deputies' wardrobes: they were instructed not to wear derbies or loud suits.

When reorganizing the hitherto rather lax office into a strong, closely knit team, he held daily staff meetings with specific departments and weekly roundup sessions on Saturday mornings beginning sharply at 8:30 with the entire staff, including all field officials. As in later Supreme Court conferences, even the most junior members were encouraged to speak. In assessing problems, a favorite Warren saying was: "Let's pick it up by the four corners and look at it."

Central records were maintained for the first time. Up-to-date files were kept on all current cases. Old prosecutions which had cluttered the office's calendar were cleared up. Information was exchanged with neighboring enforcement agencies long before the FBI set up a nationwide system to do this.

Warren, who worked long hours himself, assumed that all his subordinates would, too. Yet he rarely lauded their overtime labors. "My husband thought he was great," recalls one of the many neglected wives of the time, "He worked like a dog for Warren and loved doing so. Maybe Warren appreciated him but I never thought so—then!"

Perhaps mindful of his own law school brush with Dean Jones, Warren recruited his junior staff members from recent Boalt Law School graduates who sought *practical* experience. In hiring them, grades concerned him far less than character, intelligence and imagination. Whenever a young staff member goofed, his chief often reassuringly said: "Don't worry if it was a mistake of the head and not of the heart. That's how we learn."

The major staff project between 1927 and 1930 was a unique assignment for any law-enforcement agency: prosecuting corruption in *other* law-enforcement agencies. Warren's staff did not wait for such cases to arise in the normal course of events, but undertook their own investigations.

Sheriff Burton F. Becker was his first target. Becker, formerly the Piedmont police chief, had been elected sheriff of Alameda County on a law-and-order program in November 1926, the same election in which Warren had won his first victory as district attorney. Because these two men held the county's two top law-enforcement positions, good government surely would have been best served through their teamwork. But Sheriff Becker's open protection of bootleggers, gamblers and vice lords, with the accompanying graft, was common knowledge. A month after Becker assumed office, Warren quietly urged him to renounce his underworld connections. Becker, who turned out to be a Ku Klux Klan leader, claimed complete innocence. The abuses grew greater, and Warren repeated his warning.

"You take care of *your* office and I'll take care of *my* office," Becker angrily retorted.

Warren made a final attempt. He asked Richard Carrington, publisher of Hearst's Oakland *Post-Inquirer* to arrange a meeting with political boss Mike Kelly, who had helped elect Becker. In Carrington's presence, Warren said, "Politics is not my motive. But if Sheriff Becker doesn't clean up this mess, we'll have to seek the evidence to indict him."

Kelly decided to speak to Becker. Soon he reported back to Warren that Becker had promised to clean up everything and to cooperate with the district attorney in enforcing the law.

Becker, however, did no such thing. His open corruption grew even more flagrant, until at one point he defiantly challenged Warren to indict him.

"It took us several years to get the evidence," remembers Oscar Jahnsen. "People seemed to be indifferent. They couldn't get excited about corruption until it hit their own pocketbooks."

An Oakland street-paving scandal finally proved to be Becker's Achilles heel, for this *was* an issue that touched homeowners' pocketbooks. A small cartel of contractors who did not really bid competitively were given a monopoly by city officials to pave all of Oakland's streets. They billed the city for work that was never done. They jacked up prices outrageously. They used substandard materials instead of those specified. They charged homeowners exorbitant prices for laying small sidewalks. And, naturally, they paid kickbacks to the officials protecting their racket.

Warren asked a grand jury to indict Sheriff Becker, Public Works Commissioner William H. Parker, other public officials and the shady contractors. Warren subpoenaed all available records, but key and intermediary witnesses had either been bribed or feared to testify, and threats were even made against Warren's life.

He decided to take the case to the public. Daily, he released to the press the secret grand jury transcripts of testimony concerning defrauded victims, perhaps to embarrass witnesses who had invoked the Fifth Amendment privilege of self-incrimination. Warren was promptly accused by the defendants' lawyers of doing so illegally and being in contempt of court. Indeed, his actions did seem in clear violation of the law. Seeking to justify them, Warren pointed out that while the penal statute said that members of a grand jury may not disclose evidence, there was no specific law saying that a district attorney could not do so. Josh Eppinger, the San Francisco *Examiner*'s retired executive editor, recollects, "This was the first time that grand jury testimony was released *before* indictments were returned. Earl Warren was a tough law-and-order D. A. who fought his case in public in this highly unorthodox way." Interestingly, forty-five years later, the retired Warren was not proud at how D. A. Warren probably had broken California law.

Yet it often disheartened the future Chief Justice that some of the area's judges squeamishly disqualified themselves from the difficult case. "Judges should take the hard ones, not just high pop flies," he complained privately.

But with aroused public opinion now strongly behind him, Warren personally prosecuted the contracting racketeers. Sheriff Becker resigned. Other public officials and contractors were later convicted and imprisoned. The racket was broken and so were Becker's protection, speakeasy, gambling, prostitution and other illegal activities. In the end, Commissioner Parker, Sheriff Becker and several corrupt contractors were sent to San Quentin Prison.

A subsequent Warren crusade was launched against the entire Alameda city administration. An investigation revealed that the mayor, city manager and all except one councilman (who had suddenly resigned) were stealing city funds and conducting a shake-down racket compelling local merchants to pay protection money. The accused denied any wrongdoing until confronted with incriminating signed receipts. They then pleaded guilty and were imprisoned.

Warren's success in cleaning up such corruption enabled him to be re-elected to his second term in November 1930 by the largest majority won by any district attorney in Alameda County history. His salary was boosted to $7,200 a year, and he was elected president of the fifty-eight-member District Attorneys Association of California. When a new San Francisco D.A. took office at an $18,000 annual salary, he publicly pledged, "I'm going to try to do the kind of job that Earl Warren is doing." However, Alameda County citizens, safely sipping their whiskey in speakeasies across the bay in San Francisco, had mixed feelings about this promise.

After Earl's 1930 re-election, the Warrens moved out of their five-room apartment into a purchased three-story seven-bedroom house on Larkspur Road in residential Oakland. There, they began raising the photogenic family from which candidate Warren later derived such political mileage.

Five of the six blue-eyed children were born during a six-year, four-month period: Virginia on September 13, 1928; Earl, Jr. on January 31, 1930; Dorothy on June 12, 1931; Nina Elizabeth ("Honeybear") on October 15, 1933; and Robert on January 9, 1935.

With their doctor's blessing, Earl accompanied his wife into the hospital delivery room when each of their children was born. "My husband stayed right with me throughout and it helped a lot," reports his wife, "even though he was as white as the surgical gown the nurses gave him to wear."

Nina Warren nursed all of her babies and thriftily got through the Depression on her husband's public servant salary, by doing considerable home dry cleaning and most of her own housework.

When one child caught mumps, chicken pox, measles or whooping cough, several others would usually catch it too. Nina Warren somehow managed to handle every emergency, but when she was in the hospital giving birth to her youngest, four of the older children came down with chicken pox. Their father had to take over. He stayed home from the district attorney's office for a week, moved all of them, complete with toys, into the master bedroom, and played with them until they were well. Today they all fondly recall that happy chicken pox week.

Like many of his generation, the head of the Warren household had a strict rule: *no business at home.* He refused to see official visitors at his house and only accepted the most urgent business telephone calls from his staff. "Home is for living," he insisted. "It belongs to the family." Although he worked long and hard hours at his office in the county courthouse and would go there late at night if necessary, he never brought his official problems into his home. The Warrens' only guests were intimate friends.

When district attorneys from other areas, or representatives of the state government in Sacramento or the federal government in Washington came to Oakland to visit him, he generally took them to dinner at his town club.

"During a case, I never questioned my husband about it," recalls Nina Warren. "If I had known something, I might inadvertently have let it slip. After it was all over, though, he might occasionally mention things that had happened."

"I never discussed crime with the children," Warren once told me, "because youngsters are extremely impressionable. I've always hated crime and the sordid accompanying business of arrests, convictions and imprisonments. I never believed it was a proper picture to expose to growing children."

Late one afternoon, however, Earl Warren's public business finally invaded his home. The telephone rang and when Nina Warren answered it, an ominous voice told her to warn her husband that if he did not stop a current investigation, she and the children would be harmed.

Because she was alone in the house, she instinctively gathered her three young children together and carefully bolted all the doors and windows.

She did not stop trembling until her husband, whom she had immediately telephoned, rushed home and comforted her. Calmly, they then discussed the possibility of requesting police protection for the children, or even of temporarily sending them away. But they agreed that either of these measures would upset their youngsters. Finally, Earl Warren quietly concluded, "My dear, we can't live in fear. We've encouraged the children to live without fear. So we must too. Fear is defeat in advance."

Mrs. Earl Warren was to face many more such threats in ensuing years, including one delivered a generation later, on the morning when her husband was about to offer his eulogy in the Capitol rotunda for martyred President John F. Kennedy.

During this period, Earl Warren had kept the district attorney's office strictly nonpartisan and free of politics. But, as a twice-proven vote-getter who was acquitting himself well in public office, he did not escape the attention of state and even national Republican leaders. Nor did the fact that his loyalty to the GOP had remained steadfast since his becoming D. A.

In November 1920, six months after taking office, he voted for the conservative Harding-Coolidge ticket over the more liberal Democratic James M. Cox-Franklin D. Roosevelt slate. In 1924 he outwardly supported President Calvin Coolidge, but in the privacy of the voting booth he cast his ballot for a man whom he admired infinitely more: Progressive Party candidate Robert M. LaFollette. He knew that it was a wasted vote, but it was something that his conscience impelled him to do.

In 1928, Warren was named an alternate delegate to the Republican National convention in Kansas City, which nominated Herbert Hoover on the first ballot. Back in Alameda County, Republican Warren dutifully campaigned for the "Great Humanitarian" for whom, as president of the Hoover College Club of California, Warren had urged the "Men and Women of California Universities" to vote.

In 1932, Warren was a full delegate to the Republican National Convention in Chicago, which unenthusiastically renominated President Hoover. The Depression had engulfed the nation. With a stock market crash, vast unemployment, rising bank failures, bankruptcies, mortgage foreclosures, farm evictions, soup kitchens and bread lines, Hoover's 1928 campaign promise of "prosperity" now seemed a bitter national joke. Forty-two states, including California—and Warren's own Alameda County—voted overwhelmingly against the bewildered Hoover, though Warren loyally stood by the GOP standard-bearer whom he personally later grew to dislike. Franklin Delano Roosevelt was swept into office on a landslide. A new era was dawning for America, and a new cycle in Earl Warren's life was about to begin.

In searching retrospectively for early clues in the emerging character of the future Chief Justice, one is immediately struck by the apparent discontinuity in his personal development. Instead of evolving gradually, he seems to have progressed by sudden leaps. Perhaps the word that best fits is *transformed*: The shy Bakersfield schoolboy was transformed into the convivial Berkeley undergraduate. The ambitionless youth was transformed into the intense young lawyer. The easygoing clerk was transformed into the relentless district attorney. And yes, the lackluster law student—there is even future evidence—was eventually transformed into an unacknowledged legal scholar.

This is not to say that there were no constants in Warren's personality. Quite the contrary. But it does suggest that he demonstrated an astonishing ability to rise to new challenges. At successive stages in his early career—at Berkeley, at Boalt Hall, as a law clerk, as D.A.—he was called upon not only to do things he had not previously done, but to *be* something he had not been before. And on each occasion, he accomplished the necessary transformation with exceptional speed and success.

This ability to respond well—even brilliantly—to entirely new sets of circumstances seems to have been a trait that Warren nurtured, developed and retained until the end of his eighty-three years. Like most innate talents, it is somewhat mysterious, more easily observed than defined. Yet it is indubitably one of the keys to understanding some of Earl Warren's subsequent actions and some of the truly amazing transformations he was still to undergo.

Chapter Three

The Roosevelt Years
1932–1945

*D*uring the dozen years of Franklin D. Roosevelt's presidency, Warren moved directly into big-time politics. Although a faithful Republican, he nevertheless found much to admire in the Democratic President—his verve, his idealism, his bold experimentation and his incomparable political mastery. Indeed, there would come a time when Warren's enemies would even dub him "a Republican Roosevelt." But that was far in the future. The Warren of 1933 still had much to learn about the art of politics.

Apparently one of the first things that attracted the commoner Californian to the patrician President was FDR's sense of humor. Warren was fond of quoting Roosevelt's story about the GOP big businessman who gave a Wall Street newsboy a quarter every morning, swiftly glancing at the front page and then returned the newspaper, saying, "I'm only interested in the obituary notices."

"But the obituary page is in the middle of the paper and you don't even look at it," protested the puzzled newsboy.

"Son," shot back the businessman, "the sonofabitch I'm interested in will be on Page One!"

But while Roosevelt was beguiling and reforming a nation, Warren was making modest political progress of his own. In 1934 he was easily re-elected to a third four-year term as district attorney of Alameda County. By now, he had definitely renounced his early

55

dream of becoming a private trial lawyer. "I realized that I was spoiled for private practice because of the enjoyment I was getting out of public service," he said. "I already had had my baptism of fire."

Warren's *pro bono publico* instincts were fortified when, in a single year, 1934, he was awarded the United States Flag Association's medal for outstanding achievement in law enforcement; named to an American Bar Association Criminal Law vice-chairmanship; and invited to help launch the Bay Area's Legal Aid Society.

He was soon to learn, however, that a public figure's life is not all laudation and laurels when his ethics were excoriated and his career jeopardized in the controversial 1936 "ship murder case," the most bitter imbroglio of his public life until then. Conservatives and most California newspapers called this *cause célèbre* a "Communist plot." Liberals and leftists angrily cried "labor frameup." Three decades later, retired Chief Justice Warren regretted that he may not have observed all of the defendants' constitutional rights in this case, even though the American Civil Liberties Union never protested.

These were the facts: Chief engineer George W. Alberts of the *S.S. Point Lobos,* a freighter on the Alameda dock, was found stabbed to death in his cabin. His skull had been cracked by a two-foot printing roller and his leg nearly severed by a huge knife. Vehemently anti-union and anti-Communist, he had recently fired a crew member in a dispute concerning overtime wages.

After a six-month investigation during which Warren was frequently threatened with political reprisals, his office indicted three union officials and one "fingerman" of the Marine Firemen, Oilers, Watertenders and Wipers Union for conspiracy in Alberts' murder. Testimony revealed that two union men, Earl King and E. G. Ramsey, were accused of sending two goons to beat him "within an inch of his life." Neglecting to bring a ruler, one of the alleged assailants had misjudged the inch and beaten Alberts to death instead. The goon promptly fled the country and joined the French Foreign Legion.

The morning after the accused men were arrested, two defense lawyers came to the sheriff's office with writs of habeas corpus, only to find that the suspects were not in the sheriff's custody.

The District Attorney's office had reportedly held them all night for questioning without counsel—a procedure which the Warren Court later decisively condemned.

Warren was denounced for this, as a "reactionary enemy of organized labor" by the left wing of the newly created Congress of Industrial Organizations (CIO). During the three-month trial Harry Bridges, the articulate Australian-born leader of the leftist maritime unions, ordered several thousand pickets around the red brick courthouse daily. Other pickets, including some demanding the impeachment of the district attorney, marched in front of his home in Oakland. The threatening letters and telephone calls frightened Mrs. Warren and the children.

The trial was no model of jurisprudence. Jurors were picked from lists submitted by influential industrialists and bankers; no union members were chosen. Defense lawyers protested when the case was transferred to Judge Frank M. Ogden, who had formerly been a Warren deputy and had been elevated to the bench on Warren's recommendation. It was also later revealed that the deputy prosecuting this bitter case under Warren's direction had borrowed $25,000 from a woman juror—a fact unknown to both Warren and the defense during the trial.

Because the union officials had been accused of conspiring to commit murder, but not of actually committing it, Warren asked for a second-degree verdict instead of the death sentence. The defendants were convicted on this charge and sentenced to twenty-six years in San Quentin Prison.

In an unsuccessful appeal, the defense charged the prosecution with wiretapping and using third-degree methods, and further complained that a key prosecution witness had been on the hidden payroll of the shipping firm that owned the *Point Lobos*.

Impartial legal students of the case agreed that although there were certainly many dubious aspects to its handling which did not reflect well on Earl Warren, he did act in good faith. His prime motive had been to convict men whom he was convinced were guilty. Many unforgiving unionists, however, still contend that Warren ruthlessly played up to the antilabor, Red-baiting Establishment. As one old-timer declared not long ago, "Earl Warren was great as a Chief Justice but he was a sonofabitch as a district attorney in *Point Lobos*."

The case sharply divided California labor. At the end of the trial, Warren the politician, anxious not to lose future labor support, sanctimoniously said: "This case is not a case against union labor, but rather one against individuals who have forced themselves into a position of power among honest workers. Tens of thousands of union labor men in this state will rejoice that this case has been cleared up, and if it had not been for the assistance given by the conservative and law-abiding elements of the Fireman's Union, the crime never would have been solved."

But a majority of unionists remained unconvinced, and Warren's election two years earlier as Republican State Party chairman, was another factor tending to alienate them and left-leaning constituencies. Moreover, his problems with the left were almost immediately aggravated by the gubernatorial campaign of socialist author Upton Sinclair, now running on the Democratic ticket.

Sinclair's "End Poverty in California" (EPIC) soak-the-rich campaign was sufficiently radical that even Roosevelt and the Democratic National Committee withheld their support. Conservatives, not surprisingly, reacted with a less-than-becoming virulence. Warren, who personally did not have any particular, anti-Sinclair bias, was, by virtue of his state chairmanship, nonetheless obliged to parrot the party line on Sinclair. Dutifully, he called the Democratic candidate's proposals "half socialistic, half communistic," warning that Sinclair's election would threaten private industry and every investor, and would bring chaos to California.

This was standard campaign pap and probably would have gone largely unnoticed had it been the worst of the anti-Sinclair activities. But, alas, it was not. Right-wing Republican extremists, especially in the movie industry, launched a scurrilous campaign of personal vilification against Sinclair which approximated overkill. It infuriated the left and needlessly turned off many independents. Although Warren had no connection with these activities, he was inevitably tainted by them.

The Sinclair campaign and the *Point Lobos* case moved Warren's political image sharply to the right. Many now began to view him as a hard-nosed archconservative, ignoring—or, more likely, not knowing—the fact that in neither situation had his actions arisen from reactionary motives. This misperception of the man behind the political role was later to give rise to widespread confusion when Warren began to display an apparently inexplicable liberalism.

In the meantime, however, Warren's position within the California Republican party was stronger than ever. Sinclair's drab Republican opponent, incumbent Governor Frank Merriam, had narrowly squeaked through to victory. Warren, who had managed the campaign, though privately considering Merriam a mediocrity, was given much of the credit for the victory.

In June 1936, while his staff was gathering evidence on the *Point Lobos* case, Warren, now forty-five years old, journeyed to the Republican National Convention in Cleveland as chairman of the uninstructed California delegation. In this post, he openly battled publisher William Randolph Hearst, who sought to control the delegation. Warren was aided by the Republican publishers of the Oakland *Tribune,* San Francisco *Chronicle* and Los Angeles *Times.* Although Depression-scarred Herbert Hoover had indicated his availability again to be the candidate, the convention unanimously nominated Kansas Governor Alfred M. Landon to oppose Roosevelt's second-term bid.

National GOP Committeeman Warren obediently criticized the New Deal during the campaign. He hailed the U.S. Supreme Court's 1935 Schechter "sick chicken" decision, which declared Roosevelt's National Recovery Administration unconstitutional, and deplored FDR's "impractical experimentation" and "waste of public funds." Loyally, he saw "Landon sentiment, . . . making itself felt in California."

(Ironically, though during FDR's later Court-packing attempt the small voice of Alameda County District Attorney Warren protested that "the President had no right to destroy the Supreme Court's traditional independence," in due course, as the result of deaths and resignations, Roosevelt was able to appoint eight New Deal Justices and thus could be said to have been the principal architect of the Court that Warren would one day inherit.)

GOP euphoria soared, especially after a *Literary Digest* poll predicted victory for the "Kansas Coolidge." But Landon ignominiously lost forty-six of the forty-eight states, carrying only Maine and Vermont. FDR even swept California by nearly a million votes, showing Warren that the only way to win was bipartisanly.

When Roosevelt entered the White House in 1933, Warren was already planning his next career step upward. He decided that he wanted to be California's attorney general and vowed to reinvigorate the slumbering office, as FDR had the Oval Office. The state attorney general since 1902 had been seventyish Ulysses S. Webb. Under his easygoing stewardship the office served the governor and legislature in a passive way, largely representing the state in appealing criminal cases. It maintained no central files; encouraged little teamwork among local law-enforcement agencies; allowed cases and queries to gather dust for years; engaged in virtually no law enforcement. Because this figurehead position paid merely $5,000 a year, the attorney general was expected to supplement his income in private practice, as did Webb, who was routinely re-elected every four years with merely token opposition.

In the spring of 1933, Warren called upon the venerable Webb and told him that whenever the older man decided to retire, he would file for the position. He promised, though, that he would never oppose Webb as long as he wanted the job.

Webb thanked him for his candor, but the aged nine-term incumbent kept the aspiring Warren waiting five long years before reluctantly announcing his retirement in February 1938. Meanwhile, the farsighted Warren, noting Roosevelt's bold New Deal measures, had drafted several constitutional amendments to both modernize and strengthen the obsolete attorney general's office. These changes would transform it from a minor political sinecure into a major state office, and the California attorney general would then rank next in importance to the governor. Warren solicited the support of the District Attorneys Association, of which he was a former president, and aroused civil organizations during the 1934 election to push these amendments through the legislature.

One amendment empowered the attorney general to oversee all of the state's local and county law-enforcement agencies. Another, in making the attorney general functionally as well as officially California's highest law-enforcement officer, enabled him to supervise all other state agencies in law-enforcement. A third established a California Department of Justice—the first such state body in the nation—and a final amendment raised the attorney general's annual salary from $5,000 to $11,000 (the same as that of Justices on the California Supreme Court) and forbade him from engaging in private practice. "Warren's setting up a good job for himself," snickered political insiders. "But he needs that money to support his large family."

Ironically, as Alameda District Attorney Warren was actively preparing to run for California's highest law-enforcement position, he suffered a bitter personal tragedy that resulted from a particularly gruesome crime.

On the warm Saturday evening of May 14, 1938, Methias Warren, then seventy-three years old, was sitting in the living room of the small frame house at 709 Miles Street in Bakersfield where he had lived for forty-two years. The unkempt house was crammed with old unused furniture that he periodically removed for the tenant renters of his hundred-odd cottages which he had built and owned in East Bakersfield. He had been reading the same local evening newspaper that his son used to deliver as a boy, but had probably fallen asleep. His wife was in Oakland convalescing from a cataract operation. For several years, she had rented an apartment there near the home of their daughter, Ethel Plank.

The screened doors and windows were all open. A tenant came in at 8 P.M. to pay him the fifteen dollars' rent. This tenant was the last person to see Methias Warren alive.

The following morning, as his son was about to speak at a Sunday Masonic breakfast meeting in a Berkeley hotel, he was interrupted by an urgent telephone call from the Bakersfield police. Methias Warren had been savagely bludgeoned to death by an unknown assailant with a foot-long iron pipe presumably taken from his back yard strewn with pipes, plumbing and old stoves. Robbery appeared to have been the motive. The pipe had been found in a neighbor's yard; the victim's broken glasses were on the kitchen floor, and his empty wallet was found in a nearby schoolyard, with the other contents scattered on the street. Two pennies were found in the slain man's trouser pocket.

It was immediately rumored that this was a political murder aimed at his crimebusting son. The district attorney of Alameda County had no jurisdiction in Kern County, where the murder had been committed, but he immediately dispatched several aides to cooperate with Bakersfield authorities. On Sunday evening, before boarding a plane for Bakersfield himself, he sadly said to reporters, "This is a terrible reason to have to make a trip home."

In his Bakersfield hotel room, Warren later held a press conference. Reporters flocked there from all over the state. Speaking honestly and emotionally about his father, he broke down while sitting on the bed and sobbed. Everyone present was deeply moved, remaining transfixed. But one photographer snapped a picture. Shocked at such insensitivity, the other reporters reproachfully removed the film from his camera and exposed it to the light. No picture of this scene ever appeared. "We all felt that Warren was such a decent guy that even us bastards wanted to protect him," recollects an onlooker.

More than a hundred suspects were questioned, and several were held, but all were later released because of lack of evidence.

Warren's chief investigator, Oscar Jahnsen, after months of investigation became convinced that he had identified the murderer, a man who had been involved in business dealings with Matt Warren. But before Jahnsen could wrap up the case, overeager local authorities clumsily began to third-degree the suspect without informing him of his rights; when the man's attorney found out, he advised him to remain silent, and no conclusive evidence was found to link him to the murder.

"I blew my top when they blew the case," Jahnsen recollects, still bitter. "The Chief wanted his father's murderer apprehended, but he refused to break any of his own rules or use his office to convict a guilty man without solid, legally secured evidence. He warned us that we had to follow our strict office rules in investigating *any* murder. He even said to me later, 'Oscar, you did the right thing.' "

But Bakersfield Chief of Police Robert B. Powers, who supervised twenty-five men working exclusively on the case, believed that the culprit was an itinerant prowler. "The motive was robbery and murder was not deliberately intended," he said for years. This view was accepted by the slain man's bereaved son. Among the suspects was a San Quentin prisoner—convicted of another crime—who could have been in Bakersfield at the time. "I wanted to put a stool pigeon in his cell and plant a dictaphone there," revealed Powers. But when informed of this plan, Earl Warren flatly rejected it. "We don't break the law when trying to enforce the law," he said simply.

The slain Matt Warren, a miser-hermit according to neighborhood scuttlebutt, had hidden under his kitchen floorboards considerable cash, collected from his rentals. Some California newspaper stories described him as a tight-fisted "millionaire," "capitalist" and "real estate king." But his only son promptly disputed these descriptions, contending in a May 17, 1938, Oakland *Tribune* interview that "Father spent his life at hard work ever since he was seven years old. His only luxury in life was helping his children and grandchildren." Although estimates of Methias Warren's estate, mostly from his property, ranged as high as $177,000, according to the Sacramento *Bee*, the murdered man left no fortune.

Nina Warren, who went to the scene of the crime to dispose of her father-in-law's belongings, remembers it as being one of the saddest days of her life. Among other remnants, she found the metal forms which Methias had learned to use from his correspondence courses to half-sole his family's shoes. Years later, when Nina asked her governor husband what he wanted most for his birthday, he wistfully replied, "A pair of half-soled shoes done at home."

Although profoundly disturbed by his father's cold-blooded murder, Warren concealed his trauma in public. But, as a family friend observed, "Earl's attitude toward crime stiffened after that. He became an even tougher law-enforcement officer." The tragic memory forever engraved on the future author of the *Miranda* decision the need for improving crime prevention and local law-enforcement agencies.

Years later when I asked Chief Justice Warren about his father's still-unsolved murder, his smiling face suddenly grew stern. Understandably, the painful memory was something that he could *never* erase.

Could this memory of his own father's brutally bludgeoned head possibly have been a subsconscious reason why Chairman Warren twenty-six years later refused to release publicly the photographs and X-rays of the disfigured head of President John F. Kennedy? Surely he knew, had he done so, that they would have been instantly plastered on the front pages of newspapers and television screens throughout the world. When he sorrowfully observed the police photographs of his murdered father's head, he was relieved that they were never made public by sensationalists.

Three months before his father's death—on February 17, 1938—Warren had announced his candidacy for state attorney general. Now, shortly after his father's funeral, he stepped up his campaign. Dipping into his meager savings, he posted the necessary separate filing fees—at $200 each—to become a candidate on not only the Republican but also the Democratic and Progressive tickets. This "cross filing" was then permitted under California law since 1911 in the belief that it produced truly nonpartisan anti-"spoils system" public servants.

Oddly, this was the first election in which Warren actually ran as a Republican, despite the fact that he had always been registered as one. Candidates for district attorney in California were not required to designate their party affiliations on ballots, thanks to the earlier nonpartisan reforms of Governor Hiram Johnson, who, like Robert La Follette, the Independent maverick, had bolted the Republican party to become a Progressive. The Johnson legacy enabled Republican Warren to ride simultaneously the twin horses of partisanship and independence on the California electoral merry-go-round.

Still, as a political realist Warren saw that he needed Democratic votes to win. He well remembered how in both 1932 and 1936 Roosevelt had triumphantly swept California, and he knew that Democrats for the first time in decades now numerically dominated it. Warren expected his Republican and Progressive opposition to be perfunctory. Therefore, he concentrated on trying to capture the longshot Democratic primary endorsement in August 1938. Hopefully, he encouraged the formation of Democrats-for-Warren clubs, especially in Los Angeles, and cultivated the support of such Democratic liberals as Robert W. Kenny. Warren sent Kenny a handwritten letter affirming his commitment to civil liberties. This was made public during the campaign and helped Warren among liberal Democrats. Gone were the days when Warren had assailed Roosevelt's New Deal programs as "socialistic." Now, in campaign literature pitched to Democrats, he shrewdly echoed this nonpartisan Roosevelt statement which invited ticket-splitting:

> *Under a perfect party system of government, a bid for political favor should rest solely upon political principle and good adminis-tration. We should seek through every possible means to move toward that objective . . . They [younger voters] are less and less concerned with party emblems; they are saying more and more: "I belong to this or that party, but actually I always split my ticket." That is a happy sign for the future of America.*

Answering liberal and leftist Democratic charges that he had been an antilabor reactionary in the *Point Lobos* and other cases, Warren made speeches in labor areas championing the Bill of Rights. He promised that if elected attorney general, he would vigorously defend labor's right to picket; protect minorities against the tyranny of the majority; and oppose any official vigilantism, such as was then being ruthlessly practiced in Jersey City by Mayor Frank ("I Am the Law") Hague.

Some liberal and leftist Democrats remained unconvinced, but Warren did not lose his momentum. He maintained his campaign against corruption, sin and communism—he never came out for Motherhood but surely would have, if that had seemed necessary —and promised that under his stewardship, California would have a truly nonpartisan attorney general. While his seven Democratic opponents were busy vilifying one another, Republican Warren squeaked through with 28,000 more votes than the leading Democratic candidate. Thus, in the August 1938 primary, three months before the November election, he had sewn up the attorney general nominations of the three major parties.

Caught flat-footed, the Democrats desperately tried to defeat him with a write-in pension plan candidate in the November election. But Warren captured a million and a half more votes than his closest write-in Democratic challenger. With Republicans in the political doghouse nationally, he was the only major Republican victor to survive the 1938 California Democratic landslide which swept into the governership Culbert L. Olson, an outspoken New Dealer riding Roosevelt's coattails. Olson was elected California's first Democratic governor in forty-four years. For Warren it was his first taste of the juicy apple of nonpartisan victory.

The campaign promises of the attorney general-elect were tested on his first day in office, January 2, 1939. At 9 A.M. he arrived in his huge, wood-paneled quarters in San Francisco's new State Building. He had barely had time to inspect the red-bound law volumes or to observe the City Hall Plaza's pigeons roosting on his windowsill before he received an urgent telephone call. Warren was informed that outgoing Republican Governor Merriam had just appointed his executive secretary as a Superior Court Judge in Warren's own Alameda County, even though this man had been accused of selling pardons to Folsom and San Quentin prisoners. Within an hour, Warren had the alleged culprit in his office. Securing the man's permission to have a stenographer present, he interrogated the new "judge" for two hours. Later, he had him read and sign this transcript. It was used not only to keep the man off the bench but eventually to help put him behind bars. Warren's swift cancellation of a last-minute appointment by an outgoing

Republican Administration may have troubled some GOP politicians, but the Democratic Los Angeles *Daily News* crowed: "Official California is in for a good scrubbing behind the ears."

One morning soon afterward, Governor Olson telephoned him inquiring whom Warren planned to appoint to certain non-civil service jobs.

"Why do you ask?" Warren parried.

"Well, as governor I certainly should have something to say about the people you appoint."

"Not while *I'm* attorney general," was the reply.

This fierce autonomy hardly endeared him to the new and equally strong-willed governor, whose aides referred to the attorney general as the arrogant "Earl of Warren." The fact that the governor stood at the left flank of the Democratic party, while the attorney general still apparently stood at the center of the Republican party did not help matters.

In forming his new staff, Warren quickly fired the political deadwood and recruited new members without regard to party affiliation, until he had fifty hard-working attorneys and investigators on his team. Forbidding any of his deputies to engage in private practice, he pushed through compensating salary boosts for them, up to $700 monthly. A leading aide, Democrat William T. Sweigert, now a U. S. District Judge in San Francisco, recalls, "The Chief was a demanding man for whom to work. He was a perfectionist who treated his staff fairly. He gave all of us wide latitude and responsibility." Nonetheless, if a job was performed negligently or any disloyalty was evident, the ordinarily genial Warren could unleash devastating ire toward the offender."

The attorney general's office was departmentalized into new criminal, civil litigation, collections, tax and other divisions. The new chief quickly revitalized the office, just as he would every other one he was to occupy.

Many Warren critics insist that he became liberal only after becoming Chief Justice. However, Democrat Adrian A. Kragen, one of his former deputies and now a Berkeley law professor, recollects: "But those of us who had the good fortune to sit around the attorney general's office on Saturday afternoons when the University of California wasn't playing football and hear him discuss medical care and equal educational and economic opportunities for everyone, knew that his basic humanity was always one of his outstanding and most endearing qualities."

The staff worked out of three offices in San Francisco, Sacramento and Los Angeles. During Warren's four-year term his aides wrote approximately three thousand legal opinions for the Olson Administration and legislative officials, and were involved in nearly five hundred criminal prosecutions.

Not unmindful of their publicity value, Warren personally handled many of the antigambling prosecutions, as he had during his district attorney days. He disapproved of gambling, not because he was a bluenose, but because he knew, from his boyhood visits to the gambling houses, just how fraudulent most organized gambling was. What troubled him most was the link between professional gambling and corrupt public officials. "No one can run a big gambling establishment without paying off," Warren insisted.

Dog-track racing was the attorney general's first gambling target. He called it unsupervised gambling, and saw it as both illegal and "a plain racket." Years earlier as Alameda County D. A., he had closed the local dog-tracks, but now seven were booming elsewhere in California, unregulated by the state and protected by local authorities. "The odds are fixed and so are the dogs," Warren told his staff. "Now go out and get the evidence."

When Warren had it, he summoned to his office John "Black Jack" Jerome, an ex-strikebreaker in San Francisco and now the kingpin of the El Cerrito track. This was the only one then operating, since the seven track owners had divided up the season among themselves to avoid conflicting races. Jerome arrived at the attorney general's office with his lawyer.

Warren told him that he had enough evidence to prosecute immediately, but would rather save the state—and Jerome—the money by having Jerome close down his operation voluntarily. The closing of all the other tracks would follow.

The dog-track operator and his attorney requested a brief recess. When they returned, Black Jack asked whether he could hold that Saturday night's race and then close.

Warren, quietly amused, replied that while he could not give Jerome permission to engage in illegal activity, he did not think that his office would be prepared to act before Monday morning. Therefore, if Jerome would *really* cease operations on that Saturday night, he would not prosecute the complaint.

Black Jack got the message. After holding his final race on Saturday, he reluctantly closed. None of the other six track operators dared reopen, then or since. The sport is outlawed in California.

Horseracing bookmakers likewise inflamed Warren's Puritan zeal. Aware that this racket thrived thanks to communication facilities, Warren summoned to his office officials of Western Union, the Pacific Telephone and Telegraph Company and even its parent American Telephone and Telegraph Company. Though all obtained considerable revenue from transmitting horse-racing information, these communications officials were persuaded by Warren to cease their California racing information operations. Moses Annenberg's lucrative Nationwide News Service for bookmakers, which operated out of Chicago, promised to terminate all service to California. However, by the very next day, racing results were being transmitted by another company, by a Mexican radio station, by walkie-talkies and by bookies operating from the Nevada border at Lake Tahoe.

An overzealous Warren deputy found an old map "proving" that all of Lake Tahoe belonged to California. Warren overruled him. As he explained later, "Even if our raids there were sustained in the courts, our action would jeopardize the legality of law-abiding citizens of Lake Tahoe. Some of their marriages might be voided and some of their children might be called illegitimate." Thus, Warren's war against the bookmakers ended in an American, if not Mexican, standoff. The bookies were too tough a nut to crack.

The slot and pinball machine rackets were far easier to demolish. The attorney general's office ruled that the liquor license of any establishment harboring a slot machine would be immediately revoked. Ironically, one seemingly harmless hangout which fell into the category was old Pop Kessler's in Berkeley, where collegian Earl Warren had raised many a beer mug. Ever since, he had periodically dropped in to chat with his former host. But one day, investigator Jahnsen strolled in to confiscate the single slot machine.

"Oscar, you're not going to do that!" old Pop Kessler protested. "Earl won't let you."

Jahnsen telephoned his boss, then handed the phone to Pop. After a minute, the crestfallen Kessler slowly put it down. Then he muttered incredulously, "I never thought my friend Earl would do this to *me*."

But Warren's most spectacular antigambling battle was a naval one.

It was waged on land simultaneously against four luxury gambling ships which were anchored off the Southern California coast at Santa Monica and Long Beach. Of the four—the *Rex*, *Texas*, *Tango* and *Showboat*—the *Rex* was the biggest and most arrogant. Its rum-running owner, Tony Cornero, who was reportedly financed by the Al Capone underworld, claimed that since his ship was more than three miles from shore, it was therefore on the international "high seas" and not subject to California law. Every day hundreds, sometimes thousands, of customers were water-taxied from shore to ship to play the dice and blackjack tables, roulette wheels and "one-armed bandit" slot machines. The floating sports palace was advertised in friendly leading newspapers, on radio and billboards and even via airplane skywriting. Cash-depleted customers later complained of roughneck treatment whenever they protested that the games had been fixed, but the *Rex* and the other ships flourished, sucking millions of nontaxable dollars out of the State of California.

Warren sent Oscar Jahnsen to inform Cornero that he would be given safe escort to leave the California area. Insisting that he was legally in the clear, Cornero refused to close down his operation.

Enraged by Cornero's defiance, Warren uncovered an ancient U. S. Supreme Court decision which empowered a state to curb any "public nuisance" even beyond territorial limits. A second old state ruling was interpreted to show that even though the *Rex* was three miles from shore, it was still anchored within an ancient "Bay" over which California could claim jurisdiction. A third ruling found water taxis "public conveyances" requiring licenses to operate, which, of course, the *Rex*'s water taxis lacked. Now convinced of his legal grounds, if not waters, Warren secured a court order which enabled him to raid the floating *Rex* casino and the three other gambling ships simultaneously.

Thus began the highly publicized naval maneuver of "Admiral" Warren. In July 1939 he formed a makeshift "fleet" consisting of four patrol, fire-fighting and fishing vessels mobilized from the state Fish and Game Commission, and sixteen water taxis. His "crew" was about three hundred law-enforcement officers, including some from the Los Angeles County sheriff's and district attorney's offices. Eight sea-going state accountants and lawyers accompanied them to examine the ship's books.

From his command post on a cliff at the Santa Monica Beach Club, the "Admiral" observed the *Rex* through telescope and field glasses, communicating his orders via shortwave radiophones. Three of the ships surrendered within a few hours but the *Rex* chose to resist. At 8 P.M. on July 29, Warren issued the command for his armada to attack it!

Suddenly a snag arose. Someone—probably a crooked law-enforcement officer—had alerted Cornero to the impending invasion. The *Rex*'s defending crew drove back the invaders with streaming fire hoses, and improvised an iron gate to prevent anyone from boarding. Undaunted, Warren ordered his commandos to blockade the ship. "If they won't let us on, we won't let anybody off," reasoned the land-based lawman. "A lot of the customers must be at their jobs the next day. Some husbands are on board whose wives don't know they're with girl friends, and some wives must be there gambling while their husbands are working."

The 650 stranded patrons threatened reprisals on the tormented Cornero. Finally the compassionate invading "Admiral" permitted them to return to shore but continued blockading the *Rex* to prevent it from fleeing.

The great California naval battle had now begun to make national headlines and the House of Representatives passed a California congressman's bill making it a federal offense to operate a gambling ship off any coast of the United States. But it was not until Cornero's patience and food supplies were exhausted that he finally hoisted the white flag and surrendered more than a week later.

Climbing into a patrol cutter, the triumphant Warren led his seagoing posse and reserve land troops aboard the *Rex*. "It was like General Grant accepting Robert E. Lee's sword in surrender," recalls Oscar Jahnsen.

When the handcuffed Cornero was booked at the nearby Santa Monica police headquarters, he was asked his occupation.

"Mariner, Goddammit!" he growled.

The vanquished Cornero threatened to sue Warren for "piracy on the high seas." But his threats proved as empty as many of his patrons' pockets. Had this defense been carried out, Earl Warren would have been the only future Chief Justice in American history ever accused of such a dastardly crime.

The seized, sacked gambling money was deposited in the state treasury. Cornero was finally persuaded to reimburse the State of California the $13,200 it had expended in raiding him and to pay the State Railroad Commission a negotiated $7,500 penalty for operating unlicensed water-taxi "public conveyances," and $4,200 in taxes. Jahnsen gleefully led a demolition crew aboard the *Rex* carrying crowbars and axes to destroy the hundred dice and blackjack tables, slot machines and roulette wheels.

Despite this occasional drama, the bulk of Warren's work between 1939 and 1942 was quiet administrative civil law. His office modernized many obsolete California laws and drafted many new statutes. In encouraging teamwork between state and local communities to solve problems that were too difficult or costly to overcome alone, a major achievement was writing into law the Statewide Mutual Assistance Act, which enabled a fire or police department to cross county or town lines to extinguish a fire or stop a riot. Before the passage of this badly needed law, many homes burned because adjoining fire departments refused to leave their communities lest their firemen be injured or equipment become damaged.

The attorney general's office likewise introduced pardon and parole reforms; improved state pensions for the elderly; investigated charges of mistreatment in public and private mental institutions, orphanages and nursing homes; handled an insurance company's liquidation and solvency proceedings against a building and loan association; opposed police troopers using unmarked cars; helped abolish the bias against black prizefighters in a Hollywood stadium; and compelled California exporters to pay their lawful sales taxes, defeating their threats to move out of the state. Warren accomplished these reforms largely by dividing the state into law-enforcement areas, and starting separate regional organizations of district attorneys, chiefs of police and sheriffs.

Before the U. S. Court of Claims he won $7 million for native Indians of California under "lost" 1851–52 treaties. He spent most of March 1939 testifying before congressional committees defending California's claim to ownership of the lush oil-producing tidelands (which he was later to come to believe should be federally controlled). Simultaneously, he fought a California oil company in court to stop its illegal drilling practices. The future Chief Justice also represented California in many cases before the U. S. Supreme Court, arguing before such new Roosevelt appointees as Justices Black and Douglas, his colleagues-to-be.

In recognition of his enlightened work, in 1940 he was elected president of the National Association of Attorneys General. At that time he confided to an intimate that he would not be unhappy if some day he were named U. S. Attorney General—by a Republican President.

Meanwhile, the backstage political conflict between Democratic Governor Olson and Republican Attorney General Warren was now in full public view. Actually, it had begun on January 7, 1939, when Olson, shortly after assuming office, fulfilled a campaign promise to pardon a labor organizer, Tom Mooney, who had become something of a martyr. Mooney had been convicted in the bombing deaths of ten persons and the wounding of forty others in a July 1916 San Francisco Preparedness Day parade. Although President Wilson had commuted Mooney's death sentence to life imprisonment, many liberals, unionists and civil libertarians, claiming that he was innocent, continued to campaign for his freedom. Republicans, however, generally opposed a pardon.

The attorney general did not challenge Governor Olson's right to pardon Mooney. Instead, Warren sought to *limit* the conditions so as not to unsettle the California law-enforcement structure, upset his own rather simplistic law-and-order philosophy or "cast any unwarranted reflection upon the agencies," as he wrote Olson. The governor scorned Warren's advice. Insisting that Mooney had been framed by perjured testimony, Olson pardoned him unconditionally in a dramatic scene in which the handcuffed Mooney was brought into a cheering Assembly hearing room and had his manacles removed.

Encouraged by the pardon of Mooney, some liberals pressured Governor Olson to do likewise for the three men imprisoned in former District Attorney Warren's controversial *Point Lobos* case. After a well-publicized 1940 visit with them in San Quentin prison (which Warren promptly charged was politically motivated) the governor proclaimed that they were not "the type of men who would deliberately participate in the murder of anyone" and that the trial evidence was "conflicting and impeached." Olson then urged the State Parole Board to release the prisoners.

The usually calm Earl Warren was furious. His integrity as an upholder of the law had been assailed. The later jurist who was accused of being "soft" on crime stormed: "The governor's statement is shocking. Silence on my part would be cowardice. These men are assassins—proved to be so. . . . When offenders are convicted, we must see to it that they stay convicted . . . neither money nor influences nor promises of votes should get them out of the penitentiary."

Olsen retorted that Warren's "venom" could be "attributed only to prejudice. It cannot be reconciled with a sense of fairness . . ." Sensing that the issue was growing too controversial, he did not pardon the men, but awaited their release the following year by the parole board for time served.

The Olsen–Warren feud next erupted over an important judicial appointment. The governor named to the California Supreme Court in July 1940, Max Radin, a liberal Democrat, an Olson supporter and an eminent Berkeley law professor. The then liberal San Francisco *Chronicle* endorsed Professor Radin as a man with "a passion for justice." By contrast, the then right-wing Los Angeles *Times* deplored his "political and social views" because the compassionate Radin had once imprudently written a letter urging judicial mercy for eighteen state relief employees who had been convicted of contempt for declining to answer questions about their communist affiliations before a Red-hunting state legislative committee.

The Judicial Qualifications Commission voted two to one against Radin's confirmation, compelling the governor to withdraw the nomination. The deciding vote was cast by Warren, an ex-officio board member. Ironically, the Max Radin of 1940 was to be the ideological blood brother of the Earl Warren of 1960.

Another issue dividing these two sincere, stubborn Swedes concerned civilian defense and war preparedness. The *drôle de guerre* in Europe had ended on May 10, 1940, when Hitler launched his dazzlingly successful blitzkrieg against France and the Low Countries. France fell in June. Within a month the Luftwaffe was scourging the English Channel preparing for the impending Battle of Britain. Most Americans still favored neutrality, but the looming prospect of a total Germany victory in Europe was swiftly undermining isolationist sentiment.

The war issue cut a zigzag path across party lines in the United States. Many western liberals, eastern conservatives and southern Democrats were isolationists, while some eastern liberals found themselves agreeing with western conservatives on intervention.

Governor Olson was a pacifist and an isolationist; Warren, while not yet an interventionist, strongly favored preparedness and civil defense.

Roosevelt was actively promoting the cause of interventionism. The tenor of his public utterances became increasingly bellicose. In September, without awaiting formal congressional approval, he transferred fifty U. S. destroyers to Britain in return for Caribbean bases. The President was convinced that the course of events in Europe would eventually bring a majority of Americans around to his way of thinking, but he felt that this process might be dangerously delayed if attitudes toward involvement were allowed to congeal along domestic party lines—something that could all too easily happen in the presidential campaign in the fall of 1940, when Roosevelt would run for an unprecedented third term. For this reason, four days before the Republican National Convention in June that nominated Wendell Willkie, "The Barefoot Boy from Wall Street," Roosevelt had ostentatiously appointed Republicans Henry L. Stimson and Frank Knox to the posts of Secretary of War and Secretary of the Navy, respectively. The President's insistence that defense and foreign policy be treated as bipartisan matters was successful. Not then, or at any later time, could the Republicans ever embrace isolationism as a party issue.

Warren probably lacked Roosevelt's grasp of the larger issues, yet he was sensitive enough to the political implications of what the President was doing. National defense, preparedness for war, vigilance against potential enemy subversion—all were themes that Warren at once believed in and realized could be convered into political capital in California. He promptly became the self-appointed spokesman for the war preparedness movement in his home state.

Warren did not do this in a consistently high-minded way. He was not above denouncing the Red Menace while exhorting right-wing superpatriots to man the defenses against Nazism. Today some of his public utterances would appear to contain more than a whiff of paranoia. But in the context of the California of the early 1940s, his new public stance was well received and politically effective. Olson, whose professed pacifism was now becoming increasingly unfashionable, could only fume—with perhaps at least some justice—that Warren was merely playing the opportunist.

A year and a half before Pearl Harbor, Warren flew to Washington to participate in a Federal-State Conference of Law

Enforcement Problems of National Defense. Returning to California, he convened enforcement officials to explain its recommendations, and presented his own proposal to divide sprawling California into nine defense zones and train both officials and volunteers for any emergency. It was a bold program, worthy of an FDR.

At last stung into trying to undercut Warren's headline-snatching, Olson, by executive decree, established in 1940 a State Council of Defense, designating himself as chairman. Warren was to be merely one of a figurehead eleven-member advisory committee. That should trim his sails, the Democratic governor thought. It did no such thing.

A month later, the irate attorney general convened his own eleven-day State Defense Conference—the first in the nation—which proved to be a model for other states. Speakers and participants included local and state law-enforcement officials, Army, Navy and FBI representatives, key fire chiefs, communications specialists, radio technicians and highway engineers. The theme: an all-embracing civilian defense program to defend California against any possible emergency or disaster.

Warren next wrote and shepherded through the legislature a Uniform Sabotage Prevention Act, which quickly became known as the Warren Act. Its aim was to protect airplane plants, shipyards and other essential defense industries from saboteurs and fifth columnists. Interference with the production of defense materials was made a felony with a possible ten years' imprisonment and $10,000 fine. Moreover, streets near defense plants could be blocked off to exclude interlopers.

Organized labor worried that this act might be used to prevent picketing. Indeed, when a Los Angeles judge used it to issue an injunction prohibiting picketing in a labor-management dispute, Warren rushed down and told the judge that this was not the law's intent and that he would oppose the injunction in court. The judge promptly withdrew it, much to the relief of labor leaders.

Governor Olson played his trump card a week after Pearl Harbor. On December 14, 1941, suddenly broadening his own defense powers, he proclaimed a state of emergency. Warren immediately challenged the governor's authority to issue such a proclamation. He cited a 1929 statute which specifically permitted the governor such a right in cases of earthquake, flood, fire or other disaster—but forbade it in time of war. Retributively, the attorney

75

general persuaded the legislature to limit the governor's powers and funds under this proclamation. The governor promptly retaliated by vetoing a $214,000 appropriation (which had passed both houses almost unanimously) allowing the attorney general's office to administer the civilian defense act.

The Olson-Warren impasse, although farcical in some respects, had become too serious to be allowed to continue. The governor now refused to cooperate with his chief law-enforcement officer on even the most trivial matters. The machinery of California government itself was beginning to break down.

One afternoon in early February 1942, Warren reached the end of his patience. He rolled back his chair, donned his topcoat and dark broad-brimmed hat, slammed the door and drove home to Oakland. Confronting his surprised wife, he announced that he could not sit in his office with a war going on and do nothing. Though he knew it was a long shot, he was going to run for governor.

Warren was warned that he had only an outside chance against the entrenched Democratic machine of Governor Olson, who was seeking re-election in November 1942. He was reminded that California boasted nearly a million more registered Democrats than Republicans (2,300,000 to 1,370,000). Friends even brought him private polls to prove what an overwhelming underdog he was. Less than 20 percent of those questioned said that they would vote for him, compared to 40 percent for Olson. The remaining 40 percent were undecided.

But Warren suspected that some hidden plusses could work in his favor. First, he would be running in a nonpresidential year, and not against the invincible Roosevelt ticket which had swept California in 1932, 1936 and 1940. Second, the hostile legislature and many Democrats were growing increasingly disenchanted with Olson, as well as vocal pressure groups for state pensions, such as Dr. Townsend's movement and the "Thirty Dollars Every Thursday" lobby quaintly known as the "Ham and Eggers." The latter were making whopping demands impossible for Olson to fulfull. Third, Warren could count on wide support among the state's largely Republican newspapers, as well as impassioned patriotic and law-enforcement groups.

Nonetheless, many fat-cat Republicans, fearing that they would merely be throwing away good money, now refused to contribute to any GOP gubernatorial hopeful in California. Thus, a host of five-and ten-dollar contributions were solicited by Warren boosters for the printing of urgently needed campaign literature. The impecunious Warren did, however, accept $7,500 from a California oil company lobbyist, for which he gave a receipt. This loan would embarrass him in subsequent years when he feuded with the oil industry, and inspired some leftists to dub him "Oil" Warren.

Attempts were made to secure an influential campaign chairman. Warren's prime backer, Oakland *Tribune* publisher Joseph Knowland, urged Independent Los Angeles Mayor Fletcher Bowron to head Warren's campaign, promising to support him for the U. S. Senate two years later. When Bowron refused, his hitherto cordial relations with Warren cooled.

Despite these obstacles, on April 9, 1942, Attorney General Earl Warren, still considered by political cognoscenti as an honest cornball, announced his candidacy for governor of California thus:

> *My experience has been in the field of nonpartisan government. I have served in the Army, in the government of my city and country, and was nominated to my present office of attorney general by the voters of the Republican, Democratic and Progressive parties. And I have sought to discharge my responsibilities without regard to partisan considerations.*
>
> *I believe in the party system, and have been identified with the Republican party in matters of party concern, but I have never found that the broad questions of national party policy have application to the problems of state and local government in California . . .*
>
> *None of [our local] problems permits a solution through partisanship. They cut entirely across party lines. This is particularly true of civilian protection, which at the moment I consider to be the most vital problem either presently with us or on our immediate horizon.*

On June 4, Warren, after paying his $250 filing fees, formally cross-filed for governor on both the Republican and Democratic tickets. In the September primary, he had little difficulty winning the GOP nomination from Robert W. Jessup, a Los Angeles county supervisor, and Wallace L. Ware, a former railway commissioner. The big surprise came in the Democratic primary. There, Republican Warren rolled up a whopping 404,000 votes compared with a relatively narrow 513,000 for Olson, who had scorned to cross-file. The overconfident Olsen, however, scoffed at upstart Warren as a "political eunuch, political hypocrite, puppet pretender not fit or competent to be governor."

But Warren sensed an opportunity in the split within the Democratic ranks. President Roosevelt, during his own 1940 third-term campaign, had sent Interior Secretary Ickes to California to heal the Democratic party split. He failed. Now, the breach between pro- and anti-Olsonites was not lost on Warren. He therefore piously intoned: "Nonpartisanship with me is not merely a political creed. Nor is it a catchall for political favor. No partisanship of any kind should be permitted to interfere with the maintenance of good government. None will interfere if I am elected . . ."

Realizing that Warren, heretofore the underdog, might be making some serious inroads with his self-righteous pitch, Olson aides telephoned presidential secretary Marvin McIntyre. Could the President possibly come to California to deliver a campaign speech for New Deal Governor Olson? If not, could he send a strong endorsement? And could McIntyre urge Democrat George Creel, President Wilson's World War I propaganda chief and a 1938 Olson supporter, to withdraw his sudden endorsement of Republican Warren? McIntyre telephoned Creel three times from the White House. Each time, Creel refused to budge. He later explained in his 1947 autobiography that Warren was a "vastly superior person [to Olson] in every way."

Roosevelt was nevertheless anxious to keep a Democrat as governor of a state so vital to his war effort. Hence, McIntyre made discreet telephone calls around the state concerning the Olson-Warren race. On September 4, 1942, George Pierce Baker, son of the well-known Harvard drama professor, then with the War Shipping Administration, wrote him the following letter from San Francisco:

Dear Mac:

I promised I would let you know how I found things out here and now with the Primary over, I am stronger than ever in the conviction that it would be a mistake for the "Boss" to try and pull the rabbit out of the hat in California . . .

Earl Warren is running on a non-partisan basis and has placed himself 100% behind the President so I do not see where we have anything to gain or lose. Also, as Director for California for the Committee for the Celebration of the President's Birthday for the past five years, Warren has served with me as my Northern California Chairman.

I am writing all this to you, Mac, as I know you see clearly and I know also how much the "Boss" relies in your judgement, so I repeat again, as I told you in Washington: I think it would be an error to step in out here. . . .

After conferring with the war-harried President, McIntyre replied on September 8:

Dear George:

Thanks a lot for your nice note.

It confirmed what I am getting from numerous sources, and I think your advice is always sound.

Had President Roosevelt decided otherwise and flown to California to make one quick campaign speech for Democratic Governor Olson, or had he even sent a written endorsement, Earl Warren's public career might have ended then.

The more Warren tasted the political sweets of bipartisanship, the better he liked them. Whatever support he was losing on the far right from this policy was more than compensated for by gains on the center and on the left. Soon he was pledging Roosevelt his "unqualified support in prosecuting the war" and appearing as an advocate for the Atlantic Charter and the Four Freedoms.

In retrospect, none of this need be taken very seriously. Politicians in hard-fought races are not generally expected to be overburdened by firmly held principles. Yet they are nonetheless finally accountable for their stance in regard to certain major issues. And on one of these Earl Warren—along with Olson, Roosevelt and the nation at large—behaved abominably.

There was nothing in his earlier life that Chief Justice Warren regretted more poignantly than his vehement—even rabid—support, before and after, of President Roosevelt's Executive Order 9066 of February 1942, which authorized the forced resettlement of

Japanese-Americans into West Coast concentration camps. Widely-syndicated newspaper columnist Walter Lippmann, shortly after conferring with Attorney General Warren, wrote "The Fifth Column on the West Coast"—a week before Roosevelt signed the evacuation order.

Today it is easier to understand this Draconian measure than to forgive it. In the dreadful two and a half months since December 7, 1941, America had seen its Pacific Fleet reduced to a shambles. Many of the 2,800 casualties at Pearl Harbor were Californians who had comprised a large proportion of the U.S. Pacific Fleet. The Philippines, Guam, Wake, Singapore, Hong Kong, the East Indies, the Gilberts—in fact the whole western Pacific and southeastern Asia—had been swallowed by the Japanese war machine. The popular mood in traumatized America—and particularly California—was a dangerous mixture of fury and panic. Rumors of an impending Japanese invasion of California were understandably believed in many quarters, as were lurid tales of widespread Japanese espionage and sabotage in California war plants. In such an atmosphere, the Nisei—the Japanese-Americans—inevitably fell victim to the national and California hysteria, suffering considerable injustice and no little violence from Uncle Sam and fellow citizens, in clear official violation of their civil rights, and even more so in the brutal and indiscriminate enforcement. The fact that the evacuation elicited few demurrers anywhere in America, including the U. S. Supreme Court, cannot excuse it. Nor can Earl Warren, the future civil libertarian and erstwhile member of the anti-Oriental Native Sons of the Golden West, be excused for his historically shabby behavior. Perhaps the kindest thing that can be said for Warren and the entire nation is that both later had the grace to be ashamed.

Persecution, however, was not an issue during the 1942 Olson-Warren campaign. Olson, still confident of re-election because of the heavier Democratic registration, campaigned mostly through radio speeches. Defending his record, he cited California's booming defense prosperity, and stressed social issues, reminding voters of his state medical insurance plan and attacking the "hot cargos" legislation against goods produced by strikebreakers or by workers involved in labor disputes.

His opponent ignored these and other sensitive issues, endlessly sounding the theme of bipartisanship as exemplified by his "Leadership, Not Politics" slogan. In generalities—even platitudes—

he promised better old age pensions and tax reduction, and foretold California's great future. He avoided extremes, committed no boners and said nothing earthshaking. "No audience was ever brought to its feet cheering a Warren speech," it was said, "but no audience ever walked out on him, either."

During an intensive three-month, day-and-night campaign he stumped the nine-hundred-mile-long state from the Oregon to the Mexican borders in an open car. In a whistle-stop campaign resembling the later one conducted by Harry Truman in 1948, Warren amiably pumped the hands of tens of thousands of voters, trying to remember their names and put them at ease. He talked to people simply and sincerely at airplane and shipyard factory lunch-hour rallies; in fruit-picking fields; on great highways and dirt roads; in oil refineries and mining camps—in both heavily populated and isolated areas. "I met more Californians face to face than I ever thought there were," he later recollected. "It was more fun than a picnic."

Mostly, he traveled with only his driver, Roy McCarthy, and his close friend, movie actor Leo ("The Cisco Kid") Carillo, who told jokes, signed autographs and then introduced Candidate Warren. "I believed that without a retinue," recalled Warren, "I could cover more ground."

On other fronts, his photogenic family, especially the three daughters, were slickly injected into the campaign by his part-time Whitaker-Baxter public relations advisors, who claimed that they helped erase his grim image as a cold, two-fisted prosecutor. But the weekend before the election, Warren suddenly fired Whitaker and Baxter for issuing a press release contrary to his instructions. "Warren was always his own campaign manager without any political or public relations organization," recollected another aide, Murray Chotiner, who gained later prominence as Nixon's political mentor. "Warren was a loner, who made all the important decisions himself." Chotiner was low-geared in the campaign after Warren became disenchanted with the man's character.

Albert C. Wollenberg, now a U. S. District Judge of Northern California, recalled this Rooseveltian aspect of Warren's 1942 campaigning in the January 1970 *University of California Law Review:*

> The man's deep faith in and affection for the whole people led him
> to seek out his fellows, enjoy their company, and listen to them.

During Warren's campaigns my best laid plans had gone awry . . .
I would often find him, the last to leave the hall, or standing on the
sidewalk, chatting with an old farmer or a grizzled hobo, or
whoever else had caught his interest. He would do this as Chief
Justice, too, stopping to chat with all manner of folk, be they black
children seeking his autograph or white and proper Birchites
seeking his impeachment. From this contact came a mutual
enrichment which for Warren took the form of knowledge of and a
respect for the deepest feelings of the people. Often a local politico
who tried to tell him what hometown opinion was on a given issue
would be met with a sharp: "That isn't the case. I know what the
farmers on Willits (or Redding, or Colusa, or whatever) feel, and I
know they are right."

Warren had to assuage the fears of many Southern Californians that
he was partial to the northern region of the state. When he campaigned in Los Angeles, he boasted that he had been born there
near Olivera Street. Dead silence—no political mileage. "Then I
casually mentioned that my father was raised in Iowa," he laughingly
recollected, "That went over great because so many people in Los
Angeles originally came from Iowa!"

As election day drew closer, Olson began to worry more about
the success of Warren's homespun campaign. In their only face-to-
face confrontation, during a San Francisco radio debate on October
11, Olson excoriated his opponent's "Leadership Not Politics"
slogan, recklessly comparing it to Hitler's Führerprinzip ("Principles
of the Leader"). Warren wisely refused to rise to the bait, and Olson
ended by losing points for having taken a cheap shot.

Olson likewise assailed Warren for upholding the California
law which required schoolchildren to salute the flag or be expelled
as delinquents. Warren coolly retorted, with perfect accuracy, that
the Supreme Court two years earlier had ruled this requirement
constitutional and that he was merely doing his duty as attorney
general in enforcing the law. Olson could only reply lamely that if
that were the case, the High Court was wrong.

Years later, as Chief Justice, Warren himself would of course
have agreed completely with Olson's position on saluting the flag.
But in 1942 he was less interested in debating the actual merits of
issues than in scoring points to win an election. He knew—far better
than Olson—precisely what type of voters he was trying to reach.

They were patriotic (in the midst of a desperate total war and couldn't image anyone *not* wanting to salute the flag); and, despite their party affiliations, they were fundamentally conservative middle California. They were not likely to fault Warren's charge that the governor's attempts to pardon the *Point Lobos* convicts—"Communist radicals," as Warren called them—"was the darkest chapter of the Olson administration." The Chief Justice who was to defend passionately the constitutional rights of communists, then argued that the Communist party "should not be entitled to legal recognition in the political life of America."

Somehow, amid all the campaign uproar, Warren still found time to do serious work. To his great credit, he seldom confused the job of being attorney general with that of being a candidate.

An obscure case that arose a month before the November election is now recalled by Berkeley Law Professor Adrian Kragen: "I was a deputy general handling tax cases and was asked by the Attorney General [Warren] to come to his office," he reported in the November 1970 *University of California Law Review*. "I entered and saw assembled about five lawyers, representing one of the most powerful interests in the state, one whose support was very important to any political candidate. Attorney General Warren told me that the lawyers had requested him to drop the case. He asked me if I thought the case was important and should be continued. I answered in the affirmative. He quickly turned to the lawyers and said, 'Gentlemen, you have your answer.' "

The basic Warren qualities of integrity, sincerity and stability must have filtered through to the California voters on November 3, 1942. Winning fifty-seven of the fifty-eight counties, he defeated Governor Olson by more than 342,000 votes—1,275,287 to 932,995 —in a surprising upset. The crestfallen Olson philosophized, "Earl Warren is the slickest politician I ever met."

Stunned politicians who had scoffed at Warren's unorthodox candidacy now rushed to climb aboard the bandwagon of the "Warren tribe" (as he called his family). In the Warren landslide, Republicans captured every important statewide office except Warren's former office of attorney general—won by Democrat Robert W. Kenny. This actually pleased the incoming governor, who had privately supported Kenny.

Shortly afterward, at a private White House meeting, the President of the United States asked the new California attorney general with more than passing curiosity, "Tell me, Bob, what kind of fellow is your new governor?"

"Mr. President," chortled Kenny, "*everything* we have in California is better than anywhere else. Even our Republicans are better than Republicans anywhere else!"

On January 2, 1943, fifty-one-year-old Earl Warren was about to be inaugurated governor of California. For a brief few minutes, he stood at a Sacramento Capitol window. Vaguely, he gazed out at the flower-sprinkled grounds. In his thoughts, he was, as always, alone, though a trusted longtime aide was at his side. Below, thousands of Californians were awaiting his induction. Like a bear after a meal, the governor-to-be smiled contentedly. "I'm certainly glad that so many people came today to see me," he said.

"Don't kid yourself, Earl. Most of them came to see the *other* fellow thrown out!"

The deflated governor-elect bowed his head and grinned.

In keeping with wartime austerity, California's thirtieth governor wanted no Inaugural Ball. But after being sworn in and delivering his State of the State message, he held an "open door" reception in the Governor's Office. "Remember," he cautioned his staff, "we have no friends to reward or enemies to punish." Although the new governor was entering office with probably more state experience than any man in California history, he was doing so at a $4,000 cut in salary.

On Governor Warren's first day in office, he strolled the mile from the Executive Mansion to the Capitol. He stopped to read an engraving on a state building: "Bring Me Men to Match My Mountains." He also noticed a sign on his office door which had always irritated him whenever he had come to see his predecessor. Earl Warren's first act in office was to change the sign from THE GOVERNOR to simply GOVERNOR. "Governor is important enough," he reasoned. "*The* Governor sounds like *The* King or *The* Sultan." He also laid down a rule that anyone with an appointment must come in through the front, not the back door.

Several hours after assuming office, he was shocked to observe some strange wiring concealed in both his office and the Governor's Suite in the Capitol. An electrician who checked this for him discovered that the wiring was connected to recording devices.

Warren demanded that they be removed at once, waiting only

until the leaders of the legislature and the press had had a chance to see what he had inherited.

Reporter William P. Smith, now a Sacramento attorney, recollects, "It was quite an elaborate battery of equipment installed in a small upstairs mezzanine room within the suite and was activated by switches hidden in the Governor's desk. Warren immediately ordered all of them dismantled."

The mornings of his next few days as governor were less dramatic. Warren spent considerable time traveling from office to office, good-naturedly chatting with and shaking the hands of all employees, from secretaries to elevator operators—all of whose names he made it a point to remember.

Olson and previous governors had given their friends and political cronies special license plates which state troopers duly noted. "The incoming governor quickly stopped this practice," Robert J. Hoerner, his 1958 Supreme Court law clerk, reported in the Winter 1975 *Hastings Constitutional Law Quarterly*. "I recall his saying that he only used a siren twice in all his years as Governor of California, to get where he needed to go on time. He felt an obligation to plan ahead so as to avoid inconveniencing ordinary citizens and exercising rights which they did not have."

Similarly, even the Warren children leaned over backward not to take advantage of their father's name or position. When Jim, the oldest son, an impassioned FDR admirer, was in the Marines during World War II, instead of addressing his letters home from the Pacific to "The Governor's Mansion," he mailed them simply to 1526 H Street, Sacramento. Most of his company did not know who his father was.

Even when appointing his staff and state employees, Warren tried to carry out his campaign promise of a nonpartisan, goodwill administration. He saw politicos about state government problems but not job appointments. Determined that his appointees should be selected through merit instead of politics, much to GOP dismay he named as many Democrats as Republicans to office. He chose Democrat William T. Sweigert, now an eminent federal judge, as his executive secretary.

In selecting department heads, Warren never questioned a man's political, religious or other affiliations. A man being interviewed to head an important department said at the end of the interview, "Governor, you haven't asked me about my politics or religion: I am a Democrat and a Jew." Warren answered, "I'm hiring you only because of your qualifications for the job." Shunning the spoils system, he tried to pick the best person available for the job. His technique was to inquire of responsible national organizations and impartial experts who was the best professionally qualified individual to head a specific California agency, board or bureau— wherever he happened to live or be employed. The new governor would then cajole this person into joining his administration. Such an unorthodox technique angered many patronage-hungry Republicans who had never taken seriously Warren's nonpartisan campaign promises.

To head the new California Department of Corrections (which had inherited a series of prison scandals), Warren—the former D. A. who well knew prison conditions—wooed Richard A. McGee away from a comparable position in the state of Washington, where he had distinguished himself. The new governor reached into Ohio to secure an eminent psychiatrist-administrator, Dr. Frank Tallman, to direct California's soon-to-be-revitalized mental health program. Similarly, he persuaded Dr. Wilton L. Halverson, then Los Angeles County health officer, to become State Commissioner of Public Health at a sharp reduction in salary. He convinced Palo Alto's public-spirited Harold Anderson to leave his job as local public utility head to become California Commissioner of Public Utilities, much to the disgust of the Pacific Light and Gas Company. A great nonpolitical career engineer, Charles S. Purcell, who had supervised construction of the world-famous San Francisco-Oakland Bay bridge, was chosen to be Director of Public Works. "I darn near fell over with surprise at the appointment," he later admitted.

Olson officeholders were not lopped off wholesale, even though Warren quickly fired the entire politically oriented State Highway Commission. Likewise, perhaps somewhat punitively, he discharged capable Carey McWilliams, the outspoken Commissioner of Immigration and Housing, who had long infuriated the conservative Associated Farmers by his vocal support of migratory workers. "It wasn't necessary to fire me," McWilliams now says. "My four-year term was ending."

Warren indignantly rejected Murray Chotiner's suggestion that some campaign supporters be rewarded with posts—such as managing state office buildings or working in the Department of

Motor Vehicles—where they could do extracurricular Republican party work. And when a Republican campaign supporter boasted to his friends that Governor Warren would soon appoint him to an unsalaried but honorary position on the Fish and Game Commission, Warren was irritated and delayed the appointment. The office seeker complained to him, "I'm sure that you wouldn't want to embarrass me in front of my friends."

"You've already embarrassed *me*," snapped the governor.

Similarly, when his oil company campaign contributors heavy-handedly suggested a nominee for a key post, Warren snapped, "I'll pick my own director of natural resources—and all my other people."

A major fringe benefit for the new governor was free occupancy of the Executive Mansion in Sacramento. But when the cautious governor-elect inspected it, he would not permit his family to move in immediately. The rundown gray wooden 15-room, 5-bath structure, built in 1877 by a millionaire hardware merchant, later had been the home of journalist Lincoln Steffens' family before being sold to the state in 1903 for $32,500. Now this Victorian-Gothic monstrosity was literally falling apart. Termites had enjoyed an extended stay there; the porticos were rotting and the porches creaking; and inside, the plaster was peeling, the furniture was moth-eaten and the rugs were threadbare. Gas seeped from the old jets, and rats and pigeons flew through the third-floor attic's broken windows. In 1941 the State Fire Marshal had declared the building unsuitable for occupancy.

Recent governors had generally used it only for state functions. They had been mostly older men with grown families, who had rented hotel suites in Sacramento's lobbyist-ridden Senator Hotel while retaining their homes in the communities from which they had been elected. Tall, handsome Governor Olson, whose wife had died six weeks after his taking office, had used only a small part of the downstairs, the upper floors having been boarded up. "I was heartsick when I first looked at it," recollects the ordinarily optimistic Nina Warren. "Later, I even cried."

Governor and Mrs. Warren and their six children remained at their Oakland home and he rented quarters at Sacramento's Sutter Club until the Mansion could be renovated, if indeed that were possible. Luckily, the various state historical societies were so delighted that a large family would again occupy the Governor's

Mansion that they soon prompted the passage of legislation appropriating $4,000 for an immediate remodeling job.

Now California's First Lady went to work. On this slim budget, which had to cover building repairs as well as furnishings, she decided what could be saved, cleaned, remodeled or recovered rather than bought new. Her feet grew weary from hours of bargain-hunting in San Francisco stores. The former dress shop manager purchased inexpensive rugs, fabrics, paint, wallpaper, china and glassware. "I got a stiff neck," she smilingly remembers, "shopping for lighting fixtures."

Some structural defects proved uncorrectable. The fireplace could not be used, and because the mansion had no fire escapes, a fire ladder had to be placed in each room. Cabinets were added to the kitchen, which had none, and an additional sink. The kitchen was painted "lettuce and mayonnaise" (pale green and creamy yellow). Nina Warren kept the stove, cheerfully saying, "I was lucky to have such a big old army-type stove because I could bake six cakes in it at once!"

The five children then living at home all got separate rooms. Characteristically, Nina Warren took the smallest room—formerly a porch—and converted it into a bedroom-study for herself. It had, she recalls, a green carpet, green chenille bedspread, and cream-colored drapes decorated with green-brown maple leaves.

The state at first allowed the Warrens only $500 a month to operate the sprawling mansion, but later raised this to $1,000. The California governor's salary was $10,000 a year (compared with New York State Governor Thomas Dewey's $25,000, to which it was later raised). Nina Warren did much of the cooking, cleaning and ironing herself, since household help was difficult to secure and keep during wartime. Even when she had a cook, she packed all the children's lunches herself. When she entertained at large functions, she had to rent silver trays and tea urns from a Sacramento shop.

It took five nerve-wracking months before the "Warren tribe" could move into the mansion in April 1943. The building could now exhibit its luxurious winding staircases, sixteen-foot ceilings, hanging chandeliers, huge mirrors and cleaned Oriental rugs; but the Warren youngsters so filled the house that there was not even space for a regular guest room.

During his first year in office, Warren was still generally regarded as a "safe" conservative who soundly believed in private enterprise, states' rights and decentralized government. As such, he was hardly the hero of the left. As Carey McWilliams charged in the October 18, 1943, *New Republic*:

> *[Warren's] record on most major social and economic issues is almost a perfect blank . . . Warren is completely the creature of the Hearst-Knowland-Chandler clique in the Republican party . . . darling of the Associated Farmers . . . he had to be taught to smile, to beam, to be a good fellow . . . he had to be told that labor-baiting (old style) was passé . . . he had to be taught to mouth—and it must have been bitter tutelage for this essentially grim and hard-boiled individual—such phrases as "old age security," "collective bargaining," "social planning." The advertising boys have done a good job and he can turn in a fairly acceptable pose as a liberal statesman. But to those who know him, the performance is unconvincing . . . he has always been as he is today, a personification of Smart Reaction . . . Shirley Temple, with the same newspaper support, could make a fairly popular Governor of California.*

Thirty-one years later, a more mellow McWilliams concluded in a reassessment, "The Education of Earl Warren," in the October 12, 1974, *Nation*, that the enigmatic man who had fired him was "a most remarkable American politician who grew to greatness."

In fact, now able in his gubernatorial seat to step back from the necessities of campaigning, Warren again began to exhibit the administrative qualities which had made him such an outstanding D.A. and attorney general. Besides surrounding himself with the ablest nonpartisan advisors he could muster, he listened carefully to their counsel. Above all, he grasped with extraordinary speed that his new problems were vastly more complex than the relatively simple law-enforcement matters he had dealt with earlier.

An example of the new Warren in action appeared shortly after he assumed office. In Los Angeles, tensions between servicemen and zoot-suited local Mexican-American youths had erupted into a pattern of escalating street violence. Local authorities sought to invoke harsh measures against the Mexican-American pachuca gangs. Previously, Warren might have responded to these requests with a simple affirmative. But now he recognized that more was at stake than an uncomplicated matter of law enforcement. He sent

89

police to the embattled areas but ordered them to avoid provocations. He urged the news media to downplay reports of violent incidents and asked the armed services to declare the dangerous areas off-limits to their personnel on leave. He set up a citizens committee, headed by the Roman Catholic Bishop of Los Angeles, to study the roots of the trouble and to make constructive recommendations. And he publicly assured California citizens that "there is no reason why the good name of California should ever suffer because of a race riot." His temperate measures were strikingly effective. The violence subsided within days. Indeed, not until the Watts riots of 1965 did California again suffer any disturbances on a similar scale.

During Warren's first sixty days in office, he acted with the rapidity that characterized FDR's famous First Hundred Days. Admiringly, ex-Roosevelt braintruster Raymond Moley wrote of Warren in *Newsweek* at that time: "Not even Mr. Roosevelt moved faster in using the first bloom of his Administration to attack the toughest problems."

Warren accomplished this because he swiftly established amicable relations with the legislature, which the well-meaning but arrogant Olson had antagonized in trying to ram through his "Little New Deal" measures. This era of good feeling was keynoted in Warren's Inaugural Address, when he forthrightly challenged: "Let's cut out all the dry rot of petty politics, partisan jockeying, inaction, dictatorial stubbornness and opportunistic thinking. Let's do first things first." Privately, the new governor conferred with key senators and assemblymen of both parties, casually dropping in on them in their chambers or seeking them out on the legislature floor. Similarly, he invited lawmakers to visit him when he was in his Capitol office. In seeking support for his bills, he frequently appealed to them, "Let's forget politics for the duration, help win the war and plan for California's postwar future." He was fast learning that bipartisanship had uses beyond mere campaign oratory on a state level.

One immediate result was his success in pushing through a bill which abolished Olson's State Council of Defense. A new War Powers Act of January 30, 1943, gave far greater emergency defense authority to the delighted Warren than Olson had ever enjoyed. In event of invasion, his new California War Council could mobilize citizens for behind-the-Army service.

Warren managed to accomplish other things in 1943 and 1944. He reduced taxes—income, sales and corporation—for the first time in the state's history. During World War II, he was the nation's only governor to make a huge general tax reduction. He balanced the budget and built a $43 million reserve for California's postwar future. To mollify the Townsendites and Ham-and-Eggers, he increased old-age pensions from forty to fifty dollars a month as promised. Similarly, he raised unemployment benefits and for the first time included workers in small establishments. He boosted workmen's compensation, and increased health and welfare services. He also overhauled the pardon and parole system, which had not been changed in sixty-five years. Intensely outdoor-minded, he expanded state park and recreation facilities. For teachers, he raised the minimum pay scale. The father of six opened new child-care centers under the Department of Education, and launched a pioneer Youth Authority which sought to keep young offenders out of penitentiaries, rehabilitating them in mountain and agricultural work camps. He created a Farm Production Council to recruit workers who would harvest California's record crops for wartime use, and he sparked a public works program for hospitals and highways.

Still, the left remained chary of him. He was denounced by organized labor for signing a bill banning jurisdictional strikes and for failing to outlaw "hot cargo" legislation (the Supreme Court subsequently upheld his position on this). Although he was routinely attacked by the CIO, the more moderate AFL tended to support him.

Simultaneously, his support from the extreme right was likewise beginning to erode, especially by those who had hopefully regarded him as another Herbert Hoover. Their governor was now perceived by them as a "liberal in conservative clothing"—a charge which would be voiced more frequently during his administration.

Yet Warren was not worried. He was convinced he was doing "right" and that he was destined to find his winning constituency, not at the political extremes, but in its broad center. He continued to insist that he opposed both "counterfeit liberals and blind reactionaries."

"Warren was a lucky governor during the war years," remarked one cynic. "Because California was loaded with war industries, he could play Mr. Hero by balancing the budget, reducing taxes and still show a surplus. He didn't have the headache of the Depression years or the social cost problems of the postwar boom years."

Nonetheless, Warren's constructive acts during his first two gubernatorial years caught the eye of victory-starved Republicans who were anxious to crush President Roosevelt's almost certain fourth-term bid in November 1944. Earl Warren was a bright new star in the cloudy GOP firmament.

Before the fourth-term pot boiled, on January 20, 1944, Governor Warren telegraphed President Roosevelt about a seemingly minor matter—daylight-saving time—which amused the war-weary Chief Executive. After pressure from California farmers seeking longer harvesting hours, and school officials wanting to spare pupils from having to rise so early for their bus trips, Warren asked the President if California could return to standard time.

President Roosevelt wired back—daylight-saving time was essential to the war effort. Warren courteously wrote back that of course, he understood. A pleased President Roosevelt replied on February 7:

> *Dear Governor Warren:*
>
> *Many thanks for yours of January twenty-seventh. I am awfully glad that California is not going to make an issue on the subject of time—largely because there are a number of other states who want to take all kinds of action—some forwards, some backwards!*
>
> > *Always sincerely yours,*
> > *(signed) Franklin D. Roosevelt*

National media suddenly began to eye Warren. *Time* magazine gave him the cover and profiled him in January 1944, praising his record in California but adding that nothing in it revealed him as "a potential giant in United States history." *The New York Times* noted the strong impression he had made at the Governor's Conference in Columbus, Ohio, in June 1943.

Wendell Willkie, the 1940 GOP presidential candidate, now decided not to enter his name in the May 1944 California primaries, probably because he feared being decisively defeated by Warren. As a face-saving measure, Willkie's aides spread the story that their boss considered Warren a stooge of the right-wing "Stop Willkie" isolationists. But the truth was Warren was obviously too powerful in California to be any such thing.

Warren, for his part, was then uneasy about plunging into national politics against Roosevelt. He insisted that he merely sought to lead the California delegation to the June convention in Chicago and was not a candidate for President. "California is the league in which I will do my pitching," he declared. "I am wholly without ambition for Federal office." Although having recently reached his fifty-third birthday, Warren coyly protested that he lacked sufficient seasoning to be Chief Executive. "It's like putting on a pair of new shoes," he claimed, "If you get a bad fit, it makes you uncomfortable all over."

Thomas E. Dewey, the ambitious governor of New York, had no such qualms about age. At forty-two, he felt fully qualified to win his party's nomination for the presidency and to lead it to victory over Roosevelt in 1944. He had definitely, as Interior Secretary Harold Ickes sarcastically quipped, thrown his diaper into the ring.

In casting about for a potential vice presidential running mate, Dewey did not have far to look. As the vote-getting, middle-of-the-road Republican governor of populous California, Warren seemed ideal. A large segment of the California press agreed. Joseph Knowland's Oakland *Tribune,* Norman Chandler's Los Angeles *Times* and William Randolph Hearst's San Francisco *Examiner* all began boosting a Dewey-Warren ticket. In time, the powerhouse national Republican media—the Chicago *Tribune,* New York *Daily News,* Washington *Times-Herald* and *Saturday Evening Post*—similarly began to extol Warren's virtues at more than necessary length (the *Post* compared him to Calvin Coolidge!). Dewey and nearly everyone else assumed that Warren would gratefully accept the second spot and spent an hour trying to convince him to do so.

But Warren was not to be recruited. Dewey could not beat Roosevelt in midwar, he reasoned, and Roosevelt was not likely to run for a fifth term. Warren concluded that his time of decision would be 1948, not 1944, and there was no point in entering that future arena with a needless defeat on his record. Politely but firmly he declined Dewey's earnest request. The New York governor was nominated on the first ballot.

Dewey—especially in the light of his 1944 defeat—never fully forgave Warren, and their subsequent 1948 ticket was, at best, an uneasy marriage of convenience. But Dewey and Warren were never really compatible, either in personality or outlook. Their differences began to emerge as early as the 1944 Republican National Convention at which Warren had now accepted the role of temporary chairman and keynote speaker in a last minute shift. His opening speech—in which he never once mentioned Roosevelt's name—was considered absurdly mild by the Dewey forces. Later, when they gave him more vehement speeches to deliver, he simply threw them away. Instead, he continued to hum his usual soft-spoken, often pedestrian hymns of sweet reasonableness. Warren's GOP critics felt that his support of the Dewey campaign in California was only perfunctory.

Two weeks before the election, Warren was suddenly hospitalized in Sacramento with influenza and a kidney infection. He was compelled to cancel his speeches and vote by absentee ballot. It was no surprise to the bedridden governor of California when President Roosevelt was overwhelmingly elected to a fourth term, capturing 81 percent of the electoral votes. "That Man" impudently not only won Dewey's New York State but even Warren's California by a half million majority.

In five months President Roosevelt would be dead, and a very special period of American political history would be at an end.

For Earl Warren, the Roosevelt years were the time when his career took a sharp turn toward politics. In one sense, this direction could be seen as being his most successful years. In his trajectory from obscure local district attorney to governor of a great state and potential vice presidential candidate, he advanced farther and faster than at any period of his life.

Yet in a humanistic sense, they may have been his least successful years, for in learning to master the art of practical politics, he acquired skills which were more effective than admirable. He learned opportunistically to accept supporters wherever he found them, even wobbling his own position, if need be, to accommodate their particular interests and prejudices. He learned the uses of relatively vacuous but high-sounding rhetoric in wooing and exploiting the "nonpartisan" vote. He learned that playing to emotions could be more fruitful than appealing to reason or fair play. In short, he learned—if only temporarily—how to compromise his deepest convictions in order to attain power.

All that, of course, is in the nature of politics itself. The road to political power is seldom totally pure. Perhaps the best one can ask is that the ends to which that power is put not be dishonorable—that once power is achieved, it then be exercised with justice and wisdom.

Thus, one must restrain the temptation to over-moralize about some of Warren's less noble actions during the Roosevelt years. The ways in which he gained political power and shaped California politics do not differ greatly from the ways that it has always been gained. It is what he did with that power that provides the most illuminating key to his character, and differentiates him from others who wielded it before him—or after.

In his political ascent, Warren demonstrated the same astonishing aptitude he had always shown before when confronted with new challenges. Once again, his very personality seemed to undergo the changes demanded by the new situation. The persona of the grim, single-minded, incorruptible law enforcer gave way in a remarkably short time to that of the flexible, glad-handing, melioristic politician, capable of simultaneously courting right, left and center often with suave and platitudinous inconsistency.

Doubtless Warren learned much of his new technique from Franklin Roosevelt. For both, the posture of bipartisanship was at once an offensive weapon to undercut the unity of the opposing party and a device to camouflage a lack of coherence in their own political philosophies. Both were capable of guileful behavior, when necessary. Both were prepared to hedge on rule books or even modify constitutions to achieve a desired end. Both were brain-pickers (FDR infinitely more so), recruiting advisors from far and wide, irrespective of party affiliation. And both had a highly developed talent for conviviality, an ability to charm, to size up and make people from all walks of life feel at ease. In brief, both were formidable politicians.

Ironically, though Warren was personally acquainted with every Chief Executive from Truman to Ford, he never met the President he most resembled. Franklin D. Roosevelt was once described by Justice Oliver Wendell Holmes, Jr., as having "a second-rate intellect, but a first-rate temperament." Such a description might well have been made of Warren in 1945. Indeed, in a different sense, it might even have been applied to Warren in 1965. Yet the measure of Warren's claim to greatness perhaps lies in that difference.

However, Justice William O. Douglas, who knew both Roosevelt and Warren intimately, perceives an important affirmative aspect linking their characters. On May 6, 1977, the retired Douglas wrote to me: "Warren and FDR had many things in common. Perhaps foremost was the humanism that ran through their philosophies. Each was interested in people, not in great power groups that make up the political centers that converge on our national government."

Roosevelt died of a massive cerebral hemorrhage at Warm Springs, Georgia, on April 12, 1945. His sixty-year-old successor learned that he had become President while sipping bourbon and branch water in the office of House Speaker Sam Rayburn in Washington. Harry S. Truman was, at that time, relatively unknown to the public at large. Warren, on the other hand, knew him well and was to get to know him much better.

Chapter Four

The Truman Years 1945–1953

*W*arren had first met Harry S. Truman at national Masonic conventions in the early 1930s. Later, they saw each other at various pre-World War II Senate hearings. The two men liked one another from the start. They came from analogous, if not identical, self-made backgrounds, shared an earthy common touch in dealing with people and a perhaps simplistic moralism in facing issues. Politics did not interfere with their friendship. "Mr. Truman always considered him a good personal friend and was truly fond of him," Bess Truman wrote me in January 1977.

"Earl Warren's a Democrat and don't know it," Truman was fond of saying. "Yes, but with a small 'd,' " Warren would smilingly reply.

Uppercase Democrat Truman and lowercase democrat Warren remained good friends for the duration of their lives. Warren always liked the peppery grass-roots politician with the steel-rimmed eyeglasses, a product of haberdashery and hard knocks, an "average man" of smiling modesty, quiet efficiency and simple integrity. To Warren, Roosevelt was caviar; Truman, ham and eggs.

Warren respected Truman as a decisive man who, like himself, did not agonize over decisions. "He made his own decisions promptly and without subtlety and was totally without guile," Warren said. The Californian admired the Missourian's simplified approach to complex problems, seeing certain solutions as either "right" or "wrong." And he even esteemed Truman's somewhat corny habit of occasionally pulling from his wallet these idealistic lines from Tennyson's "Locksley Hall":

> *Till the war drums throbbed no longer*
> *And the battle flags were furled,*
> *In the Parliament of Man*
> *The Federation of the World.*

Warren met Truman again in April 1945, shortly after the new Chief Executive had suddenly become President. Truman had come to San Francisco to open the United Nations Conference. As host governor, Warren escorted the President in the parade from the airport, visited with him over a drink at his hotel suite and delivered the welcoming address at the opening session. Warren, who had never been overseas, now found himself exposed to international problems for the first time, and fascinated by this conference aimed at establishing a new world order. Although the state legislature was in session, requiring the governor to be at his desk at 9 A.M., he regularly drove the ninety-three miles from Sacramento to San Francisco in the afternoon so as to be able to attend every evening and many other sessions of the conference. He seldom returned to Sacramento before three in the morning, and when the conference ended on June 26, he was an impassioned internationalist.

On August 6, 1945, the same day that an American atomic bomb killed 70,000 persons in Hiroshima, California's aged Senator Hiram Johnson died. It was rumored that Warren would resign as governor so that his successor could appoint him to fill Johnson's unexpired Senate term. Right-wing Republicans, including many bankers and the Associated Farmers of California, who were beginning to grow apprehensive about their unpredictable governor's progressive programs and latent liberalism, welcomed the possibility of getting this "nonpartisan" out of Sacramento. But Warren, his eye now on the presidency, realized that he would have greater leverage in 1948 as a veteran governor than as a junior senator. He therefore quickly ended the speculation, piously declaring that he had too much unfinished work yet to do in Sacramento, and that he was in fact leaving for Washington soon with six other governors to confer with President Truman on postwar reconversion problems.

Before leaving, he nominated for the vacant Senate seat Major William F. Knowland, thirty-seven-year-old son of the conservative Oakland *Tribune* publisher who had long been Warren's political patron. Knowland, soon to be the youngest man to sit in the Upper Chamber, was not at the time even in the state; he was stationed at the Army Historical Section in Paris. Before the war he had been a state legislator from Alameda County, but his most important qualification now was that he was his father's son. The appointment was a simple political payoff, and one about which Warren would come to feel increasingly uneasy, for young Knowland, who was at least as conservative as his father, would continue to move to the right during all the years when Warren was moving to the left. To his credit, Knowland always remained politically loyal to Warren, even when named Republican floor leader in 1953. But his world view came to diverge so sharply from Warren's that finally almost no common ground existed between them. Remembered as "The Senator from Formosa" because of his ardent championship of Chiang Kai-shek, Knowland died a suicide in February 1974.

Liberal Dr. Russel V. Lee, of the Palo Alto Medical Clinic, recollects, "When I later got to know Earl Warren better, he said wryly that he regretted having appointed Bill Knowland instead of me to the Senate." Dr. Lee, who had supported Governor Warren's unsuccessful fight for a compulsory California health insurance program adds, "I was one of the few doctors in the state who was on Warren's side, and got myself in hot water with the organized medical people because of this."

Indeed, this was Warren's most bitter gubernatorial battle. He astounded both friends and foes in his January 1945 message to the legislature urging a comprehensive prepaid medical and hospital care program for all California workers and their families. This would have been the nation's first such program, and the plan was for it to be financed by a 3 percent payroll tax shared equally by workers and employers. A cent and a half of every worker's dollar earned would have been deducted and matched by the employer.

"Socialism!" cried the American and California Medical associations. Warren retorted that it was insurance, not socialized medicine, and insisted that under his program patients would be able to choose their own physicians and that, contrary to the charges of his opponents, California doctors would not become state employees. "My bill may not be the best one," argued Warren, "but it's only to help doctors come up with a better one. They should take the lead before the state and federal government do." After his health bill was crushed by a $3 million campaign financed by organized medicine and political conservatives, he sadly remarked: "I don't understand how people can kill this kind of bill and still live with their consciences."

Health insurance care for everyone had been a deep and growing concern of Earl Warren's ever since his father had told him as a boy about his uncle's death in Chicago. Warren's own mother had had many steep medical bills before she died in 1941 after a series of eye operations. The two children of his widowed sister spent considerable time in hospitals, as did his own daughter Honeybear, who later contracted polio. As a father of six children, he had been shocked by his heavy medical and dental bills. As a periodic hospital patient himself, even for several weeks during 1945, he had occasion to reflect: "The average worker can afford to die better than he can afford serious illness! If the bills hit *me* this hard on a governor's salary, how can the man who earns so much less pay his medical bills, especially for an unexpected and prolonged illness?"

Some cynical Warren watchers, however, insisted that the proposal was a political ploy. They argued, somewhat lamely, that the governor well knew that he could never push his plan through the legislature but could emerge from the fight as a champion of the medically oppressed "little people."

The battle over Warren's health insurance bill—years before Medicare—had at least one significant side effect. He was deeply angered by the virulence of the well-financed right-wing attack, conducted by letter-writing campaigns and newspaper, radio and billboard advertising. Heretofore, he had been fairly successful in not antagonizing—or permitting himself to be antagonized by—his ultraconservative constituents. Now, both began to look at each other with growing hostility. Ten months later and three thousand miles away, Harry Truman fought a similar battle. In November 1945, the President tried to persuade Congress to pass national health insurance legislation, the Murray-Dingle bill, over the heated opposition of conservatives and the AMA. Like Warren, the President lost, and he was likewise to remain bitter over his defeat.

This was not the only important social legislation proposed by Warren and defeated by the Republican-dominated California legislature in 1945. The governor's pioneer State Fair Employment

Practices bill—a major step toward ending discrimination in hiring against minority groups as well as women, and the nation's first such state bill—did not attract nearly as much public attention as had the health insurance proposal. Indeed, there was hardly a fight. The legislature handily quashed it and a similar CIO-sponsored bill. The evening of the day his innovative bill was defeated, the governor consoled himself with several stiff bourbons and determined to fight again another day.

Nevertheless, Warren's record during the year following Roosevelt's death was by no means solely one of frustrated effort. While President Truman was desegregating the U.S. Armed Forces, Warren, despite considerable opposition, was similarly successful in desegregating the California National Guard. "In neither instance," he recalled mildly, "was it readily accepted, but it was eventually accomplished."

He also won a harder battle against one of the state's most powerful lobbies. To reduce California's automobile fatality rate that was among the nation's highest, Warren proposed an increased gasoline tax that would finance a ten-year highway- and freeway-building program. The oil, trucking and bus lobbies vehemently fought the measure. But Warren was adamant. He insisted that this was the only way to ease the five thousand miles of congested two-lane roads which he considered both obsolete and dangerous.

To thwart the proposed Warren legislation, the oil companies simultaneously raised the price of gasoline three times during a six-month period. Only when Warren requested the U.S. Department of Justice to investigate their actions as possible collusion or violations of the antitrust laws did they pull back. Suddenly, their opposition to his highway improvement bill collapsed. The governor then mobilized sufficient public support to compel the reluctant legislature to enact a bill authorizing a 1½ cent per gallon additional tax increase. Ever since this pioneer measure, California motorists have been driving on some of the world's best highway-freeway systems.

But the oil, trucking and bus industries—like the medical profession—never forgave their gubernatorial adversary. Now Warren could add these groups to his growing list of enemies.

In April 1946, Warren announced his candidacy for re-election to a second four-year term. He suspected that 1946 was a "Republican Year" because of widespread dissatisfaction with Truman. He also

knew that California Democrats were embroiled in fierce inter-
necine warfare. Once again, Candidate Warren, the White Knight of
Nonpartisanship—in state but not national politics—dusted off his
hoary campaign cry, and simultaneously mounted both the Republican elephant and the Democratic donkey, proclaiming: "I am a
Republican and shall seek the support of voters of both parties . . . I
am not interested in machine politics . . . I have not tried to build a
political machine. No man should be permitted to be both governor
and a politician boss. . . ."

In the June primary, where he cross-filed, he easily won the
GOP nomination 10-to-1 from a conservative banker who withdrew, charging that Earl Warren lacked both "courage and character." But Californians were astounded when Republican Warren
also captured by a 163,000 margin the Democratic nomination
from his friend, popular Attorney General Robert W. Kenny.
Warren won fifty-six of the fifty-eight counties. Never before in
California history had a governor won such bipartisan support.
Thus, the November election was a mere formality. Warren had
won a second term by knocking out his main opponent in the first
round. Denouncing Warren as a "fake liberal," the CIO Political
Action Committee, Harry Bridges and the California communist
paper, *The People's World,* had supported Kenny, even though the
state AFL had endorsed Warren. But nearly everyone else seemed to
want the affable Warren, who became the first California governor
in thirty-two years (since Hiram Johnson) to win a second term.
Despite having opposed his health insurance proposal, the Los
Angeles *Times* editorialized that Warren's landslide stemmed from
"the character of the man."

The witty Kenny later quipped: "I went eight rounds with Earl
Warren and never even mussed his hair. The worst part was that he
won the Democratic as well as the Republican nomination. I'm not
saying that Earl Warren capitalized on that large and beautiful
family of his, but they were everywhere. I once complained to him:
'Are we running against each other for governor or is this a fertility
contest?' "

Obviously, there was more to it than that. Warren's performance in the gubernatorial seat had favorably impressed numerous Californians. Although his support from right-wing Republicans was now eroding, he was still solid with the center and the

liberal wing of his own party. Among the influential (if fickle) independent electorate, he remained the overwhelming choice. No less important, there was little in his record that mainstream Democrats could fault. Thus, he had ingeniously created for himself an exceptionally broad centrist constituency. His opposition was largely relegated to the extremes of left and right, which could find no common ground to mount a coordinating attack upon his benevolently activist position.

Warren's national image had likewise continued to improve. In 1944, Republican and Democratic stategists had considered him primarily a successful vote-getter from a key state. Now observers in both parties were assessing him as not only a formidable politician, but as a strong and skillful leader. "I first began to take serious note of Earl Warren," his friend Harry Truman wrote many years later in the *University of California Law Review,* "when as Governor of the politically turbulent state of California he revealed a unique capacity to govern with firmness, decisiveness, independence and, what was most characteristic of him, a deep concern for the rights and aspirations of all the people—especially those who were less privileged."

So smashing was the 1946 Warren triumph that it overshadowed lesser political contests in the state. But one election, then of only local importance, was destined to have far-reaching future significance for Warren, Truman and, indeed, the entire nation. The Democratic incumbent seeking re-election from the Twelfth Congressional District, which embraced much of Los Angeles County, was Representative Jerry Voorhis, an idealistic liberal congressman whom Washington correspondents had voted the "best west of the Mississippi." Voorhis had supported Warren on the health insurance proposal and in his battle with the oil and trucking industries over the gasoline tax. Warren, not surprisingly, therefore strongly favored his re-election.

Running against Voorhis was an unknown but ambitious lawyer without previous professional political experience. At thirty-three, Richard M. Nixon had been a Lieutenant Commander in the Navy, a $3,200-a-year attorney in the U.S. Office of Price Administration and an unsuccessful applicant to the FBI. At first he seemed a most unlikely choice to unseat the veteran Voorhis. But he quickly displayed a remarkable talent for effective campaigning (some called it a talent for demagoguery and smear tactics). One day Nixon visited Warren headquarters in Los Angeles requesting that the governor issue a statement endorsing his candidacy and disavowing an earlier letter that Warren had sent praising Voorhis' work. Warren refused. But without this, Nixon defeated Voorhis in an upset. The long-term antipathy between Warren and Nixon began here, at the outset of Nixon's political career. It was to grow very much deeper with the passage of time.

In 1946, however, the fifty-five-year-old Warren was concerned with what to him were more important matters than the election of a freshman congressman. There were, for example, the problems of resettling and rehabilitating both the 850,000 returning California servicemen and the thousands of Nisei whose internment Warren, with the campaigner's freedom from responsibility, had once so aggressively advocated. (He now emerged, ironically, as a champion of Japanese-American civil rights, providing them police protection and denouncing as "atrocious" any efforts to interfere with their return into California society.) On behalf of these and other groups, he sought to curb the soaring cost of rents precipitated by the sudden postwar population boom. His rent control legislation, passed at a special session of the legislature which he summoned in July, anticipated by several months President Truman's Federal Rent Control Law—another example of how similarly the two men reacted to certain social issues.

Thanks to Warren's prudent wartime fiscal policies, California had built up a huge state surplus. Now he urged the legislature to use it constructively, without political pork barrels. Pomona Assemblyman Ernest Geddes, no Warren man, told me at the time, "The Governor will sign a good bill even if it's sponsored by a political opponent, and veto a bad bill which his own crowd are pushing." When a rider to the bill, calling for a $90 million appropriation for sewers and sanitation, was passed over his veto, Warren was furious at what he felt was the hidden graft. Even though his vetoes were sometimes overridden, none of the ten thousand bills he signed as governor was ever declared unconstitutional by the courts.

Warren's diligence resulted in many solid accomplishments of which Californians today are the beneficiaries. He built more schools and hospitals than any governor in U.S. history. To help his alma mater, the University of California (from which all of his six children graduated) become one of the world's great institutions, he secured $120 million for needed construction. "There should be no tuition at any level of education in California," he vowed—a view he held for the rest of his life despite rising operating costs. While reducing taxes, he pushed through increased pensions for the aged and blind. He set aside more funds for crippled children, and after the war he continued California's 300 state-operated child-care centers for low-income working mothers, administered by local boards of education, which every other state had callously scrapped after V-J Day. At the same time, he broadened public health, mental health and disability insurance programs; improved medical care for the mentally ill; overhauled the state's penal system; reorganized its industrial relations program; widened unemployment insurance; and built up a nonpartisan civil service system, promoting more employees than had any previous governor of California.

"He felt the people of the state were in his care and he cared for them," reminisces Edmund G. (Pat) Brown, a subsequent Democratic governor. "As the best governor that California ever had, Earl Warren faced the problems of social responsibility and growth and met them head on."

"Growth," indeed, was a Warren watchword during his 1946–50 term—before California became the nation's most populous state. Probably his proudest recollection of his years as governor was that, during that time, his state was able to absorb five million new arrivals "without any confusion or discord whatsoever," as he later put it. I remember visiting with him in Sacramento one day after the war. He was sitting at his huge rosewood desk, made by San Quentin prisoners, and rhapsodizing: "California will continue to grow. Nothing can stop it. Our great concern must be *how* it grows. Where on earth have so many people been integrated into a commonwealth in so short a period of time?"

Warren's concern for California's future was reflected in his conservation programs for the state's natural resources, which included soil conservation, timberlands preservation and development of protective fish and wildlife measures. Ironically, his attempt to curb air pollution statewide failed because shortsighted Los Angeles lawmakers—with self-serving assists from the oil, trucking and bus companies—argued that this was a "local problem." Although his fight for state public power was beaten by the private utilities, he championed the federal program.

Senator Henry M. Jackson told me: "I recall quite vividly as a congressman Warren's fight, while governor of California, to protect the Central Valley Authority. This was the government agency within the Department of the Interior that managed water and power operations. Warren took a strong stand in making that power available to the publicly owned utilities in California in opposition to the Pacific Gas & Electric Company. His stand was a most courageous one—another example of his dedication to the protection of the public."

Human resources, too, concerned the father of six children. When cannery owners tried to work their young women employees after midnight, the governor stopped this, protesting, "I wouldn't want my daughter Virginia, or anybody else's daughter, walking home from a cannery at three o'clock in the morning."

Keeping an eye on Washington, he admired the way President Truman was growing in office. When conservative Republicans sharply attacked him for echoing the Truman "Welfare State," he snapped: "I'm not afraid of the word welfare. Any party that is, doesn't deserve to win an election. If I were a private citizen, I'd be mad at my government if it wasn't concerned with my welfare. Isn't that what the Preamble of the Constitution says: '. . . to promote the General Welfare'?"

Liberal Illinois Senator Paul H. Douglas, a former educator, wrote me shortly before he died, "I first met Earl Warren in 1947 at a University of California dinner in Berkeley. I was tremendously impressed with him and could see *why* we Democrats could never make any headway against him." Another admirer, Los Angeles Congressman Thomas M. Rees, whimsically observed, "Earl Warren was one of the reasons that I began my political career as Republican. When I discovered that most Republicans weren't like him, I became a Democrat!"

Although Warren tended to agree with Harry Truman on most issues, including the Marshall Plan and aid to Greece and Turkey, he was considerably disturbed by the President's 1947 loyalty program, one of the noxious early weeds of the burgeoning Cold War. Warren was certainly anti-Communist and well understood the danger of highly placed security risks. Yet he simultaneously sensed that compulsory loyalty oaths, intrusive investigations into the political and personal backgrounds of government employees and the accompanying security mania could easily degenerate into Bills of Attainder. Although he reluctantly accepted the notion that loyalty oaths could be required of state employees, he inconsistently resisted when the California Un-American Activities Committee demanded the same of all University of California faculty members and employees. Warren mobilized a majority of the twenty-four Regents to reject this requirement, supported by U/C President Robert Gordon Sproul and the bitter opposition of Bank of America president Mario Giannini and Hearst's San Francisco lawyer, John Francis Neylan, among others. Retired Judge Victor R. Hansen, then a Regent, now recalls: "Governor Warren had appointed or reappointed a substantial number of the Regents who had opposed him on the Loyalty Oath issue."

"Any Communist would take this oath and laugh," Warren insisted. "Faculty members already have taken the statutory loyalty oath required by the State Constitution."

Sixty-eight faculty members who refused to sign the additional Loyalty Oath had been fired. However, the California Supreme Court later upheld their refusal to do so, as Warren had predicted it would.

One way in which Warren contrived to avoid becoming the political victim of the controversial stands he frequently took was through his adroit use of the media to explain his positions. His news conferences, though rarely resulting in state-shaking, front-page banner headlines, were a blend of geniality and reserve.

"I held two open press conferences each week of my nearly eleven years as governor," Warren once recalled. "One was a morning conference for the afternoon papers, and the other was an afternoon conference for the morning media. I believed in the right of the people to know what their public officials are doing. I also believed that it would help me in their appraisal of my work. If the news media did not approach me, I approached them."

Once, when the San Francisco *Examiner* published an editorial about a Bay bridge issue which Warren thought had distorted the facts, he marched into the newspaper office unannounced. "He came in and pounded the table and showed us *why* we were wrong," recalls executive director Joshua Eppinger. "He made such damn good sense that we changed our editorial position."

However, M. L. Stein, a former *Examiner* reporter, now journalism dean at California State University in Long Beach, recollects: "I found Warren frosty and reserved to representatives of the *Examiner,* which he disliked perhaps because of Hearst. After one of his speeches, I tried to pull a piece of information from him which we knew would be announced sooner or later, but I wanted it sooner. He said to me: 'Mr. Stein, the *Examiner* is not going to determine when this information will be released!' End of my interview."

Warren's success with the local news media was now beginning to be reflected in the Republican national press. Even at this early date, forces were gathering for the next presidential election. The Republicans were convinced that 1948 would at last be their year. They had control of both houses of Congress in November 1946, and had been giving Truman a rough ride ever since. The controversial President had been far less successful than Warren (for one) in building either popular or influential intraparty support, and Republican strategists now considered him an easy mark in '48 ("To err is Truman" went a popular taunt of the times.)

Warren, either out of natural caution or because he understood Truman better than most, was not so confident. He warned that a Republican victory was far from a sure thing. Nevertheless, he decided that 1948, unlike 1944, looked like a good time to make a bold entry into national politics.

There was no question but that he would go to the Republican National Convention as California's favorite son. Any possible doubt had been settled as early as November 13, 1947, when he won the party primary and control of the state delegation unopposed. Now he wore a conventional Republican fedora with no Democratic hatbands. But to be a favorite son, even from a powerful state, is not the same as being an active leading contender for the nomination. Warren had no national political organization or wealthy campaign backers to help him seek delegate support from other parts of the country. And even if he had, it would have been a difficult quest; for despite his favorable press notices, Warren still had a comparatively low national recognition factor, especially in the East. According to a January 1948 Gallup poll, 38 percent of the nation's Republicans were "not familiar with him" and another 14 percent had "no opinion" about him. Hence, he declined to enter any primaries, or permit supporters to enter his name, or actively seek the support of delegates from other states. "My strategy is no strategy," he said to me then. At his hotel headquarters during the convention, he "campaigned" by having sun-kissed California maidens wearing "Win With Warren" banners dispense free orange juice.

Such hopes as he had were those of the typical dark horse

candidate. They depended entirely on whether or not a convention deadlock developed. Gamblers bet 4-to-1 odds against him. But in the event of, say, a Taft-Dewey standoff, the big California delegation could be decisive and Warren could emerge as the king-maker. In such a situation, he might again be offered the vice presidential slot, or perhaps even the presidential nomination itself. On such imponderables did his future depend. He was, as he put it himself, "A dark horse without even a touch of bay."

But even dark horses must play the game. Warren was now courting an exclusively Republican constituency: the delegates to the convention, and all of the major candidates at once. He could hardly expect his habitual bipartisan or nonpartisan tactics to be welcomed by *that* crowd. Furthermore, he had to beware of identifying himself too closely with the particular positions of any one major candidate—or, at any rate of doing so too soon.

Thus, the unorthodox Warren now became the most orthodox of Republicans. He muted his internationalism and solemnly pronounced himself dedicated to such pieties as sound fiscal management, balanced budgets and lower taxes. He even risked his AFL support at home by signing a bill banning jurisdictional strikes and by endorsing the Taft-Hartley labor law, a brainchild of one of the major candidates (Taft) and cynosure of conservative Republicans everywhere.

About all the announced candidates, no matter how great their differences, he had nothing but good to say. If pressed too hard by reporters about his own position, he would resort to such non-answers as "What can I say that hasn't already been said by Dewey, Vandenberg, Stassen and the other candidates?" (Incidentally, Nixon, in his 1978 memoirs, admitted that he favored Stassen, despite it being customary for junior congressmen to support their governor's favorite son bid.) About other potential dark horses, Warren was amiably evasive. He yielded to no one in his admiration of Eisenhower, but hadn't the General repeatedly said that he wasn't a candidate? And MacArthur? "I admire his military genius."

In any event, this backstage campaigning went for naught. There was no convention deadlock that June. Dewey came to Philadelphia with sufficient strength to capture the nomination easily on the second ballot. The California delegation could not decide the outcome but only endorse it, and Warren could not make or unmake any kings.

Dewey's position though, was not as strong as it appeared. His convention triumph had largely resulted from heavy campaign spending and efficient staff work. His popularity with the Republican rank and file was less certain. His personality lacked warmth; Midwestern and Western Republicans still associated him with the dreaded Eastern Establishment; and, of course, he had been decisively defeated by Roosevelt just four years earlier. Truman might look like a sitting duck, yet there was no point in taking chances. Republican strategists concluded that Dewey needed a popular, politically successful Westerner to balance the ticket. Obviously, Warren was that man.

Now Warren had considerable misgivings. To have been able to *command* the party to give him the vice presidential nomination would have been one thing; *to be commanded* by the party to take it was something else. If Dewey were elected, Warren would be cut off from his California power base without having exchanged it for genuine national power; and when Dewey's term of office ended, Warren's political hopes might end with it. Moreover, there was the unspoken thought—real enough in Warren's mind—that Truman might win. There was no reason why Warren should risk besmirching his political record with a needless defeat. Most important, deep down he really didn't like Dewey very much. But as Justice Douglas wrote me in May 1977, "Warren liked the common touch that Truman had."

Still, Warren was in no position to gainsay the party's will. It was none too delicately pointed out to him that, should he refuse the vice presidential nomination, he could forget about the party supporting any future bid he might make for national office. Even closer to the bone, it was hinted that the Republican Party in California might—just might—look for a new standard-bearer.

Presidential nominee Dewey did not make the same mistake this time with Earl Warren that he had four years earlier. At midnight on June 25, 1948, Warren had returned to his Warwick hotel room to snatch some sleep. At 2:30 A.M. his telephone rang. It was the authoritative baritone voice of the newly selected Republican presidential nominee. Would Governor Warren please come immediately to his room in the Bellevue-Stratford Hotel a few blocks away for a private chat? When the sleepy Californian arrived, Dewey was alone, dressed in a bathrobe. He immediately asked his visitor to be his running mate, so as to balance the ticket.

Warren replied that he did not really want to be Vice President, spending his time just calling balls and strikes in the Senate.

Dewey declared that he would not expect a man like Warren to do just that. Rather, he envisioned the Californian as a real working partner in the Administration. The New York governor eloquently outlined the ways in which he intended to broaden the Vice President's duties. No longer would it be a mere figurehead role. The man who expected to be the next President of the United States then pulled out his best card. He told Warren that he needed him to help carry out the party platform, a more liberal one than what the Republican Congress would want: endorsing the United Nations, sponsoring programs for civil rights, controlling inflation, creating more public housing and raising minimum wages. They would not just be talking liberal but acting conservative, Dewey assured Warren, and he would need him as a full partner to help put through that great program for America. "It isn't just a ceremonial job," Warren later recalled him saying. "You'll sit with the Cabinet and be a real Assistant President."

Warren listened attentively, thanked Dewey but did not commit himself. He mentioned that the lowly vice presidential position then paid merely $20,000 a year. As governor of California, he was earning five thousand dollars more and had two big fringe benefits: the rent-free governor's mansion plus a contingency fund. He had no private fortune. He had always lived solely on his public salary.

Dewey replied that a Republican Congress would soon raise the Vice President's salary and probably even give him an official home, such as Blair House across from the White House, which the State Department long had used to house visiting foreign dignitaries.

The two men talked for nearly an hour. Still Warren did not accept. He asked for just a few hours to mull it over. But Dewey was adamant: He needed a definite answer immediately.

Realizing that he could not *twice* refuse the vice presidential nomination, Warren reluctantly accepted, then strolled back to his hotel to wake his wife and tell her the news. She was not happy about it.

At breakfast with the California delegation, he told them of Dewey's offer. Many present, including Senator Knowland, insisted that he still refuse and hold out for the presidency in 1952. Finally Warren phoned the news to his thirteen-year-old son Bobby. "Vice President?" the boy inquired. "Is that good, Dad?"

111

"Yes, I think so," answered the nominee.

A sharp difference in the respective human qualities of the two Republican standard-bearers was observed as each was presented to the convention delegates. J. Raymond Bell, now chairman of the U.S. Government's Foreign Claims Settlement Commission in Washington, recollects:

> *Dewey waved to the packed auditorium, ignoring the woman who stood at his side. On any great occasion in any man's life, it is instinctive for him to reach for, or embrace the one female who shares his life. Not so with Dewey. That glaring omission seemed to be communicated to the gathered Republicans and, ostensibly, to those who saw the event on television.*
>
> *Earl Warren, on the other hand, did that which was natural with him. He not only embraced Nina Warren, but made it quite clear that she was very much part of the moment.*
>
> *Minor? I doubt it, for I have always remembered that moment as have many, many others. It is a human quality that people associated with Warren.*

When he stepped to the convention rostrum after being unanimously nominated, Warren did not come bearing a prepared acceptance speech. "For the first time in my life," he told the delegates, "I know what it feels like to be hit by a streetcar. Before you change your mind, let me say that I accept your nomination. You've all heard enough speeches." A cynical reporter, who did not know Warren's true feelings, cracked: "Sure, he means *A Streetcar Named Desire.*" Concluding his brief remarks, Warren pledged to work with Dewey "to make this a humane government, a fair government, an efficient government and, above all, a government of integrity from top to bottom."

After Warren's acceptance, some political observers on the floor muttered that this was a "kangaroo ticket"—stronger in the back than the front. As George E. Reedy, later Lyndon B. Johnson's press secretary and now dean of journalism at Marquette University, recollects:

> *I was on the convention floor as a reporter for the United Press when it adjourned and discovered, to my surprise, that many of the delegates were somewhat gloomy about the Dewey nomination and*

thought they would do better if Earl Warren had had the top spot. I distinctly recall one delegate saying at the top of his voice: "If we could only turn this ticket upside down we might go someplace."

It was somewhat surprising because the conventional wisdom at the time was that Dewey not only had the nomination sewed up even before going to Philadelphia but that he was a sure-fire winner in the coming campaign. Out of curiosity, I asked a number of the delegates about it and found out that a surprising number had voted for Dewey reluctantly, but did not like him because of his cold personality. They did like Earl Warren, though.

I was covering the convention for *This Week* magazine and received a similar impression. I still vividly recall the joint press conference which the two GOP candidates held in the Bellevue-Stratford hotel ballroom. Dewey, his temper frayed, barked at the reporters and nervously parried their questions.

In sharp contrast, when Warren faced the news corps several minutes later, he answered questions both more humbly and more candidly, and often ended by inquiring cordially, "Does that answer your question?" Thomas E. Dewey made the headlines that day, but Earl Warren made the friends.

Later over their Scotches, long-memoried reporters who thought the ticket should have been reversed, with Warren instead of Dewey heading it, recalled the classic 1924 exchange between President Coolidge and maverick Idaho Senator William E. Borah. Anxious to have Borah as his vice presidential running mate, Coolidge telephoned him, saying, "Senator, I'd like to have you on the ticket with me."

"In which position, Mr. President?" retorted Borah, who promptly disqualified himself with his answer.

Nevertheless, nearly everyone deemed the Dewey-Warren ticket invincible—most of all candidate Dewey and least of all candidate Truman, who was far behind in the pre-election polls.

The President had offered the Democratic vice presidential nomination to both Eleanor Roosevelt, then a United Nations delegate, and Justice William O. Douglas. Both declined. Finally, it was accepted by genial seventy-one-year-old Kentucky Senator Alben W. Barkley (later called the Veep) who chuckled, "I'll take it, but don't pass it around like a cold biscuit anymore."

Instant campaign biographies of all the candidates were

rushed into print. The first book about Earl Warren, written by novelist Irving Stone and subtitled *A Great American Story*, was an extension of his May 10, 1948, *Life* magazine profile. The last chapter of this slim volume, "The Assistant Presidency," was optimistically pitched to "Vice President" Warren's future role with "President" Dewey.

The campaign was complicated by the emergence of two new splinter parties: a Progressive Party on the left, headed by former Vice President Henry A. Wallace with Idaho Senator Glen H. Taylor as his running mate; and a States' Rights "Dixiecrat" ticket on the right whose presidential nominee was South Carolina Governor J. Strom Thurmond. It was believed that both parties would drain votes from the Democrats, still another reason for Republican optimism. Virtually all of the pollsters—some as early as October 1— predicted a sweeping Dewey-Warren victory.

Warren, however, continued stubbornly to play the wet blanket. He repeatedly cautioned his aides that a Republican victory was far from certain. None agreed. Lieutenant Governor Goodwin Knight of California was so confident, he recalled, that he "could hardly wait to move into the governor's mansion in November." But Warren, who did not trust the conservative Knight— and when he was away even locked up in a safe bills that he planned to pocket veto to prevent Knight from signing them—told back-home aides: "Keep an eye on Goody." When Dewey visited California, Warren urged him to take a strong stand on water development, but the GOP nominee refused to do so. Instead, he arrogantly referred the media to an earlier speech he had made on the subject in Oklahoma.

As the Republican presidential campaign progressed, it became clear that Dewey's lofty assurances of an active presidential-vice presidential partnership had been based less on reality than on the exigencies of the moment. Now that Warren was in the bag, however, he was expected to do what was required of him and keep out of Dewey's way. Warren was in fact so totally excluded from Dewey's inner circle that he was not even kept informed of the New York governor's speaking schedule, but had to obtain it through the intercession of a reporter friend.

For his part, Warren—perhaps reflecting the ambiguity of the separate, shaggy dog role in which he was now cast—conducted a campaign so uncharacteristically relaxed that the Dewey forces privately accused him of slackness. He spoke widely and often, making a ten-thousand-mile swing through thirty-six states, but without ardor or anger—thus presenting a sharp contrast to Dewey's furious tirades against the alleged villainies of the Truman Administration. While Dewey's opponents were likening him to a malevolent groom on a wedding cake, the mild-mannered Warren was once again intoning the vague bipartisan speak-no-evil sonorities ("Good Americans are to be found in both parties. . . . Both parties at times have served their country well") that had been his stock in trade in Sacramento. Perhaps the kindest thing that could be said of these not exactly earth-shaking speeches was said by Pierre Salinger, then a reporter for the San Francisco *Chronicle*: "Earl Warren can pronounce publicly a platitude with the reassuring tone of discovery, as if, with God's help, he had stumbled onto hitherto unsuspected but eternal verity." Perhaps one reason for this is that the Dewey braintrust muzzled their vice presidential candidate who refused to deliver any of their canned speeches. As Warren sadly remarked in a long-distance call to his friend, Walter P. Jones, editor of the Sacramento *Bee* and the McClatchy newspapers of California: "The just won't let me speak my mind."

Probably more of an asset to the campaign than anything Warren said were the handsome female members of his family. Mrs. Warren; Virginia, nineteen; Dorothy, seventeen; and Honeybear, fourteen; became national figures and the envy of many another aspiring politician.

Harry Truman, who had resisted being "dumped" as a hand-me-down President, and "Missouri Jackass," as many right wing Republicans were calling him, swung back furiously at his GOP opponents even before the sparsest crowds. He blistered the "good-for-nothing Republican 80th Congress," "the gluttons of Wall Street" and even, most unfairly, called Dewey a "Hitler fascist." The belligerent Truman drew laughs in New Haven, Connecticut, and undoubtedly farm votes in Terre Haute, Indiana, when he jeered at a published photograph of Dewey and Warren at the former's Pawling, New York, farm: "Speaking of cow stables, I saw Dewey's picture with Governor Warren leaning on a gate. That gate was upside down! Dewey didn't know which way to put the gate up! I spent the best ten years of my life on a farm. That picture was a fake!"

As the Warren train whistle-stopped its way across country,

newspapers were tossed onto it at different stops. A daily press digest of Truman's inflammatory remarks was prepared for Warren. "The Governor, a mild, decent, and tolerant human being," reminisces J. Raymond Bell, "would slowly shake his head as he read Truman's diatribes, look up and plaintively ask, 'Did the President *really* say those things?' "

Truman walked a tightrope in referring to Warren because of his respect and genuine friendship for the Californian. Clark M. Clifford, a key adviser on the Truman train, recollects: "President Truman's comments about Tom Dewey may not bear repetition but he always said that Earl Warren was a splendid human being with good instincts."

The following excerpt from an August 5, 1948, press conference held by the President back in Washington illustrates the delicate balance that Truman tried to maintain:

> Q. *Mr. President, in California, I believe, you said that Governor Warren was a Democrat and didn't know it. Have you changed your mind on that?*
> A. *He evidently is a thoroughbred Republican. He was nominated for Vice President. (Laughter). I don't think the Republican platform agrees with his views, however.*

By mid-October 1948, Warren sensed that Truman's gamecock combativeness was making sense to the American people. The President crisscrossed the country in his 30,000-mile campaign. Before sparse crowds, the self-educated man who had never gone to college derided Dewey's "high road" campaign, ridiculed the Henry Wallace splinter party and shunned the Dixiecrats as if they were wilted azaleas. "Everybody's against me but the people," cried the underdog President.

But Warren did not really grow alarmed until his wife said to him clearly that she thought Truman was going to win. However mixed his feelings about the vice presidency, he certainly did not relish the prospect of being defeated in a national election. Previously, he had perhaps avoided facing the issue squarely in his own mind. But now that the situation seemed to have reached a crisis point, he apparently at last decided to make a belated fight.

As Warren's final campaign days assumed a much sharper, more aggressive tone, he urged Dewey to borrow a leaf from the

President's book and use the remaining time to humanize Dewey's own campaign through more face-to-face encounters with voters. Dewey paid as little heed to that sound advice as he had to most of Warren's counsel, which—had he taken—might have changed the outcome. He was assured of victory, he said, and scorned to demean himself by "getting down into the gutter" to scrap with Truman. Instead of behaving like a campaigning candidate, he was already assuming the airs of an elected statesman, going so far as to leak to the press his tentative Cabinet choices.

Dewey was spared those weighty decisions by the events of November 3, 1948. In the greatest upset in the history of American presidential politics, Truman swept the country, 303 electoral votes to 189. In a final irony, it was late-tabulated returns from Warren's own California—along with those from Ohio and Illinois—that decided the President's victory.

When the dust of the "election-day miracle" had settled, Warren hardly knew whether to be disappointed or relieved. He was dismayed and hurt that he had not been able to carry California for the Republicans, losing it by less than 18,000 votes. It was the first election that he had lost in twenty-two years. Yet he undoubtedly meant it when he told reporters in Sacramento: "It feels like a hundred-pound sack has been taken off my back." He undoubtedly meant it, too, when he remarked to a close friend in private, "I was a hick ever to have let myself run with Dewey."

Halfway across the country in Independence, Missouri, Truman again exulted, "Earl Warren's a Democrat and don't know it." Years later, in 1960, Truman would tell me, "Sure, it would have been a helluva lot harder beating Warren than Dewey." Truman and Warren were to become close friends the rest of their lives while the Warren-Dewey relationship was to become coolly uncomfortable.

The downcast Warren now had to look to his own future. He was nearly fifty-eight years old and his defeat—especially in California—had seemingly dealt a lethal blow to all his political prospects. "Warren's all washed up," his enemies crowed. He toyed briefly with the idea of trying to line up a lucrative job in private industry after his term as governor ended. He received several positive responses to his feelers—one from a large insurance company and even one from a leading oil company—but Warren was not basically business-oriented. The idea of making money as an end in itself actually bored him. Lieutenant Governor Goodwin Knight recalled, "I once explained a deal I was involved in. I started telling him how to make a fast buck this way. Before I realized it, he had fallen asleep."

Although public service had become Earl Warren's life, he flirted with other possibilities. He was offered the enticing, lucrative post as Commissioner of Baseball (a job he probably would have enjoyed) but he finally turned it down because he saw no compelling challenge in it. He was rumored to be a prospect for a possible U.S. Supreme Court Justiceship (presumably so that Truman could remove him once and for all from California politics). But the President filled the next two vacancies with political cronies—Attorney General Tom Clark (later to be characterized unfairly by Truman as "the dumbest man I ever met") and Indiana Senator Sherman Minton—so talk of a Warren Supreme Court seat faded away.

In the meantime, conservative enemies in California, sensing Warren's weakness both political and psychological, pressed him hard to undo the liberal legislation that had characterized the first two years of his second term. This pressure must have been precisely what he needed to lift his dejected spirits. He at once put the 1948 campaign and his sense of being hemmed in by undesirable options behind him, and faced the new battle with gusto—becoming, in fact, more progressive than ever. Vigorously he resisted all attempts to modify his health insurance and FEPC programs; renewed his attacks on the oil, liquor, small-loan, highway and other lobbies; bombarded the legislature with new proposals; and, to the chagrin of most right-wing Republicans, took a strong stand against the rising tide of McCarthyism in the state. "The fact that McCarthy is a Republican," he said, "does not mean that he speaks for our party. I dislike blanket accusations against *any* individual or group." Inevitably, the charge that Warren was "soft on communism" was voiced more loudly and frequently than ever, not least by Senator Joseph McCarthy himself.

By the end of 1949, the year that had begun so badly for him, Warren had recovered his good spirits. He had improved his political position in California to such an extent that he began to consider seriously running for an unprecedented third term. He was reluctant to leave the state in the hands of a reactionary successor such as "Goody" Knight, who probably would scuttle his progressive postwar programs, and also because he realized that still being governor two years hence would keep him in the 1952 presidential limelight. On February 2, 1950, he suddenly announced (without first telling Lieutenant Governor Knight, whom Warren's opponents were encouraging to unseat him) that he would be a candidate for a third term as governor of California in the November 1950 election.

The announcement was hardly greeted with unanimous joy. Right-wing Republicans, anxious to remove him from Sacramento, urged Warren to seek the vacant U.S. Senate seat in 1950 against liberal Democratic congresswoman Helen Gahagan Douglas. The popular Warren could have easily won this seat, neutral observers agreed. However, the man whom party conservatives were trying to hustle off to Washington surmised that his chance for the 1952 presidential nomination was greater as Governor than as Senator Earl Warren.

Even if Warren was willing to forego the Senate race, ambitious Representative Richard Nixon, who had captured national headlines during the recent Alger Hiss trial, leaped at the opportunity to be the Republican Senate nominee. He became the darling of the California GOP right wing—the beneficiary not so much of pro-Nixon as anti-Warren sentiment. An $18,000 fund was set up on his behalf, which he would later have to defend in his famed "Checkers" speech.

Nixon and his campaign manager, Murray Chotiner, concocted an ugly smear campaign against the patriotism of Mrs. Douglas, whom they dubbed the Pink Lady. Nixon aides appeared at Warren rallies asking this planted question: "Governor, are you for Nixon or Douglas?" Warren, who was infuriated by the Nixon-Chotiner tactics of character assassination, would retort, "I don't believe in package deals. I don't make it a policy of endorsing candidates for *other* offices. I'm interested in only one campaign—my own."

Surprisingly, Nixon at first felt the same way. Before the primary, he flew up to Sacramento to see the governor and suggested that they conduct separate campaigns. Warren replied, "I've always operated that way." But after the primary, Nixon again came to the state capital but now suggested, "I think we should have a packaged Republican ticket." Smilingly, Warren answered, "No, Dick, I prefer your original argument of separate campaigns."

"Nevertheless, there was a great deal of pressure put on Earl Warren to come out for Nixon," reports Amelia R. Fry, director of the Earl Warren Oral History Project in Berkeley. Horace Marsden Albright, Warren's conservative college classmate and friend, told me that he asked Warren, "Aren't you really going to help Nixon?" Warren snapped, "Oh, let Nixon take care of himself!"

Ironically, instead of seeking a third term, had Warren chose to become California's junior senator himself in 1950, he would probably have delayed Richard Nixon's rise to power and perhaps even have eliminated a future President from the national political scene.

Warren easily won the Republican gubernatorial nomination because no one dared to oppose him, even though Knight desperately wanted to. Yet his position with respect to election was weaker than ever before. Now the Republican right was thoroughly disaffected, and he could not win the Democratic nomination as he had in 1946.

His Democratic opponent was James Roosevelt, California businessman and eldest son of the late President. The Roosevelt name was still magic in California, which FDR had carried all four times. The Roosevelt aura was deemed unbeatable—as would be said of the Kennedys in the 1960s—and particularly so in a state where Democratic registration outnumbered Republican by more than a million. Candidate Roosevelt's mother, Eleanor, even flew out from New York to campaign for her son. Chivalrously, Warren observed, "It's only natural for a mother to speak for her son. How can I argue with a mother about her boy?"

Eleanor Roosevelt liked Warren personally, but she bitterly resented the fact that President Truman—out of high regard for Warren—had refused to support her son in either the primary or general election. By contrast, Truman did endorse Congresswoman Douglas in her Senate race against Nixon, whom the President called a "no-good sonofabitch who hopes to become President some day." So enraged was Jimmy's loyal mother with the man she deemed an ingrate that, as a result, she nearly resigned as a United Nations delegate, reports her biographer Joseph Lash.

It was a campaign lacking concrete issues. Roosevelt, unable to criticize Warren's progressive record, was reduced to charging that his opponent was a political opportunist ("an agile political performer who floats through the air with the greatest of ease in the hope that he will please"). Warren carefully maintained his liberal stance (he made much of repudiating the proffered support of rabble-rousing reactionary Gerald L. K. Smith) and concentrated on explaining to voters why there was nothing inherently wrong in his seeking a third term: Certainly no Roosevelt could complain about that! Since he had lost most Democrats and organized labor—his longtime AFL supporters had switched to Roosevelt—he was now obliged to try to confect his winning plurality from a coalition of moderate Republicans and independents.

The "Jewish vote" never became an issue but it was recognized by Warren strategists. Warren's campaign manager, Victor R. Hansen, recalls in his unpublished memoir of the campaign:

> In the Fairfax section of Los Angeles and other areas of high Jewish population, we found that Jimmy Roosevelt showed real strength. Some Jewish leaders told us that President Roosevelt was generally popular with those of the Jewish faith. Therefore, they should honor his son by voting for him. We were not satisfied with this answer. Governor Warren had never been accused of being anti-Semitic—there never was even a hint of this. We opened regional campaign headquarters in the Fairfax area using many Jewish volunteers and some paid workers.

Perhaps the greatest asset to Warren's campaign, however, was an adventitious event unrelated to California politics. In late June 1950, the Korean War broke out. By early fall it loomed as an American disaster. Sensing growing public alarm over the possibility of a total defeat in Korea, Warren began again to harp on his old World War II theme of the need for wartime bipartisan unity and for making plans for the emergency defense of California. Absurd as this might seem in retrospect, it was not believed to be so at the time by many Golden Staters. The quick succession of disillusioning and frightening events that had precipitated the Cold War were fresh in nearly everyone's memory; the Soviet takeover of Eastern Europe, the swift rise of Communist parties in Western Europe, the guerilla warfare in Greece, the theft of A-bomb secrets and the Berlin blockade. World peace now seemed a fragile dream indeed. Although relatively few feared that North Korea planned to invade California, many seriously wondered whether the Korean conflict might not be the opening of World War III.

One can only speculate on how helpful this war scare was to Warren. But whatever the reasons, he won a smashing victory in November. He beat FDR's son by more than a million votes, sweeping all fifty-eight counties, including Roosevelt's own Los Angeles County, and even received more than a million votes than Nixon had in being elected to the Senate. It was the greatest electoral triumph in California history. Years later, Jimmy Roosevelt did go to Congress, where he strongly supported Chief Justice Warren's decisions, and reflected about that election long past: "The voters of California showed excellent judgment in re-electing Earl Warren over me."

Ironically, Election Day, November 7, 1950—the time of Earl Warren's greatest triumph at the polls—was one of the darkest days of his life. Before he and Mrs. Warren had departed for Oakland to vote that morning, their doctor had said that their youngest daughter, blonde seventeen-year-old Nina—nicknamed Honeybear by her father because as a baby she had looked like a small cuddly koala bear he had seen at the zoo—had symptoms of the flu: headache, nausea and fever. The Warrens left home reluctantly. Later that day they received a phone call telling them that Honeybear was being rushed to Sutter Hospital in Sacramento; what had seemed only the flu was actually spinal poliomyelitis. On the breakneck eighty-mile ride home—which seemed the longest of their lives—Earl and Nina Warren quietly prayed.

Honeybear's father refused to leave her bedside to receive any calls, even from his staff, until late that evening, when he was assured that she was going to live. Only then did he care to learn—much later than millions of California voters—that he had been overwhelmingly re-elected governor: The public man had been superseded by the grief-stricken father. On her hospital bed Honeybear weakly said to her mother, "Take Daddy home and make him rest—he'll be a wreck otherwise." To her father she moaned, "Oh, Daddy, I've spoiled your day!" Warren found a lonely corner and wept.

Twelve days later, the middle Warren daughter, Dottie, was being driven home from a college fraternity dance when her escort's car plowed into a truck that had stopped at a railroad grade crossing in a heavy fog. Her date, a fellow University of California at Davis student, was unhurt, but Dottie had been hurled violently against the dashboard. To save the family from unwelcome publicity, the driver took her home, as she had insisted, rather than to a hospital. But when her father was awakened and saw his daughter's condition, he immediately rushed her to the city's emergency clinic, where she was found to have a punctured lung and five broken ribs. In the morning, her father insisted that her name appear on the police accident list, where it belonged, governor's daughter or no. "For the next few weeks," recalls Mrs. Warren, "we kept shuttling back and forth between Honeybear in the Sutter and Dorothy in the Mercy hospitals."

Honeybear was lucky. The paralysis did not move upward in her body and in time she was able to leave the hospital to begin her long recuperation at home. During the first month of her illness, the family had received about 10,000 cards, letters and telegrams, including one from President Truman; Mrs. Warren affixed these to ribbons with which she decorated Honeybear's room. Until the girl was able to begin exercising her legs, her brothers took turns carrying her up and downstairs. When the exercises began, the whole family exercised with her. Recovery was slow, but it was complete. By May 1952, she was well enough to be crowned Queen of the Shenandoah Apple Blossom Festival by Bernard Baruch. The fact that Honeybear's medical bills had amounted to considerably more than Warren's salary was probably the least of his considerations on that happy occasion.

The wave of public sympathy over Honeybear's illness indicated once again what an extraordinary asset Warren's family was to his political career. The girls—Virginia, Dorothy and Honeybear (hardly anyone called her Nina anymore)—were better known than the boys—James, Earl, Jr. and Robert. Like their mother, they were all highly photogenic and exuded an aura of unspoiled wholesomeness. Together, the Warrens seemed the very image of the 1950s' popular ideal of the American family. And whatever reservations one may have about that ideal, there was nothing phony about the Warren family's "togetherness."

Earl Warren doted on his children. He avoided weekend engagements so that he could be with them and even renounced Sunday golf in their favor (although, to be sure, former California Senator Thomas Kuchel reports that in Warren's hands "a number two iron constituted a dangerous weapon"). Birthdays, frequent as they were in such a large family, were made much of, and Christmases were downright Dickensian. When the children were young, every morning before going to work their father would pile them all into the family car and take them for a ride around the block. On Sundays, after Sunday school, he would usually take his "tribe," as he affectionately called them, on rollicking picnics to give their mother a rest. The family always vacationed together—usually at their Santa Monica beach cabin, where they enjoyed catching grunions.

The Warren youngsters all developed distinctive personalities. Teenage Jim, for example, was an impassioned FDR admirer and for years kept a picture of President Roosevelt in his room alongside one of his father. Although friends often teased Republican Warren about the political split in his family, he smilingly insisted, "Jim is old enough to make up his own mind."

Warren very early encouraged his children to swim, fish, hunt, ski, ride and enjoy water sports. Earl Jr. excelled in the latter. Despite a childhood heart murmur, he became a topflight all-year-round swimmer, scuba diver and champion skin diver. In La Paz, Mexico, in 1949, equipped only with goggles and flippers, he speared a forty-two-pound Golden Cabrillo (bass), setting a world record. The other children were similarly athletic.

They all took private swimming lessons at Sacramento's Del Paso Country Club. "For a long time, I never knew who the Warren kids were," recollected instructor Harry Stevens. "None of them ever mentioned it. But one day young Earl said to me, 'You never met my father, did you?' I said, 'Where is your father?' Well, you could have knocked me down with a feather when our big fine governor grabbed my hand, smiled and said, 'Coach, you're doing a fine job with our children and they all think a lot of you. We often talk about you at home and we all appreciate your excellent instruction.' Since then, I've thought that we'd have a lot less juvenile delinquency if there were more parents like Earl and Nina Warren."

The Warren youngsters all attended Oakland's unsegregated public schools. Several years before the Supreme Court school desegregation decision, I asked Governor Warren how he had taught his children about differences in race and religion. Thoughtfully, he replied, "Who can forget the derisiveness of such terms as 'Shanty Irish, Dago, Polack, Kike, Squarehead, Heinie' and others, or the heartaches they caused until these minorities became indistinguishable from the rest of the population?" He paused and then added, "I have often searched my memory to recall how Mrs. Warren and I began to teach our children to be considerate of others. I don't believe there was any formal beginning. It seemed to us that the problem is not so much to teach children to be tolerant as it is to protect their young minds from being poisoned by an atmosphere of intolerance. Children come into this world entirely free from prejudice and without knowledge of races or creeds. They start learning immediately and their porous minds instinctively absorb the emotional as well as the reasoning atmosphere that surrounds them. If their home life reflects not only affection but also the dignity and quality of each member of the household and a like attitude toward neighbors, children will react accordingly."

The Warren family discipline was mild but effective. Neither Earl nor Nina Warren ever spanked any of their six children. "We never had a childhood situation which couldn't be handled by logic rather than anger," Warren once said. "A child can't help resenting unfair or harsh treatment especially if it's for something he doesn't fully understand. Mrs. Warren and I found it far more effective to 'tune out' on balky children. This didn't mean that we denied them anything, including their good-night kiss. But they quickly sensed from our attitudes that we were annoyed, and sooner or later a child would generally say, 'Daddy (or Mommy), you're angry at me?' We then quietly discussed the matter and the child worked out for himself or herself what was wrong and what to do about it. This method, we believed, was much better than threats or spanking. Children have a natural sense of justice."

There was little rest for Governor Warren from normal parental problems as his youngsters entered teenagehood. Once when visiting him in his office in Sacramento, this reporter asked him: How come the governor's home telephone number was listed in the public telephone directory?

"With three teenage daughters, I have no choice," mirthfully explained the man who always disapproved of unlisted telephone numbers.

Little wonder the Warren family was so attractive to voters. With their vivacity, warmth, gentleness, mutual respect, healthy good looks and plain old-fashioned decency, they were the prototype of middle-class virtue. Warren's political enemies could no more attack such an image than show public disrespect to the flag. They insinuated without conviction that the image was too perfect by half, but actually, most probably believed it was true—as, indeed, it seems to have been.

Certainly Warren's concern for children was very real, as was evidenced by one of his most remarkable achievements, little-known outside of California: the 300 child-care centers operated by the State Department of Education for children of working mothers. They were mostly housed in public schools and administered by local boards of education in fifty-one school districts. The cost was met by the state and by parents' fees of two to six dollars weekly per child, which were uniform throughout the state.

The federal government had financed these day-care centers during World War II, but scrapped the program on March 1, 1946. California alone continued them on a widespread scale, largely because its warmhearted governor knew—long before Head Start, Follow Through and similar programs were born—how desperately they were needed, even during peacetime, to hold families together, keep them off relief, and reduce divorce, delinquency and family tensions. In 1971, President Nixon, despite the existence of almost 26 million children with working mothers, vetoed a child-care bill claiming it would "weaken" families.

Every June, at the eleventh hour, just as the legislature was adjourning, Warren cannily wrangled several million dollars out of it to continue the child-care centers for another year. "If you don't appropriate funds for them," he warned, "children will show up some *other* place in your budget as state charges."

I was assigned to research these centers for the normally pro-Warren *Saturday Evening Post* and wrote an article about them, titled "Schools That Save Families." The editors cynically demanded that I rewrite my affirmative article in a more flip, critical tone along the lines: "Here's another nutty idea coming out of California." I refused. The article was published, substantially as I wrote it, in another national magazine. Later, when I explained the reasons for my magazine switch to Warren, he sadly said, "You did the right thing, Jack. World War Two and the present Korean war merely reminded us of the permanent need for these centers as long as women with children work."

Warren's pioneer Youth Authority was another unique California victory for children. Hailed by the American Law Institute, it has since been adopted by other alert states. Before Warren fought it through the legislature, California youngsters who ran afoul of the law were generally hustled off to state reform schools, or even tossed into prisons or county lockups with hardened criminals. As a district attorney, Earl Warren had observed that all many teenage offenders needed for rehabilitation was some of the understanding and guidance they had lacked at home. Now, instead of incarcerating teenagers with adult felons, the California Youth Authority gave them psychiatric treatment and then placed them in outdoor rural or mountain camps to be rehabilitated.

Regional affairs likewise concerned Warren. In 1950, he was elected chairman of the Western Governors' Conference, after long serving on the executive committee of the National Conference of Governors and Council of State Governments. Here, he was among the first to urge fellow governors to support statehood for Alaska and Hawaii. Now he conferred frequently with other governors of the eleven western states on Pacific Coast interests. Warren often appeared before congressional committees in Washington on behalf of cherished Western interests such as upholding state control of tidelands offshore oil resources. But he lost that fight. President Truman vetoed a bill "giving" these treasures to California, Louisiana and Texas, insisting that they were federally owned—a view later accepted by the Warren Court.

The future Chief Justice was enormously proud of his own California judicial appointments. Bar officials agree that Warren significantly improved the quality of the California bench statewide. During his nearly eleven-year term, he appointed almost two hundred and fifty judges. "If I ever had to practice in California," he quipped, "I couldn't appear before seventy percent of the judges because I appointed them." All except one were subsequently elected to continue on the bench.

So single-minded was Warren's quest for judicial excellence that in reviewing the qualifications of potential appointees he refused absolutely to consider certain matters he considered irrelevant. Such "irrelevancies" included party affiliation, race, religion, sex or even the possibility that the chosen candidate would not accept the seat. Apparently Warren was never more beguiling than when explaining to a successful, respected member of the bar why he should leave his lucrative practice for a lower-paying judicial appointment. Louis H. Burke, now a retired Associate Justice of the Supreme Court in California, recalls that when Warren first approached him in December 1951 about a vacancy on the Superior

Court of Los Angeles County, Burke thought the proposal flattering but absurd. A twenty-year specialist in municipal and government law, he was then immersed in work for two counties and at least six major cities and "had not been in a courtroom for at least fifteen years." But Warren's mind was made up. To Burke's surprise, he found himself being sworn in within a matter of days after Warren's initial phone call.

Whatever the secret of Warren's persuasiveness, it resulted in a decidedly nonpartisan upgrading of the California judiciary. Nearly half of Warren's appointments were Democrats, and among them were the first black and first Japanese ever to sit on California benches.

Crime continued to be one of Warren's preoccupations. Unlike New York Governor Dewey, he eagerly collaborated with Senator Estes Kefauver's Special Committee to Investigate Crime in Interstate Commerce when that body held hearings in Los Angeles and San Francisco in 1951. Indeed, since 1949 he had had a similar body, the State Crime Commission, operating in California. Since crime commissions are never popular with attorneys general, who tend to view them as infringements on the prerogatives of the office, it is not surprising that when Democrat Edmund G. "Pat" Brown was elected attorney general of California in 1950, he tried to have the Crime Commission disbanded. It is equally unsurprising, in view of Warren's strong feelings on crime, that he talked Brown out of it. "I'm glad I had the good sense to accept [Warren's arguments]," Brown said many years later. "I made a better attorney general and, subsequently, governor because of it."

Even in the governor's chair, Warren kept a cocked eye upon the status of his earlier prosecutions as attorney general. When Tony Cornero reappeared in Santa Monica harbor sporting a new gambling ship (*The Lux*) with the approval of a new Los Angeles County district attorney, Warren was enraged. Instead of calling out the National Guard, he wrote to President Truman, urging that *all* gambling ships be banned in *all* coastal waters of the United States. Truman's legislative aides sparked such a bill through Congress which the President swiftly signed for his pleased California friend.

On April 11, 1951, Commander in Chief Truman stunned the world by suddenly firing General Douglas MacArthur for insubordination. The brilliant five-star general was relieved of his Far East command because he insisted upon conducting his own foreign policy, one which could ignite World War III, Truman believed.

In California, as elsewhere, storms of protest arose. The California legislature passed a resolution condemning the President. The Los Angeles City Council adjourned "in sorrowful contemplation," terming the MacArthur dismissal "a political assassination." Flags were flown at half-mast in many parts of California. In San Gabriel, Truman was burned in effigy. A Hollywood wag asked a bartender: "Give me a Truman beer—it's like any other beer except that it doesn't have a head!" When Old Soldier MacArthur flew back home to address Congress before "fading away," he stopped off in San Francisco, where he was wildly greeted by an estimated one hundred thousand Californians.

Warren did not host the welcome. Privately, he agreed with President Truman on the constitutional supremacy of the civilian over the military. But in public, when pressed for comment by reporters, he hedged: "The President had a right to do so. Whether he acted wisely is for history to determine."

In August 1951, Warren flew to Tokyo, where he received a top-level briefing from MacArthur's successor, General Matthew B. Ridgway. Years later the retired Ridgway recalled his pleasure in meeting Warren: "I was at once charmed with his open, frank, warm personality. Afterwards, I met him but once—accidentally on a Washington street—as he was taking one of his customary walks. His instant recognition of me, after a lapse of years, and his cordial greeting, was just the way I remembered him in Japan."

While there, Warren impulsively invited a group of young Japanese farmers to come to California to learn American farming methods. The offer was quickly accepted, and in 1952 the first group of ninety young farmers arrived. Warren had the University of California agricultural extension division oversee their training program and arranged for the California Farm Bureau, through its growers, to assist. This program is now in its twenty-seventh year. To date, several thousand young farmers from Japan have enjoyed a year's agricultural training in California thanks, perhaps, in large measure to the penitent conscience of the man who had sparked Japanese internment a decade earlier.

Several weeks after returning from Japan, Governor Warren, with President Truman sitting beside him on a flag-draped dais, welcomed delegates from fifty-two nations to the Japanese Peace

Treaty Conference at San Francisco's War Memorial Opera House. In his speech, televised nationwide, Warren said: "Peace is a way of life which leaves no room for hatred, greed, rancor or arrogance. . . . Progress in this world has never been made by grinding people down. . . ."

Nevertheless, with another presidential election year looming, Warren could not afford to be too openly supportive of Truman. Scandals in the Truman Administration—trivial compared with those of later administrations—and the dreary horror of a stale-mated war in Korea had tremendously eroded Truman's popularity. The Republicans, determined to avenge their 1948 humiliation, were closing in for the kill. Despite his personal fondness for the President, Warren dutifully joined the fray. He denounced Truman's efforts to seize and operate struck steel plants in March 1952, and told *U.S. News & World Report* in May that he considered the administration to be riddled with "corruption, chiseling and favoritism" and that the low morale in government now constituted a national danger. As a political veteran, Harry Truman doubtless saw these attacks by his friend as routine.

For Warren, however, 1952 could hardly be a routine election year. He was now sixty-one years old, with perhaps no more than another decade of active political life ahead of him. It was not clear whether he could tempt fate again by running for a fourth term in California, and in any case, he was not sure that he wanted a fourth term. If he was ever to make a serious bid for the presidency, this seemed to be the time.

He felt that he had a reasonably good chance, too. A July 1951 Gallup Poll reported that Warren could defeat President Truman by a 52 to 29 margin. The Mystery Candidate, of course, was General Dwight D. Eisenhower, then commanding NATO in Paris. America's most popular military leader since Ulysses S. Grant, Eisenhower was still playing coy with both Democrats and Republicans who wished him to be their standard-bearer. After Ike had brushed off Truman's offer to make him the 1952 Democratic nominee, the Missourian inaccurately scoffed, "That fellow doesn't know any more about politics than a pig knows about Sunday."

The cautious Warren had intended to wait until spring 1952 before formally announcing his candidacy. However, a well-financed, well-organized anti-Warren movement was taking shape within his own party. Many conservative California Republicans were determined to junk him and back Ohio Senator Robert ("Mr. Republican") Taft. As a pro-Taft speaker at an Associated Farmers dinner in San Francisco had said, "We're here to bury Earl Warren, not to praise him."

On November 14, 1951, at a Sacramento news conference, Earl Warren announced that he would actively seek the Republican presidential nomination. At Truman's White House news conference in Washington the following morning, this exchange took place:

Q. Mr. President, what do you think of Governor Warren's announcement?
A. Governor Warren is a fine man. I once said that he was a Democrat and didn't know it. (laughter)
Q. Does that still go, Mr. President?
A. Still goes.

The same day at a Los Angeles news conference, Senator Nixon said: "General Eisenhower and Senator Taft are the front-runners, with Governor Warren the strongest dark horse. . . . But the country does not know too much of where Warren stands and he lacks strength among the people who nominate outside of California."

In California, the governor was finding that his strength was far from total. "Anybody except Warren," cried his right-wing Republican opponents, who sought to defeat him in the California primary and thus prevent his being California's favorite son at the July convention in Chicago. The anti-Warren slate was led by Bakersfield Congressman Thomas H. Werdel, who was closely allied with the oil lobby sparked by B. M. Keck, millionaire president of the Superior Oil Company. They attracted a variety of anti-Warrenites, including conservative doctors, upholders of the loyalty oath and many others who for whatever incoherent reasons, considered their governor a "socialist."

Warren had no political stake in trying to replace Taft as the darling of this right wing, and certainly no taste for it. Once again, his strategy was to seek the support of independent voters and moderates in both parties—taking the bold middle course, as some cynics put it. A sampling from his campaign oratory during this period illustrates his forthright approach:

> *Too many people fail to make the distinction between socialism and social progress. Lincoln once said that the trouble with certain people is that they can't distinguish between a chestnut horse and a horse chestnut.*
>
> *We must establish ourselves as a party of the people, a party that is not overinterested or underinterested in any class or group of people in our country.*
>
> *Our party should not shun the terms "civil liberties" or "social justice." The Constitution was not ratified until assurance was given that civil liberties would be guaranteed in the Bill of Rights. And the term "social justice" is not evil. It comes to us from the Holy Bible.*
>
> *A Republican alliance with Southern Dixiecrats is a disgraceful thing which violates every civil rights principle for which the Republican party has stood since Lincoln's time.*

Recognizing that his knowledge of international affairs was inadequate, Warren engaged an expert in that field to prime him. "He was a German with an accent—but not Kissinger—who spent several weeks in our office preparing position papers for the governor," recalls an aide.

Warren's preoccupation with politics resulted in California losing one of America's most valuable private art collections. Walter C. Arensberg was urged to donate the collection to the University of California (UCLA) by his friend novelist Irving Stone, who, in turn, asked Warren to request it from Arensberg. "This is outside my training," demurred Warren. "How can I ask for something that I don't understand?" Stone rushed some books to him on modern art but the busy governor was still puzzled. Instead, on faith Warren asked the UCLA chancellor to take steps to acquire the collection. Arensberg told the university's art officials that he wanted a special building built for the collection and that eighty percent of it must be on display at all times—a demand unable to be met. Thus, the collection, now worth millions of dollars, went to the Philadelphia Museum of Art while the governor was deep in less artistic matters.

Warren had intended to open his primary campaign at a

Republican State Committee dinner in San Diego in early December 1951. But the evening before, he suddenly suffered severe intestinal distress and was rushed to the hospital. When a series of tests several days later revealed a malignancy, doctors removed much of his intestine. He remained hospitalized for two weeks.

After this surgery, Taft diehards spread rumors that Warren was dying of cancer. The governor's physicians issued a statement that no malignancy remained. Nonetheless, at a private pro-Taft meeting of thirty-five other doctors, called by AMA president Dwight Murray, a longtime Warren foe from Napa, California, this gossip was repeated. Former President Herbert Hoover, a Taft devotee who attended that meeting, was reported to have said: "You don't have to be concerned about Warren. I know the doctors who operated on him. They opened him up, took a look, and sewed him up again." In his own memoirs, Warren bitterly wrote: "The implications of that kind of story were well understood."

Vulgar jokes were bruited about Warren, and even his integrity was now questioned. I was then in California and heard from an outraged Old Guard Republican that on a golf course, Warren recently had been handed a golf bag containing $92,000 in cash as a bribe. Later, I checked and found that Warren had not even been on a golf course for a considerable length of time. When reports of this hate talk got back to the convalescing Warren, he angrily termed them "venomous" and "scurrilous."

After the usual Christmas holiday with his children and multiplying grandchildren, Warren flew to Hawaii with his wife and daughter Honeybear to recuperate for his coming campaign. While he was there, on January 7, 1952, Dwight Eisenhower stopped playing the reluctant bride. He now decided that he had been a lifelong Republican and announced that he was returning to the United States to seek the GOP nomination. Although Warren had never met Ike, he now responded to press queries: "I have great admiration for General Eisenhower as both a soldier and citizen, but I am in the race to stay."

Nonetheless, Taft supporters now charged that Warren was merely a "stalking horse" for Ike to help defeat the Ohio senator in a holding action. As a reward, they said, he had been promised a Cabinet position or the first Supreme Court vacancy. Warren quickly denied this, claiming, "Nothing that I have ever said or done would indicate that assumption. I have made no alliance with any other candidate and shall make none." Asked what the Republicans needed to win in November, Warren cracked: "More votes."

In May 1952, though Eisenhower was still in Paris, his name was entered in the Oregon primary. On May 18, Warren cabled Eisenhower: "I congratulate you on your tremendous vote in the Oregon presidential primary. It was a great tribute to you. Sincerely . . ." The following day, Ike replied, "Dear Governor Warren: Your telegram was handed me just a few minutes after takeoff from Orly Airport for The Hague. While a few months ago the occasion for such a message would have seemed inconceivable to me, and entirely beyond the scheme of things that I had planned for myself, it is nonetheless one of the most heartening messages I have received in many weeks. I hope that some day, in the reasonably near future, I shall have the opportunity to thank you personally for it and tell you how much it meant to me this afternoon. My best wishes to you. Sincerely . . ."

Had his choice been limited to Eisenhower or Taft, Warren would have preferred Eisenhower. The Californian could not forget Taft's insensitivity in human relations during the 1948 campaign. When Warren's train had chugged into Cincinnati, he was handed a telegram from Taft explaining that he was unable to welcome the vice presidential nominee because he had to attend a Republican State Committee meeting in Columbus. Nor had he assigned any other Republican official to greet the infuriated Warren—it was the only place on his tour that he was so snubbed.

Yet Taft and Warren had a healthy respect for each other. The Californian declined to oppose Taft in the Ohio primary in May, rationalizing, "Ohio is the home state of Senator Taft and he is certainly entitled to that delegation if he wants it." Similarly, Taft feared to contest Warren personally in the California primary in June, preferring to operate through the anti-Warren Werdel slate.

Warren's attitude toward Taft had been evident a year earlier in June 1951, when I visited his office. Glancing at the map of California painted on one wall and a map of the world on an opposite one, I teased, "Governor, you really don't consider California a part of the world, do you?"

A twinkle crept into his blue eyes. Then he pointed to a front-page headline in that morning's *New York Times* air edition that I was carrying in which Taft was quoted as saying that the United States should stay out of Europe. "I wish some members of my party thought about the world once in a while," Warren said.

Warren decided to risk opposing the better organized and financed Taft machine in the important Wisconsin primary in May, which had traditionally been a political cemetery for many presidential hopefuls. Eisenhower chose to stay out of this crucial primary in which Senator McCarthy was an inflammatory issue. Although Taft and Stassen intensively campaigned daily for a month, Warren flew there only on weekends because of a busy schedule in Sacramento. Taft won twenty-four Wisconsin delegates. Warren captured the other six, thanks to La Follette family support. Harold Stassen, who already seemed politically shopworn even at a youthful forty-five, despite his Minnesota geographical propinquity, surprisingly received none. Warren, who lost to Taft by merely 26,000 votes, later said: "If I had spent more time campaigning and even a little money, I probably would have won."

Encouraged by this Wisconsin showing, Warren returned home to prepare for the sticky California primary on June 3. There, more than a million dollars in Southern California alone had been spent by the oil lobby to defeat him. But the governor's ten-year popularity enabled him to beat the Taft-oriented Werdel slate by a margin of nearly 2 to 1. It was hardly Warren's most spectacular California triumph, but at least he now possessed the state's seventy convention votes plus Wisconsin's six, the latter delegates being treated as pariahs by the Taft forces.

Nonetheless, Warren did not have California in his pocket. Freshman Senator Nixon, who, with all other California delegates, had signed a pledge on March 22 to support Warren's candidacy, had been scheming from at least early May with Eisenhower's key aides, Thomas E. Dewey and Herbert Brownell, to undercut Warren. As a reward, Nixon hoped that he might be offered the vice presidential nomination.

Curiously, Nixon in his memoirs, neglects—or is ashamed—to reveal how he could not-too-secretly *campaign for* Ike while *pledged* to Warren. On page 83, he writes: ". . . I had already informed Knowland and Warren of my decision [to support Eisenhower]." If indeed he ever had, this incredible revelation would have been news to both Warren and the loyal Knowland until their dying days. To be charitable, it may well be that Nixon is not deliberately lying this time. He merely may be suffering from a lapse in memory. After all, as Nixon himself admits at the beginning of his book, ". . . memory is fallible and inevitably selective."

What is historically well-documented, though, are some of Nixon's anti-Warren antics during the 1952 campaign.

Before the July 7 opening of the Republican National Convention in Chicago, Nixon tabulated the results of a mail questionnaire sent under his congressional frank at taxpayers' expense. He had asked 23,000 California Republicans to name "the strongest possible Republican candidate for President." The results were predictable in this loaded question: Eisenhower, of course. Nixon's poll was "reluctantly" leaked to the media. Warren, understandably, was infuriated, since this revelation lessened his favorite-son status and diminished his strategy to emerge as the compromise candidate in the event of an Eisenhower-Taft deadlock which Warren and many others considered a real probability.

Still, an exhilarated air permeated Warren's campaign train, the Sacramento Special, as the Warren daughters sang and danced with the delegates, wearing orange-colored "W" baseball caps, amid the piano-playing in the lounge car.

Nixon, who had been in Chicago a week before the convention's opening, flew from there on July 4 to board the Warren train at Denver, the night before it was due in Chicago. He and his political mentor, Murray Chotiner, moved among the delegates, hand-pumping and whispering that Warren did not have a prayer and that they should climb aboard the Eisenhower bandwagon *now*. When Warren heard about this seeming doublecross, or "great train robbery" (as some jokesters described it), he was infuriated. Certainly he was willing to throw his votes to Ike *if necessary*, but he scorned sharing any credit with Nixon, whom he deemed an unprincipled upstart.

Nixon furtively left the Warren train at the last stop before Chicago at the suburb of Cicero. Picked up by a waiting automobile, he beat the train to Chicago. When the train arrived at its downtown destination, buses were waiting to transport the delegates to their hotel. Oddly, these buses sported "Eisenhower for President" banners, because Ike's campaign representatives had managed to pay for their rental. "I tore off those banners and put up our Warren ones," recalled Warrenite Oscar Jahnsen. "We weren't going to ride through Chicago with Eisenhower banners! When I told the governor about this, he was mad as hell. He thought that Nixon and Chotiner had pulled this fast one." Oddly, too, Senator Nixon was absent when the photograph of the California delegation was taken upon arrival and when it later caucused at its headquarters in the Knickerbocker Hotel.

Warren had several other surprises, too. Soon after arrival, he paid a courtesy call upon Eisenhower. The doorkeeper admitting him to Ike's suite was Murray Chotiner! Afterward, when Warren visited Taft, the Ohioan desperately pleaded with him for California's seventy votes promising Warren "any job" he wanted in a Taft Administration, except possibly Vice President, which he already had offered to General MacArthur.

As the convention opened, dark horse Warren faced a dilemma. The Eisenhower forces were shrewdly offering a "fair play" amendment. This move challenged the credentials of sixty-eight pro-Taft delegates, especially those in the Texas, Georgia and Louisiana delegations, to vote on another hundred disputed seats. Taft, long the symbol of Republican rectitude, was now crassly maneuvered into being branded a vote vandal. A phony rumor—perhaps launched by the Eisenhower forces—spread throughout the convention that Taft, in an act of desperation, was going to throw his votes to Warren in order to stop Ike.

Warren's dream of a longed-for convention stalemate was to defend Taft in this squabble or, alternatively, to split the seventy California votes equally between Eisenhower and Taft—as pro-Taft Senator Knowland had strongly urged. But when the moment of decision arrived, Warren's self-interest surrendered to his principles. Because he believed in the morality of the fair play amendment, he could not bring himself to support Taft. The California delegation cast its entire seventy votes for the amendment, thereby probably assuring Eisenhower's nomination.

Even so, the contest was surprisingly close. On the first and only ballot, Eisenhower received 595 votes; Taft, 500; Warren, 81; Stassen, 20; and MacArthur, 10. When Stassen switched to Eisenhower, it was all over, and the Republicans had their presidential nominee. Shortly afterward, they had their vice presidential nominee, for Richard Nixon was ready and eager to claim his reward—six brief years after first running for office. Perhaps Warren's only consolation was that he could now appoint someone he trusted to Nixon's vacant Senate seat.

Two weeks later, on July 21, the Democrats held their convention in Chicago. President Truman, having announced his intention not to seek re-election, attempted unsuccessfully to persuade Chief Justice Fred M. Vinson to run, while simultaneously refusing to endorse the candidacy of aging Vice President Alben Barkley. In the end, the convention settled on the sophisticated, witty governor of Illinois, Adlai E. Stevenson. Whatever his private thoughts, Truman told the enthusiastic convention, "You have nominated a winner and I am going to do everything I can to help him win."

Warren had mixed thoughts about Stevenson. The two men had known one another since 1945, when they had met at the San Francisco Conference on the United Nations Charter. Warren liked Stevenson's moderate liberalism, his humor and his elegant personal style, but he doubted that the Democratic nominee would prove to be a formidable vote-getter. Personal feelings aside, Stevenson had to be viewed as extremely vulnerable to a well-conducted Republican campaign.

But would Warren actively participate in such a campaign? Many Republican insiders feared that he would not. He had no personal stake in an Eisenhower victory and he was still angry at what he considered Nixon's betrayal. Plainly, it was time for Eisenhower to intercede. In September, he telephoned Warren to arrange a meeting in Denver on the 15th. Precisely what passed between the two men in their two-hour talk is disputed. Presumably Eisenhower suggested various appointments for which Warren might be considered in return for Warren's commitment to campaign vigorously for the Eisenhower-Nixon ticket. The possibility of Warren's being offered the first Supreme Court vacancy was most likely the main option discussed. Reassured, Warren returned from Denver to tell waiting reporters that he now intended to wage an all-out campaign on Eisenhower's behalf.

And so he did. He worked far harder for Eisenhower than he ever had for Dewey. He campaigned in eleven western states. There his assignment was to reassure voters—particularly Democrats and Independents—about Ike's unknown views. One may wonder how well Warren—or even Eisenhower—understood them. He told farm groups that Eisenhower favored rural electrification, public power, soil conservation and price supports. He told labor groups that Ike was a good friend of unions—always had been. He told mountain-state voters that the Kansas-born candidate championed reclamation and redevelopment projects. And so on. At least he never had to tell voters that the national idol was for Motherhood and against sin; everybody knew that when Ike grinned.

On September 17, when Nixon's campaign was at Pomona, California, near his native Whittier, Warren concluded his introduction of him by saying: "I now present to you the next President of the United States." Warren's embarrassed correction was lost amid the audience's loud laughter and handclapping. Was this a Freudian slip? Certainly Warren well knew of Nixon's presidential ambition long before this vocal slip.

But a family mishap a week later troubled Warren infinitely more. While he was campaigning for Eisenhower elsewhere, his wife, Nina, was closing the family's summer cottage at Santa Monica. As she was sorting out the family's belongings in the garage, she reached out for something and a 350-pound marble slab fell directly onto her right foot, breaking all the bones. Nina Warren's three daughters were in the cabin, just a hundred yards away, but none of them heard the crash, or her cries, because a civil defense siren then sounded. "I could have yelled my lungs out and nobody would have heard me," she recalls. With great effort, she crawled back to the cabin and was rushed to the hospital. The accident prevented Nina, who was placed in a cast, from accompanying her husband on his campaign tour. Dwight and Mamie Eisenhower telephoned Mrs. Warren in the hospital, attempting to cheer her.

Despite Warren's public enthusiasm for Eisenhower, he began to have mounting misgivings about the Republican candidate. He had no great objection to the General's expressing himself primarily in vacuities and platitudes. Warren did that himself. It was part of the game of politics. Nor, probably, since Warren was no stylist, did Eisenhower's talent for mangled syntax grate unduly on his nerves. But his more substantive policy actions could not be so easily overlooked. Warren was disheartened by the ease with which Eisenhower accepted an ultraconservative manifesto issued by disgruntled Taft Republicans and swiftly dubbed by Stevenson "The Surrender of Morningside Heights." Moreover, Warren was seriously disturbed by Eisenhower's failure in Milwaukee to defend his old colleague and benefactor, General George C. Marshall, against Senator McCarthy's charges of treason. He was angered by Ike's attack on national health insurance. Nor was he pleased by the persistent rumors that Eisenhower was seriously considering appointing General MacArthur Secretary of Defense. Perhaps hardest of all to accept was the minor scandal that erupted over the campaign monies given to Richard Nixon by his right-wing supporters in California. Matters were hardly improved when Dana C. Smith, the uninhibited treasurer of the "Nixon Fund," announced, "Warren has never sold the free enterprise system, and Nixon has always done what we wanted."

Perhaps sensing Warren's uneasiness, President Truman shrewdly went out of his way to treat the Californian with kid gloves. Warren, to the dismay of fellow Republicans, responded in kind. At Davis, California, on October 3, Warren raised GOP eyebrows by his exceptionally friendly welcome to President Truman, who was speaking there on behalf of Adlai Stevenson. Warren joined the whistle-stopping train three stops earlier so that he could visit with his friend, Harry Truman, who warned him: "Earl, you aren't doing yourself a bit of good traveling with *me*." Warren beamed and continued to joke with Truman. Before the Davis speech, a Truman aide asked Warren if he had any objection to being photographed with the President.

"Please don't embarrass the governor," Truman interjected. "He was nice to come here from Sacramento to meet me."

"It is never embarrassing for a Governor of California to have his picture taken with a President of the U.S.," replied Warren, as he posed gladly. Then, introducing Truman, Warren quipped, "The only thing wrong with my friend, President Truman, is that he's a Republican and don't know it!" Truman grinned broadly. Warren then concluded, "Now, I leave you Democrats to your own devices!" and departed without hearing Truman's pitch for Stevenson.

At San Francisco the next day, Truman said: "At the Republican convention last July, it seemed that the dinosaur wing of the Republican party had suffered a real defeat. If they had nominated your good governor, Earl Warren, it would have been clear that the National Republican party was on the way to give real recognition to its much abused liberal wing. But they turned away from your great liberal governor and chose another Californian who is not worthy to lace his shoes. . . ." When later asked by reporters whom he was referring to, the plain-talking Truman retorted: "Nixon! He's a no-good lyin' sonofabitch!"

At Oakland, California, later that day, Truman added: "I was welcomed yesterday by your fine governor, Earl Warren. I have genuine respect for your governor, and also a great deal of sympathy. He has been under attack by some of the same special-interest lobbies that are always after me. I was afraid that the Republican Convention was going to nominate your governor to be their candidate for President. That would have given the Democrats something to worry about, sure enough. But the Republicans didn't do it. Earl Warren is too much of a liberal for them. He ought to be a Democrat."

At Redding, California, the following morning, Truman contined: "I feel sorry for that little band of liberal Republicans who dreamed that the General would become their champion. Men like Earl Warren . . . must find it hard to listen to what he has to say these days."

The Republican National Committee chose not to ignore these Truman "compliments." It tried to persuade Warren to disavow them. He refused. "No votes were ever lost by being courteous," Warren maintained.

The nonpartisan governor was even hospitable to Stevenson in absentia. When the Democratic nominee visited Sacramento, Warren was campaigning for Eisenhower out of state. Yet he arranged for Stevenson to be able to speak on the Capitol steps and even offered the use of his office. This was the beginning of the subsequent Warren-Stevenson friendship.

But if Warren disdained to stoop to the scurrilities used by some fellow Republicans, Nixon did not. Twelve days later, he called Truman, Stevenson and Secretary of State Dean Acheson traitors—something for which none of them ever forgave him. In public, Warren remained entirely loyal to Eisenhower. Rather than lambast the Truman Administration or the Democratic record, he concentrated upon Eisenhower's virtues, especially his humanity. For example, on an October 31 Chicago television program (the 1952 campaign was the first in which TV played a significant role), Warren introduced the General by saying that voters "are interested in a warm-hearted government and they know you will make a warm-hearted President."

Warren was probably right. More important than the fact that, after twenty years, people were weary of having Democrats in the White House; more important than popular dissatisfaction with the Korean war; more important than the peccadillos of some Truman cronies; more important even than any of Eisenhower's stated policies (including his promise to bring a speedy end to the war in his "I shall go to Korea" peace cry) was the overwhelming aspect of the man's undoubted personal magnetism. Americans in 1952 wanted to vote *for Eisenhower,* not for his program or against his opponents.

And vote they did. Eisenhower won by a landslide, capturing all eleven states where Warren had campaigned. He ran six million popular votes ahead of Stevenson, scoring 449 electoral votes to his opponent's 89. Sadly, the disappointed Stevenson quoted Lincoln: "I feel like the little boy who stubbed his toe: I'm too old to cry, but it hurts too much to laugh."

Thus, the Republicans swept triumphantly into office and the Democrats were out. And so, in a sense, was Earl Warren. The White House would be closed to him for at least the next eight years; clearly, barring some unforeseen accident, Eisenhower would again be the Republican nominee in 1956. By 1960 Warren would be nearing seventy—too old to be an ideal candidate—and in the interim he would be hard put to keep himself in the public eye and to maintain a sufficiently strong base of political power so that he could command the party's attention as a potential candidate. Even in the dubious event that he could successfully run for a fourth term in California, he would still be out of office before Eisenhower or, inconceivably, his Democratic successor had completed the 1956–60 presidential term. If he had been a wholly political animal such as Nixon and many others, early in the campaign he would have made a "deal" to accept the vice presidency under Eisenhower in return for California's seventy votes. Had that speculative "if" in history occurred, most likely there would have been no Nixon presidency, no Watergate and no Warren Court. But to return to stubborn reality, it appeared very much as though the governorship of California would remain the highest elective office that Earl Warren would ever attain.

At least he could look back with satisfaction at what he had accomplished in that office. His capacity for rising to new challenges had meant that he had grown steadily while in public life—enlarged with experience. Having mastered the art of winning elections, he had moved on to master the art of executive leadership. In terms of prosperity, social service, law enforcement, freedom from corruption, government efficiency, future planning, and a general aura of optimistic well-being, California was an infinitely better place in 1952 than it had been in 1942. Even in the face of California's traditional penchant for political extremities, Warren had been extraordinarily successful, despite some right and left wing hostility, in muting factionalism and creating a kind of California consensus.

Although perceptible to only a few observers of the national political scene in 1952, considerable evidence already existed in Warren's record that he would have made a *good*—even if not a *great*—President. A philosophical dimension still seemed lacking—the difference, perhaps, between an able leader and an outstanding statesman. It would have been impossible to foretell in 1952—perhaps as much so for Warren as anyone else—whether latent in his character lay the seeds of true greatness.

By a nearly fortuitous sequence of events—when another type of unexpected lightning struck—the years of the Eisenhower presidency were to provide an answer.

Chapter Five

The Eisenhower Years: 1953–1961

On November 5, the day after the election, Governor Warren wrote President-Elect Eisenhower a congratulatory letter. The General's victory, Warren predicted, was "a great omen for the future of our country . . . the American people will now participate in the solution of our problems with renewed enthusiasm."

At the January 20, 1953, Inauguration parade, however, Warren was mildly irritated by the display of military power. Because both the Korean conflict and the Cold War with the Soviet Union were still raging, the Californian considered this an inappropriate demonstration by a new peace-seeking President.

Warren's most tangible and immediate gratification from the Eisenhower victory was the opportunity to fill Nixon's vacant Senate seat with Thomas H. Kuchel, his loyal friend and state controller since 1946. Kuchel, who subsequently served in the Senate for sixteen years, remembers, "Warren laid down one basic rule for me to follow, the same one he gave every man or woman he appointed to public office: 'Tom, always determine what should be done for *all the people you represent.*'" Possibly to forestall any Nixonian back-biting, but more likely just on a warmhearted impulse, Warren took the unusual step of writing a recommendation of Kuchel to Eisenhower: "He is as clean in his politics as in his way of living. He is serious, fair and friendly . . . thoroughly committed to your governmental philosophy and leadership." Eisenhower seemed genuinely pleased when he replied, "You were very kind and thoughtful to tell me something about your recent appointee. . . . It is always so good to hear from you and I hope to see you often." Was Warren trying to advise the new Chief Executive that Kuchel was a high-minded individual unlike Vice President Nixon?

Relations between the President and the Governor had never been—and would never be—better. Each, to be sure, had some reservations about the other. During the campaign, Warren had begun to fear that Eisenhower might occasionally be more pliable than principled. In turn, Eisenhower had been concerned over what he thought was Warren's stolidity and lack of forcefulness. Yet they seemed to need each other. Warren was still, at least until 1954, the most powerful political leader west of the Rockies; and in the long run, the future of Warren's public career probably depended upon whether Eisenhower would offer him a suitable appointment. Beyond these professional considerations, the two men liked each other. In manner and outlook, though perhaps not in deeper aspects of character and conviction, they were remarkably similar: friendly, open, outwardly placid, paternal, moderate, unaffected, unintellectual and middle-class. Though not intimate friends, they appeared to get along with one another very well.

Perhaps in recognition of this, Eisenhower asked Warren to be one of the United States' special representatives at the Coronation of Britain's Queen Elizabeth II in June. The other representatives were Generals Omar Bradley and George C. Marshall, the delegation chairman, and Mrs. Fleur Cowles, wife of the publisher of *Look* magazine. The surprised Warrens were delighted to accept. Earl, Nina and, inevitably, their three daughters attended and tremendously impressed their hosts—possibly because they so perfectly conformed to the sentimental European stereotype of American innocence. "Governor Warren's family radiated apple-pie Americanism," Mrs. Cowles somewhat condescendingly reported. "None of the Warren family had ever been abroad before, and their excitement and pleasure was infectious."

The Warren boys, mildly chagrined at having been left behind, took their revenge. One day in London, Mrs. Warren received an ominous letter from Earl Jr. in Sacramento reporting that the white Governor's Mansion was so dirty it was being painted gray; that a blight had destroyed the lovely camellia trees outside her bedroom window; that pigeons had somehow crept into the empty mansion and were nesting in the entrance hall. Knowing how his mother had loathed cats ever since she had been scratched in the face by one in childhood, young Earl solemnly continued: "Somebody also inadvertently locked a stray cat in the house, but we were only able to find a few small spots on the rug which really don't show much. The one in your bedroom is the worst." Apparently the elder Warrens believed every word of this nonsense until the girls began to laugh. "We must have been more homesick than we knew," Mrs. Warren recalls.

The Warrens planned to follow the London visit with a vacation trip to Scandinavia, but first the governor had to fly back to California to adjourn the legislature and act on an accumulation of bills awaiting his signature which he feared the lieutenant governor might attempt to veto in his absence. On his way back to London on July 13, he stopped off in Washington to visit Eisenhower and Attorney General Herbert Brownell at their request.

Ostensibly Warren was to report on his Coronation trip, but in fact he had sent the President an extensive written report thirteen days earlier. The real purpose of the separate meetings with Brownell first at a Statler Hotel luncheon, and Eisenhower later that afternoon was more significant. Warren informed Brownell that, after returning to California from his Scandinavian trip, he planned to announce immediately that he would not run for a fourth term.

Brownell asked whether he would be interested in the position of solicitor general, which the new Administration was having difficulty in filling. Warren asked for time to think it over.

At the subsequent social visit with the President and Mamie, the conversation consisted mainly of small talk about the Coronation. Though nothing was said about it, neither had forgotten their pre-election talk in Denver the previous September 15, 1952, about the possibility of a Supreme Court appointment. Probably even fresher in their respective minds was Ike's spontaneous telephone call to Warren in late November 1952 before he left for Korea, informing him that he was appointing Brownell attorney general but that he *definitely* planned to offer the governor "the first available vacancy on the Supreme Court." Since then, the Washington grapevine had buzzed with rumors that ailing Associate Justice Felix Frankfurter would soon resign. When a California newsman asked Frankfurter if this were true, Frankfurter, miffed at not having been consulted, snapped, "Tell your governor that it is not my desire to keep him off the Court."

Although Warren probably realized that accepting the solicitor general interim position before being named to fill the "first Court vacancy" would refresh his rusty law that he had practiced as attorney general years before, in greater probability he had been thinking about a possible Supreme Court appointment ever since the Denver meeting. Had he concluded that he had a mission to fulfill on the Court? Or did he merely suppose in some general way that he was competent to discharge the duties of that eminent office?

It is doubtful that Warren as yet had a comprehensive vision of what he might achieve on the Court. He was a great public servant and a good executive but he was no legal theorist. Much of his background was that of a law-enforcement officer: one who carried out the law without permitting himself to be too much distracted by questions concerning its equities or long-range social effects. As governor he had, of course, been responsible for *framing* considerable legislation, much of it notable for its social concern. Yet its inspiration seems in nearly every case to have been more pragmatic—a specific response to a specific need—than theoretical. His interests in upgrading the caliber of the California judiciary had been totally free of ideology. His sole criterion in making judicial appointments had been competence, balance and fairness in decision-making. He probably saw his own potential role on the Supreme Court in similar terms. Most likely he would have objected to any suggestion that he might have a "mission" on the Court; the only mission he could imagine would be to do the job as best he could. He might have been surprised at the notion that such a modest objective could nonetheless produce revolutionary effects.

After Warren left the White House on July 13, his Court appointment was still only a *possibility*—certainly not a matter of immediate concern. Frankfurter seemed in no hurry to resign. Presumably there would be plenty of time to reflect on the matter. Meantime, there was still a vacation to be taken.

Five days after arriving in Sweden, Warren wrote a three-page handwritten letter to President Eisenhower from the Gyllene Uttern restaurant near the town of Granna thanking him for his hospitality. "I really felt the need of a vacation," he admitted, "but after two weeks of relaxation I feel as if I could return to work with enthusiasm. It is amazing what even a short time away from an office desk will do for a person. . . . The only sad note on our trip has been the reported serious illness of Bob Taft. I do hope his condition is not as serious as indicated by the news dispatches. . . ."

On July 31, the day that Warren wrote this letter, Senator Taft died from a rare form of cancer. The Ohioan, a hitherto healthy sixty-three-year-old dynamo, had felt a stiffness in his hip on April 19, while golfing in Augusta, Georgia, with President Eisenhower. The mortal seriousness of his swift-ensuing illness could not be kept from him. Gifted, obstinate, and brusque in style, Taft had, since childhood, yearned to follow into the White House his father, William Howard Taft, the twenty-seventh President of the United States (1909–13) and later the tenth Chief Justice of the United States (1921–30). A gracious loser, Bob Taft had become a loyal Senate liege of the military hero who had bested him. Before dying, the methodical Taft had named conservative Senator Knowland, Warren's onetime protégé, as acting Republican floor leader.

In Sweden, Governor and Mrs. Warren and their daughters spent three weeks (July 26 to August 18) touring the country, visiting relatives and rediscovering old family traditions and memories. Some forty relatives met the Warrens at Strand, the farm where Earl's mother had been born, in the tiny village of Stratjara in the northern province of Hälsingland. In Visby, off the southern Swedish coast, they visited the room where Nina Warren had been born in her father's Baptist Immanuel Church. In southern Malmö, birthplace of Nina's mother, the California visitors were welcomed by the provincial governor and scores of Nina Warren's cousins and their children. At a huge family reunion, Governor Warren cut the *spettekaka*, a local pastry baked over an open spit. After visiting the nearby university town of Lund and port of Helsingborg, the birthplace of Mrs. Warren's father, the American tourists motored up to Stockholm. There, at a dinner given by the Swedish Foreign Office, Earl Warren—an immigrant's son who had made good in the Land of Opportunity—was awarded Sweden's highest civilian honor, the Grand Cross of the Royal Order of the North Star. Among the most interesting aspects of Sweden, to Warren, were its social security and other welfare measures and its civilian defense setup, which included a new A-bomb-proof public shelter.

Moving on to Norway, where Methias Warren had been born, Earl was welcomed "home" by scores of dignitaries and the press. In Stavanger several dozen "Varran" relatives convened to greet him in the banquet hall, and in Oslo, the American governor was invited by the Foreign Office to visit its new Kjeller reactor plant.

The Warrens ended their seven-week vacation in France and

Spain. Before leaving Europe, Warren cabled Brownell the enigmatic words that he was willing to accept the solicitor-general post, since no Supreme Court appointment seemed immediate. Brownell sent a return cable, via the U.S. Embassy in Stockholm, expressing in equally coded language, both the President's and his gratification at Warren's acceptance. Soon after returning, Governor Warren announced on September 3 in Sacramento that—unlike Franklin Roosevelt—he would not seek a fourth term. "The people of California should be first to know in order to have ample time to select my successor," he stated. This decision, he piously insisted, was predicated "on my firm and long-standing belief that a periodic change of administration is essential to the continued health of our representative system of government." When asked about his future plans, Earl Warren was silent.

Five days later, Chief Justice Vinson, who had served seven lacklustre years, suddenly died of a heart attack at the age of sixty-three. If Warren had announced that he would not be a gubernatorial candidate *after* Vinson's death, it would have been a gauche act alien to Warren's nature.

Frederick Moore Vinson, an inimitable raconteur, quipped that he always had been close to the law because he had been born in a Louisa, Kentucky, jail superintended by his father. Before being named to the High Court by his friend Harry Truman following the death of Chief Justice Harlan F. Stone in June 1946, Fred Vinson had had a wide political and governmental background. The man lived and breathed politics. He had been a congressman for nearly seven terms (1923–29 and 1931–38) and had become a fiscal expert on the Ways and Means Committee. As a reward for supporting Roosevelt, in 1938 Vinson was appointed to the United States Circuit Court of Appeals in the District of Columbia. During World War II, he was made, successively, Director of Economic Stabilization, Federal Loan Administrator, Director of War Mobilization and Secretary of the Treasury before named to the High Court.

The easy-going Vinson was given the center seat to heal the Court's feuding factions, especially the open hostility between Justices Jackson and Black. Jackson had desperately wanted to be promoted to the Chief Justiceship. But Black threatened to resign in this event. President Truman, after conferring with Charles Evans Hughes, the eighty-four-year-old retired Chief Justice, decided to appoint someone from outside the Court to bring harmony. He chose the patient, politically shrewd Vinson, Truman's genial, poker-playing friend.

Unhappily, Vinson failed to unify the bitterly divided Court. During his final term, 201 dissenting opinions were filed—eighteen by Vinson himself. Besides personal feuds, the Vinson Court was racked by prolonged absences, partly because its Chief provided little leadership. Frankfurter was even heard to mutter about his Chief: "Damn fool!" A poor opinion writer, Vinson often left the task to his clerks. Even the number of opinions by the other Justices sharply declined. In 1950 the Vinson Court rendered fewer decisions than in any year in an entire century.

Seldom did the Vinson Court rule in favor of civil liberties or free speech. Typically, Vinson wrote the majority opinion upholding the conviction of Eugene Dennis and other Communist Party leaders for violating the Smith Act. The Court championed federal and state authority, and loyalty programs over individual freedom, with Black, Douglas and Murphy invariably dissenting. Vinson himself dissented in his Court's decision overruling President Truman's steel-seizure attempt. In other ways, he remained steadfastly faithful to the President who had appointed him.

Vinson, whom historians later rated a "failure" as Chief Justice, died a disappointed, unhappy man. His goodwill proved inadequate to a position which was simply too big for him.

Eisenhower, merely eight months in office, did not relish the unexpected task of having to replace Vinson. Apparently he had never taken his promise to Warren as seriously as Warren had. In any case, it had never occurred to the President that the "next Court vacancy" might be that of Chief Justice. "Neither he [Warren] nor I was thinking of the special post of Chief Justice," Eisenhower wrote ten years later in *Mandate For Change,* "nor was I definitely committed to any appointment." In his own memoirs, published fourteen years after Eisenhower's, Warren testily wrote: "The General's recollection and mine do not fully agree, but my part in the selection of a replacement for Vinson was so simple that there would be little room for faulty memory."

Eisenhower's strong personal first choice for the center seat was John Foster Dulles, but the dour secretary of state, a man who felt that he had a mission outside the Court, respectfully declined, according to Eisenhower. Next, in return for services rendered and because he was a party elder statesman, Thomas Dewey was informally sounded out. But he now rejected talk of *any* federal position for himself on the grounds of advanced age (he was only fifty-one) and a desire to return to private life after leaving his New York governorship. Some observers suspected, however, that fear of nonconfirmation by a Democratic Senate influenced Dewey's decision. Eisenhower was not unduly distressed by Dewey's attitude and thus never specifically offered the Chief Justiceship to him, according to Attorney General Herbert Brownell and James C. Hagerty, Eisenhower's press secretary. Warren was Eisenhower's next choice. But certain formalities still had to be observed before this could be made known to the retiring governor.

The task of "finding" a suitable Chief Justice was entrusted to Brownell, a key Eisenhower campaign brain truster and former Republican National Committee chairman. At least three distinguished jurists were announced publicly as being considered seriously: Arthur T. Vanderbilt, Chief Justice of the New Jersey Supreme Court; Judge Orie Phillips of the Tenth United States Circuit Court of Appeals in Denver; and Judge John J. Parker of the Fourth United States Circuit Court of Appeals in North Carolina. John W. Davis, the highly respected attorney and 1924 Democratic presidential nominee, was likewise mentioned. "Most of these prospects were automatically eliminated either because of advanced age or a record of unsound health," wrote Eisenhower later.

The elevation of an Associate Justice to the top seat was also pondered. The only Republican then on the High Court, Harold H. Burton, was suffering from Parkinson's disease. At first, it was thought that Burton might serve a few years as Chief Justice until Warren, as an Associate Justice, could acquire the necessary Court experience to succeed him. But this notion was rejected because Burton, though a liberal decent man, was an amiable mediocrity who seemed neither personally nor judicially potent enough to shepherd or harmonize the contentious Court.

In a secret breakfast meeting at the Harvard Club in New York, attended by Harrison Tweed, president of both the Association of the Bar for the City of New York and the American Law Institute; John Lord O'Brian, of the blue-chip Washington law firm of Covington & Burling; and Judge Charles E. Wyzanski, Jr., now senior district judge of the U.S. District Court in Boston, it was suggested that Robert Jackson be granted his long-cherished hope and be promoted to the center seat. "We were aware that Eisenhower had promised the first Court vacancy to Earl Warren," recollected Judge Wyzanski. "But we hoped that the promise could be fulfilled by elevating Jackson from Associate to Chief Justice, and giving his Associate Justiceship to Warren. With that hope, the two others went to Washington to ask Herbert Brownell to convey their views to the President." Brownell admits having given this recommendation serious consideration.

Jackson had been the chief prosecutor at the Nuremberg trials following World War II. General Eisenhower liked the idea of promoting someone from the Supreme Court ranks. Wasn't that how he himself had risen from major to five-star general in such a relatively brief period? Promotion was the Army method of advancement. But Jackson had two strikes against him: His bitter public feuding with Hugo Black would not bring harmony to the Court. Second, Eisenhower was reminded that Jackson had once been a militant New Deal Democrat who had argued for Roosevelt's "Court-packing" plan in 1937. The President's aides now convinced him that the center seat *must* be given to a Republican. Thus, the trail kept leading back to Warren through a process of elimination.

Eisenhower's conservative elder brother, Edgar, a Tacoma lawyer, assured the President that Warren was a "leftist tool." By contrast, Milton, Ike's liberal younger brother, then president of Pennsylvania State University, advised him that Warren was a spokesman for right-wing reactionaries. The President was much reassured; he invariably believed that the path of wisdom lay somewhere midway between his brothers' opinions. Indeed, the more Eisenhower thought about Warren, the better the Californian seemed suited to the Chief Justiceship. Though the President felt that he owed Warren nothing politically, he still remembered the Californian's crucial help in defeating the "Fair Play" amendment of the Taft forces. His image seemed perfect: honest, safe, unimaginative, "progressive-conservative," popular, scandal-free. Insofar as Warren had ever taken positions on issues involving the Court—Roosevelt's Court-packing scheme, Truman's efforts to seize the steel industry and federal control of tidelands oil resources—Eisenhower saw nothing to criticize. Warren could be depended upon not to rock the boat with controversial decisions, and also thanks to his infectious goodwill, perhaps even to heal some of the Court's conflicts.

However, Warren had one major drawback: He lacked judicial experience. He had never sat on any court, not even a police court as had the young Hugo Black. Warren supporters reminded the President that three of the greatest Chief Justices—John Marshall, Roger Taney and Charles Evans Hughes—had come to the High Court directly from politics without ever having served on any bench.

Ironically, at a White House breakfast less than two weeks before Vinson died, Eisenhower had casually asked California Representative William S. Mailliard, who had been Warren's secretary, whether Warren would really want to sit on the Supreme Court.

"Yes," Mailliard recalls replying. "He might be bored as an Associate Justice, but he's such a good administrator he would be very happy as Chief Justice."

Other Warren-for-Chief-Justice promoters now included Vice President Nixon and Senate Majority Leader Knowland, two strange California bedfellows. When Vinson died, Knowland was in Karachi, Pakistan. Thomas Kuchel, California's junior senator, telephoned him, urging him to fly back to Washington immediately because Warren was being considered for Chief Justice. Knowland arrived shortly thereafter.

Nixon and Knowland called on the President together to urge the appointment, insists Justice Douglas. Nixon's motives appear to have been uncomplicated: Despite Warren's announced intentions not to run for a fourth term, Nixon was convinced that the only way to *ensure* that Warren would not continue to be a power in California politics was to remove him from the scene. Knowland's motives probably were more mixed. Like Nixon, he detested Warren's "liberalism" and feared his popularity; but unlike the Vice President, he still had warm personal feelings toward his onetime benefactor, even though Warren had been cool to him since the convention because of Knowland's pro-Taft inclinations. Knowland would be glad to see Warren out of California politics, but he wished him well and thought he would be truly happy with the Chief Justiceship.

Although Eisenhower was not unduly moved by the back-home concerns of his two petitioners, he appreciated the thrust of another Nixon argument: Warren still could not be entirely counted out as a 1956 presidential candidate. This threat, admittedly, seemed remote to the President. Yet one could not be absolutely certain which way the political winds would blow three years hence. Would it not be wiser now to separate Warren from his obvious constituency?

Both argument and inclination were moving the President strongly toward the Warren appointment. But among his advisers there were some dissenters, such as Sherman Adams, Ike's Man Friday. A Los Angeles newspaper, referring to Adams, headlined a September 1953 story: "Top Ike Aide Stops Warren High Court Bid." Adams disclaimed this dissenting role in his 1961 book, *First-Hand Report.* Six years later, however, in a Columbia University Oral History memoir, Adams reflected that Warren's "make-up was abstruse and difficult to understand. Warren was a strange person. As I came to know him better, I came to the conclusion I thought the intellectual intrigue which beset him was probably a facade. He was aloof. I am satisfied that Eisenhower never understood Earl Warren any more than the rest of us. Nor do I think that he ever took time to discover how Warren's mind worked. I doubt if Eisenhower at any time ever understood the intricate mechanism of the Warren mind. If he had known Warren better, he certainly would have hesitated appointing him."

On Eisenhower's orders, Herbert Brownell felt out Warren in a trial-balloon telephone conversation focusing on whether he would accept an Associate Justiceship. The California governor insisted upon fulfillment of the Eisenhower-Brownell promise of the "first vacant seat"—which now happened to be the Chief Justiceship. Brownell reported, "I can't get that bullheaded Swede to change his mind."

In little more than a week, the Supreme Court would begin its busy fall term. When a High Court is left leaderless, its dissensions invariably multiply. The perplexed Brownell weighed the alternatives again: Should he advise the President to offer Warren the coveted center seat? Or should he urge Eisenhower to promote one of the sitting Supreme Court Justices—Burton or even Jackson—to the top spot, as Roosevelt had elevated Associate Justice Harlan Stone in 1941?

While Brownell was pondering this question, General Eisenhower directed him to fly to California secretly to learn more about Warren's "record of attainments as a lawyer, as district attorney and

154

as attorney general of California." As Eisenhower later wrote, "I needed the conclusions of a qualified lawyer on the matter."

But this was really only window dressing. Brownell had known Warren and his qualifications for many years—after all, the New York attorney had been Dewey's campaign manager in both 1944 and 1948—and as attorney general, Brownell could swiftly examine the FBI dossier on Warren. He could hardly "investigate" the California governor on such a hurried trip because Warren would be the only person he would have time to interview.

Meanwhile, in California, prospective nominee Warren was well aware that Eisenhower's decision was fast approaching. To avoid reporters' embarrassing questions even by telephone, he decided to go deer hunting with his sons at a friend's isolated hideaway on Santa Rosa Island off the Santa Barbara coast. There, he received a wireless message on Friday, September 25. Would he please immediately telephone Attorney General Brownell in Washington? An airplane took him to the mainland and he arranged to meet Brownell two days later.

On early Sunday morning, September 27, Brownell flew to McClellan Air Force base, ten miles outside Sacramento. He arrived at 8 A.M. and was whisked into a private room where the governor was awaiting him. Warren later remembered the meeting as having lasted about an hour. Brownell says an hour and a half. But reporters insist that it lasted about three hours.

At first Brownell said that the President was considering appointing Warren to the Supreme Court but wanted a man with more judicial experience to be Chief Justice. Politician Warren smiled and remained silent. This was an old cat-and-mouse game to a hard-bargainer who felt that he now had the President boxed in.

Pleasantly, Warren remarked that he would be honored to be a member of the Supreme Court. Contrary to popular belief, nothing was said about his being Chief Justice or Associate Justice, both Warren and Brownell have insisted in separate memoirs. Yet Warren pointedly reminded Brownell that he had been promised "the first vacancy," would prefer this immediate appointment to an interim one as solicitor general, and was generally sympathetic to the goals of the Eisenhower Administration.

Sighing, the President's emissary reluctantly played the card for which the other poker player was waiting. The tone was more solemn now. "I am authorized to offer you the Chief Justiceship of the United States, providing that you can take your seat a week from tomorrow [Monday, October 5]."

Warren beamed broadly.

"Herb, that's a helluva thing to say to the Governor of California."

"That's the condition of the offer, Earl."

"I accept it."

No issue that might come before the Supreme Court was discussed, claimed Brownell in an August 1975 memorandum to the Earl Warren Oral History Project in Berkeley. But skeptical Southern senators immediately insisted that they must have discussed the school integration and other civil rights issues.

Another skeptical note about the official Warren and Brownell versions has been recorded, surprisingly, by Merrell F. ("Pop") Small, Governor Warren's administrative secretary from 1945 to 1953. On November 15, 1972, he wrote to Amelia R. Fry, the project's director, that he doubted Warren

> . . . *would have gladly accepted appointment as an associate justice, and would not have insisted upon being named Chief . . . I cannot remember whether Warren ever actually said to me that he insisted with Brownell upon being appointed Chief Justice, but this certainly has been the strongest possible impression with me these twenty years . . . I wrote in the Sacramento* Bee *of June 7, 1970, that he held out for the highest job . . . and nothing was said by him about it then or since. . . .*

Warren in his memoirs fudges about this. The retired Chief Justice insists that he would have gladly accepted an Associate Justiceship and that "Nothing was said about my becoming Chief Justice" by either himself or Brownell. What occasioned author Warren's published sensitivity? Was he concerned about his historical "image"? Certainly his octogenarian memory—like that of all of us—was not infallible, several intimates have pointed out.

Whatever the facts, Brownell immediately flew back to Washington. "The Attorney General, on his return," Eisenhower later wrote, "gave me a helpful report, and I decided to name Governor Warren Chief Justice."

The nineteen days of speculation were over. That Sunday evening—to test public reaction—Brownell invited six meticulously selected reporters from newspapers friendly to the Administration to his home for "background information, not attribution"—a news-dispensing practice that exhilarates favored Washington correspondents but enrages the uninvited. Brownell then "leaked" the news of the forthcoming Warren appointment. Understandably, it was rushed into print the following morning.

On Tuesday evening, September 29, at nine P.M. in the Executive Mansion in Sacramento, California, Governor and Mrs. Warren were sitting in his bedroom. The governor was reading; Nina Warren was stitching a hem on a dress of Virginia's. The telephone rang. The governor answered it. After he had finished speaking briefly, his wife looked up. As she recalls, she asked who the caller had been.

There was a long silence.

Finally, her husband murmured, "Oh, Herb Brownell."

Silence. Then, "Oh, he said that the President was going to announce my appointment as Chief Justice at his press conference tomorrow morning."

Earl Warren's brow puckered. His mind was three thousand miles away, in Washington. If he harbored any dominant thought then, it might have been that it had been nice to hear the news from Herb Brownell, but wasn't it strange that the President had not called to give him the news personally?

Early on the morning of September 30, the thirty-fourth President of the United States announced at his overflowing news conference that he was nominating Earl Warren to be the fourteenth Chief Justice of the United States. Since Congress was not then in session, it would be a recess or interim appointment [which was dated October 2, 1954] until the Senate could confirm the nominee. With familiar charm, the President began by saying, "I could start off, I think, by confirming something that is certainly by no means news any more." Adding that his nominee had "no ends to serve except the United States and nothing else," he predicted that Earl Warren "to my mind will make a great Chief Justice."

A negative note was injected by Raymond "Pete" Brandt, the highly regarded St. Louis *Post-Dispatch* bureau chief, who was irritated by the attorney general's "leak" to competitive newspapers. Without mentioning Brownell's name, he needled the Chief Executive: "Is it going to be the policy of this Administration to leak such important news only to *friendly* newspapers?" Unprepared for this cantankerous query, the President replied that he could not answer this question right away. But if any "trusted subordinates" had leaked news for what they deemed proper purposes, he certainly would not interfere with them. Even more awkward—although unknown to reporters—was the curious fact that Eisenhower had never taken the trouble to inform Warren personally of the appointment. Warren knew nothing except what Brownell had told him. [Warren in his memoirs wrote with charitable vagueness: "I have tried very hard to remember whether it was Attorney General Brownell or President Eisenhower who made the call. . . ."]

Thus, the newly appointed Chief Justice heard the news of his elevation on the radio as he was finishing breakfast at 7:30 A.M. Sacramento time (10:30 A.M. in Washington). Promptly, he sent this telegram:

> THE PRESIDENT
> THE WHITE HOUSE
> DEAR MR PRESIDENT: YOUR DESIGNATION OF ME TO BE CHIEF JUSTICE OF THE SUPREME COURT HAS JUST BEEN ANNOUNCED OVER THE AIR. WITH FULL APPRECIATION OF YOUR CONFIDENCE AND OF THE RESPONSIBILITY IMPOSED, I GRATEFULLY AND HUMBLY ACCEPT. YOU MAY BE SURE THAT I WILL DO MY BEST TO INTERPRET THE CONSTITUTION FAIRLY AND TO DEFEND IT FAITHFULLY AGAINST EVERY ENCROACHMENT. SINCERELY
> EARL WARREN

Late that afternoon, he received this reply:

> THE HONORABLE EARL WARREN
> GOVERNOR OF CALIFORNIA
> SACRAMENTO, CALIFORNIA
> THANK YOU VERY MUCH FOR YOUR FINE TELEGRAM. AS YOU ALREADY KNOW, I REACHED THE DECISION TO MAKE YOU CHIEF JUSTICE BECAUSE OF MY DEEP CONVICTION THAT YOU ARE UNIQUELY QUALIFIED TO SERVE OUR COUNTRY IN THAT HIGHLY IMPORTANT POST. PLEASE REMEMBER ME KINDLY TO YOUR FAMILY.
> DWIGHT D. EISENHOWER

In his more formal acceptance statement later on that same day, Warren announced that he would resign as governor of California in four days and take his oath when the High Court convened the following Monday morning. "The President has designated me to be Chief Justice of the Supreme Court and I have wired him my humble acceptance," he wrote. "I will apply myself to the task with the very best that is in me and will compensate for any limitations with industry and faithfulness to the cause of constitutional government in America."

Actually, the new Chief Justice had misstated for a second time the correct title of his forthcoming position, for he was now the Chief Justice of the United States and not merely of the Supreme Court, because he would, in addition, preside over the nation's entire judicial system.

However, he characterized his new title correctly by Saturday, October 3, in a succinct handwritten letter to Frank Jordan, California Secretary of State: "In order to accept the office of Chief Justice of the United States, I hereby resign as Governor of the State of California effective at 12 o'clock midnight, October 4, 1953. Sincerely, Earl Warren."

The harried governor had four days to terminate his California affairs. Before leaving office, he signed nineteen clemencies. One was a full pardon for labor organizer Ernest Ramsey, whom Alameda County District Attorney Warren had convicted sixteen years earlier in the controversial *Point Lobos* case. Other official final acts included appointing John F. Aiso of Los Angeles as California's first Japanese-American judge and Helen MacGregor, Warren's longtime secretary, to the Youth Authority Board. Shortly before resigning, in a bill to increase all state salaries, he requested that the governor's not be included. "My salary has been raised from $10,000 to $25,000 since I took office and that is sufficient," he wrote, not altogether to the delight of future California governors.

The reaction to Warren's appointment was generally favorable. It was widely assumed that an upright, respectable, moderately progressive, if uninspiring, Republican was being rewarded for party loyalty. He would preside over a no-nonsense Supreme Court which would blend with the middle-road Eisenhower Administration philosophy, most observers believed.

The *American Bar Association Journal,* with a prescience which later troubled its parent organization, contended, "[Warren] has a keen and well-trained legal mind and is not easily fooled. The nation will discover this in due course, as California did."

The legal profession and the news media widely praised the new Chief Justice's character, ability and administrative skill, though duly noting his lack of experience as either a federal, state or even local judge. It was the first time in forty-three years that a man without any prior judicial experience had been named to head America's highest court. Only thirteen men before had been Chief Justice. Vinson had insisted vainly that he was not the "unlucky" thirteenth but instead the twelfth Chief Justice, arguing that John Rutledge [1789–91], although nominated, had never been confirmed. Warren was the first governor to be named directly to the center seat.

"[Warren] is honest and highly intelligent," editorialized *The New York Times.* "He is liberal and humanitarian when basic issues must be faced. If rancor exists on the High Bench—as unhappily it does—there is no person better qualified than Earl Warren to soothe and mollify." Even the New York *Daily News'* peevishly right-wing columnist John O'Donnell predicted that Warren's philosophy would coincide with the Republican Party's desire to hold their newly won Southern support and further forecast that he would uphold "traditional racial segregation." This fond hope was shared by such ordinarily shrewd Georgia senators as Walter F. George and Richard Russell, who based their judgment upon Warren's earlier anti-Japanese stand.

Other politicians in both parties lauded him. Republican Thomas E. Dewey said that his onetime rival would make "a superb Chief Justice." Democrat Adlai Stevenson exulted. "It is an excellent appointment"—as if astonished that Eisenhower could have such uncommon good sense!

James C. Petrillo, American Federation of Musicians president, telegraphed congratulations: "From a Union Clarinet Player to Chief Justice of the Supreme Court of the United States is Quite a Jump." In his note of thanks, Warren handwrote this P. S.: "My regards to the brothers of the federation. Their kindness to me has always been more than a onetime poor clarinet player deserved."

There were also some scattered, though subdued, dissents from both the right and left. An Old Guard San Francisco lawyer complained, "Earl Warren's decisions will sound like he's running for President or Assistant God." Senator Barry Goldwater deplored the appointment of a man who hadn't "practiced law in twenty-five years and was a socialist." *U.S. News and World Report* publisher David Lawrence, radio commentator Fulton Lewis, Jr., and columnist Raymond Moley generally deplored this "leftist" appointment. Simultaneously, liberal writers in *The Nation* and *New Republic*, citing the nominee's right-wing and antilabor actions, indicated skepticism that Earl Warren could ever be concerned with protecting human rights or civil liberties.

Both Edgar and Milton Eisenhower protested to their brother. On October 1, the day after the nomination, the Chief Executive wrote to his conservative older brother, who was then staying at New York's Lexington Hotel:

> *Dear Ed:*
> *What you consider to be a tragedy, I consider to be a very splendid and promising development. . . . I wonder how often you have met and talked seriously with Governor Warren. This I have done on a number of occasions, because from the very beginning of my acquaintanceship with him, I had him in mind for an appointment to the high court. . . . To my mind, he is a statesman. We have too few of these. Many people condemn him because of a particular medical plan he advocated for California. On this point, I would have, of course, disagreed with him—but I find that, at least, he never advocated such a thing nationally. I get a bit weary of having the word "political" used with respect to such decisions. These appointments get my long and earnest study, and I am not trying to please anybody* politically. *Not only do I want nothing— I never did! So it is useless to talk to me in such terms.*

Eight days later, he wrote another "Personal and Confidential" letter to his liberal younger brother Milton, who had forwarded a letter from a former Office of War Information official claiming that the Warren appointment was spearheaded by "reactionaries."

> *I believe that we need* statesmanship *on the Supreme Court. Statesmanship is developed in the hard knocks of general experience, private and public. Naturally, a man occupying the post must be competent in the law—and Warren has had seventeen years of practice in* public *law, during which his record was one of remarkable accomplishment and success, to say nothing of dedication. He has been very definitely a liberal-conservative; he*

represents the kind of political, economic and social thinking that I
believe we need on the Supreme Court. . . .

On Sunday, October 4, 1953, the Chief Justice-designate and his wife boarded a United Airlines plane for Washington. Their noontime departure was delayed a half hour because so many well-wishers came to see them off. At the last minute, Nina Warren had decided to accompany her husband to witness his induction. Originally, she had planned to stay behind to pack. However, in their nearly thirty years of sharing, it seemed only proper for her to be with him now. The plane arrived in Washington at ten o'clock that night—barely fourteen hours before Warren was to be sworn in. Vice President Nixon and Attorney General Brownell reportedly met them at Washington's National Airport, but the Warrens chose to accept a ride to the Statler Hotel with Supreme Court Clerk Harold B. Willey and the Marshal, T. Perry Lippitt, Warren wrote in his memoirs. Strangely, Brownell in his memoir, wrote for history that President Eisenhower had met the new Chief Justice at the airport!

Warren had brought along an old black robe which he wore at academic functions. But he was told that it was not satisfactory for this solemn occasion, so he had one rented early the next morning from a Washington cap and gown shop which claimed to have robed all except two Supreme Court Justices since 1926. "It was a sample size 44 robe, the largest and longest we had in stock but still too small around the shoulders for Chief Justice Warren," explained proprietor George F. Tudor. "He didn't complain, though. He wore it a week until we finished making the new size 48 one for him, which cost $110. This was presented to him by California's two senators, in accordance with Court custom. Like most Justices' robes, it swung loosely two to four inches up front and ended about seven inches from the floor. This was long enough to look dignified but short enough so that he wouldn't trip over it."

On Monday morning, October 5, at 10 A. M., the new Chief Justice arrived at the white Greek-style Supreme Court building, even though his swearing-in was not scheduled until noon. He was as eager as a high-school boy preparing for commencement. His chauffeured limousine—provided for the ceremony—inconspicuously brought him to the rear basement entrance used by the Justices. Suddenly, he remembered a promise made to airport photographers the previous night. To fulfill it, he strolled around to the front of the building with its eight huge Vermont marble columns and engraved inscription: "Equal Justice Under the Law." He gazed at them as well as at the two seated figures representing Justice and Authority facing the Capitol across a plaza park. He ambled up the steps smiling and waving as the grateful photographers clicked away.

President and Mrs. Eisenhower attended the noon ceremony. It was the first time that either they or Mrs. Earl Warren had been inside the Supreme Court building. All three were stunned by the breathtaking courtroom—perhaps the most magnificent room in Washington, with its twenty-four gleaming Ionic columns of Siena marble and its forty-eight-foot-high walls of ivory marble brought from Spain. One wall depicts nine law-givers who lived before Christ, including Moses, Solomon, Hammurabi and Confucius; the opposite wall portrays nine who lived after Christ, including Justinian, Mohammed, Blackstone and Marshall.

Two oaths were administered to the incoming Chief Justice in the only important remaining American ceremony conducted without the presence of television, radio, or modern electronics. The first, the traditionally private Constitutional Oath, was taken in the sacrosanct Conference Room behind the bench with merely the eight sitting Justices present. It was administered by Associate Justice Hugo L. Black, the senior jurist in service. Warren pledged to "support and defend the Constitution against all enemies foreign and domestic . . . and bear true faith and allegiance to the same."

Precisely at noon, the Marshall pounded his gavel on a wooden block. Everyone rose. The red velour curtains behind the bench parted in three places and the eight leaderless Justices filed through them, in pairs, as if in a Greek drama. They took their respective seats, leaving the center one vacant. The courtroom audience could then be seated.

After the Crier made the traditional announcement that the "Honorable Court" was in session, Justice Black announced the death of Chief Justice Vinson and said that a memorial service would be held later in the term. Then Clerk Harold Willey administered the Judicial Oath to the incoming Chief Justice, who raised his right hand and repeated: "I, Earl Warren, do solemnly swear that I will administer justice without respect to persons, and do equal right to the poor and to the rich, and that I will faithfully and impartially discharge and perform all the duties incumbent upon me as Chief Justice of the United States, according to the best of my abilities and understanding, agreeable to the Constitution and the Laws of the United States. So help me God."

The Marshall then escorted the new Chief Justice to his high-back black leather chair in the center of the elevated bench. While stepping up to it, the neophyte jurist tripped over his long borrowed robe. A major mishap was averted when he quickly recovered his balance. "Yes, I guess that I literally stumbled into the Court," he later chuckled. The chair was pulled out by a black-knickered, fourteen-year-old page boy, too short to see over the top of it. Shortly afterward, the Court adjourned until the following Monday.

"What do you remember most about the ceremony?" I later asked Earl and Nina Warren.

"It was so short!" they both laughingly agreed.

"Perhaps the most lonesome and awesome day of my life was when I arrived at the Supreme Court," Warren later told me. "Moving from the governorship of a state growing at the rate of a thousand persons a day, to the deliberative work of the Supreme Court was an experience that one must undergo to appreciate. All my life I had been dealing with people and their problems. Now on the Court, I knew that I would rarely see a litigant. And my experience in federal courts had been very limited because most of my practice had been in state courts."

In retirement, he admitted to his friend Dr. A. L. Sachar, Brandeis University chancellor, "I arrived on four days' notice, with no preparation or knowledge of anything that was before the Court at that time—some four hundred pending cases or those that had come in during the summer months." Yet, as usual, he managed to rise to the occasion. Justice Douglas recollects, "He asked Justice Black to preside at the first few Conferences, stating the issues involved in petitions for *certiorari*, and leading the discussions on argued cases. After a few weeks, Earl Warren felt more comfortable and thereafter presided over all Conferences and all of our public sessions."

But the gossip along the Washington cocktail circuit was that Warren was in way over his head. When I asked Justice Douglas much later if this had been true, he replied, "Earl Warren definitely was not in over his head in the work coming to his desk as Chief Justice. He was well trained as a lawyer and had a nose for the relevant facts in a case."

When an old California friend, Judge Oliver D. Hamlin, requested an autographed photograph, Warren inscribed it: "In memory of days when neither of us was judicial or judicious." But the new Chief had to be both during a bizarre episode commencing his first week in office. A bitter election for Mayor of New York was raging. Candidate Robert F. Wagner charged anonymously that a high lawman in Washington was interceding to get Joey Faye, a notorious labor racketeer, released from prison. Reporters besieged Warren for a quote, but the old politician knew that the best he would get from the press would be a "Warren denies" headline. To avoid the media, he cut off his hotel telephone and entered the Supreme Court every morning through the basement in an automobile. "I sat tight and suffered in silence," he recollected. Finally, he turned on his television set one evening shortly before the election when Wagner was holding a news conference.

"Was Chief Justice Warren the man you referred to as being implicated in the prison scandal?" a reporter asked.

"Oh, no," Wagner replied. "I've never met him but understand that he is a very fine man who would never be involved in anything like *that*."

During his early court days, the new head of the nation's most powerful judicial body amazed the tribunal's employees by strolling around the building introducing himself, shaking hands and chatting with court officials, law clerks, secretaries, elevator operators, gardeners, barbers, cleaning women and others, even more earnestly than he had in all of his previous positions. "He shook more hands in one day than some Justices had in twenty years," remembers Information Officer Bert Whittington. "In a few days, he knew everybody's name and some of their backgrounds."

When moving from the governor's chair to the Supreme Court's center seat, Warren's real income was reduced, even though he was entitled to a $900-a-month pension for his long California service. As Chief Justice, his initial salary was $25,500—only $500 more than he had been receiving as governor. However, in Washington he lacked major fringe benefits, such as free occupancy of the Governor's Mansion. There were other differences as well. For one thing, the size of his seven-person Court staff was appreciably smaller; as governor he had had available a large, diversified staff assisted by state consultants and researchers. Now his entire staff consisted of two secretaries, three law clerks and two messengers.

Mark W. Cannon, the Supreme Court administrative assistant, recalls, "It was a personal staff smaller than that of a freshman congressman."

Moreover, as a Justice he could not defend his decisions—the Court's formal written opinions were supposed to speak for themselves. Governor Warren had been able to use news releases, interviews, speeches and private conferences to explain his actions or statements. But a Supreme Court Justice cannot talk back.

A less obvious difference, but one that was bound to be trying to a man of Warren's gregarious temperament, was his new position's professional seclusion. A Justice is severely restricted as to the people with whom he can discuss pending cases. Seldom can he confront litigants directly. Their cases are generally presented by counsel or in written briefs. "In all my years on the Court, I saw only one or two actual litigants," Warren once recollected wistfully. Raymond Bell, a former campaign aide remembers: "Several years after he had been made Chief Justice, I visited him in his chambers. After twenty minutes I said, 'Governor (some of us still called him that), I feel I am intruding on your heavily booked time.' He urged me to stay, saying, 'We lead a rather lonely life here, and it is always good to have a chance to visit with friends.' "

The Court, all of whose members except Warren had been appointed by Presidents Roosevelt and Truman, was composed of diverse and difficult men ranging in age from Frankfurter's seventy-one to Clark's fifty-four. Clark was the only one whom the new Chief knew, dating from early 1942 when the Texan, as a U.S. Department of Justice representative, had conferred with him about the Japanese internment. Some of the Justices were brilliant; others, mediocrities; most were prima donnas. Philosophically, they ran the gamut from extremely liberal to extremely conservative. In several cases, their ideological differences were compounded by bitter personal animosities. Black, for example, made no secret of his contempt for Jackson; Douglas and Frankfurter were barely on speaking terms. Warren would need all of his considerable political skills and robust good will to persuade this divergent group to get the work done and the cases decided.

All of the Justices had fairly fixed views, unlike the new Chief, who seemingly had no ideology, no preconceived plans, no grand designs.

The all-out liberals were Hugo Black, the first New Deal nominee, an ex-Klansman, crusading Alabama U. S. Senator and First Amendment diehard; and William O. Douglas, a former Yale law professor, chairman of the Securities and Exchange Commission, and impassioned conservationist, mountain climber and world traveler.

The moderates were Robert H. Jackson, a onetime U. S. attorney general under FDR and Internal Revenue Bureau general counsel; Tom C. Clark, an ex-attorney general and poker-playing pal of Truman; and Sherman Minton, a dour, undistinguished former Seventh Circuit U. S. Court of Appeals jurist and sometime senator from Indiana.

The conservatives were Kentucky's aging Stanley Reed, a former solicitor general and onetime New Dealer who had moved sharply to the right; Harold H. Burton, a plodding former Republican senator from Ohio and ex-Mayor of Cleveland; and the brilliant Felix Frankfurter, who had been an ultraliberal as a Harvard law professor and a founder of the American Civil Liberties Union, but who had grown increasingly conservative on the Court.

The principal arena where Warren would mix with his fractious brethren was at the Saturday Court Conference (which he later changed to Friday). This all-day meeting was regularly held in an elegant oak-paneled room adjoining the Chief Justice's chambers. In the center, beneath a crystal chandelier, was a long mahogany table at which the Justices sat, the Chief at the head. Flanking a large fireplace and lining all the walls were rows of leather-bound law books. Hovering over the scene was a solitary portrait of red-robed John Marshall.

Although a telephone had incongruously been installed in the room, it was never used during Warren's sixteen years as Chief Justice. Whenever the Justices convened, no one, not even a clerk, stenographer or messenger, was permitted to penetrate the heavily bolted door into their Conference Room. Their deliberations could be interrupted only for the most urgent reason. On these rare occasions, by tradition it was the most junior Associate Justice in service who would open the door. Tom Clark, who filled this role for some years, cracked: "I'm the highest paid part-time doorkeeper in America." Thus, Friday, November 22, 1963, Arthur Goldberg was the first Justice to learn that the President of the United States had been shot.

The Chief Justice would open the discussion of each case

under review, briefly stating the facts and the issues to be decided upon. If he were persuasive and respected, his summary would go a long way toward determining the course of the ensuing discussion. Then, in descending order of seniority, each of the Associate Justices would comment on the case without being interrupted. If a vote was taken, the order of precedence was reversed, with the most junior Justice casting the first ballot—the rationale being to ensure that juniors would not be influenced by the votes of their seniors.

Although a majority vote was necessary for a verdict, only four votes were required to grant a *writ of certiorari*: an acceptance that the Justices will hear oral arguments on a case which they believed merited review. On "hot" cases, there was much jockeying.

If the Chief Justice was in the majority on a Conference vote, he could either write the Court's opinion himself or assign it to one of his concordant brethren. But if he was in the minority, the writing of the opinion would fall to the senior Associate Justice on the majority side (who could, if he wished, assign it to someone else in the majority). Justices in the minority could, of course, write dissenting opinions. Similarly, members of the majority could elect to write concurring but separate opinions.

Preliminary drafts of the majority opinion, printed in the secret basement printshop—before today's computer—were circulated among the Justices for comment by both supporters and opponents. Occasionally, a well-reasoned dissent circulated at the same time was so persuasive that it succeeded in changing a minority into a majority opinion. Legal and writing skills were thus at a premium. The indefatigable Douglas once reportedly drafted both the majority and the dissenting opinions on a single case, which report Douglas modestly insisted to me was "slightly exaggerated."

Warren was no stylist. He wrote his opinions in simple, nontechnical language. Moreover, he had a weakness for indulging in moral or philosophical digressions that were sometimes only debatably connected with the pertinent written law. Yet unlike Vinson, who assigned most of his opinion-writing to his clerks ("he wrote with his hands in his pockets," said a colleague), Warren worked hard at his writing. He always wrote his first draft in longhand on a yellow-lined pad. This he would circulate among his clerks, asking for opinion and comment. Then he would redraft— often several times. Only when he was satisfied himself would he permit his fellow Justices to read his text. After receiving their suggestions, he would prepare further drafts until, at last, the final draft was ready. The results may not have been art, but they certainly proved to be history.

Facing the Court when Warren arrived were such important issues as school desegregation, tidelands oil, the Taft-Hartley labor legislation and the Fair Trade laws. There was also an overwhelming mass of more mundane matters: Should professional baseball be exempted by Congress as a sport? Are TV and radio giveaway programs lotteries—hence illegal? Can a book club advertise that a book is "free" when you must buy four books a year to own it? Is a manufacturer of liver pills deceiving its customers? Can Charlotte, North Carolina, ban Sunday movies? One month after Warren had been on the bench, he wrote his first opinion, which was also the Court's first one of that term (*Voris* v. *Eikel*). In a state workmen's compensation case, the Warren opinion, reversing the Court of Appeals, unanimously upheld a longshoreman who, injured in a ship fire, had neglected to have his claim filed within the prescribed time period. Warren wrote that the statute should be "liberally construed . . . in a way which avoids harsh and incongruous results."

But in other early cases Warren took positions (for which he later privately professed regret) that displayed a tendency toward the status quo which Eisenhower must have found reassuring. In *Irvine* v. *California*, for example, three months after he had arrived on the bench, Warren joined the conservative majority—casting its deciding vote—in upholding police wiretapping of a gambler's premises, denying that evidence so obtained from a hidden microphone, without a warrant, was illegal. Similarly, shortly afterward, in *Barsky* v. *Board of Regents*, he sided with conservatives in agreeing that a New York physician had *not* been denied due process of law when his medical license had been suspended in reprisal for his having refused to turn over to authorities the membership rolls of an organization then on the attorney general's subversive list. And in *Galyan* v. *Press* Warren again supported the conservatives who argued that an alien could be deported on the grounds that he had once been a Communist party member, even though this membership had been legal at the time.

These early decisions are curious in the light of Warren's subsequent judicial record. Perhaps he felt so insecure in his new position that he wanted to be identified with the majority. Perhaps he was trying to conform to Eisenhower's implicit wish that he not rock the boat. Or perhaps—and there is some evidence for this—he was still in awe of the most brilliant and articulate of the Associate Justices, the constitutionally conservative Frankfurter whose wife quipped: "Felix has two faults. First, he always strays from the point and second, he always comes back to it."

Whatever the reasons, Warren's debut on the Court seemed not only undistinguished, but tinged with timidity, conformism and even callousness. To be sure, few outside the Court noticed this. But Warren *himself* appeared to have been troubled. It is impossible, of course, to document what may have been going on in his mind and heart at that time (in later references to this period he would only speak vaguely and sadly of "feeling my way" and "going along with the others.") However, judging from the extraordinary speed with which his judicial position changed—and even repudiated some of these early decisions—it is reasonable to hypothesize that he must have been undergoing a crisis of conscience.

Before Warren could become wholeheartedly involved in Court cases, he had to face Senate confirmation. This proved less of a formality than anyone had expected.

On January 12, 1954, the President routinely sent the Warren nomination, along with more than a hundred lesser appointments to the Senate. He had not anticipated the antagonism of the new chairman of the Senate Judiciary Committee, Republican William "Wild Bill" Langer of North Dakota. Although Langer had nothing against Warren personally, he was disgruntled because he believed that the Eisenhower Administration was not giving his state sufficient patronage in the federal appointments of judges, postmasters and the like. The Warren appointment, he decided, was to be his bargaining weapon.

In opposing the Warren appointment, Langer was aided by Mississippi Senator James Eastland, who now feared that the Californian might vote to end segregation in Southern schools. Eastland's fears had been aroused by Warren's first major speech as Chief Justice in February at the Columbia University bicentenary, where he had lambasted McCarthyism and defended "dissent and free inquiry."

Chairman Langer scheduled Senate subcommittee hearings. Nominee Warren declined an invitation to appear. The American Bar Association and California State Bar, among others, endorsed his appointment. But more than 200 objections were filed. Spokesmen for such groups as the American Anti-Communist League, Christian National Crusade and American Rally testified against Warren. Charges were made that he had "a 100 percent record of following the Marxist line," had "permitted organized crime" to flourish in California, had "wilfully protected corruption" there, had "knowingly appointed dishonest judges," and had been "under the domination" of California liquor lobbyist Artie Samish.

Caught off guard, the infuriated Eisenhower suddenly became an impassioned Warren partisan. "Earl Warren is one of the finest public servants this country has ever produced," he announced. "If the Republicans as a body should try to repudiate him, I shall leave the Republican party. . . ." Other party big-guns were quickly mobilized against Langer's maneuver. The accusations were "completely fantastic and untrue," claimed Vice President Nixon. "The biggest lot of tommyrot ever brought before a Senate Committee," declared Senator Arthur V. Watkins of Utah, Eisenhower's principal spokesman on the Langer subcommittee. Joining the defense chorus were nearly all Republicans and many Democrats, including Adlai Stevenson, who deplored "the sorry example of the baseless charges brought against our honored Chief Justice."

Langer had reaped a whirlwind. He stubbornly held his ground, but no one else on the subcommittee had such temerity; Langer's was the sole opposing vote—and when the matter came up before the entire Senate, not even Langer voted in the negative. Warren was confirmed by a voice vote on March 1. Eisenhower had given the Congress an impressive demonstration of his personal power, and Warren was able to take office in an atmosphere of almost total, if somewhat nervous, consensus. Having won his victory, Eisenhower, in a masterly gesture of *noblesse oblige*, gave Langer precisely the patronage he had been seeking. Justice Douglas, who knew both men well, wrote me in May 1977: "Warren never said anything unkind about Langer to me, nor did Langer ever say anything unkind to me about Warren."

Thus, five months subsequent to his recess appointment, Earl Warren was confirmed as Chief Justice of the United States. The

Congress and country would not have to wait anywhere near that long to discover what sort of a man they had confirmed in that high office.

For more than a decade, the Supreme Court had avoided ruling on the explosive desegregation issue, but it refused to go away. Five desegregation-related cases had been scheduled for reargument before the Court only two months after Warren ascended to the bench. One was *Brown* v. *Board of Education of Topeka, Kansas*.

At first the new Chief Justice gave virtually no indication of what position he might take. He asked few questions in Court but asked many others of fellow Justices at Conferences, lunches, and even at such extracurricular events as football and baseball games. He was particularly inquisitive of the three Justices who came from states maintaining segregated schools—Black of Alabama, Reed of Kentucky and Clark of Texas. Although he avoided committing himself at Conferences, he pressed his brethren to seek unanimous positions in preliminary discussions. But he never bullied. On the contrary, he made full use of his considerable gifts of tact, humor and persuasion. Yet he was quietly determined that this time, if possible, the Court would face the issue and find a common ground for a ruling.

The immediate cause of this judicial soul-searching was one Linda Brown, age eleven. Linda had been attending a racially segregated school twenty-one blocks from her home in Topeka, Kansas. Her father, Reverend Oliver Brown, petitioned the Topeka School Board to let Linda attend a white school which was only three blocks away from her home. The petition was denied. Brown took the matter to successive Kansas courts, challenging the constitutionality of the Board's ruling. By the time the case had reached the Supreme Court, it had been linked to other similar cases arising in Delaware, the District of Columbia, South Carolina and Virginia.

The basis for the School Board's defense was an 1896 Supreme Court decision, *Plessy* v. *Ferguson*, in which the Court, by a vote of 8–1, had denied that black Homer Plessy had the right to sit in a railroad coach reserved for white passengers. According to Justice Henry Billings Brown, author of the majority opinion, so long as Plessy could avail himself of equivalent facilities elsewhere on the train, he had no grounds for demanding access to the facilities reserved for whites. Thus was born the doctrine of "separate but equal," a criterion the Court had subsequently applied to segregation cases involving *all* public facilities. Now, if the Warren Court were to uphold Linda Brown's claim, *Plessy* would have to be overturned. And the doctrine of "separate but equal"—called "Jim Crow" by critics—would have to be cast aside and a way of life would have to be undone.

The chief counsel representing the Browns and the other plaintiffs was the NAACP's husky, forty-five-year-old Thurgood Marshall, destined one day to be a Supreme Court Justice himself. His formidable opponent was the distinguished corporation and constitutional lawyer, John W. Davis, majestic in his striped trousers and cutaway. The nearly eighty-one-year-old Davis had been the Democratic nominee for President in 1924, had served as ambassador to Great Britain (George V called him "the most perfect gentleman I have ever met") and had argued more cases before the Supreme Court than any man in the twentieth century.

Davis' eloquent arguments dwelt on principles and precedents. Since 1896 the *Plessy* doctrine of "separate but equal" had been reaffirmed by the High Court no less than seven times and by the Congress literally hundreds of times. There was, moreover, the doctrine of the states' and local rights to be considered: It was constitutionally unsound for the Supreme Court to invade these rights by trying to act like a "glorified Board of Education." Nor could it be held that "separate but equal" was incompatible with the Fourteenth Amendment, since twenty-three states which had ratified the amendment had nonetheless enacted segregation laws. "No man," said Davis solemnly, "will treat with indifference the principle of race. It is the key to history."

Marshall's arguments tended to be less precedential and less emotional, stressing rather the inequities of the given situation. He flatly denied that the School Board's ruling was consistent with the Fourteenth Amendment's guarantee of "equal protection under the law" since, in fact, hardships had been imposed upon segregated black students. He likewise cited the findings of social scientists on the adverse effects that segregation has on children's motivation to learn. If this latter argument was not necessarily the purest form of legal discourse, it was nevertheless sufficiently persuasive to prompt Warren later to include in his written opinion a controversial footnote relating to one of Marshall's cited sources, Swedish sociologist Gunnar Myrdal's book on the race problem, *The American Dilemma*.

For weeks the Court heard these and other oral arguments, read voluminous briefs and, above all, searchingly discussed the case in Conference. Warren took special pains neither to force the pace of the discussions nor to permit his fellow Justices to commit themselves to any position too early. Typically, he wasted no time himself orating about the subject. He desperately wanted the issues implicit in *Brown* to be met with consensus. Bit by bit, and to the surprise of some of the Justices, a consensus did begin to take shape. "It was created slowly and patiently by an understanding Court," Chief Justice Warren told me in July 1955. After retiring, he reminisced in greater detail:

> There was some division in the Court. But a lot of thought had been given to it before this was reargued. In order that we not get polarized on this great issue and not be able to work it out in a unanimous way, we decided that we would not vote on how we stood. Without committing ourselves one way or another, we continued to discuss Brown *and the other cases. Week after week, I found time to put them on the agenda for discussion. Each Justice would pick a point which he thought was debatable and we discussed it in that light without anybody announcing how he felt one way or another. By the end of February, it seemed to me that we had thoroughly discussed the issue. I inquired if they were ready to vote. In late February, they said yes. We took a vote early in March. It was unanimous against the "separate but equal" doctrine. The fact that we did not polarize ourselves at the beginning gave us more of an opportunity to come out unanimously on it than if we had done otherwise.*

This modest summary hardly conveys the importance of Warren's role in achieving that unanimity. It was not nearly as easy as he made it sound. Retired Justice Douglas wrote me in May 1977: "The only thing that was unique about *Brown* v. *Board of Education* was that the decision was unanimous. If the case had been argued under Vinson's last days, I fear the decision probably would have gone the other way."

Judge Charles E. Wyzanski, Jr., senior judge of the U. S. District Court in Boston, later told me: "On May 18, 1954 [the day after the decision] I was lunching with Felix Frankfurter in his chambers when the Justice showed me—without letting me read them—the galley proofs of his and Jackson's separate opinions in *Brown* v. *Board of Education*. Warren as Chief Justice had persuaded these not-very-easily persuaded jurists to abandon their separate concurrences, which they had carried so far as to get them in printed form. I do not believe that the majestic Hughes or the chuckling Taft could have rivaled Warren's performance in cajoling colleagues during his first years as Chief."

The new Chief Justice was acutely aware that on such an explosive issue a divided decision might do more harm than good. If some Justices wrote separate, even though concurring opinions, it could confuse the meaning and diminish the total effect of the ruling. For this reason, Warren took pains to convince the more reluctant Justices that the *principle* of the decision could be separated from its *implementation*. This delay would give needed time for Southern wrath to cool while simultaneously laying down the new law of the land. Warren and his brethren recognized that integration would be a slow and painful process. No judicial ruling could end overnight an educational practice which had prevailed for nearly a century. This separation of principle from enforcement was probably what made a unanimous decision possible.

On Monday morning, May 17, it was evident that something extraordinary was brewing. Surprisingly, Justice Jackson, who had been absent from the Court for a month and a half convalescing from a heart attack, left his hospital bed that morning to assume his seat. Warren, who had visited Jackson in the hospital early that morning, had told him it was unnecessary for him to come but Jackson overruled his Chief. Mrs. Earl Warren, who attended with her daughter Virginia and a visiting nephew, insists, "My husband never mentioned anything to me that morning. I happened to be in the Court to attend the luncheon which Justice Douglas was giving for the Belgian ambassador, Baron Silvercruy." The press, in its Supreme Court basement quarters, was not handed the customary advance copies of that Monday's decisions.

At 12:52 P.M. the Chief Justice slowly began reading his comparatively brief eleven-page opinion. In direct, simple words, he read to a hushed audience the High Court's unanimous decision: "We unanimously conclude that in the field of public education the doctrine of 'separate but equal' has no place." When he read the word *unanimously*, sighs swept the courtroom. This would immediately affect the lives of twelve million schoolchildren in seventeen Southern and border states, and four others which then permitted segregated schools, including President Eisenhower's native Kansas. The decision flatly outlawed segregated public schools as a clear violation of the Fourteenth Amendment's "equal protection" clause.

Implementation came a year later in deference to traditional Southern customs. On May 31, 1955, Chief Justice Warren again read for a unanimous Supreme Court his opinion that desegregation of public schools must be carried out with "all deliberate speed"—an old admiralty phrase which recalcitrants seized upon as a device for delay.

The sources of Warren's personal commitment to the principle of school desegregation, and its depth, are easier to speculate about than to document. Although he recognized that others might disagree, he never for a moment doubted the moral rectitude of the decision. All the lessons he had received in childhood—the imperative of fair play, the cherished immigrant notion that universal education is the key to social equality, the irrelevance of race as a criterion for judging human beings—these and other assumptions constituted for Warren first principles. They were the things by which the validity of arguments are proven, not the things which arguments prove. In that sense he took the principle of *Brown* for granted.

Not so others. The decision raised a storm of controversy which persists to this day, primarily in the form of the school busing dispute. Even many Northerners who endorsed the principle behind *Brown* worried about whether the Court's action might not have been precipitous. "These people were not racists," Warren later remarked sadly, "They were not unfriendly, they were simply uninformed or unthinking. I have no doubt that in the aggregate they constituted a large segment of our citizenry."

Understandably, it was at first in the white South that the opposition was most violent. Mississippi and South Carolina threatened to abolish public education in their states. James F. Byrnes, Governor of South Carolina and himself a retired Supreme Court Justice, angrily proclaimed that "The Court didn't interpret the Constitution; it amended it," and went on to imply that the present members of the Court were the tools of communism. More than a hundred Southern senators and representatives signed a "Southern

Manifesto" pledging to defy the "stab-in-the-back" Supreme Court decision, just as South Carolina's John C. Calhoun had shouted "Nullification" a century earlier. Warren was castigated as another Thaddeus Stevens. The only Southern senator who refused to sign the "Southern Manifesto" was Lyndon Johnson, who, as Senate Majority Leader, shrewdly explained that he could not take sides on such a divisive issue.

One evening wc oden crosses wrapped in oil-soaked rags were burned on the lawn of Chief Justice Warren's Sheraton Park Hotel. "Impeach Earl Warren" signs became a familiar sight everywhere in the nation, particularly in the South. They were the first sight that greeted Warren in September when he disembarked from his plane in Virginia en route to Williamsburg, where he had been invited to speak in honor of Chief Justice John Marshall at the College of William and Mary Law School. He was not greeted either by Virginia's Senator Harry F. Byrd (who had invited him) or Governor Thomas B. Stanley, both of whom boycotted the event.

Eisenhower was dismayed. The desegregation decision had taken him by surprise. Whatever he thought of it privately, he had no illusions about the turmoil it would cause. Deep festering social sores had been lanced. Before they healed, considerable enmity and violence probably would ensue. This was precisely the kind of thing he had appointed Warren *not* to do.

Yet now the President was caught in the middle. Eisenhower had sworn to uphold the Constitution and obey the law. Now it would be impolitic in the extreme to let it be thought that he opposed desegregation in principle. He tried to make the best of an unpleasant situation by indulging in veiled public grumbling ("You can't change people's hearts just by laws . . . If you try to go too far too fast, you're making a mistake") coupled with pieties about doing his duty ("It makes no difference whether or not I endorse it. What I say is, the Constitution is as the Supreme Court interprets it and I must conform to that"). But neither proponents nor opponents of the decision were mollified by this waffling. As liberal columnist Marquis Childs wrote, the President sounded "like a police officer who must wait for a riot call before he can intervene in a family quarrel."

Some partisans of the decision, after discreetly conferring with Warren, urged the popular President to throw the moral

177

prestige of his office behind the ruling to make its enforcement easier. Warren strongly believed that such presidential action would help avoid racial strife. One suggestion was that Eisenhower make a television appeal to the nation for patience and understanding. Another was that he summon a national conference of white and black moderates to Washington. But the Chief Executive chose to do nothing. Not even a full-page May 31, 1954, *Life* magazine editorial moved Ike to try to fulfill its praise. Optimistically headlined "The President is already showing us how we can best make the Court's decision work," it included the amazing line: "Dwight Eisenhower has put more personal effort into solving the race problem than any President since Lincoln."

Eisenhower's silence merely afforded ammunition to the Court's enemies. "President Eisenhower's tepid reaction without any effort to commend the decision's fairness or lead public opinion undercut Southern liberals," recollects North Carolina's Eli N. Evans, now a New York foundation official whose father had then edited the Durham, North Carolina, *Morning Herald*. Other liberal Southerners remember how word was cynically passed around the South by a U. S. Department of Justice attorney who assured angry segregationists: "The President doesn't agree with the Supreme Court decision."

Not until nine years later—three years after leaving office—did Eisenhower show any public support of the decision. In his 1963 memoirs he wrote: "There can be no question that the judgment of the Court was right." The retired President then added some words which indicated that he still did not fully understand the unique gifts of his first Supreme Court appointee:

> *Some of those who disliked the decision directed their criticism against the Chief Justice on the theory that because of his position it was obvious that he was responsible for the Court's decision. . . This criticism, too, I have always discounted; the Chief Justice had been on the bench such a short time—he was its newest recruit—that I do not believe he would possibly have exercised the amount of influence ascribed to him over this group of men, who are notable for the independence and variety of their views. . . .*

The belated endorsement of the Court's decision was not merely the wisdom of hindsight. Eisenhower's foot-dragging was more a result of political caution than of ideology. He behaved, in Warren's view, more like a figurehead chairman of the board than an active President whose job it was to move the nation forward. Although Ike's heart was in the right place, there were limits as to how high a price he was willing to pay for the sake of his conscience. Actually, he had encouraged the stamping out of bigotry in the Army long before Truman's Armed Forces desegregation decrees were enacted. The President, moreover, took umbrage at Charles Wilson, his Defense Secretary, for refusing to permit black members of the Civil Rights Commission to be guests at the Montgomery, Alabama, Air Force Base. But in moral terms, the quantum leap from such small skirmishes to the major battle implicit in *Brown* was beyond him.

The President well understood that this was only the beginning. As Justice Tom Clark later observed, "*Brown* started a rash of school cases that soon led into other segregated areas such as public accommodations, transportation, restaurants and so forth." It had opened the floodgates not merely to school desegregation but to one of the most profound and far-reaching struggles for equal rights in American history.

Years later, in a lecture at Notre Dame in 1972, the retired Warren observed:

> With the late 1950's came a new stage in the history of race relations in America. After a temporarily moderate response to the Brown *decision, several Southern states gradually moved to the point of open resistance to Federal desegregation orders. From approximately 1957 to 1960, progress toward desegregation of the South's public facilities slowed. Beginning in 1960, Negroes in the South openly resisted the stalling tactics, using protest strategies of their own, such as sit-ins, freedom rides, and other nonviolent demonstrations. The violent reactions in some Southern states to these strategies and to efforts by the Federal government to enforce desegregation produced a national response of shock and horror, which in its turn gave its stimulus to the growing movement for full-scale civil rights for Negroes. By the early 1960's, the struggle for Negro equality had become the principal domestic issue in the Nation.*

Any hope that Eisenhower may have had of keeping the presidency aloof from this struggle were foredoomed. By June 1957, two months after he had assured reporters that he could not "imagine any set of circumstances that would induce me to use Federal troops," he was obliged to order the 101st Airborne Division (led by Major General Edwin A. Walker, later of John Birch Society fame) to restore order to the Little Rock, Arkansas, Central High School, after Governor Orval Faubus had scorned to obey a Federal Court order for a token integration of nine black students. Even then, rather than justify his action on the basis of the landmark *Brown* decision, the circumspect President instead cited the law passed in 1792 to stop Shay's Rebellion. (Warren, in contrast, summoned a special summer term of the Supreme Court to rule directly, swiftly and unanimously on the Little Rock case in *Cooper* v. *Aaron*.) Yet not all the wishing in the world could turn back the clock on what the Warren Court had set in motion—and would sustain for at least two decades.

Warren was deeply troubled about other problems in the spring of 1955. Senator Joseph McCarthy had at last received his just deserts at the hands of the U.S. Senate which in December 1954 had condemned him for contemptuous, insulting and abusive behavior. But the intolerant, hysterical passions upon which McCarthyism had fed were still very much alive in the land. The frightening pressures of the Cold War had not abated despite the Korean conflict having finally simmered down to an uncertain truce. Freedom of speech and opinion were everywhere being assaulted by the orthodoxies of professional patriots. And Earl Warren, like many other men and women of vision and good will, felt duty bound to speak out in defense of the Bill of Rights.

In a series of speeches on numerous college campuses during the spring of 1955, the Chief Justice repeatedly sounded one theme: the need to tolerate dissent. His words not only illuminate the man's deepening personal beliefs but foreshadow the spirit that would animate the entire Court on future civil rights decisions.

At Washington University in St. Louis in a "Blessings of Liberty" speech, the Chief Justice warned—with Senator McCarthy's witch-hunting still in mind—that in seeking to preserve traditional American liberties, "the danger of erosion is greater than that of direct attack."

At the University of Illinois he warned against the peril of uncritical acceptance of shibboleths: "Truth cannot be acquired from the 'spot news' of the day or through the gossip of the cocktail hour. . . . Above all, it calls for a habit of serious reading to learn the lessons of the past which, after all, are the best guide for the conscience. . . ."

And at the University of Michigan he reminded his audience that, "Conformity is no special virtue. Sometimes nonconformity is exactly the antidote needed to remedy a situation." He recommended to his listeners the advice Disraeli had once given a young friend: "Associate yourself with a just but unpopular cause."

Warren ended his college tour with a speech at the La Follette centennial held at the University of Wisconsin, and on the following day, June 20, Chief Justice and Mrs. Warren flew to Europe to spend six weeks touring Sweden, Norway, Denmark, Finland, Luxembourg and, finally, India. Warren brought along stacks of legal homework and one white 17½-inch-collar Dacron shirt, which Mrs. Warren washed each night. He delivered speeches in Copenhagen and Helsinki; lunched with German Chancellor Konrad Adenauer and met with Germany's Constitutional Court; and "sat" on Norway's Supreme Court. He likewise fulfilled a youthful ambition by seeing, at a point not far from the North Pole, the midnight sun on the longest day of the year. In August, the Warrens flew back to California to visit their children and grandchildren.

The Chief Justice wanted to relax before the busy fall term would begin in October. That March, conservative John Marshall Harlan, the second Eisenhower Court appointee, had succeeded Robert H. Jackson, who had died. A Republican New York Circuit Court judge and former Wall Street lawyer, Harlan's grandfather and namesake had served on the High Court from 1877 to 1911. For the urbane new Associate Justice's surprise fifty-sixth birthday luncheon given him by colleagues, Mrs. Earl Warren baked one of her angel food cakes.

In the fall of 1955, at the Chief Justice's instigation, the Supreme Court underwent a series of small modernizations. A long-overdue public-address system was installed so that the spectators in probably the world's most majestic courtroom could better hear the proceedings. Similarly, a tape-recording machine was belatedly introduced to enable the Justices to play back the oral arguments in their chambers. And finally, the Court clerk acquired a typewriter for docket entries. For more than a century and a half, they had been entered in longhand.

Some tradition was not tampered with, however. The Colonial-style white goose-quill pens on attorneys' tables, handcut by Lewis Glaser of Charlottesville, Virginia, were not replaced. Lawyers who argued cases before the top tribunal and sought souvenirs customarily pilfered these pens—replicas of those with which the Founding Fathers had written the Constitution.

Warren received from Congress some perquisites for himself and his fellow Justices. Chief Justice Stone (1941–46), when working late in the Marble Palace, had sometimes been driven home in the Supreme Court's pickup truck. Now Warren finally wheedled out of Congress—after undergoing the embarrassment of being driven to a White House dinner in a mistakenly-sent airport station wagon—an official chauffered automobile for his private use, an amenity the Vice President, Speaker of the House, Cabinet heads and assorted military and civilian bureaucrats had long enjoyed. The former California politician also coaxed out of Congress an automobile for the official business use of fellow Justices. Furthermore, he managed to convert a fourth-floor room into a gymnasium where sedentary Justices could exercise on a rowing machine, stationary bicycle and wall pulley weights.

The Chief Justice's salary was raised in March 1955 to $35,000 (the customary $500 more than for the other Justices) in a general congressional pay-raise bill. What probably prompted this Supreme Court boost was the dismaying revelation that Chief Justice Vinson had died penniless, even though he had refused offers of up to $250,000 a year to join industry. Unlike some public figures who already possessed private fortunes, Earl Warren never had or sought any. He had reared his family of six children solely on his public salary, invariably refusing to accept any fees for his speeches or writings. His sole nest egg was a California pension of approximately $10,000 a year which right-wing columnist Westbrook Pegler demanded be taken away from him.

Whatever Warren's feelings about a potential appointment to the Court may have been in 1952, by 1955 he had become entirely happy in his judicial seat. After years of the rough-and-tumble of professional politics, at last he held a position that was stable, secure and, above all, morally significant. Still, politics had not yet renounced its claim upon him—if it ever could.

On Saturday morning, September 24, 1955, the free world was shocked to learn that the seemingly healthy President of the United

States had suffered a coronary thrombosis and was in an oxygen tent in the Fitzsimmons Army Hospital in Denver.

After the convalescing President briefly returned to Washington in November 1955, it appeared that he would not run for re-election in 1956. This prompted many Republicans—noting pollsters' prognostications—to turn to Chief Justice Warren as their next strongest candidate. All the polls reaffirmed that he could defeat any Democratic nominee. But Warren was more embarrassed than flattered by the "Will-Warren-Step-Down-from-the-Court?" newspaper speculation and vain efforts by national magazine editors to pay him handsomely for *any* statement.

Anxious to flee the capital gossip-grinder, the Chief Justice spent late December 1955 with his family in California. During Christmas week, he drilled with his National Guard regiment in Oakland and spent several days hunting at his friend Wallace Lynn's ranch in Colusa.

The Warren-for-President speculation finally ceased on February 29, 1956, when President Eisenhower announced that he would seek a second term. "My answer [is] positive, that is, affirmative," he declared.

Nonetheless, after Ike's June 9 ileitis operation—two months before the Republican convention—talk about his "disability" recurred. But who was to define this condition? Who would decide when a Vice President should perform presidential duties? And who would determine when and if a President had recovered sufficiently to resume his duties?

Eisenhower himself said that a constitutional amendment was necessary. But former Presidents Truman and Hoover insisted that Congress should be the sole judge of a Chief Executive's "disability." Senator Fulbright proposed that if Congress determined a President to be incapacitated, its resolution should be submitted to the Supreme Court, which would then decide whether such a condition existed. Swiftly, Chief Justice Warren wrote Fulbright smothering this hot potato by insisting that the Court should not be party to any such decision.

The problem soon became academic. The President recovered sufficiently to crush Adlai Stevenson again by 457 to 73 electoral and nine million popular votes.

In defeat, Stevenson won Earl Warren's admiration far more, paradoxically, than had Eisenhower in victory. The Chief Justice believed that the articulate Illinois lawyer reflected the conscience of the country better than the inert General. Stevenson's self-deprecating, introspective nature appealed to the warm Warren. In 1952 the California Republican had esteemed the Democratic candidate's grace and wit, especially when under attack ("Eggheads of the world, unite! You have nothing to lose but your yokes!"). In 1956 Warren welcomed the Stevensonian scorn of Nixon and McCarthy, especially when it took the form of labeling the Vice President a "white-collar McCarthy." He relished Stevenson's championing of civil liberties and the right to dissent, his prophetic advocacy of a test ban treaty and his "quality of life" philosophy. Warren rejoiced when the campaigning Stevenson, in sharp contrast to Eisenhower's silence, said what Warren himself fervently believed about the desegregation decision but dared not express publicly:

> *I do not agree that the Supreme Court exceeded its proper authority on school segregation. I think rather that these rulings are correct interpretations of the Constitution . . . The office of President of the United States has great moral influence . . . and I think the time has come when that influence should be used by calling together white and Negro leaders from the areas concerned in the South to explore ways and means of allaying these rising tensions . . . Such a conference would strengthen the hands of the thoughtful and responsible leaders of both races . . . The prestige of the President could curb the tensions in the South . . . It should be exerted before the situation gets any more serious.*

Stevenson's gallant concession statement likewise moved the sentimental Chief Justice: "There are things more precious than political victory," he said. "There is the right to political contest. . . . What united us is deeper than what divides us—love of freedom, love of justice, love of peace. Remember . . . a wise man said: 'A merry heart doeth good like a medicine, but a broken spirit dryeth the bones.' "

Warren's growing admiration for Stevenson was symptomatic of something that probably neither Eisenhower nor Warren fully understood at the start of the new presidential term. The President and his Chief Justice had such similar personae that their profound philosophical differences were for a long time less noticeable—even to the two men themselves—than they might otherwise have been. Issues, not words, soon would reveal the growing gulf that separated the men. These issues were already materializing and, although neither man was perhaps aware of it, the decay in their relationship had already set in.

However embarrassing the *Brown* decision may have been for the President politically, he could not have interpreted it as a personal affront. On the contrary, privately and in the abstract, he probably agreed with it. But on some other issues, he had not only disagreed but felt that Warren was approaching personal confrontation— something the General was temperamentally disposed to regard as disloyalty.

These issues primarily concerned Warren's astonishing about-face on the subject of criminal justice in general, and the federal government's internal security programs in particular. For the Chief Justice, who had now veered 180 degrees from his early conservative positions on *Irvine* v. *California* and *Barsky* v. *Board of Regents*, was becoming an impassioned defender of the rights of the accused.

Warren's first major clash with the government had occurred in June 1955, in the case of *Peters* v. *Hobby*. Dr. John Peters, a Yale Medical School professor, had been dismissed from his job as part-time consultant to the U.S. Public Health Service and had been barred from other federal service because the Federal Loyalty Review Board had found "reasonable doubt" about his loyalty. Peters protested that he had never been a communist; that he had twice been given security clearance by the Health Service; that he had never been afforded an opportunity to defend himself against unsworn statements to the FBI; and that he had not even been permitted to know who his accusers were.

Customarily, such cases are briefed and argued for the U. S. Government before the Supreme Court by the solicitor general. However, to the acute embarrassment of Attorney General Brownell and President Eisenhower, Solicitor General (later Judge) Simon E. Sobeloff had refused to argue this case on the grounds that the government's position was conscienceless. At the last minute, an ambitious forty-seven-year-old assistant attorney general had stepped forward and volunteered to present the government's case in Sobeloff's stead. He was Warren E. Burger, and his action won him the enduring gratitude of Eisenhower, Brownell and Nixon.

Within a year he had been appointed to a vacancy on the U. S. Court of Appeals in the District of Columbia, and in time President Nixon would appoint him to be Earl Warren's successor.

Burger may have helped save the government's dignity, but he lost the case. In a 7–2 decision the Court ruled that Dr. Peters had been wrongfully dismissed and ordered the Civil Service Commission to expunge the Loyalty Review Board's findings from its records. Although the Court sidestepped ruling directly on whether a federal employee had a constitutional right to confront his accusers, the thought was implicit and little doubt was left as to the direction in which the Court was moving. Reflecting upon Warren's participation in the case, Justice Douglas later wrote, "He was more alert than anyone I knew to make the government obey the mandates of due process and beyond."

A year later, in April 1956, in *Pennsylvania* v. *Nelson*,the Court had even gone so far as to rule in favor of an admitted communist—at least to the extent of saying that he could not be tried in a state court for sedition, which is neither a local nor a state offense. Although this ruling had not challenged the federal government's powers directly, it dealt a sharp blow to the entire internal security program, depriving the government of many judicial and law-enforcement allies within the forty-eight states. The author of the federal law (the Smith Act) defining sedition, conservative Virginia Representative Howard Smith, bitterly denounced this decision.

Several months later, the Court had struck again at the government in a case involving five communists convicted under the Smith Act. In *Mesarosh* v. *United States*, the Court ordered a retrial on the grounds that the FBI's key witness, a paid informer hired to infiltrate Communist Party meetings, was suspected of having lied. In his scolding majority opinion, Warren lectured the representatives of the Justice Department as if they were errant schoolboys: "The dignity of the United States Government will not permit the conviction of any person on tainted testimony . . . [We must] see that the waters of justice are not polluted. The government of a strong and free nation does not need convictions based on such testimony."

These Warren Court decisions not only interfered with the government's freedom of action and annoyed President Eisenhower personally, but they also exposed the administration to a new tide of criticism from the political right. As a paunchy but still-swinging Senator McCarthy droned to the Senate in June 1956: "Warren has become a hero to the *Daily Worker* . . . I don't say that he is a Communist himself, but there is something wrong with him . . . It was extremely unfortunate that he was ever confirmed as Chief Justice." At a Senate Internal Security Committee hearing, McCarthy engaged in this vaudeville exchange with Mississippi Senator James O. Eastland, the new chairman of the Senate Judiciary Committee, which controlled the Supreme Court's appropriations:

> Eastland: *The Supreme Court seems to be issuing one pro-Communist decision after another.*
> McCarthy: *You're so right.*
> Eastland: *What influence is there except that some Communist influence is working within the Court?*
> McCarthy: *Either incompetence or the influence you mention.*

Eastland proposed a constitutional amendment requiring Supreme Court Justices to be confirmed every four years. Echoing South Carolina Senator Strom Thurmond, several Southern legislatures passed resolutions demanding that Warren and Justices who had voted with him be impeached immediately for "high crimes and misdemeanors."

Thus, at the beginning of Eisenhower's second term, his feelings toward his Chief Justice were somewhat less than worshipful. And if the President feared that Warren's future Court behavior would not improve the administration's composure, his fears were soon realized. On June 17, 1957—only five months after the Inauguration—the Warren Court handed down three additional decisions that struck at the rights of both Congress and state legislatures to "investigate" private citizens and at broad interpretations of the term "sedition" under the Smith Act. Since all three cases involved the issue of communism, anti-Warrenites promptly memorialized June 17 as "Red Monday."

The first case, *Watkins* v. *United States*, concerned a United Auto Worker organizer who had refused to answer questions by the House Un-American Activities Committee. His silence had resulted in his conviction for contempt of Congress. But the Supreme Court, in a 6–1 decision, reversed the conviction. Warren's majority opinion consisted largely of a long, somewhat rambling discourse on the history of Congress' abuse of its investigatory powers. "There is no congressional power to expose for the sake of exposure," Warren defiantly wrote. Congress is not "a law enforcement or trial agency." If Congress were to assume the limitless right to question witnesses about their beliefs or associations, the results could be "disastrous": Free-born Americans might grow fearful and seek safety in only "orthodox and uncontroversial associations."

Warren's legislative scolding was somewhat gratuitous. Actually, the *Watkins* case was decided on narrow legal grounds. Because the committee had failed to explain to the defendant the "pertinence" of its questions, he therefore had not been afforded a fair opportunity to determine whether he would have been within his rights in refusing to answer. Thus, his conviction was invalid under the "due process" clause of the Fifth Amendment.

The Chief Justice's motives, however, for departing from strict technicalities in his opinion were obvious: He was serving notice upon Congress—as he already had on the Eisenhower Administration—that henceforth the Court would be fearless in defending individual rights during the current investigative procedures by *all* branches of government. Warren furthermore was declaring that the Court did not recognize that the communist issue in any way modified these rights. Congressional patriots, understandably, received this unsubtle message with a mixture of gloom and fury.

The second "Red Monday" decision, *Sweezy* v. *New Hampshire*, unfurled a similar message to state legislatures. Professor Paul Sweezy had been convicted of contempt of the New Hampshire legislature for having refused to answer questions concerning his past political associations; his wife's affiliations with Henry Wallace's Progressive Party; the beliefs of some friends and colleagues; and whether he had "taught" socialism in his University of New Hampshire lectures.

The Court reversed this conviction, 6–2, on the grounds that the professor's privacy and academic freedom had been invaded. Once again Warren asserted that "mere unorthodoxy or dissent from the prevailing mores is not to be condemned: The absence of such voices would be a symptom of grave illness." This opinion so infuriated the New Hampshire attorney general that he attempted to persuade the National Association of State Attorneys General to denounce the Warren Court decision at its next meeting—but without success.

The third "Red Monday" case, *Yates* v. *United States*, concerned the convictions of fourteen West Coast communists under the Smith Act. In a 6–1 decision, the Court threw out the convictions of five and ordered retrials for the other nine. Several issues were involved, but the key one was how far the Smith Act could go in defining what constituted seditious activity. The convictions had been based largely on the charge that the defendants had "advocated" the overthrow of the government, and, *ipso facto* because they were avowed communists, had "organized" to that end. But the High Court ruled that mere abstract advocacy of overthrow was not in itself illegal: There had to be actual incitement or recruitment. Moreover, the word *organize*, as used in the Smith Act, would apply only to the formation of a *new* organization, not to former membership in the Communist Party, which had been legal. Oddly enough, the *Yates* opinion, which right-wing critics were quick to denounce as "sanctioning treason," was written by the conservative Harlan. Apparently Chief Warren's influence was making itself felt among his brethren.

Later that same June, Justice Brennan wrote the opinion in another case—*Jencks* v. *United States*—in which communism was likewise involved. New Mexico labor leader Clinton S. Jencks, as required under the Taft-Hartley Act, had sworn that he had never been a Communist Party member. But on testimony confidentially given a trial judge by the FBI, Jencks was convicted of having lied. The judge denied Jencks's request that he be permitted to see the FBI testimony so that he could prepare a defense. Ruling 8–1 that Jencks had been denied his rights under the Sixth Amendment (specifically the right of an accused "to be confronted with the witnesses against him"), the Court reversed the conviction. Like *Yates*, this decision outraged the Justice Department. Attorney General Brownell spoke darkly of *Jencks* having created "an emergency in law enforcement." FBI Director J. Edgar Hoover angrily said he would refuse to prosecute rather than open his files.

Despite pressure from the Eisenhower Administration and other quarters, the Warren Court never backtracked in its refusal to permit "national security" (or, still less, simple anticommunism) to be used as a pretext for infringing upon individual rights. The following year, in *Kent* v. *Dulles*, the Court again slapped the government's knuckles by decreeing that Secretary of State John Foster Dulles (whom Eisenhower would have preferred as Chief Justice) could not legally deny a passport to Rockwell Kent to attend a World Council for Peace conference in Helsinki merely because of the artist's refusal to file an affidavit concerning his present or past membership in the Communist Party.

And so it went, in similar ruling after ruling, on the Warren Court for the next eleven years.

History has yet to vindicate Warren on many issues, but most Court-watchers now would probably concede that his steadfast defense of individual rights during the McCarthy-Cold War era was admirable. Martin F. Richman, one of Warren's three 1956–57 law clerks, now a New York attorney, recollects: "It was typical of the Chief's reaction to an injustice to get right to the heart of it. He had a clear idea of where he wanted to go in a particular case and how to achieve the just result." Reminiscing about those days from the vantage point of retirement, Warren told a University of Georgia Law School audience in 1973: "The late Senator Joseph McCarthy . . . was demeaning people all over America by calling them to the witness stand and compelling them to admit that, even years before, they knew someone whom the Senator claimed was a communist . . . In that era, the John Birch Society, by their words, and the Senator, by his actions, portrayed President Eisenhower as a 'dedicated communist.' "

Ironically, back in 1957 President Eisenhower had privately grumbled to friends about what he deemed his appointee's judicial "stupidity." This complaint was picked up by the Washington cocktail circuit. Soon it made public print. When it did, the President of the United States wrote this amazing letter on June 21, 1957:

> *Dear Mr. Chief Justice:*
> *As I have told you, I rarely read beyond the headlines on the front page of my newspaper. However, I was told this morning that some enterprising reporter has a story that at a private party I severely criticized the Supreme Court, expressing anger. I have no doubt that in private conversation someone did hear me express amazement about one decision, but I have never even hinted at a feeling such as anger. To do so would imply not only that I knew the law but questioned motives. Neither of these things is true.*
> *So while resolving that even in private conversations I shall be*

A Warren family portrait taken in 1894 in Los Angeles, when Earl was three. From the left: his mother Chrystal, Earl, father Methias and sister Ethel, seven. (Courtesy Lamson Studio)

Earl Warren was eleven in 1902 when this snapshot of him and his dog, Spot, was taken in Bakersfield. (Courtesy McCurry Foto)

In 1917 Warren enlisted in the Army as a private. A year later, when this picture was taken, he was a cadet in Officers Training Camp. (Courtesy McCurry Foto)

Virginia, the first of his six children, was born September 1928 during Warren's first elected term as District Attorney of Alameda County. (Courtesy California State Archives)

By 1938, when Warren won the Attorney Generalship of California, his handsome family had already become a formidable political asset. From the left: Mrs. Warren, Dorothy, Virginia, Earl Warren, Earl, Jr., Nina (Honeybear) and Bobby. (Carl Bigelow, Oakland *Tribune*)

The (now considerably enlarged) Warren family at a Christmas gathering in 1954.

At the 1949 California State Fair, a portly Governor Warren encounters an unfriendly weighing machine. (Courtesy William P. Smith, Jr.)

A life-long devotee of outdoor sports, Warren here returns from a hunting expedition at Christmas 1954 on the California ranch of his friend, businessman Wallace Lynn. (Courtesy Mrs. Earl Warren)

Under the critical eye of baseball-enthusiast Warren, President Eisenhower throws out the first ball of the 1953 season. This picture seems laden with ironies and prophecies. Warren was then still Governor of California. The man he would soon replace, Chief Justice Vinson, is seated in front of him. To Warren's right stands future President Lyndon B. Johnson. To Warren's left, just behind Eisenhower, is Representative Joseph W. Martin, Jr., whose Massachusetts power base later would be fatally eroded by the Warren Court's "one-man-one-vote" decisions. Next to Martin, half hidden by Clark Griffith's hat, is Warren's long-time nemesis, future President Richard Nixon. On the right, baseball greats Bucky Harris and Casey Stengel look on. (Courtesy National Baseball Hall of Fame)

The Warren Court, December 1965. Seated from left are Tom C. Clark, Hugo L. Black, Chief Justice Earl Warren, William O. Douglas and John H. Harlan. Standing from left are Byron R. White, William J. Brennan, Jr., Potter Stewart and Abe Fortas. (Courtesy National Archives)

The New Yorker *cartoon, which appeared a full ten years after the* Brown *decision had first rocked the country, is emblematic of the controversy that always surrounded the Warren Court.* (Drawing by Lorenz; © 1964 The New Yorker Magazine, Inc.)

Warren and the Court were given a White House dinner on Wednesday evening, November 20, 1963— two days before President Kennedy's assassination. (Courtesy National Archives)

The Warren Commission appointed by President Lyndon B. Johnson to investigate the assassination of John F. Kennedy. Representative Gerald R. Ford, Representative Hale Boggs, Senator Richard B. Russell, Chairman Earl Warren, Senator John Sherman Cooper, lawyer John J. McCloy, former CIA Director Allen W. Dulles and General Counsel J. Lee Rankin. (Courtesy Ackad-Scurlock Studio)

Retired Chief Justice Warren chatting with students at the University of Notre Dame's Center for Civi *Rights in April 1972.* (Courtesy University of Notre Dame)

In July 1973, a year before his death, the retired Warren participated in a ceremony of considerabl *symbolic significance: the swearing in of Tom Bradley, first black Mayor of Los Angeles.* (Courtes Harry H. Adams)

more careful of my language, I do want you to know that if any
such story appeared, it was a distortion.
With warm regard,

As ever,
(Signed) Dwight D. Eisenhower

Prudently, Warren delayed answering this letter. He was not altogether certain that it required an answer. When he flew to California, he thought about it, and pondered the matter still further while on a trip to Independence, Missouri, to help dedicate the Truman Library with former President Herbert Hoover and Eleanor Roosevelt. There, on July 6, he hailed "Mr. Truman's Presidency . . . his character as a man of action: tireless, fearless and decisive"—an assessment he did not share of his appointer. New York Governor W. Averell Harriman recollects: "Chief Justice Warren's speech about President Truman was one of the most completely laudatory statements of any public official that I have ever heard." Eisenhower was irritated by both his Chief Justice's remarks and his presence at the Truman shrine because he was still privately anguished by his presidential predecessor's less than laudatory attitude toward him.

After returning to Washington, the Chief Justice had by now framed a reply to President Eisenhower in his mind. On July 15 he wrote:

Dear Mr. President:

Your letter of June 21st, concerning the gossip column, arrived just as I was leaving for the Pacific Coast to spend a few days with my children. Realizing that they would still be writing similar things at the time of my return, I postponed answering it until now.

It was considerate of you to write, but it was in no sense necessary. Those of us who have long been in public service know that some columns are written in ignorance and others to deceive. Whatever the reason, if unfounded, they should be ignored.

So far as some of the articles about our recent opinions are concerned, the writers could not possibly have written them unless there was a deliberate purpose on their part to deceive. While in

*other positions, I could and did speak out to counteract such
statements. Here we do not respond regardless of what is said. We
must live with what we write and are contented to do so. Some
of the things which were written about the Court are as silly as
those they have written about the purpose of your civil rights bill
and your action in the Girard case. I am sure the only thing for us
to do in such instances is to tune out on them and trust to the future
to vindicate both our actions and intentions.*

*Nina and I are leaving Wednesday for London with the
American Bar Association, and we are looking forward to a
pleasant visit. I hope that you and Mrs. Eisenhower will have a
refreshing vacation at your new summer home.*

*Sincerely,
(Signed) Earl Warren*

The letter was read to Attorney General Brownell on the telephone
Afterward, a White House memorandum to the President stated:
"Mr. Brownell said he thought this was a very friendly letter and was
glad to know about it (he sails on the same boat to England)."

The Warrens, Brownells and other legal luminaries sailed on
the *Queen Mary* to England to attend the late July convention of
the American Bar Association which would also celebrate with the
British bench and bar our joint civil liberty heritage. One early
morning, while standing at the deck railing, the sun was blazing
pleasantly on Warren. Then suddenly, the sun had changed direction: Warren noticed that the boat was turned around. He asked
Captain G.H.G. Morris why.

Luther Huston, the *New York Times* Washington bureau chief,
sauntered over to inquire, "Mr. Chief Justice, what's the trouble?"

"Oh, a naval ship was torpedoed over there," explained
Warren, summarizing the captain's information.

Huston immediately cabled the facts to his newspaper. Later,
he laughingly told me, "I'm probably the only reporter in history
who ever used a Chief Justice as a leg man!"

At the London convention where the Chief Justice was to
speak, an American Bar Association report was unexpectedly read
accusing the Warren Court of aiding communism in its recent civil-
liberty decisions. Warren was not the only infuriated person in
attendance. Winston Churchill rose to the Court's defense. He
reminded the several thousand delegates that "the United States

Supreme Court has been the guardian and upholder of American liberty. Long may it thrive!"

After the convention, Warren journeyed to Dublin for a holiday. There, he was awarded an honorary degree by the National University of Ireland. While in Ireland, he remembered the light-hearted debate that he had engaged in for many years with his friend Bartley Cavanaugh, the former Sacramento city manager, over the relative numbers of Irish and Swedes in Dublin. On his way home to Washington, he checked into the New York hotel where Cavanaugh was staying. Donning his academic robe, the dignified Chief Justice of the United States strolled up the hall as other hotel guests gaped. He held a Dublin telephone book in his arm. Impishly, with his documentary evidence in hand, he presented to his astounded friend the tabbed telephone book exclaiming, "I told you, Bart, there were as many Warrens as Cavanaughs in Dublin!"

More solemnly, shortly afterward in New York, the Scandinavian Warren switched from modern Ireland to ancient Israel in his sociological research. At the Jewish Theological Seminary, the Chief Justice sat down with scholars, including Dr. Louis Finkelstein, the president, at a three-day weekend conference on judicial decision-making. Protestant Earl Warren donned the traditional black yarmulke (skull cap) at the Sabbath services. "I wish that I could speak to you in the words of a scholar," he remarked, "but it has not fallen to my lot to be a scholar in life. I have been in public life for forty years. Since that time, I have been doing the urgent rather than the important. I was always jumping from one thing to another without the opportunity to explore any one thing to its roots." Not surprisingly, some views of Talmudic scholars such as Dr. Norman Lamm, now head of Yeshiva University, later turned up in the footnote opinions of Chief Justice Earl Warren. "Among other things," Warren later reflected, "I learned that double jeopardy and self-incrimination in our Fifth Amendment cases came from the Old Testament."

But soon it was back to his learning seat on the bench, where last fall a new liberal Justice had been appointed and this fall there would be a new conservative one.

Sherman Minton, once a militant New Dealer but an ineffectual conservative during his eight years as a Truman-appointed Justice, had resigned in 1956 because of ill health. Curiously enough, William J. Brennan, Jr., a quiet, hard-working liberal judge on the New Jersey Supreme Court, was appointed in October of that year to the vacant seat. A month before the 1956 election, the Eisenhower brain trust had deemed it politically prudent to name (1) a Democrat and (2) a Catholic (the "Catholic seat" had been vacant since Frank Murphy's 1949 death and a promise had been made to Cardinal Spellman of New York to name a Roman Catholic). Brennan was enthusiastically endorsed by the bar associations and New Jersey Chief Justice Arthur T. Vanderbilt. During Brennan's Senate confirmation hearing the only dissenting vote was cast by Senator McCarthy, whose methods Brennan had denounced at Irish Society meetings. This appointment—which Eisenhower later privately termed "my second Supreme Court mistake"—added another voice to the Warren-Black-Douglas liberal wing. Felix Frankfurter, the Court's conservative leader, under whom Brennan had studied at Harvard Law School, quipped about his junior colleague: "I always encouraged my students to think for themselves but Brennan goes too far!" In some of his monumental future decisions, Brennan later played a brilliant pizzicato violin to his Chief's massive sometimes clangorous cello.

President Eisenhower looked elsewhere for his fourth Supreme Court appointment after the aging conservative Stanley E. Reed retired. In March 1957 he had named Republican Charles E. Whittaker, a Missouri Federal Circuit Court judge to the seat. A corporation lawyer of limited outlook, Whittaker proved neither intellectually nor physically equipped for the Associate Justiceship. "When Whittaker found the life of the Supreme Court not to his taste, the Chief took care in the assignment of opinions to ease the burdens of his brother Justice," recollects Warren clerk Graham B. Moody, Jr. Whittaker lacked the legal wisdom of such learned conservatives as Frankfurter or Harlan. Five years later he resigned because of inability to keep up with the Court's demanding workload. Surprisingly, Whittaker then not only criticized the Supreme Court itself for "usurping" powers but even some of the Justices. In 1965 he joined the General Motors legal staff. Nonetheless, in a charitable tribute to Whittaker in the 1962 *Texas Law Review,* his compassionate former Chief Justice wrote, "He refused to leave time for any diversion."

It was indicative of Eisenhower's growing displeasure with Warren that the President now made a heavy-handed point of stressing the need for prior judicial experience in candidates for all his subsequent Supreme Court appointments, "I told the attorney general," he wrote in his memoirs, "that I would not thereafter appoint anyone who had not served on a lower federal court or a state supreme court."

It was indicative, also, of the President's failure to understand Warren's character. He seems to have imagined that his problems with his Chief Justice arose somehow from Warren's professional incompetence rather than from any deep-seated differences in conviction. Alistair Cooke, the perceptive British observer of the American scene, says that "The apotheosis of Earl Warren was something that baffled Eisenhower until the day he died." The President's seeming lack of insight into the *meaning* of Warren's performance adds credence to this observation.

Warren's disillusionment with Eisenhower was also proceeding apace. The jurist still liked the President personally and well understood that Ike's successive illnesses were inevitably eroding his administrative efficiency. But Warren was becoming increasingly impatient with what he considered the escapist inattention, indecisiveness and insensitivity with which Eisenhower treated many important domestic problems, often delegating them to others, particularly to Chief of Staff Sherman Adams. (This was all the more irritating to Warren because the President still displayed an undiminished vigor in dealing with foreign affairs.) Above all, Warren was angered by the President's continued failure to implement the Court's desegregation decisions. On this point he was unyielding. Whatever political pressures the President might have had to face, whatever predisposition he might have toward seeking compromise solutions, Warren brushed aside. The decisions were right, they were law and they required active support. "It is a delicious irony," wrote Anthony Lewis of *The New York Times,* much later, "that a President who raised inactivity to a principle of government should have appointed a Chief Justice for whom action was all."

Paradoxically, as relations between the two men worsened, both made greater diplomatic efforts to avoid an open break. Throughout the remainder of 1957 and on into 1958 the President took special pains to entertain the Warrens as frequently as possible at the White House. Warren in turn acceded amiably to such ceremonial Presidential requests as accepting the chairmanship of a committee to establish an "Armed Forces Institute" within the Smithsonian Institution, of which Warren was Chancellor. And both men bombarded one another with polite, if insignificant, correspondence at the slightest pretext, such as a birthday or other event of little moment.

Eisenhower's refusal to permit a public breach to develop between himself and Warren required some political courage. Anti-Warren sentiment in Congress and throughout the nation had never been more vocal. During the 85th Congress in the 1958 Court term, desperate legislative efforts were made to curb the Warren Court's jurisdiction and even reverse some of its rulings. In the Senate, Warren supporters, by merely a 41-40 vote, beat down a sweeping bill curtailing the Court's powers which had passed the House of Representatives 241-155. Majority Leader Lyndon B. Johnson persuaded several senators who opposed the Warren Court to be "absent" or "unavoidably detained on official business" in the cloakroom, barbershop or lavatory during the crucial vote. Outside Congress, the John Birch Society's vituperative "Impeach Earl Warren" campaign had reached its zenith.

Since the most bitter opposition to Warren centered among conservative Republicans and angry white Southerners, and since Warren's most ardent supporters generally were confirmed liberal Democrats, President Eisenhower might have made political capital by publicly disapproving the Court's decisions. But Eisenhower—if not the Republican party—resisted any such temptation. Perhaps the President did not want to admit that he had made a mistake in appointing Warren. Perhaps he valued the support of liberal Republicans too much to risk offending them. Or perhaps—and this is what one wishes to assume—he was too honorable to stoop to such disloyalty.

Not all of the opposition to Warren came from outside the Court. Justice Felix Frankfurter had grown more conservative and cantankerous and now became increasingly hostile to Warren's activism. Gone were the days when Frankfurter could write, as he had after the *Brown* decision, "Dear Chief: This is a day that will live in glory—a great day in the history of the Court—I congratulate you." Now Frankfurter attempted to enlist the aging Harlan (whose eyesight was so poor that Warren made special efforts to curtail the reading assigned to him) in an opposition coalition. But this was only partially successful; by and large, the Warren Court still eschewed any factionalism, and the friction between Frankfurter and Warren remained primarily personal.

196

Once in open court, a young attorney, failing to understand a Frankfurter query, began to stutter. Helpfully, Warren took over, asking Frankfurter, "Mr. Justice, do you mean . . .?" as he paraphrased the question in simpler words. Not even a Chief Justice could do that to a man who deemed himself the most learned Justice on the High Court. Frankfurter smirked, put his finger to his nose, gazed at his Chief contemptuously before finally answering, "Yes, Mr. Chief Justice, that is *precisely* what I mean."

The Frankfurter scorn even later erupted at one Friday afternoon Conference that surviving Court personnel still remember with dismay. Frankfurter had been pontificating upon his pet theme: that the Court should neither try to "make law" (the privilege of the legislature) nor dispense justice (the function of the lower courts), but should confine itself solely to the *interpretation* of the law. Warren, who generally let these orations pass without comment, this time mildly demurred on constitutional grounds. The nettled Frankfurter rounded on him furiously: "You're the worst Chief Justice this country has ever had." The other Justices looked away in embarrassed silence. After a moment, Warren calmly proceeded to the next order of business. "That remark was much more a reflection on Felix than on the Chief," one Justice sadly commented later. According to Judge Charles E. Wyzanski, a friend of both Warren and Frankfurter, this incident confirmed what Warren had long suspected: that in deciding what role the Court would play he would have to choose between the Frankfurter and the Black philosophies. He chose Black—"the right choice," in Wyzanski's words.

In October, Eisenhower made his fifth and final Court appointment. Potter Stewart, an Ohio Circuit Court judge, replaced the retired Burton. At forty-three, Stewart became the Court's youngest Justice. Stewart still gratefully recalls that when first arriving at Washington's Union Station at 7 A.M., he and his party of six were met by the Chief Justice and his waiting automobile. Neither dogmatically liberal nor rigidly conservative, the flexible Stewart soon became known as the Supreme Court's "Swing Justice." His swing vote would be increasingly important, for Warren no longer represented the middle ground in the Court's thinking. Contrary to the more circumscribed Frankfurter-Harlan philosophy, Warren now believed that the Court must not only review the letter of the law, but also accept cases in terms of equity and long-term social effects. Robert J. Hoerner, Warren's 1958 clerk, recollected (in the Winter 1975 issue of the *Hastings Constitutional Law Quarterly*):

> ... *during the 1958 term, the Chief largely convinced himself that his more activist judicial philosophy was appropriate for the High Court. He went into the 1959 term with more inner peace and confidence in the propriety of judicial implementation of his own views than he had in his earlier terms. The seeds of* Escobedo, Miranda *and* Reynolds *had begun to germinate.*

Ralph J. Moore, Jr., Warren's 1959 clerk, added that during the following term:

> ... *the Chief ... wrote opinions for the Court in a series of cases that dealt principally, not with broad constitutional issues, but with the kinds of problems lawyers encounter in everyday practice—Federal tax procedure, Federal estate taxation, state property taxation, FHA mortgage priorities, and application of the Fair Labor Standards Act, Railway Labor Act, Interstate Commerce Act, and Robinson-Patman Act. The Chief's workload was substantial ...*

Moreover, the Chief Justice grew increasingly concerned with how to improve Federal and state courts. Many state judges bitterly complained that the Warren Court needlessly encouraged the review by Federal district judges of too many of their criminal justice decisions. The Conference of State Chief Justices joined the public attack upon the Warren Court in 1958–59, contending that it lacked judicial restraint. Result: a decade of strained relations between Warren and state judges (as well as the American Bar Association, with whom Warren was already feuding). One Midwestern state judge grumbled, "Our job is to keep our legal machinery oiled with an oil can and to keep the wheels from scratching. We don't need anybody to sell us new machinery!"

In some major economic cases, the Warren Court reversed not only state but lower Federal courts. For example, a lower court decision involving the Eisenhower Administration was negated by a 1960 Warren Court ruling which enraged both industry and the legal profession (just as had the Warren Court's 1956 decision breaking up the General Motors-DuPont association as a violation of the anti-trust laws). Here, the U.S. Atomic Energy Commission had engaged the Mississippi Valley Generating Company to build a Memphis-area steam power plant. During its construction, a congressional committee investigated this business deal, which soon became better known as the Dixon-Yates scandal (after the two presidents of the utilities involved). The Eisenhower Administration was denounced for engaging a private company to construct this plant instead of the government's own Tennessee Valley Authority. Under attack, the contract was cancelled by President Eisenhower. The rejected company sued the Federal government for $2 million for work already completed and for legal fees. The company won judgments in Federal district courts until the appeal reached the Supreme Court.

There, Earl Warren's majority opinion denied the company's claim for repayment of the $2 million, plus more than a million dollars in legal fees. His grounds? Investment banker Adolph Wenzell, the government's dollar-a-year consultant who had advised awarding the contract, was vice-president of a Boston financial firm which seemingly would have profited from the deal. Calling this a conflict of interest, the Chief Justice quoted Scripture: "No man can serve two masters."

Warren's concern with equity was nowhere more apparent than in his opinions on a series of "little people" cases during the 1959–60 term. He wrote a blistering dissent when the Court affirmed the conviction of a Jehovah's Witness for refusing Army induction (the defendant had been given no hearing to plead his conscientious objection). Similarly, Warren enthusiastically joined Black's dissent when the Court upheld the taking of Indian lands secured by treaty (". . . great nations, like great men, should keep their word"). Furthermore, he voted with the majority in denying Louisville's attempt to justify a $10 fine for a misdemeanor conviction of a black man which was obtained without any evidence.

Thus, as Eisenhower's second term drew to a close, Warren continued to fulfill the expectations of both his enemies and his advocates. The *Brown* desegregation decision had not been a fluke, nor the result—as the President seemed to have hoped—of Warren's judicial ineptitude. Since then, the Chief Justice had revealed himself to be a committed activist. All his decisions had been consistent with this orientation. He no longer spoke for the entire

Court, but was firmly positioned on its liberal wing and often in the dissenting minority. Nonetheless, his fellow Justices—Frankfurter apart—now so liked and respected their Chief that he remained the Court's most influential member, constantly guiding it toward broader and more soul-searching interpretations of its responsibilities with greater clarity of mind and firmer leadership.

Until the end of his administration, Eisenhower continued to behave toward Warren with classic courtesy. Yet neither man had any illusions about how far apart they had drifted. Once the President left office, their relations cooled perceptibly. The retired Chief Executive pointedly failed to invite the still-sitting Chief Justice to the dedication of the Eisenhower Library at Abilene in May 1962, and Warren never visited it at any time during the next twelve years of his life (although he was a frequent visitor to the Truman Library in Independence and the Johnson Library in Austin).

It was Eisenhower who, in an unguarded moment, first gave public indication of the depth of their estrangement. In 1964, the former President told Ralph Cake, a Republican national committeeman from Oregon, not only that he had never wanted Warren as Chief Justice (he was, he insisted, only honoring a promise made by Brownell), but that he regarded the appointment as "one of the two biggest mistakes I made in my Administration." The remark was widely quoted. It is not altogether clear what or who Eisenhower then believed his other mistake had been. Perhaps that does not matter, because he was soon quoted as calling the Warren appointment "my *biggest* damn-fool mistake."

By contrast, Warren was always far more scrupulous in voicing any criticisms of the President. He had, of course, never concealed his dissatisfaction with Eisenhower's failure to enforce or even to endorse *Brown* until after he had left the White House. But the Chief Justice usually avoided making more general characterizations of the President. Typical of his approach is this fragment from a luncheon conversation with a friend in Washington in 1973, in which Warren said, "The real trouble with Eisenhower was that he never really understood the meaning of the law."

"Why don't you write about that in your autobiography, then?" he was asked.

"Oh, I don't want to get into that. He's dead and couldn't answer back.

The fever chart of the Eisenhower-Warren relationship was an ironic counterpoint to Warren's evolving performance as Chief Justice. As Warren's stature grew, Eisenhower's regard for him correspondingly sank. If only Warren had been content to play the role of moderator or steward on the Court—instead of leader—presumably Eisenhower would have continued to hold him in high esteem.

Was Eisenhower's opinion of Warren (and that of many other observers) conditioned in part by stereotyped thinking? The President and the nation at large viewed Warren as a newly-fledged extremist liberal. Conservatives abominated this apparent metamorphosis. Liberals applauded it. And the President, who professed to dislike ideological extremes, deplored it.

But how accurate, really, was this perception? Were not Court-watchers imputing to Warren an ideological consistency that was not really there—at least not in a conventional sense? Actually, Warren was anything but an ideologue. Throughout his entire public career he had repeatedly shown that he was capable of being "liberal" on one issue and "conservative" on another. This was the "unpredictability" of which Eisenhower and his aides—and so many of Warren's earlier critics—had complained.

Both Eisenhower and, in earlier times, Warren had been called "middle-of-the-roaders." Indeed, this was what had attracted Eisenhower to Warren in the first place. But this imprecise phrase masked a profound difference between the two men. Earl Warren's "middle road" stretched far wider than Dwight Eisenhower's. In some ways, it was an eight-lane California freeway compared to an Abilene county dirt road.

Much as Eisenhower decried ideological formulations, he responded to them; Warren did not. Eisenhower tended to take his bearings from opposing extremes of opinion and then to steer a middle course between them. In this behavior, he was consistent and predictable. By contrast, Warren tended to respond first to his own conscience. In this he was consistent but quite unpredictable to those who were, in David Riesman's phrase, "other-directed"—the President included. "If a man does not keep pace with his companions," wrote Thoreau, "perhaps it is because he hears a different drummer." The quality in Warren that seems to have eluded so many of both his detractors and defenders was his genuine independence of thought.

To be an independent thinker is, of course, no guarantee of greatness. During the Eisenhower years, Warren had given undeniable proof of his independence, but whether that independence was coupled with true wisdom had now become a subject of furious national debate. In the coming years, Warren's behavior would do nothing to lessen the violence of that debate.

Chapter Six

The Kennedy Years 1961–1963

*T*he Republican nomination of Richard Nixon on July 27, 1960, as their presidential candidate, was half-hearted and, some party strategists felt, possibly dangerous. Despite being Eisenhower's heir apparent, he enjoyed little of Ike's popularity, even among conservative Republicans, his main power base. Presumably Nixon would be highly vulnerable to a strong Democratic challenge, even one by the twice-defeated Adlai Stevenson, Warren and many others believed.

But the Democrats, displaying their traditional penchant for meeting political opportunities with disarray, nominated a candidate seemingly encumbered with liabilities. John Fitzgerald Kennedy was disconcertingly young, politically provincial and a Roman Catholic. As the hard-driving Kennedy himself quipped, "If I were Protestant, governor of a big state and fifty-five, I could sit back and let the nomination come to me." On the other hand, he was vigorous, handsome and intelligent, and had a beautiful wife. Best of all, he had behind him vast financial resources, talented campaign aides and the relentless energies of ambitious old Joseph Kennedy's colossal clan. ("It isn't the Pope that bothers me," Harry Truman reportedly once remarked, "it's Pop.")

John Kennedy shrewdly used all of these assets during the rugged primary races to capture the nomination. But overcoming his liabilities to win the election was another matter. In the end, it was probably Nixon's weakness—especially as a glowering, heavy-bearded television campaigner—rather than the crisp, clean-cut Kennedy strength that enabled JFK to emerge victorious. At that, a scant 113,057 popular votes separated the two candidates. It was the closest election of the century. During the campaign, Kennedy himself wisecracked: "I got a wire from my father that said, 'Dear Jack. Don't buy one vote more than necessary. I'll be damned if I'll pay for a landslide!' "

Chief Justice Warren's attitude toward this election was, if not exactly typical of the nation's quandary, symptomatic of it. Despite his misgivings about his party's right wing, as a Republican, Warren probably would have preferred a Republican to a Democratic administration. He did not know Kennedy well. He vaguely remembered having met John Kennedy, then a young journalist, at the 1945 opening of the United Nations in San Francisco, and having again seen him when both he (as governor of California) and Kennedy (now as a U.S. Senator) were awarded honorary doctorates of law at Catholic Villanova University in Pennsylvania in April 1957. But now, he saw little hard evidence that the young man would make a good President. He saw considerable evidence, on the contrary, to indicate that any influence Joe Kennedy might exert over his son most likely would be bad for the country. Yet he finally voted for Kennedy because he could not bring himself to vote for Nixon. In his Supreme Court chambers during the campaign, he gravely said to a visiting California intimate, "Nixon is a *bad* man." The remark brimmed with melancholy rather than bitterness, indicating his assessment of the Republican nominee's character.

Thus, it was with mixed feelings—half wary, half hopeful—that the sixty-nine-year-old Chief Justice prepared for the swearing in of the 35th President of the United States on January 20, 1961. Privately, he joked: "This will be only my second swearing in of a President. Maybe this time I'll be able to look around and really enjoy it. Four years ago, I was so nervous I didn't see a damn thing!"

Indeed, there was a great deal to see. The nation's capital had been brought to a standstill by the heavy snow of the past two days. Three thousand servicemen and civilians toiled all night to plow away eight inches of it on the Capitol Plaza. Inauguration morning, though, was clear but cold. At 11:30 A.M., President Eisenhower, barred from serving a third term by the Twenty-second Amendment, and President-elect Kennedy stepped into a waiting limousine which transported them along Pennsylvania Avenue to the Capitol. The oldest man (seventy) ever to serve as President would soon turn over the nation's leadership to the youngest man (forty-three) ever elected to that office.

At 12:30 P.M. the Chief Justice asked the mop-haired incoming President, who had removed his coat and top hat, to place his hand on a Kennedy family Douay Bible and repeat the oath of office. Thus, the first Catholic President of the United States was sworn in by a onetime Methodist whose High Court was then battling bigotry in all forms.

After being sworn in, the new President warmed the heart of not only the Chief Justice but of other millions throughout the free world with his now classic Churchillian words: "Let the word go forth . . . to friend and foe alike, that the torch has been passed to a new generation of Americans. . . . Let us never negotiate out of fear. But let us never fear to negotiate. . . . Ask not what your country can do for you—ask what you can do for your country. . . ."

Warren's initial misgivings about Kennedy were not reciprocated. The President seems to have entered office full of admiration for the Chief Justice, telling intimates that he deemed the Warren appointment possibly the greatest accomplishment of his predecessor's administration. He soon took a step to convey his sentiments to Warren. Less than two months after Kennedy became President and shortly before the disastrous Bay of Pigs invasion, Earl Warren reached his seventieth birthday. The Chief Justice's past and present law clerks threw him a surprise birthday dinner at Washington's Metropolitan Club. Earl Warren was astonished when President Kennedy marched in unannounced during the cocktail hour to pay his respects. They chatted briefly, including mention of their respective large families. Asked by the President how many grandchildren he had, the Chief Justice quipped: "Sixteen and I'm afraid to open the morning mail!" Several days later, on March 20, the party-crasher received this letter:

My dear Mr. President:
May I express to you my deepest thanks for dropping in at the

birthday party for me Saturday evening. It was very thoughtful and gracious of you to do so, and I want you to know that I personally appreciated it very much.

All of the law clerks were thrilled to have an opportunity to meet you. I am sure it is an occasion they will not soon forget.

With best wishes for your continued success in the high office you occupy, I am

Sincerely,
(Signed) Earl Warren

Equally gratifying, and more significant, were Kennedy's oral assurances to Warren that his administration intended fully to support all Court rulings, past and future, including desegregation, in precisely the way that the Eisenhower Administration had not—and to move the nation forward. Senator Edward Kennedy later reminisced:

The first change of Administrations during the Warren Era found a new commitment to social justice. The Executive worked in tandem with the judiciary, taking strong initiatives in civil rights, and laying the groundwork for an upheaval in criminal and civil justice by focusing on the problems, ventilating them, and proposing administrative and legislative reforms. By the end of the first decade of the Warren Court, Congress also began to complete what the Court had started.

The first milestone Warren Court decision during the Kennedy Administration was *Mapp* v. *Ohio*, in which it reversed the conviction of Dollree Mapp, a Cleveland woman. When police illegally began to search her apartment without a warrant, she snatched the blank sheet which detectives had spuriously flashed and stuffed it into her bosom before being handcuffed. Thanks to Warren's influence, the High Court ruled in an opinion written, surprisingly, by conservative Tom Clark, that any "evidence unlawfully seized" can never be admitted at trial or used against a defendant; it violated the "unreasonable searches and seizure" clause of the Fourth Amendment. Most law enforcers protested the ruling, arguing that evidence is evidence regardless of the way it is obtained.

The principal instrument for enforcing Supreme Court decisions was, and is, of course, the Department of Justice. When the

President appointed as attorney general his younger brother Robert, Warren's misgivings about the Kennedy clan briefly revived. Apart from the question of nepotism, Bobby's lack of experience was all too obvious. ("What's wrong about my giving Bobby a little legal experience *before* he goes out to practice law?" the debonaire President cracked to newsmen.) Yet Warren soon became reconciled to the appointment. The Chief Justice, in fact, was delighted when young Attorney General Kennedy—along with the President—publicly denounced the John Birch Society. The younger Kennedy's intellectual gifts, moral seriousness and tough-minded idealism went a long way toward compensating for his youth and inexperience. Of his willingness to enforce the law—even, at times, ruthlessly—there could be little doubt. This would be important to Warren, for the upcoming Court Term of October 1961–June 1962 was scheduled to hear arguments on two issues so explosive that the High Court would need all the support it could muster.

The first was the 1962 reapportionment case of *Baker* v. *Carr,* which Warren later would call the most important opinion rendered during his sixteen years on the Supreme Court. Attorney General Kennedy hailed it as "a landmark in . . . representative Government." This case was launched by disgruntled Tennessee voters who complained that recent population shifts had made obsolete a 1901 state law prescribing how seats in the state assembly should be apportioned. Because of this law, they were being unfairly represented and therefore deprived of their constitutional rights, they argued. A rural county with a bare 2,340 voters had one representative while a city county with 133 times more voters had only seven.

This Tennessee law was, of course, by no means unique. Geographically-biased representation was a time-honored, though little-advertised, fact of American political life. Just as in England's old "Rotten Boroughs," it was the principal means by which American politicians with small rural constituencies retained their power against the multitudinous votes in big cities and growing suburbia. It was the basis for gerrymandering countless election districts so that entrenched political parties and machines could survive the vagaries of statewide elections. It was also a way of preventing rising urban ghetto populations from acquiring too much political clout in state politics. In short, people living in cities and suburbs had little voice in how they were being governed, even though the nation was no longer predominately rural in character.

And any U.S. Supreme Court ruling that tampered with this weighted representation—and none ever had—could unbalance a political structure long considered sacrosanct.

Yet that is *precisely* what the Warren Court boldly did. In a 6-2 decision, it upheld the protesting Tennessee voters, affirming that hereafter all voter representation must comply with the "one-man-one-vote" principle. This, the Court ruled, was the proper interpretation of the constitutional provisions that representatives "shall be chosen by the people of the several states" and that all citizens should have equal protection under the law. By thus enfranchising millions of hitherto unrepresented voters in cities and suburbs, it overruled the way that virtually all state legislatures had been filling their seats.

Justice Brennan wrote the courageous 161-page opinion in *Baker* v. *Carr*, with Warren enthusiastically concurring. Ailing eighty-year-old Frankfurter, soon to retire, wrote a defiant farewell dissent for himself and Harlan. Frankfurter had long adamantly opposed the Court's involving itself in any cases with strong political implications—"political thickets," he called them. He excoriated the *Baker* decision as "a massive repudiation of the past."

Oddly, many politicians at the time seem to have failed to grasp the far-reaching import of the decision, which would have made some of their seats illegal. The Court was saying, in effect, that the legislatures of nearly all states were illegally constituted and that their seats now must be reapportioned on the basis of population rather than geography. As a result, many "safe" election districts would evaporate, many local political machines would lose power and many personal political careers would end. The awful truth dawned only when the Warren Court spelled out the practical ramifications of the "one-man-one-vote" ruling in later cases—notably in *Reynolds* v. *Sims* in 1964, where Warren himself wrote in the majority opinion these memorable words: "Legislators represent people, not trees or acres. Legislators are elected by voters, not farms or cities or economic interests."

When the message finally sank in, the reaction among old-time politicians in and out of Congress was understandably violent. Representative William Tuck of Virginia rushed an anti-"one-man-one-vote" bill through the U.S. House of Representatives, only to see it narrowly killed by the Senate. Everett M. Dirksen, the Republican Senate minority leader, proposed a constitutional amendment that would give voters a choice between the Warren Court decisions and the traditional prevailing apportionment methods. The Dirksen Amendment was strongly supported by, among others, the Council of State Governments, the American Farm Bureau, the National Grange, the National Association of Manufacturers and the United States Chamber of Commerce. But it was opposed by many labor and liberal groups, such as the AFL-CIO and the Americans for Democratic Action (ADA), League of Women Voters and National Municipal League. It failed to pass the Senate by a mere seven votes, thanks largely to the indefatigable efforts of Illinois Senator Paul H. Douglas, assisted by Wisconsin's William Proxmire and Indiana's Birch Bayh.

Even while opponents in Congress were waging their bitter, unsuccessful campaign against "one-man-one-vote," the states had begun complying with the new law. Contrary to Frankfurter's fears, a quiet revolution was occurring in America's political power structure. For example, populous cities such as Hartford, the capital of Connecticut, would never again be represented in the state's lower house in exactly the same ratio as such villages as Union (population: 383). Rurally-dominated state legislatures no longer could ignore the urgent economic, fiscal, social and other problems which bedeviled their cities. And the power bases of some of the nation's most entrenched political figures—for example, former House Speaker Joe Martin of Massachusetts, House Rules Committee Chairman Howard W. Smith of Virginia and Post Office and Civil Service Committee Chairman Thomas Murray of Tennessee— would be fatally eroded.

Warren rode serenely above the uproar created by the Court's legislative reapportionment decisions. The only thing that seemed to matter to him, then and later, was the intrinsic merit of the principle involved. "If *Baker* v. *Carr* had been in existence fifty years ago," he insisted, "we would have saved ourselves acute racial troubles. Many of our problems would have been solved a long time ago if everyone had the right to vote, and his vote counted the same as everybody else's. Most of these problems could have been solved through the political process rather than through the courts. But as it was, the Court had to decide."

Paradoxically, in reapportionment, Chief Justice Warren had overruled Governor Warren. Back in 1948 in California he had defended the grossly unequal method of selecting legislative seats, even though the Los Angeles area, then having approximately five million inhabitants, had the same single voice in the Sacramento Senate as a northern mountain county with merely 50,000 residents. But thanks to the Warren Court decisions, in 1965 and 1967 California made significant changes in the way it selected assembly, senatorial and congressional seats.

Naturally, it is easier to be more noble as a Chief Justice for fifty states than a governor of merely one of them. In retirement, Warren admitted, "In California I went along with the thought that we should leave well enough alone. It simply was a matter of political expediency. But I saw the situation in a different light on the Court. There, you have a different responsibility to the entire country."

Recognizing its responsibility, the Kennedy Administration was quick to support the *Baker* vs. *Carr* decision. The following January, in a kindred case challenging Georgia's archaic county unit method of choosing legislators (*Gray* v. *Sanders*), Attorney General Kennedy vigorously opposed it in his first appearance before the Supreme Court as a prosecuting lawyer. This was additional indication of the growing ideological bond between the White House and the Marble Palace.

A second explosive Warren Court decision—particularly difficult for the Catholic Kennedys—was the ruling in June 1962 which outlawed compulsory school prayers (*Engel* v. *Vitale*), reaffirming instead the traditional American separation between Church and State. In a 6-1 decision, the top tribunal held that reading the Bible or even the Lord's Prayer in public schools was unconstitutional. ("It was no business of Government to compose official prayers for any group of American people to recite.") Bluntly, the Warren Court tabooed a simple, seemingly innocuous twenty-two-word New York State Regents Prayer for public-school children which read: "Almighty God, we acknowledge our dependence upon Thee, and we beg Thy blessings upon us, our parents, our teachers and our Country."

The opinion was written by Justice Black, a former Alabama Baptist Sunday school teacher, who based it upon the First Amendment's freedom of religion clause which the Court ruled was extended to the states by the Fourteenth Amendment.

This decision aroused a nationwide hurricane of protests from religionists, legislators and parents who wanted their children to secure religious instruction in the schools. Not since the 1954 school desegregation ruling had the Warren Court been condemned so bitterly. In the "Impeach Earl Warren" movement the Chief Justice was now excoriated as "anti-Christian" as well as "pro-Communist."

Former President Hoover and Eisenhower, New York's Francis Cardinal Spellman, Los Angeles' James Cardinal McIntyre, Evangelist Billy Graham and Congressman Gerald R. Ford, among others, swiftly denounced what many termed the "Godless Supreme Court." Mississippi's pro-segregation president of the American Bar Association rationalized that if school prayers were unconstitutional, so were the words "In God We Trust" on U.S. coins. Honey-tongued Illinois Senator Dirksen thundered: "Almost *anything* can be taught in the schools. They teach sex education today . . . they teach communism . . . ballet dancing. You name it and they have it. But they do not mention prayer—the pipeline to the Almighty . . . What a strange thing!" The Hearst newspapers urged a constitutional amendment to negate the ruling.

However, Roman Catholic President Kennedy quickly defended the decisions. Counseling restraint and support of the Warren Court, he pointed out that there was a very easy remedy, and that was "to pray ourselves . . . we can pray a good deal more at home, we can attend our churches with more fidelity, and we can make the true meaning of prayer much more important in the lives of all our children."

A year later, the *Engel* decision was reinforced by another Warren Court ruling (*Abington [Pennsylvania] Township School District* v. *Schempp*). This opinion, written by Presbyterian Tom Clark, again declared that no state could compel Bible reading or recitation of the Lord's Prayer in any public school without violating the First Amendment. During the hearing on this case, Abington's young lawyer, Philip W. Ward III, argued: "If the period were an hour, people might think the school is teaching religion instead of morality."

"Is one hour of morality unconstitutional but ten minutes all right?" deadpanned the Chief Justice.

In a kindred Maryland case, the Chief Justice uncharacteristically jabbed at Frances Burch, Baltimore's city solicitor: "In schools in Hawaii, where the majority of the students are of Japanese or Chinese descent, would you say that it is proper to have a Buddhist ceremony there and make all the Christian children participate? Or should their parents request that *they* be excused?" Later, in cross-examining Maryland Attorney General Thomas B. Finan, Warren persisted: "Why must we make an issue between Christianity and atheism? Are you saying that the only ones who should be asked to be excused [from prayer and Bible-reading] are atheists?"

Seven years later, in retirement, Warren reminisced, "The floodgates were opened. It was not long before there were fifty constitutional amendments in the House of Representatives to override these decisions." *Newsweek* magazine at the time counted 147.

Although he wrote none of the school prayer opinions, the Chief Justice was the prime target of the denunciations. Earl Warren was castigated as "anti-God," "a Godless communist," "Bible-hating atheist" and "servant of the devil" by countless critics. Some pickets carried placards saying: "In God We Trust—Not Earl Warren." But his namesake son, Sacramento Municipal Court Judge Earl Warren, Jr., insists: "My father was the most religious man I ever knew. He was raised on the Bible."

Benjamin R. Swig, one of Warren's closest friends who owns San Francisco's Fairmount Hotel where the Warrens often stayed, recollects: "After he retired, I discussed these school prayer decisions with him. He disliked them because he felt that it was good that people said their prayers in school or any time. But he said that he had no alternative. He had to live up to the Constitution." Indeed, in the church-state issue, Warren was a strict constitutionalist.

Amid all the furor, the Chief Justice could laugh at a newspaper cartoon portraying a college student saying to a classmate, "I don't care what Earl Warren says. I *always* pray before an exam!"

Two vacancies arose on the Supreme Court during 1962. Justice Whittaker resigned suddenly in March because of ill health. President Kennedy's first thought was to appoint black Judge William Henry Hastie, then on the U.S. Court of Appeals for the Third Circuit, former dean of the Howard University Law School and Governor of the Virgin Islands. On reflection, however, he concluded that such an appointment might be premature and the Kennedy Administration might be criticized for seeking to woo black voters.

Instead, after Attorney General Kennedy had conferred with Chief Justice Warren, the President nominated on March 30 his friend Byron Raymond "Whizzer" White, who joined the bench on April 16 after being confirmed by the Senate five days earlier. The forty-five-year-old White had been an All-American halfback at the University of Colorado, a Rhodes Scholar, a Yale Law School graduate, a Naval officer, a law clerk to Chief Justice Vinson in 1946–47, and a successful Denver corporation lawyer. During the 1960 campaign, he had worked hard for JFK. In 1961, as deputy attorney general under Bobby Kennedy, Whizzer White had skillfully withstood the mob fury while defending the Freedom Riders in Montgomery, Alabama. When appointing him to the High Bench at Bobby's strong recommendation, President Kennedy declared that White had excelled in everything that he had ever attempted. Skeptics irreverently called him "Jack Armstrong."

For Chief Justice Warren, however, this New Frontiersman quickly proved a major disappointment; White soon began voting with the conservatives more frequently than with the Court liberals, especially in civil liberty and criminal justice cases.

Five months later, in September 1962, Kennedy made his second and final Supreme Court appointment: Secretary of Labor Arthur J. Goldberg to succeed Felix Frankfurter. From Warren's point of view, it was an excellent choice, for Goldberg quickly gave the activist wing (Warren, Douglas, Black and Brennan) its narrow 5-to-4 majority. Before appointing Goldberg to the traditional "Jewish seat" previously held by Brandeis, Cardozo and Frankfurter, President Kennedy had also considered nominating Harvard Law Professor Paul Freund and Abraham A. Ribicoff, his recently designated Secretary of Health, Education and Welfare. All three were acceptable to Warren when Bobby Kennedy assessed these possible choices with him beforehand.

Ten months after Goldberg ascended the High Bench, President Kennedy asked him to arbitrate an acrimonious July 1963 railroad dispute. Before doing so, he scrupulously sought the Chief Justice's clearance, telephoning Warren in Athens, where he was attending the World Bar Association convention. Although reluctant to involve any Supreme Court Justice in the Executive branch's activities, Warren agreed because of Goldberg's unique labor background, which included having been the former general counsel of the United Steel Workers of America and a key figure in the merger of the American Federation of Labor (AFL) and Congress of Industrial Organizations (CIO).

Two years and eight months later, however, Warren lost Goldberg when he was wheedled by President Johnson into resigning from the Supreme Court to succeed the suddenly deceased Adlai Stevenson as United Nations Ambassador.

One minor Kennedy decision irritated the Chief Justice. In rearranging the White House ceremonial seating list for dignitaries, he now placed the Speaker of the House and President of the Senate above the Chief Justice in the "Precedence List," in conformity with the new Presidential Succession Act.

Chief of Protocol Angier Biddle Duke had the unpleasant task of breaking this news to the Chief Justice.

"I don't give a damn who sits above or below the salt," Warren protested. "But I am deeply concerned that the Court as an institution not be downgraded, especially nowadays when it is under so much attack."

"The President is only trying to adjust the old custom to reflect the new law," explained Duke.

"Well, please tell the President for me that I do not construe the law as making the legislative branch superior to the judicial."

More gratifying to Warren was the latest development in the tortuous saga of Richard Nixon's public career. To virtually everyone's surprise, the former Vice President decided to run for governor of California against the popular Democratic incumbent, Edmund "Pat" Brown. After conferring with his father, Earl Warren, Jr., now at thirty-two a successful Sacramento lawyer, promptly bolted the Republican party in order to become Brown's campaign vice-chairman. The depth of his—and presumably his father's—animus against Nixon was revealed in his answer to a newsman's question: "Nixon, through back-door politics and for political gain for himself, pulled the rug out from under us in 1952. He wronged my father and the whole state." Although Nixon had rebuked the John Birch Society for calling Eisenhower a "dedicated agent of the communist conspiracy," he was strangely silent about its insistent demand to "Impeach Earl Warren." Young Earl Warren then remarked, "This is something our family has been watching with great interest."

Young Earl's father got into the act because he dreaded the possibility of a Governor Nixon controlling his state. As Chief

Justice, of course, he could not engage in politics, but he accepted an invitation in October 1962 to dedicate a building in Oakland. Though the former California governor never mentioned Nixon or Brown by name in his speech, he indirectly endorsed Brown by criticizing Nixon's campaign program.

Shortly before the election, Warren was interviewed in the El Mirador hotel in Sacramento by Richard H. Rodda, the political editor of the Sacramento *Bee,* who recalls: "It was very frustrating. He steadfastly refused to discuss politics for publication. He would only be quoted on trivia—the World Series or the beauty of the trees below us." Finally, Warren leaned forward and said, "Now, Dick, off the record, do you think Pat Brown can beat Nixon?"

"It will be close but I think Brown will win," replied the reporter.

With a glint in his eye, Warren happily retorted, "I think he's going to beat the hell out of Nixon! I can just feel it. I can't get involved, of course. But Nixon has to be stopped."

"We were alone in the room," adds Rodda. "I pressed for permission to quote him but he refused. While he did not go into details on his animosity toward Nixon, the expression on his face as he savored a Brown victory was revealing. I repeated this story to my boss, the late Walter Jones, one of Warren's closest friends, who said: 'Sure, Warren hates Nixon's guts!' "

Nixon's eventual crushing defeat by Brown, and its embarrassing aftermath (Nixon blamed the bias of the press for his loss and announced his retirement from politics, telling reporters, "You won't have Nixon to kick around anymore") elicited little sympathy from the Warren family.

By contrast, the Chief Justice had no hesitancy in openly and enthusiastically lending his support to Democrat Adlai Stevenson. In July 1962 both had been guests on Agnes Meyer's yacht on a ten-day European-Asiatic cruise, along with, among others, future *Newsday* editor William Attwood. The following month, UN Ambassador Stevenson asked Chief Justice Warren for a letter of recommendation for admission to the New York bar. Warren promptly wrote the Committee on Character and Fitness:

> *As Circuit Justice for the District of Columbia Circuit, I have been requested to express my opinion of the professional ability and character of Honorable Adlai E. Stevenson in connection with his application for admission to the Bar of the State of New York.*

This I am happy to do, based on years of acquaintance with him and on observation of his governmental and legal activities. He is, without question, a man of the highest character and a lawyer of outstanding ability. Trained in the law at Harvard and North-western Universities, he has practiced with distinction in Illinois and in the District of Columbia. His outstanding public service as Governor of Illinois and as our Ambassador to the United Nations is, I am sure, too well known to you to require enumeration. In the fields of corporate, public and international law he is outstanding both as a lawyer and as a citizen. I heartily endorse his application.

Sincerely,

(Signed) Earl Warren

On August 30, the grateful Stevenson thanked his endorser:

Dear Earl:
I have your letter and I am most grateful for your flattering letter to the Committee on Character and Fitness of the Supreme Court of New York. If you don't go to heaven for charity, I hope you won't go anywhere else for anything else.
Our journey together is one of my imperishable memories, and I wish there could be another and more leisurely opportunity to travel with you and that beloved and sainted Nina.
I yearn to see you both.

Cordially yours,

(Signed) Adlai

A month after the opening of the Court's October 1962–June 1963 term, Warren delivered a curious but illuminating speech at the Louis Marshall Award Dinner at the Jewish Theological Seminary in New York. Observing that "Law floats on a sea of Ethics," the Chief Justice recommended that perhaps a new profession, that of Ethics Counsellor, should be created: Attorneys and judges, he implied, were too often preoccupied with the law at the expense of equity and morality. Perhaps he was merely alluding, in somewhat novel language, to the traditional role of clergymen. Yet one may be pardoned for suspecting that he was simultaneously referring to what he deemed the ideal role of the Supreme Court should be. Certainly it was in this spirit that the Warren Court rendered its next major decision on March 18, 1963.

Clarence Gideon was a penniless fifty-one-year-old drifter. Convicted in 1960 of intent to burglarize a Panama City, Florida, poolroom, he was serving a five-year sentence in a Florida jail. The problem was that Gideon had never been represented by an attorney at his trial. He had been too poor to hire one and the Florida court had denied his request that one be appointed for him. By extraordinary chance, Gideon's petition requesting review, handwritten and misspelled on prison stationery, came to the attention of the Chief Justice. Sensing that a basic constitutional issue was involved, Warren, who had championed the public defender concept in California, decided that the Supreme Court should take up Gideon's case.

The issue stemmed from a 1942 decision, *Betts* v. *Brady,* in which the High Court had upheld a Maryland verdict denying legal counsel to a farm worker who subsequently received an eight-year prison sentence. Writing for the majority, Justice Owen J. Roberts had held that "appointment of a counsel is not a fundamental right, essential to a fair trial." But a minority consisting of Black, Douglas and Murphy had dissented bitterly, pointing out that the Sixth Amendment specifically said: "In all criminal prosecutions the accused shall . . . have the assistance of counsel for his defense."

Warren was now determined to set constitutional matters straight. He not only urged his brethren to grant *certiorari* and hear the Gideon case, but set in motion a search to find a first-rate attorney who would volunteer to try it. The lawyer who accepted the Court's invitation and who eventually prevailed for Gideon was Abe Fortas, later himself to become a Supreme Court Justice.

The Court's unanimous decision, appropriately assigned to the eager Justice Black, overturned Gideon's conviction on grounds that vindicated the Black–Douglas dissent back in 1942. There was no question of attempting to determine Gideon's guilt or innocence. Instead, the Court ruled that the procedures adopted by the lower court had been so defective as to make a determination of guilt impossible. Thus, the happy Gideon soon afterward could be photographed shooting billiards in the same poolroom he had once been accused of breaking into. Guilty or innocent, he had unwittingly become the vehicle for the reassertion of a fundamental American right—that every person is entitled to counsel in a criminal proceeding.

Since then, *Gideon* v. *Wainwright* has been called one of the Warren Court's best decisions, a case perfectly exemplifying Earl

Warren's approach to justice. As California Congressman James C. Corman aptly put it, "The case offended his basic sense of fairness. It was shocking to him that there should be one law for the rich and another for the poor." And, indeed, in later years Warren derived considerable satisfaction from *Gideon,* although he always spoke of it with characteristic matter-of-factness: "It interpreted the Constitution to say exactly what it said."

Although the *Gideon* decision was generally well received throughout the nation, it did nothing to assuage the fury of Warren's multiplying enemies. The racial tensions exposed—though hardly *created,* as Warren-haters charged—by *Brown* continued to fulminate in a pattern of rising violence. There had been a flurry of ghetto riots during the summer, ominous precursors of the coming explosions that would occur in Watts, Newark, Detroit and elsewhere; and the University of Mississippi, by illegally attempting to prevent the enrollment of a black student named James Meredith, had compelled the President in September to send Federal troops to Mississippi to protect Meredith's rights.

Except for the Mississippi case, Kennedy's promised support of the Court's desegregation ruling thus far had been confined largely to words and gestures (such as making a point of personally attending the opening session of the new Court term on October 2). This was not due to his lack of commitment. Actually, the President had been so beset with Cold War crises during the first two years of his administration that he could devote little time to grappling with the civil rights crisis at home. As one disappointed civil rights activist put it, "I wish the President would take the 'r' out of 'Cuber' and put it back into 'vigah.' "

But now at last the civil rights issue had begun to engage the President's full attention. The marching, picketing and public demonstrations of blacks and Freedom Riders in both the North and South during the past two years were now reaching a crescendo. In April, sparked by Dr. Martin Luther King, Jr., blacks in Birmingham marched peacefully for forty days; over 2,500 of them, King included, were arrested. And already plans were afoot for the biggest demonstration of all, a march on Washington, to the Lincoln Memorial, to be led by King and scheduled for August.

Meantime, in June, another crisis erupted when Alabama Governor George Wallace defied the Federal government by refusing to permit the admission of three black students to the University of Alabama. Once again the President was obliged to use force. He quickly federalized the Alabama National Guard both to prevent violence and to keep the guard out of Wallace's control.

That evening, June 11, as Warren sat glued to his television set, Kennedy informed the nation that comprehensive new civil rights legislation was now the nation's highest priority. A week later he sent to the Congress the toughest, most far-reaching civil rights bill since the Civil War. He asked for new laws to ensure equal access to the services and facilities of hotels, restaurants and other public establishments "engaged in interstate commerce"; to empower the attorney general to initiate school segregation suits; to end discrimination in all jobs financed by Federal funds; and to create a Community Relations Agency to mediate race-related disputes. Now the President had more than fulfilled his promise to Warren. Three months earlier on Warren's seventy-second birthday, the President had written him: "Although it is not possible for all of us to be your clerks, in a very real sense we are all your students."

Warren, meanwhile, had written the majority opinion in a May 1963 case which had overturned the convictions of civil rights demonstrators and had concurred in earlier kindred rulings upholding peaceful protest and opposing exclusion of blacks from private restaurants located on state-owned property.

While Congress agonized over the President's civil rights package, the Chief Justice's attention was temporarily switched elsewhere. On September 27, ground was broken for the Earl Warren Legal Center, a new wing of Boalt Hall, at the University of California School of Law in Berkeley. The pleased 1914 alumnus turned the first spadeful of earth. Seven fellow Justices of the U.S. Supreme Court looked on, as did all members of the Supreme Court of California.

Occupying 11,300 square feet on several floors, the Warren wing was planned to house new classrooms; a library; academic office facilities; a 500-seat auditorium; two conference rooms; a display room and a dozen research offices. The $2 million cost had been met almost equally by state appropriations and private contributions. The biggest single gift, mostly for the adjoining dormitory, was $500,000 from Countess Folke Bernadotte; widow of the United Nations negotiator killed in 1948 in Palestine, and her brother, Hiram Edward Manville, Jr., of Reno, in memory of their late father.

That same week, the State Bar of California, then holding its annual convention in San Francisco, chose the tenth anniversary of Warren's appointment as Chief Justice to honor him. Inevitably, pickets outside the building carried the now-familiar "Impeach Earl Warren" signs and others distributed new hate-Warren literature. Nevertheless, the guest of honor retained his good-natured dignity. To do otherwise, he felt, would have demeaned the Supreme Court. "How good it is to be back home—right where I started from," he opened his address.

Among the congratulations was the following September 23 letter:

> *Dear Mr. Chief Justice:*
>
> *I hope that you will permit me to make this brief out-of-court intrusion into the ceremonies which are being held this week by your brethren of the Court and by the Bar in recognition of the full decade you have served as Chief Justice.*
>
> *You have presided over the work of the Supreme Court during ten years of extraordinary difficulty and accomplishment. There have been few decades in our history when the Court calendar has been crowded with so many issues of historic significance. As Chief Justice, you have borne your duties and responsibilities with unusual integrity, fairness, good humor, and courage. At all times your sense of judicial obligation has been unimpaired by criticism or personal attack. During my time as President, I have found our association to be particularly satisfying, and I am personally delighted that during this week you will receive not only the acclaim of Californians, but also the respect and affection of all Americans whose common destiny you have so faithfully helped to shape throughout your public career.*
>
> *Sincerely,*
>
> *(Signed) John F. Kennedy*

On Wednesday, November 20, 1963, the annual White House reception for the Supreme Court was scheduled. That day also happened to be the thirty-eighth birthday of Attorney General Robert Kennedy. Late that afternoon, his Department of Justice staff threw him a surprise birthday party before Bobby and his wife, Ethel, were driven to the White House reception.

Jacqueline Kennedy did not plan to attend. She was secluded

in Bobby and Ethel's Hickory Hill, Virginia, estate, convalescing from the death of her prematurely born son, Patrick Bouvier Kennedy, in August.

Mrs. Earl Warren had agreed to substitute as President Kennedy's hostess for the nine Justices and their wives, and the two retired Supreme Court members. But Jackie Kennedy suddenly changed her mind and decided to put in a brief appearance.

Before the formal downstairs reception in the East Room, which would be attended by more than five hundred persons, including lower Federal court judges, Department of Justice and White House officials, the Supreme Court Justices and their wives were entertained privately in the second-floor living quarters. The President sat in a rocker holding a daiquiri and amiably exchanging small talk with the Justices and their wives.

The twenty-four-year-old bride of Justice Douglas, Joan, a 1962 graduate of Allegheny College, obviously ill at ease, strolled over to chat with the President. So did Mrs. Potter (Mary Ann) Stewart, who likewise had never met the President and very much wanted to. The Chief Executive was his usual gallant self, especially with the ladies, but his mind, according to his sensitive sister-in-law Ethel, seemed elsewhere.

Very possibly he was thinking about the trip he was scheduled to take to Dallas thirty-six hours hence. He was going there in a dutiful attempt to heal the bitter Democratic breach in the Lone Star State between partisans of conservative Governor John B. Connally and liberal Senator Ralph Yarborough—with Vice President Lyndon B. Johnson in the middle.

Chief Justice Warren, sitting comfortably on a sofa and starting his second martini, well knew the rough-and-tumble of state political feuds. He called over jovially, "Watch out for those wild Texans, Mr. President. They're a rough bunch." The President smiled.

The informal gathering ended when three Army, Navy and Marine aides appeared. The American flag and blue-and-gold presidential banner were carried to the stairway. The President rose from his rocker and moved to the head of the stairway. Behind him stood the Chief Justice and Mrs. Warren. Justice and Mrs. Goldberg were directed to their positions at the end of the judicial line, followed by Attorney General and Mrs. Robert Kennedy. The President's wife returned to her bedroom. The band thumped "Hail to the Chief" as the judicial procession marched into the East Room for the formal reception, followed by spirited dancing on the waxed floor.

A day and a half later, on Friday, November 22, at 1:34 P.M., Chief Justice Warren was presiding over the weekly Conference in the sacrosanct oak-paneled room. The relaxed Justices had recently returned from lunch one flight above and were seated in their respective name-plated high leather chairs. They were beginning to discuss a series of reapportionment cases, including *Reynolds* v. *Sims,* for which the Chief soon would assign himself to write the majority opinion.

Suddenly there was an exceptionally sharp knock on the door. It indicated an unusually urgent message. Instead of the customary page, a troubled Mrs. Margaret McHugh, the Chief Justice's private secretary, handed a note to the junior Justice nearest to the door, Goldberg. He quickly transmitted it to the Chief Justice without reading it.

"He read to us the simple tragic statement that President Kennedy had been shot," recollects Goldberg. "He got very pale and his voice broke. It was the first time that I ever heard his voice break. Without a moment's hesitation, he adjourned the Conference. And then the Chief and all of us crowded around a transistor radio and later a television set. We did not know how fatal the shot was. We remained until hearing the tragic news."

Years later, the Chief Justice, whose own father had been senselessly murdered a quarter century earlier, reflected, "This was the saddest day, the saddest week and saddest year of my life."

At 2 P.M. (EST), the President of the United States was pronounced dead. At 2:15 P.M., Lee Harvey Oswald killed Dallas police officer J. B. Tippit. At 3:38 P.M., Lyndon B. Johnson was sworn in as thirty-sixth President of the United States. At 6:05 P.M., the silver-blue and white Air Force One plane landed at Andrews Field, returning President Kennedy's body to Washington.

Together with other key invited government officials, Warren nervously waited at Andrews Air Force Base outside Washington. After observing the newly widowed Mrs. Kennedy descend the ramp shortly after 6 P.M., her eyes reflecting horror and pain, he later said to his own wife, "There was that brave girl, with her husband's blood still on her, and there was nothing that I could do—*nothing.*"

On the rain-drenched next morning (Saturday), the weary

Chief Justice and his wife were invited to attend the private 10:30 A.M. White House Mass for the family and friends in the East Room. At 2 P.M. the other eight members of the Supreme Court, led by senior Justice Black, arrived to observe President Kennedy's casket in the East Room, the scene, only two and a half days earlier, of the festive Supreme Court reception. Along with millions, the Chief Justice was numbed by this unbelievable event. His mind drifted back to his swearing in less than three years earlier of this youthful President, hatless in the January frost, whose head now had been shattered by an assassin's bullet.

Shortly after 9:00 P.M. that Saturday evening, the Chief Justice was jolted from his dazed state by a surprising telephone call from the bereaved widow of the fallen President. Would he speak briefly at the Capitol rotunda the following day when her husband lay in state? In an almost inarticulate reply, the Chief Justice said that he would. Later he learned that the two other speakers, selected after considerable White House, congressional and family pondering over protocol, were Senate Majority Leader Mike Mansfield of Montana and House Speaker John W. McCormack of Massachusetts.

The Chief Justice immediately marched into his study, where he spent several hours trying to write a draft of his proposed eulogy. At midnight, he wearily stopped. Not liking what he had written, he decided to get up early the next morning and start anew. On Sunday, after a listless 6:30 A.M. breakfast, he resumed his writing. He remained riveted to his desk all morning, painfully trying to compose his tribute. At 12:25 P.M., as he was polishing his final draft, which had been typed by his wife, his daughter Dorothy rushed in. "Oswald was just shot!" she cried.

The Chief Justice irritably put down his pencil and wiped his glasses. This was no time for games.

"Don't pay any attention to all those wild rumors, dear."

"But, Daddy, I saw it on television!"

The Chief Justice soon did, too.

The Warrens arrived at the Capitol shortly before the horse-drawn caisson bearing the flag-draped casket of the slain President on a black catafalque reached there at 1:50 P.M. A black riderless horse in reversed boots—symbol of the fallen leader—walked behind the caisson, which was drawn by six white horses. "Hail to the Chief" and a Navy hymn were quietly sounded.

At 2:02 P.M., Senator Mansfield began to speak, eloquently

and affectionately, directing his tribute to the brave widow. Speaker McCormack's somewhat colorless talk followed. Then Warren's turn came.

For a man accustomed to concealing his innermost feelings in public, the Chief Justice's brief words in the fifteen-minute ceremony were an unusually emotional panegyric. To him, the Kennedy assassination was a traumatic personal, as well as national, tragedy. Few events during his seventy-two years had affected him so profoundly. "It was like losing one of my own sons," he later remarked. Justice Douglas confirmed this in May 1977: "The Chief's attitude toward JFK could be called fatherly. He thought the world of the man and spoke very frequently of him in affectionate terms." As Warren said, in part:

> *What moved some misguided wretch to do this horrible deed may never be known to us, but we do know that such acts are commonly stimulated by forces of hatred and malevolence such as today are eating their way into the bloodstream of American life. What a price we pay for this fanaticism!*
>
> *It has been said that the only thing we learn from history is that we do not learn. But surely we can learn if we have the will to do so. Surely there is a lesson to be learned from this tragic event.*
>
> *If we really love this country; if we truly love justice and mercy; if we fervently want to make this Nation better for those who are to follow us, we can at least abjure the hatred that consumes people, the false accusations that divide us and the bitterness that begets violence. Is it too much to hope that the martyrdom of our beloved President might even soften the hearts of those who would themselves recoil from assassination, but who do not shrink from spreading the venom which kindles thoughts of it in others?*

Three minutes after Warren's plea for a renunciation of hatred, the networks announced that Oswald was dead. The next day, shortly before the funeral services for the martyred President at St. Matthew's Cathedral, Warren received an anonymous telephone call warning that his own life was in jeopardy if he dared to walk behind the President's casket in the mourning procession.

Far from receding, the forces of hatred and malevolence about which the Chief Justice had warned were everywhere gathering strength. For American society as a whole, the remaining years of the 1960s would be remembered as being among the most rancorous and violent in recent history. And Earl Warren would continue to be one of the epicenters about which these forces would swirl.

Chapter Seven

The Johnson Years: 1963–1969

Lyndon Baines Johnson had automatically become the thirty-sixth President at 2 P.M. (E.S.T.) when John F. Kennedy died, according to some constitutional scholars and to former Presidents Truman and Eisenhower. Chief Justice Warren, however, when consulted, insisted that the administering of an oath of office was a legal necessity. Thus, at 2:40 P.M., Judge Sarah T. Hughes of the U.S. District Court in Dallas, formally swore in the new Chief Executive.

Such grave insistence upon observing traditional formalities contrasted with the nightmarish mood of a nation disoriented by shock and grief. No one seemed willing to agree with Dallas Police Chief Jesse Curry's reported remark that since Oswald was now dead, the Kennedy murder was "a closed case." Although Camelot-on-the-Potomac had ended, the nation and world were convulsed with suspicions and doubts. Conspiracy theories burgeoned. Nearly every social, political and ethnic group from left to right began to speculate about the possible guilt of someone else: white segregationists, black extremists, American communists, Texas millionaires, the Russians, the Cubans, the CIA, the FBI and so on. Even President Johnson was suspected of being implicated in some way.

The requirements of both stable government and exploitative politics converged in a demand that the assassination be thoroughly and publicly investigated, lest the Eternal Flame in Arlington smother the survivors. President Johnson moved first. On November 25, he asked his friend Texas Attorney General Waggoner Carr to summon an open all-Texas Court of Inquiry, with Leon Jaworski as chief counsel, to investigate the murder. Perhaps LBJ hoped that by this preemptive maneuver he might both contain speculation and influence the course of the investigation. If so, he was being naïve.

Congress was determined not to be left out of the act. On November 26, Senator Everett Dirksen, the Republican leader, announced that a Senate investigation of the murder would be conducted by a special committee headed by James O. Eastland, chairman of the Judiciary Committee. Not to be upstaged, the following day the House of Representatives swiftly attempted to create a similar committee of its own. Now President Johnson, sensing that his Texas Court of Inquiry gambit—with a proposed open hearing before a justice of the peace—and the contemplated competing congressional probes would inevitably fail, announced that he had directed the FBI to prepare a detailed public report that would give "the facts and all the facts." One of the jurisdictional difficulties was that murder—even of a President—then was a state, not a Federal, crime.

Attorney General Kennedy, understandably, was both too distraught and too hostile to his slain brother's successor to be consulted about any of this investigatory politicking. But the second and third officials in the U.S. Department of Justice—Deputy Attorney General Nicholas D. Katzenbach and Solicitor General Archibald Cox (of later Watergate fame)—were horrified by these proposed probes. So was the President's bosom friend, attorney Abe Fortas, who conferred with Katzenbach and Cox. All three agreed that any all-Texas investigation might result in a whitewash and congressional inquiries might very well become political yoyos before the November 1964 election. Any investigation, they agreed, must be bipartisan and composed of eminent public figures of unimpeachable integrity.

At first, beleaguered President Johnson still clung to the idea of appointing a commission composed entirely of Texans. However, Fortas, together with Yale law professor Eugene Rostow, Secretary of State Dean Rusk and columnist Joseph Alsop, convinced him that any all-Texas inquiry would be too parochial and would jeopardize public acceptance of its findings. Fortas conceived a plan for an extraordinary blue-ribbon national commission which President Johnson finally accepted.

On Friday morning, November 29, Katzenbach and Cox visited Chief Justice Warren in his chambers. They started to explain the President's intention to create such a commission. The nation's highest judge interrupted them: "If you are asking my permission to have an Associate Justice of this Court serve, I have no intention of giving my approval."

The Department of Justice visitors replied that they had come to ask the Chief Justice himself to serve as chairman of this presidential commission. "Then *a fortiori* I won't serve!" exclaimed the head of the top tribunal. "Please tell the President that I am sorry but I cannot properly undertake this assignment."

Warren protested that he opposed any use of sitting Supreme Court Justices by the Executive branch, if the independence of the judiciary was to be preserved. "Justice Roberts was criticized, you remember, for going to Hawaii to investigate the Pearl Harbor attack," Warren reminded his visitors. "And many were critical of Justice Jackson for leaving the Court for a year to go to Nuremberg to be chief prosecutor at the Nazi trials." The Chief Justice went on to lecture his amazed callers on the unfortunate political participation of five Supreme Court Justices who sat on the fifteen-man President's Commission named to settle the 1876 Hayes-Tilden presidential election.

Warren then suggested several individuals—including two retired Supreme Court Justices—whom he believed could effectively chair any Kennedy Assassination Commission. "I let it go at that," he recollected afterward. But hard-driving Lyndon Johnson did not.

"About two hours later that afternoon," remembered Warren, "I received a telephone call asking if I could come to see President Johnson right away about an urgent matter."

En route to the White House, the Chief Justice had determined to reaffirm his irrevocable No to the President's request. But upon arrival, Warren was given the famed "Johnson treatment" privately in the Oval Office.

The President spoke gravely of the desperate need to restore public confidence. He hinted darkly at the possibility of dangerous international repercussions, including a possible nuclear war killing sixty million Americans in the first strike. He invoked Warren's sense of duty and patriotism. He told the Chief Justice (undoubtedly stretching the truth) that he had already secured promises from Senators Russell and Cooper and from Representatives Ford and Boggs, as well as from Allen Dulles of the CIA and John McCloy, former U.S. High Commissioner in Germany, to serve on the commission—but only if Warren would be its chairman. He alternately wheedled, bullied and promised. By the end of the interview, he had succeeded in making Warren feel that to refuse the President would be a betrayal of a public trust. As a man-to-man persuader, Lyndon Johnson had no equal. His trump card was: "Mr. Chief Justice, you were a soldier in World War I. There's nothing you then did that compares with what you can now do for your country. As your Commander-in-Chief, I am ordering you back into service." Tears filled Warren's blue eyes as he reluctantly accepted the assignment. With Warren in the bag, the artful President now had an easier time convincing the other men he had mentioned that they too should serve on this commission.

"I don't believe I ever considered anyone but Chief Justice Warren for chairman," Johnson later wrote in his memoirs. "I was not an intimate of the Chief Justice. We had never spent ten minutes alone together, but to me he was the personification of justice and fairness in this country."

Late that same afternoon, November 29, 1963, President Johnson signed Executive Order 11130 creating the seven-man President's Commission on the Assassination of President Kennedy (which, two weeks later, Congress and the President signed into Public Law 88–202). The Order said:

> *The purposes of the Commission are to examine the evidence developed by the Federal Bureau of Investigation and any additional evidence that may hereafter come to light or be uncovered by Federal or state authorities; to make such further investigation as the Commission finds desirable; to evaluate all the facts and circumstances surrounding such assassination, including the subsequent violent death of the man charged with the assassination, and to report to me its findings and conclusions.*
>
> *The Commission is empowered to prescribe its own procedures and to employ such assistants as it deems necessary. Necessary expenses of the Commission may be paid from the "Emergency Fund for the President." All Executive departments and agencies*

are directed to furnish the Commission with such facilities, services and cooperation as it may request from time to time.

The same day, a six-paragraph White House press release concluded: "The President is instructing the Special Commission to satisfy itself that the truth is known as far as can be discovered, and to report its findings and conclusions to him, to the American people and to the world."

Warren's fellow Justices frowned on his accepting this extra assignment. "Hugo Black and I expressed to Warren our misgivings," Justice Douglas wrote me in 1977. The 1964 Court was deep in one of its busiest terms. Its docket was bulging with important cases. But the Chief then answered his protesting brethren, "I just couldn't turn the President down."

Scores of Americans wrote to President Johnson protesting the Warren appointment. Few praised it. The criticism came mainly from small towns and reflected a disapproval of "the warren court" (often spelled sarcastically in lowercase). Typical examples:

Earl Warren is a defender of Communists and should be dropped from the Commission before its findings are reported to you . . . In his Capitol Rotunda speech about President Kennedy, he made no reference to a Divine Being. This proves that Warren is an atheist . . . He is a One Worlder and has prejudged the case saying that right-wing extremists did it when everyone knows a Marxist committed the crime . . . Chief Justice Warren has so much power it makes me feel panicky . . . This will be a coverup job of some kind . . . Why hasn't the investigation been allowed to be handled by the able legal system of the State of Texas?

Presidential Assistant Lawrence F. O'Brien sent all of these Warren-haters this form reply:

Your recent letter has been received by the President and read with appreciation. He has directed me to thank you for giving him the benefit of your views and comments regarding Chief Justice Earl Warren.

The White House received almost no complaints about any of Chairman Warren's six fellow commissioners.

All were deemed men of lofty rectitude, integrity and sound judgment. They were busy, highly regarded, prestigious persons of diverse backgrounds, abilities and philosophies. Four were Republicans. Two were Southerners. One came from a border state.

Conservative bachelor Democratic Senator Richard B. Russell of Georgia had served continuously in the Senate for thirty years. At sixty-six, he was the influential chairman of the Armed Services Committee. An articulate opponent of the desegration decisions, Russell had been sought by President Johnson to serve with Warren on the commission as a sign of national unity.

Liberal Republican Senator John Sherman Cooper, sixty-two, later Ambassador to India and Nepal and a U. S. delegate to the United Nations, had been a county and state circuit court judge in his native Kentucky.

Middle-road Democratic Representative Hale Boggs, fifty, of New Orleans, the Majority Whip, was first elected to Congress in 1940 at twenty-six. After a World War II stint, he was returned to the House of Representatives, where he had served ever since.

Conservative Republican Representative Gerald R. Ford of Grand Rapids, fifty, was the new chairman of the House GOP Conference. He had been cited by the American Political Science Association as one of the House's most effective members. Earlier, in 1950, the U. S. Junior Chamber of Commerce had named him one of the ten outstanding young men in the United States.

Allen W. Dulles, seventy, the conservative Republican brother of late Secretary of State John Foster Dulles, had been replaced in 1961 as director of the Central Intelligence Agency when President Kennedy entered office. During World War II Dulles had worked for the Office of Strategic Services (OSS), and had recently published his book, *The Craft of Intelligence*.

Republican lawyer John J. McCloy, sixty-eight, had been High Commissioner for Germany (1949–52), president of the World Bank (1947–49), Assistant Secretary of War (1941–45) and chairman of New York's Rockefeller-dominated Chase Manhattan Bank. During the Cuban missile crisis, he had headed a presidential team which had negotiated with the Soviet Union.

When this elite group first convened on December 5, its initial task was to select a General Counsel. Chairman Warren's first choice was Warren Olney III, his longtime California friend, but Olney was not acceptable to all of the commissioners. Warren then suggested

J. Lee Rankin, a fifty-six-year-old former U.S. assistant attorney general and solicitor general. A Nebraska Republican, he had effectively represented the Eisenhower Administration before the Warren Court where he had successfully argued the *Brown* and Little Rock school desegregation cases. Rankin was unanimously accepted by the commissioners and given a free hand in hiring as assistant counsel fourteen highly independent attorneys. Recruited nation-wide—mostly outside of government—they were paid $100 a day on a consulting arrangement. Twelve other younger legal staff members were engaged on a $75 daily basis. All worked indefatigably, on different aspects of one assassination, except for one figurehead assistant counsel, a former police official, who was never discharged because of Chairman Warren's concern over adverse publicity.

One of the hardest-working assistant counsel was Norman Redlich, a brilliant, unassuming, thirty-eight-year-old New York law professor at New York University, now its dean. Redlich, an authority on civil liberties, capital punishment and taxes, wrote or edited major portions of the final Warren Report, including what critics deem its most controversial sections.

Another little-publicized but valuable staff member was Howard P. Willens, then on loan from the Justice Department criminal division, now a Washington attorney.

One young lawyer, who whimsically characterized himself as a "Goldwater Republican," turned up at an early staff meeting sporting a long beard. The clean-shaven Warren grumbled to Rankin, "Tell him to shave it off. We don't want the public to think we've hired hippies or beatniks." Infuriated, the bewhiskered barrister wrote a long protesting letter to the chairman. Conceding that the recalcitrant attorney indeed had a constitutional right to his hirsuteness, Warren then pleaded with Rankin: "Lee, please tell him that I would personally appreciate his shaving it off just for the duration of our investigation." Mollified at having persuaded the nation's Chief Judge to reverse an autocratic ruling, the rebel appeared at the next staff meeting minus his beard.

At a closed session of the seven "blue ribbon" commissioners, Gerald Ford cited the FBI file on two staff lawyers and urged that they be immediately discharged. But the civil libertarian Chairman refused to do so, passionately defending the two accused staff members. Warren, in fact, excoriated the FBI "raw material" smears of individuals generally and gave a future President of the United

States an elementary lesson on the Bill of Rights. "Earl Warren was never more glorious," recollects an insider.

The lawyers and entire commission secured two floors of space in the new Veterans of Foreign Wars building at 200 Maryland Avenue N. E., across from the Supreme Court. The commission was given an unlimited budget and access to all government investigatory assistance. A scale model of the assassination site, together with film projectors and other equipment, was installed in the building's basement by the FBI.

Wearing two administrative hats, Warren divided his time between the commission and the Supreme Court. He tried to schedule commission hearings when the Court was not sitting. Formerly, each morning he had enjoyed strolling down Connecticut Avenue toward the Court until his driver picked him up. But after assuming the commission chairmanship, he was driven in his limousine because of the time pinch. Rising at 6:30 A.M., he tried to work for an hour before breakfast. At 9 A.M., he often conducted commission business before strolling across to the Marble Palace to open Supreme Court hearings at 10 A.M. When his Court duties were completed, he generally returned to commission headquarters. There he presided over sessions or examined documents, testimony, staff suggestions and findings, many times until late in the evening.

"The Chief would sometimes work until long past midnight and yet be the first to show up the next morning," recalls Rankin. "I began to worry about his health in trying to do two full-time jobs at once."

The commission quickly became known as the Warren Commission even though the Chairman always called it "The Kennedy Commission." Insiders, however, invariably observed, "Warren *is* the commission." Every important administrative problem—and there were many—came to his attention. He had to make countless decisions, some of which proved wrong. He was faced with resolving many of the confusions and contradictions in the FBI, Secret Service, Dallas Police and other reports, which he could not always do. To the former Alameda County district attorney, the commission was a national—instead of county— Grand Jury. Any conventional trial was impossible because the main suspect, Lee Harvey Oswald, was dead. If Oswald killed Kennedy, the full answer to why he had done so died with him, erased by Ruby's avenging bullet. However, Mark Lane, then a little-known

New York attorney, telegraphed the commission that he wished to be appointed Oswald's "defense counsel." Warren persuaded fellow commissioners to deny this request because they were an "impartial fact-finding body"—not a trial court restricted by court procedure and rigid rules of evidence. No adversary proceeding was involved. Since there was no prosecuting attorney, no defense counsel was needed.

Warren invited the American Bar Association president, Walter E. Craig, now Chief Judge of the U. S. District Court in Phoenix, Arizona, to attend the hearings or to send representatives, to ensure that the commission adhered to "the basic principles of American justice."

Judge Craig observed, in a March 1976 letter to me:

> *While I did not always agree with Mr. Warren's conclusions on any given topic, I, nevertheless, respected them because of his sincerity and beliefs. During the years I knew him I can think of no instance where any decision he made was based on anything but his sincere belief in that conclusion, nor do I know of any instance where selfishness was in any way the motive.*
>
> *For a person to have lived in public life as long as Earl Warren, one would suspect that he would develop a pretty thick skin. Contrary to such a belief, in my opinion, Mr. Warren was probably the most sensitive man I have ever met. He was sensitive to criticism; he was sensitive to courtesy, and he was sensitive to lack of courtesy. His sensitivity was not one of diminution of personal pride, but rather a very sincere feeling. Possibly this sensitivity to the words and actions of other people was one of the many attributes which made Earl Warren a man apart from others.*

Although invited, the American Civil Liberties Union did not send a representative to the hearings. Its officers did confer with commission staff members over witnesses' constitutional rights which, of course, deeply concerned the Chief Justice as well.

But Warren convinced his fellow commissioners that the hearings should be private executive sessions closed to the public. Hearsay testimony, if publicized, he reasoned, could harm not only "innocent parties" but jeopardize Ruby's constitutional right to a fair trial, which had been postponed until February 3, 1964. Witnesses, however, could speak to the news media *after* the hearings, if they wished, Warren ruled.

Some early staff conflicts, too, had to be mediated by Chairman Warren. The assistant counsels were articulate maverick primarily trial attorneys, who heatedly argued on which witnesses to call, how to interrogate them and which areas to pursue.

Originally, Warren had hoped that the commission could complete its investigation and submit its report within three months, as President Johnson desired, so that the assassination would not become a November 1964 election issue. Warren soon realized, however, that even a June 1 deadline was impossible.

"We all want to do this job fast," the chairman remarked in his greeting to the first staff meeting in mid-January 1964, "but it is more important that we do it *right!*"

Rankin added, "Truth is our only client."

Leon D. Hubert, Jr., then an assistant counsel, and now a Tulane University law professor, remembers: "The Chief asked general questions or invited general inquiries and gave the impression—and I think it was real—of intense earnestness. He was keenly interested in what he was doing and showed it. He exuded a very warm human kindness but he was not overawing."

"The Chief was tough-minded but very fair-minded with all of us," Redlich recalls. "He could grasp, organize and assess complex facts quickly. That was part of his genius."

Instead of hiring or training its own investigators, the commission decided to forego this time-consuming and expensive task. It chose to utilize the facilities of those government agencies already involved—mainly the FBI and Secret Service, as well as the CIA, State Department, Justice's Immigration and Naturalization Service and Treasury Department. However, Commissioner McCloy warned: "There is a potential culpability here on the part of the Secret Service and the FBI, and their reports, after all, human nature being what it is, may have some self-serving aspects in them." Warren urged that the FBI and Secret Service findings be double-checked with independent outside experts in such fields as ballistics, fingerprinting and handwriting—which commission lawyers did.

After the commission began its work, the Senate, House and State of Texas dropped their proposed investigations. Texas' Leon Jaworski, though, was invited to attend all of the commission's sessions. "Once the Chief Justice assumed the assignment," recalls

Jaworski, "he gave it learned and dedicated leadership. I was very much impressed with the thoroughness of the investigation. He presided over every session except when an irreconcilable conflict occurred with his duties as Chief Justice."

Three other Texans—Attorney General Carr, Dallas County District Attorney Henry Wade and his first assistant, Bill Alexander—flew to Washington at Warren's request on December 16, 1963. As Carr recalls the conversation, the chairman's first question was to Alexander, a tough, plain-talking prosecutor.

"Can you tell us what you know about the actions of Mr. Jack Ruby the night after the assassination," asked Warren.

"Well, Mr. Chief Justice, my investigation has shown that Mr. Ruby went to his apartment in Oak Cliff in an emotional state. He paced back and forth in his living room, shortly getting back in his automobile and heading downtown to his strip joint called the Carousel. On the way, he noticed a billboard. He stopped his car, got out, walked over to the billboard and looked at it, and then went back to his car to get a camera. He returned to the billboard and took several pictures of it. Thereafter, he got back into his car and went to his strip joint."

"You forgot, Mr. Alexander, to tell us what was on the billboard which was so important to Mr. Ruby," pressed Warren.

Alexander, slumped down, embarrassed. Finally, he found his tongue.

"Well, Mr. Chief Justice, the billboard said: 'Impeach Earl Warren.' "

The silence in the room became thick. Alexander drew himself up in his seat and in his smoothest courtroom manner drawled, "But, Mr. Chief Justice, it was just a little bitty old sign. It didn't amount to nothing."

"All of us, including Mr. Warren, roared with laughter," recalls Carr. The tension melted.

"Well, Mr. Alexander," said the chairman with a broad smile, "those signs always look a lot bigger to *me* than to anyone else! "

The following month, a bombshell struck the commission. The sound and smoke from it still reverberate fifteen years later.

On Wednesday morning, January 22, 1964, the commission was informed of a rumor that Lee Harvey Oswald had been a $200-a-month FBI undercover agent from September 1962 until the assassination. This information was telephoned to the flabbergasted Rankin by Texas Attorney General Carr, who revealed that he had heard it from Dallas District Attorney Henry Wade, a former FBI agent.

Chairman Warren, whose mind could hardly have been on Supreme Court matters the rest of that day, immediately called an emergency meeting of the seven commissioners at 5:30 P.M. that day. Congressman Ford was summoned out of a House Military Affairs Subcommittee meeting to attend. John J. McCloy flew down from New York. "I can never recall having attended a meeting more tense and hushed," Ford later said.

The shocked commissioners agreed to request both Carr and Wade to fly from Texas to Washington to confer with Warren and Rankin immediately. At 7:30 P.M., the meeting broke up with all the commissioners and Rankin determined not to discuss this rumor even with their wives. Warren skipped dinner. An hour later, he was the long-scheduled speaker at the dedication of the Smithsonian Institution's National Museum of History and Technology.

A day and a half later, on Friday morning, January 24, Carr and Wade arrived in Washington to confer secretly with Warren and Rankin. Although neither Texan could document the rumor's original source, both offered "information" about Oswald's alleged employment as FBI agent S. 179. They reported having heard this indirectly from two Texas newsmen and a Dallas assistant district attorney.

On Monday, January 27, a closed-door executive session was held. The seven commissioners, Rankin and a stenographer were present. The transcript was kept top secret and not declassified by the National Archives (under the Freedom of Information Act) until nearly nine years later on June 12, 1974—less than a month before Earl Warren died.

"We have a dirty rumor that is very bad for the commission," began Rankin, "very damaging to the agencies that are involved and must be wiped out insofar as possible to do so by this commission."

Warren suggested going to the rumor's sources to see if there was any substance to the claim.

A spirited discussion ensued. Should FBI Director Hoover be asked directly about the truth or falsity of the rumor, or should it be investigated independently of him?

Former CIA Director Dulles offered some cynical seasoned counsel: If Oswald really *was* an FBI employee, the person who recruited him certainly wouldn't tell.

"Wouldn't tell it under oath?" asked Warren incredulously.

"No, I wouldn't think that he would tell it even under oath," repeated Dulles.

"Why?"

"Agencies do employ undercover men who are terribly bad characters," explained Dulles.

Congressman Boggs urged that Hoover be given an opportunity to clear the FBI *before* the commission began to investigate.

"We must go at this thing from *both* ends," interjected Warren, "from the end of the rumormongers and from the end of the FBI. If we come to a cul-de-sac—well, there we are. But we can report on it."

Rankin recommended that the commission inform Hoover of what they had heard and tell him that "We would like to go ahead and find out what we could about these—"

"Well, Lee," cut in Warren, "I wouldn't be in favor of going to *any* agency and saying, 'We would like to do this.' I think we ought to know what we are going to do and do it—and then take our chances one way or another. The fair thing to do would be to try to find out if this is fact or fiction."

Some pro-FBI commissioners, including Ford, voiced concern that the supersensitive Hoover might think the commission was investigating *him*.

"We *are* investigating him, that is true," said Warren. "I don't believe we should apologize or make it look that we are in any way reticent about making any investigation that comes to the commission."

After this exchange had been leaked back to the FBI director by Ford, it festered the mutual hostility between Warren and Hoover which had been sparked by the Chief Justice's earlier civil libertarian rulings.

On February 6, 1964, FBI Director Hoover submitted an affadavit to the Warren Commission flatly denying that Oswald had ever been a paid employee or informant of the FBI. Fourteen years later, the release of the 80,000-word FBI "raw file" on the assassination seemed to confirm that Oswald never had been an FBI agent or informer. The CIA made a similar denial, presumably after searching its records.

Later, when Assistant FBI Director Alan H. Belmont testified before the Warren Commission on May 6, he offered to leave the bureau's "entire" Oswald file with it.

"I am not going to look at it," ruled Chairman Warren.

Senator Russell asked to examine it.

"And *you* are not going to look at it either," added Warren before his amazed fellow commissioners and the staff. The chairman softened this decision, explaining, "Well, the same people who would demand that we see everything of this kind would also demand that *they* be entitled to see it. But if it is a security matter, we can't let them see it."

A week later, on May 14, Hoover personally testified before the commission. Again, he categorically denied that the unstable Oswald had ever had any FBI affiliation whatsoever, and insisted that the FBI had no reason to believe that this Marxist "loner" was capable of violence.

Warren has been widely criticized both for accepting the FBI and CIA denials at face value and for refusing even to look at the FBI's Oswald file. There is, however, no evidence that the old California prosecutor did the former, and considerable reason to doubt that the proffered file would have revealed anything substantive. It subsequently was disclosed in 1976 that the FBI *did* withhold, "lose" or destroy at least one document pertaining to Oswald's violent nature. Yet, in the prevailing 1964 climate of suspicion, Warren's somewhat high-handed treatment of the matter may legitimately be thought insensitive.

Warren also has been rebuked for not having questioned more forcefully the commission's first witness on February 3, Oswald's widow, Marina. Indeed, the commission seemed to have behaved toward the attractive twenty-two-year-old Russian-born woman with untoward solicitude—so much so that one observer quipped: "It was a performance of Snow White and the Seven Dwarfs." Redlich was moved to write an angry intra-office memorandum calling for further interrogation on the grounds that Marina had "lied to the Secret Service, FBI and this Commission repeatedly on matters of vital concern to the people of this country and the world."

But Warren, a father of three grown daughters himself, found Marina an appealing if confused young woman. Marina herself told me in 1978 that "like all really great persons, he made me feel *kak doma* (at home). The Chief Justice was not just a gentleman but a gentle

239

man." Warren maintained the same friendly relaxed attitude toward Ruth Hyde Paine, Marina's Quaker benefactress, who now recollects, "Rather than create an adversary atmosphere, he set the stage for a cooperative endeavor to help me get at all the relevant facts I could possibly recall." Apart from this, Warren had another reason for putting Marina at ease, which he later privately admitted. The chairman feared that Oswald's widow might have collapsed while testifying. If so, worldwide headlines would have resulted, perhaps with pictures showing Marina being transported to a hospital in an ambulance. Soviet propaganda then might have vilified the Warren Commission as a "fascist star chamber."

At the end of the second day of Marina's four-day testimony, the ordinarily circumspect Warren made a colossal blunder.

"Will all the commission's testimony and exhibits be made public?" reporters asked.

"Yes," responded Warren forthrightly, "there will come a time. But it might not be in your lifetime. I am not referring to anything especially, but there may be some things that will involve security."

The news media widely publicized the first two sentences but mostly omitted the final qualifying one. Critics were quick to cry "cover-up."

Mark Lane, the most vocal of the commission's critics in both the United States and Europe, had questioned its motives from the start. A shrewd, indefatigable lawyer-lecturer and onetime New York State assemblyman, Lane contended that the commission's actual purpose was to conceal the truth for patriotic reasons and that its members—whether consciously or otherwise—would therefore ignore any leads indicating unpleasant conspiratorial truths. Lane's adversaries called him obsessive, a sensationalist and profiteer who used faulty logic and manipulated evidence.

When Oswald's erratic mother, Marguerite, testified on February 10, Lane turned up before the hearing requesting to serve as her attorney even though she already had one present who said he would withdraw if Lane became a co-counsel.

"Mrs. Oswald, what is your wish?" inquired Chairman Warren.

"Well, Mr. Lane is just here for a few hours . . . He is catching a four o'clock plane out. . . ."

"Either he represents you or he does not."

"No, sir, he does not represent me."

"Then we will excuse Mr. Lane."

Lane protested, "Mr. Chief Justice . . ."

"Mr. Lane, now really, either you are here as the attorney for Mrs. Owsald or you are not entitled to be in this room—one of the two."

However, on March 4, 1964, Lane was invited as a private citizen to testify about his own investigations and theories. At the start, he requested that he "be able to secure a copy of the transcript of my testimony tomorrow," and that the hearing be "open to the public and to the press." A foxy twinkle crept into the eyes of the old California politician. He agreed that Lane had the same right "as any witness would have to request that." He adjourned the hearing, saying it would be reconvened in the auditorium downstairs in a few minutes. There, in the huge, virtually empty auditorium, witness Lane had his desired "public" hearing—the only one of the 552 commission witnesses who requested this publicity.

Lane testified that on the evening of November 14, 1963—eight days before the assassination—a two-hour meeting had been held in Ruby's Carousel Club attended by Ruby, Patrolman Tippit and Bernard Weissman, a carpet salesman who had placed an anti-Kennedy advertisement in a Dallas newspaper on the morning of November 22. Lane refused to name his "source" on grounds that he had not been given permission but said that he would try to obtain it. He never did so, despite recurrent requests by commission staff members.

Lane left for Europe saying that only from there would he be able "to inform the American people." The commission paid his return passage so that he could testify again on July 2, but once more he refused to name his "source." This prompted Warren to say: "Until you give us the corroboration that you say you have, we have every reason to doubt the truthfulness of what you have told us." British barrister A. L. Goodhart later wrote: "This must be the first time in history that a Chief Justice of the United States had deliberately accused a lawyer of telling an untruth . . . In England Mr. Lane would have been sent to prison if he had refused the commission's demand for an answer."

Warren himself in his memoirs bitingly commented:

One of the lecturers and writers who claimed to have knowledge of a conspiracy between Oswald, Ruby, the slain officer J.B. Tippit, and others, and said he could produce the names of people who could prove it, was twice called before the Commission and questioned about the matter, but refused to give us any information. The last time, in order to make certain that we had all the facts, we brought him back from Europe to testify, but again to no avail. Yet he continued to write and lecture on the subject to his financial benefit.

Nonetheless, if Lane was stronger on speculation than on hard evidence, he raised some awkward questions which persist to this day. It was not Lane, but what he stood for, that had to be dealt with. Probably the questions he raised were bound to have been raised by someone, sometime.

Chairman Warren displayed infinitely greater compassion on March 10 toward a more obscure witness—an 18-year-old Dallas young man named Arnold Rowland.

The youth testified that he had been awaiting the motorcade near the Book Depository Building. At least 15 minutes before it arrived, he glanced up and noticed a slender dark-haired white man holding a high-powered rifle with a telescope sight at the southwest corner of the sixth-floor window. He mentioned this to his wife, Barbara, who was looking elsewhere. But when the young couple looked up again, the man with the rifle was gone from their vision. Young Rowland believed that this must have been a Secret Service agent protecting the President.

"We had seen in the movies before where they have security men up in windows and places like that with rifles to watch the crowds," Rowland testified. "We brushed it aside as that at the time and thought nothing else about it until after the event happened." Ironically, a policeman was standing merely twelve feet away from them at the time.

"Why didn't you tell that policeman about this?" Rowland was asked.

The youth did not answer. Instead, he burst into uncontrollable tears. Chairman Warren called a recess.

"Don't you think I've asked myself *that* a million times?" Rowland cried convulsively. "Every time I go to sleep at night and wake up, I ask myself that question. I can't sleep afterwards! Just think: *I* could have saved President Kennedy's life and didn't! I feel guilty every time I think about it! I wish I was dead and President Kennedy was still alive!"

Overcome with remorse, the young man wept hysterically. A

pin-drop could have been heard in the hushed room between his heavy sobs. No one seemed to know what to say or do.

Then the seventy-three-year-old Warren, father of three sons himself, arose. He marched over and placed a comforting arm around the youth's shoulder.

"Mr. Rowland," Warren softly addressed him, "you *must* not feel this way. There are people in this room who are older and wiser than you are. They probably would have acted exactly the same way. I know that *I* would have. Most of us would have behaved as you did. You can't go through your life carrying this terrible guilt feeling. You're not being fair to yourself."

"There wasn't a dry eye in the room," recollects Redlich. "It was an unforgettable memory watching the Chief handle this delicate situation like a skilled psychiatrist."

The young man stopped sobbing and slowly regained his composure. Cheerfully, Warren inquired, "Have you done any visiting in Washington while you've been here?"

"I've tried but walked my feet off, sir."

"Well, we'll take care of that. I'll have my chauffeur drive you around this afternoon."

The hearing was resumed. The commission completed questioning him, finding some of his other testimony inaccurate or difficult to corroborate. Then the limousine of the Chief Justice of the United States picked up a tormented Dallas youth who had failed to prevent—as he might have singlehandedly—the assassination of the thirty-fifth President of the United States.

Most of the criticisms of the commission's findings concern 1) Oswald's past history and associations and 2) the ballistic and medical evidence relating to the crime itself. On both matters even today some of the unanswered questions persist murky and complex, especially over Oswald's alleged "Cuban connection."

Texas Governor John B. Connally, Jr., was one of the chief sources of the controversy over the ballistic evidence. Sitting in the right front jump seat of the Kennedy limousine, Connally was shot in the chest, wrist and thigh. On April 24 Connally testified before the commission that he had been wounded *after* he had heard the first shot and had turned back toward the President. It was "not conceivable," he said, that both he and the President had been hit by the *same* bullet. Yet apparently this "single bullet" was later reported to have been found intact on Connally's stretcher at Dallas' Parkland Hospital. (Conspiracy theorists, ex-Congressman Allard Lowenstein among them, were quick to suggest that this bullet may have been planted there.)

According to Connally, there had been three shots. The first hit the President, the second Connally and the third, the President again. All the shots, Connally insisted, came from the same place: behind his right shoulder, from the direction of the Book Depository where Oswald was supposed to have been. Connally himself did not doubt that Oswald was the assassin, but his testimony raised problems, because many contended that Oswald did not have time to fire three shots. Obviously, if Connally and Kennedy were not hit by the same bullet, there would have had to be more than one gunman. On the other hand, if they were not hit by the same bullet, claim "multiple assassin" adherents, why was no evidence of the first bullet, which pierced the President's throat, ever found?

To this, Commissioner McCloy angrily told me: "Why, Connally didn't even know he was hit until the next day! His doubts about the 'single bullet' are naïve. And as for those other people who talk about 'puffs of smoke' at the grassy knoll, they are either liars or ignorant. There haven't been any 'puffs of smoke' like they say since the Gettysburg battle during the Civil War."

Still, three-bullet-theory advocates still argue that the famed 8-millimeter film of amateur photographer Abraham Zapruder confirmed their contention. However, to any objective person who has studied the film, its evidence is at best ambiguous. It lacks a sound track, unfortunately, but Zapruder himself, who was filming at the edge of the grassy knoll, believed that all three shots came from the Book Depository.

Mrs. John F. Kennedy's June 5 ten-minute testimony at her Georgetown home—in which only she, Warren, Robert F. Kennedy and Rankin were present—likewise might have shed additional light, critics have argued. Chairman Warren concluded that it did not. Although Rankin wanted to pursue the questioning, Warren cut him off after ten minutes, saying protectively, "No, this is the story and that is what we came for." Moreover, for what he indicated were reasons of tact, Warren refused to permit Jacqueline Kennedy's entire testimony, such as the description of her husband's wounds, to be published—a decision that conspiracy theorists persist in viewing as sinister.

In the end, the commission concluded that there had been

three shots and that Oswald had fired all of them. At first, Warren himself had difficulty believing the "single bullet" theory. Only after he reviewed the medical evidence of the Kennedy-Connally wounds and the extensive ballistic tests of the controversial bullet at the U. S. Army Laboratories in Edgewood Arsenal, Maryland, did he accept it. All the "multiple assassin" theories then seemed less plausible to him. [Other independent tests by the FBI and later by CBS, and Columbia University's Dr. John Latimer support the "single bullet" theory.]

Nevertheless, Warren displayed what many considered an amazing high-handedness with respect to the autopsy photographs. He viewed both the twenty-odd photographs of President Kennedy's wounds and the dozen rolls of X-ray photographs in private, stubbornly refusing even to let other members of the commission see them. Dr. James H. Humes, the senior pathologist present at the Bethesda Naval Medical Center autopsy, was then permitted to testify before the commission without ever producing these photographs. "I think if there is one thing I would do over again," says John J. McCloy now, "I would insist on those photographs and X rays being produced before us. We were perhaps a little oversensitive to what we understood were the sensitivities of the Kennedy family. All Warren said to us was 'Don't worry, I'll take care of it. I'd hate to see the President's mutilated head on the front page of nearly every newspaper in America and many in the world.' "

In fact, these disputed pictures have never been released to the public. They remained in the Kennedy family's possession until November 1966, and then were turned over to the National Archives with the stipulation that they were not to be shown to anyone for five years, and thereafter only to authorized government personnel. No amount of petitioning under the Freedom of Information Act has succeeded in securing their release. Warren always defended his suppression of these pictures as "the proper thing to do." But he did not help matters by referring to the suppressed pictures as "damned interesting" in the presence of such outsiders as Chief Protocol Officer Angier Biddle Duke one afternoon at the White House when both were waiting to see the President separately. "I didn't dare ask him what the photographs revealed," says Duke. "Now I wish I had."

Chairman Warren had decided to withhold this crucial autopsy material as early as March 16, 1964.

Why?

Solely because of concern over protecting the feelings of the Kennedy family? Because Bobby Kennedy had fibbed to the Warren Commission about his slain brother's Addison's disease? Out of his desire to protect national security? From an old-fashioned sense of propriety? Or might there have been another subsconscious reason—the recollection, perhaps, of the gruesome police photographs of his own murdered father's mutilated head back in 1938?

Whatever the reason or reasons, after viewing the photographs Warren was unable to sleep for many nights, he later admitted. He feared that release of them would prove profitable to ghoulish promoters who would use them in conjunction with other assassination memorabilia to exhibit to morbid thrill-seekers for a fee.

To prevent this, Warren recommended that the U.S. Government purchase the assassination weapons, clothes and other artifacts from the lawful owners. And he did what he felt was his part by suppressing the ghastly photographs of the President's disintegrated head. Warren deeply regretted that the Zapruder film, because of legal technicalities, could not be purchased or commandeered so as to prevent bootlegged copies from later being shown on commercial television.

Conspiracy theorists have inevitably fastened like limpets on this gray area of the photographs. They point darkly to the abrupt way the President's body was whisked away from Texas medical authorities before a Dallas autopsy could be performed and flown back to Washington, where the examination was conducted in the Bethesda Naval Medical Center. They charge that this, together with the suppression of the pictures, indicates some sort of "cover-up for reasons of state." But if the purpose of the Warren Commission was to reassure the public, this would certainly have been less than ideal public relations.

Still, Warren was alert to *some* need for commission public relations. An overzealous staff lawyer spent more than a month in the Dallas police station basement trying to determine how Jack Ruby had been able to enter there in a few seconds or minutes. This staff member even bullied those he was interrogating, snapping at one: "I think you're lying!" When word of this reached Chairman Warren, he immediately ordered that the man be brought back to Washington on the next plane. The culprit was reprimanded for his behavior and assigned another task.

On Sunday morning, June 7, Warren flew to Dallas to question

Jack Ruby in the county jail. Present also around the long narrow table were Commissioner Gerald Ford, Rankin, associate counsel Arlen Specter, Joseph Ball, a stenographer, and Ruby's lawyer, Joseph H. Tonahill. Ruby wore sandals and a white jumper with several missing buttons. When Ruby noticed Specter, he asked: *"Du bist a Yid?"* ("Are you Jewish?") Warren, who understood this elementary Yiddish, smiled. Ford considered Ruby tense and balky, but Warren patiently questioned Oswald's killer for much of the nearly four hours, courteously and tactfully trying to win his confidence. When Ruby was unable to read a document shown to him, the Chief Justice loaned Ruby his glasses. Desperately anxious to learn firsthand whether Ruby had any prior link with Oswald, Warren skillfully fielded Ruby's rambling discourse.

At the start, Ruby, who three months earlier had been convicted and sentenced to death in a Dallas court, demanded that he be given a lie detector test, which incidentally commission associate counsel David W. Belin had been strongly urging.

Warren, knowing that polygraph tests were not admissible in courts of law, pleasantly replied, "If you and your counsel want any kind of test, I will arrange it for you." (The polygraph test was given to Ruby a month later.)

Ruby complained that Warren should have brought him to Washington six months ago. "Well, Mr. Ruby, I will tell you why we didn't," Warren said. "Because you were then about to be tried and I didn't want to do anything that would prejudice you in your trial."

"Chief Warren, your life is in danger in this city, do you know that?"

"No, I don't know that."

"I would like to talk to you in private."

"You may do that when you finish your story."

Denying vehemently that he ever had known Oswald or officer Tippit, Ruby insisted, "I am as innocent regarding any conspiracy as any of you gentlemen in the room."

After hearing Ruby out, Warren and all the others present were convinced that his alleged meeting with Tippit and Weissman in his strip joint had never taken place. To the old California prosecutor, one of the most persuasive pieces of evidence that Ruby's murder of Oswald was a purely impulsive act after he had observed a smirk on Oswald's face, was the fact that Ruby was waiting at a Western Union counter to send $25 to one of his strippers, whom he did not particularly like, at precisely the moment that Oswald was scheduled to be transferred from the city to the county jail. Ruby had no way of knowing in advance of the accidental hour-and-twelve-minute delay in this transfer.

Until Ruby died of cancer in January 1967 in prison, he steadfastly maintained that he was no conspirator; that he had killed Oswald solely in a desire to spare Jacqueline Kennedy from the ordeal of a Dallas trial at which she would have been compelled to be a witness.

Earl Warren believed Jack Ruby. But millions of people throughout the world to this day still do not.

Instead of testifying before the commission, some individuals, such as President and Mrs. Johnson, just furnished statements. Former Vice President Nixon was informally interviewed, not under oath, in his law office on February 28, 1964, by John F. Malone, Assistant FBI Director in charge of the New York office. In his memoirs, Nixon writes that he had flown to Dallas on November 20 to attend a board meeting of the Pepsi-Cola Company, one of his firm's major clients, and that "Early on the morning of November 22" had flown back to New York shortly before President Kennedy's motorcade arrived. What he neglects to mention is the fact that Malone reported to the Warren Commission: "Mr. Nixon advised that the only time he was in Dallas, Texas, during 1963 was two days prior to the assassination of President John F. Kennedy." Although probably only a lapse in memory on Nixon's part, this discrepency, a trivial footnote to history, has never been explained.

On June 17, the Warren Commission concluded its questioning of 552 witnesses and began to assess the results, along with the 25,000 FBI and 1,500 Secret Service interviews and 3,100 exhibits. The commission's original June 30 deadline obviously could not be met. Neither could its extensions to July 15 or August 1. The independent lawyers who were writing the report could not be rushed even by the Chief Justice of the United States, who forsook his planned summer vacation in California. As Burt Griffin, an associate counsel, recollects, Warren finally asked the staff: "Have you found anything that shows a conspiracy?"

Griffin, now a Cleveland judge, adds: "He had twenty-six people investigating and we couldn't say we had found anything. I think that this man who had been a prosecutor for so many years looked back and said: 'I have never had so many investigators work on a case for so long and come up with nothing here. Let's get this thing out!' "

The commission lawyers were assigned to draft specific areas of the report. It seemed an endless task. Some chapters were revised more than a dozen times, especially during late August and over the Labor Day weekend, in the determination to release it before the November presidential election. Much of the writing and rewriting was done by Redlich and Willens, who often toiled 18 hours daily under Rankin's painstaking supervision. Because Warren sensed that the report required an historic as well as investigatory and legal character, he had added a historian to the staff in late February.

Until the Kennedy assassination, the killing of a President had never been a specific Federal crime, despite the murders of Lincoln, Garfield and McKinley and the attempts on the lives of subsequent Presidents. Two Warren Commission lawyers, after drafting some recommendations, showed this line to the chairman:

The Commission recommends to Congress that it adopt legislation which would make the assassination of the President and Vice President a Federal crime punishable by death. *[my emphasis]*

Warren, the old California law enforcer, wrinkled his brow before thoughtfully inquiring, "Do we really need those words 'punishable by death'? A lot of people strongly feel the other way and I have two minds on the subject myself. Shouldn't we leave the death penalty issue up to Congress? Our report is going to be controversial enough without getting into this area." Thus, the three words were stricken from the list of recommendations.

Squabbles, not suprisingly, erupted among many of the lawyers. Wesley J. Liebler wrote a twenty-six-page memorandum to Rankin objecting to parts of the assassination chapter.

"No more memorandums," Rankin protested. "The report has to be published."

"I spent a long day going over the Marina [Oswald] section with him, Redlich and Willens," said Liebler in September 1975, to television moderator David Susskind. "Substantial changes were then made."

On September 4 galley proofs were distributed to the seven commissioners.

Three days later, Commissioners Boggs, Cooper and Russell flew to Dallas to make a final check of the areas connected with the assassination and to re-question Marina Oswald at the Dallas Naval Air Station.

Senator Russell was troubled by the report's conclusion that Oswald was not involved in any conspiracy. Russell demanded an asterisked footnote in the text noting his objection. "But Warren was determined to have a unanimous report," Russell later revealed. "Warren wouldn't hear of it. He finally took that part and rewrote it himself."

Contrary to popular belief, the Warren Report did finally leave the door slightly open, even if only a crack, to the possibility of conspiracy: "The Commission has *found no evidence* [my italics] that either Lee Harvey Oswald or Jack Ruby were part of any conspiracy, domestic or foreign . . . that anyone assisted Oswald in planning or carrying out the assassination." It then added:

> *Because of the difficulty of proving negatives to a certainty, the possibility of others being involved with either Oswald or Ruby cannot be established categorically, but if there is any such evidence, it has been beyond the reach of all the investigative agencies and resources of the United States and has not come to the attention of the Commission.*

The "single bullet" theory continued to trouble Russell, Cooper and Boggs, but not Ford, Dulles and McCloy. In what became a "Battle of the Adjectives," Ford sought to call the evidence "compelling." To the skeptical Russell, it was merely "credible," while Warren accepted the McCloy compromise word "persuasive."

The commission concluded that Oswald alone had fired three shots—all from the rear, within a 5.6-second time span. The single bullet struck both Kennedy and Connally. Another missed. The fatal bullet hit the President in the back of the head.

When Russell and Boggs threatened to file a minority report, Warren consented to insert the word "probable" in some instances of investigative certainty.

Ford and Boggs, who were J. Edgar Hoover admirers, spiritedly sought to keep out of the report any criticism of the FBI. But Warren overruled them. The Warren Report—unprecedentedly for a U. S. Government document—rebuked the FBI for its "unduly restrictive view" in failing to warn the Secret Service that Oswald, who was under FBI surveillance, was working in a Dallas building on the presidential route. The Secret Service and Dallas police were also sharply scolded.

It was a unanimous report. No dissenting or minority opinions were filed. "The Chief put everything in focus for us," reflects Redlich. "We kept asking ourselves thousands of times: *'Who else* could possibly have done it if Oswald didn't do it alone? Is there one single thing that we haven't done that we *should* have done? ' Near the end, things got very tense. The Chief would often break the tension by talking about baseball—such as a great catch he once saw Willie Mays make. But we all knew that he was carrying the burden more than any of us—and alone. We could divide up our responsibilities. But not him. He set up all our guidelines and procedures, read most staff memos and every line of testimony. He was the man in the middle between the commissioners and the staff; between all of us and the White House. And all this time, he was performing his demanding job as Chief Justice. What an extraordinary man!"

On Thursday, September 24, 1964, President Johnson received this one-sentence letter:

> *Your Commission to investigate the assassination of President Kennedy on November 22, 1963, having completed its assignment in accordance with Executive Order No. 11130 of November 29, 1963, herewith submits its final report.*

The letter was signed by Earl Warren with the signatures of the six other commissioners following. Its ten-month task completed, the Warren Commission dissolved itself after a cost to the U. S. Government of $1,200,000. Its staff disbanded and gave itself no farewell party. Only Willens remained to work on the twenty-six volumes of hearings. Like the Supreme Court when rendering a decision, the commission had no intention of publicly defending its verdict in what historians probably will agree was the most documented and intensive study of any crime in American history. President Johnson tucked the 888-page report (385,000 words and 158 illustrations) into his briefcase to read over the weekend at his Texas ranch. Here he could relax, away from the rigors of his current campaign against

Republican Senator Barry Goldwater in the presidential election that was now only five weeks away.

Warren flew to California for a brief holiday before the new Supreme Court term opened. He was fully satisfied with the report, as he indeed would be, despite all the criticism, during the next ten years of his life. It was the truth as this old California lawman knew, believed and understood it. Not until three years later was he informed of the CIA attempts on Castro's life—a fact which his fellow commissioner Allen Dulles, a former CIA director, had neglected to tell him. He never lived to learn of an FBI suppression of an Oswald letter.

Upon arrival in Sacramento, Chairman Warren acknowledged to reporters, "This was a depressing job for ten months. I'm glad it's over."

"Would you consider heading another commission after you retire from the Supreme Court?"

A broad smile swept over Earl Warren's relieved face. "I certainly wouldn't solicit it," he replied.

On Sunday, September 26, the Warren Report was released to the world under its official title: *The Report of the President's Commission on the Assassination of President John F. Kennedy*.

Shortly after the Government Printing Office published the uncopyrighted Warren Report, at least six commercial publishers reprinted it—Bantam Books and Popular Library in paperback within a week. Hardcover editions were issued immediately afterward by Doubleday, McGraw-Hill, the Book-of-the-Month Club and the Associated Press. *The New York Times* republished it as a forty-eight-page supplement on September 28. Many of the publishers retitled the report coverlining it: "Report of the Warren Commission on the Assassination of President Kennedy."

Two months later, on November 23, the Warren Commission's twenty-six volumes of testimony and exhibits, weighing fifty-four pounds and containing more than ten million words, was released to the public. At first, Chairman Warren had had some misgivings about publishing these voluminous hearings and exhibits because of the expense. However, after impassioned pleas by his staff, he reversed himself.

The immediate general reaction throughout the United States was that the Warren Commission had performed a painful task with great skill. Grief-stricken Americans, seeking reassurance, had *wanted* to believe the official U. S. Government investigation of the tragedy. The Warren Commission appeared to bring stability in a time of national trauma. Termed a monumental achievement, the Warren Report was widely praised by the majority of the nation's news media. Typically, *The New York Times* on September 28, 1964, called it:

> ... *comprehensive and convincing. ... The facts ... exhaustively gathered, independently checked and cogently set forth—destroy the basis for the conspiracy theories that have grown weedlike in this country and abroad. Readers of the full Report will find no basis for questioning the Commission's conclusion that President Kennedy was killed by Lee Harvey Oswald acting alone.*

Insofar as one immediate purpose of the report was to reduce public suspicion to manageable levels, it was probably successful. At first, most Americans, if not totally persuaded by the commission's findings, at least *tended* to believe them. Public speculation about conspiracy declined perceptibly. Increasingly, this became the preoccupation of peripheral groups rather than of the mass of U. S. citizens. And since many of these remaining activist skeptics could easily be dismissed as ignorant, self-serving or of dubious sanity, the term "assassination buff" acquired distinctly derogatory overtones in the popular mind. But not all the "buffs" could be dismissed as fools or knaves. By the end of 1964, some were producing a disturbing body of literature that might be called the "first-generation critique" of the Warren Report.

One curious "defense" of the report was the handiwork of future President Gerald Ford. A mere week after the report had been issued, and more than a month before the release of the full twenty-six volumes of the commission's hearings and exhibits, *Life* magazine published an article by Congressman Ford (fee: $5,000) purporting to tell the inside story of how the commission had operated. Two weeks later, Ford and the late John R. Stiles, his campaign manager and assistant on the commission, signed a contract with Simon and Schuster (advance: $10,000) for a book-length expansion of the *Life* article. According to editor Peter Schwed, the 250,000-word finished manuscript, titled *Portrait of the Assassin*, was delivered to the publisher within a month. Obviously, the book had been begun well before the commission report had been released, possibly even before the commission had reached its final conclusion. "Ford's office asked for copies of the executive session transcripts daily, which none of the other commissioners did," recollects a commission staff lawyer.

Neither in the *Life* article nor in his book did Ford dispute the commission's conclusion that Oswald was the lone assassin. But because Ford's literary labors appeared to make him a teller of tales out of school, Warren was almost as annoyed as if Ford had filed a public dissent. From the Chief Justice's point of view, Ford's behavior constituted an unconscionable breach of decorum and Warren did not hesitate to let Ford know of his displeasure.

In later years Ford himself seems to have had second thoughts. When nominated for the Vice Presidency in 1973, his testimony on the "top secret" information contained in his book was conflicting. The tenor of his remarks was regretful: "I cannot help but apologize if the circumstances are such that there was this violation, but there was certainly no intent to do so." There is no reference to *Portrait of the Assassin* in President Ford's official biography.

In September 1977, retired President Ford wrote to me:

> *Chief Justice Earl Warren did a superb job as Chairman of the Warren Commission. The outstanding staff was primarily his handiwork. He was a firm but fair presiding officer in handling the numerous and diverse witnesses. The unanimity of the Commission was achieved through his leadership. The Commission Report, which I still stand by, and which has withstood attack from all sides, is a tribute to his legal ability, his integrity, and his leadership.*

Although interesting in retrospect, Gerald Ford's book caused little stir when it was published in May 1965. By then, the tide of the "first-generation critique" was approaching a flood, and Ford's mild ripple was submerged in an international torrent of newspaper and magazine articles, books, TV and radio programs—predominantly critical of the commission's findings.

Outside America, and particularly in Europe, it was assumed that the Warren Report was a whitewash designed to cover up some dark conspiracy whose revelation would prove embarrassing to the U. S. Government. This theme was highlighted in best-selling books published in England, France, Germany, Italy and Sweden. In London a "Who Killed Kennedy?" Committee was formed by ninety-two-year-old philosopher Bertrand Russell and Oxford historian Hugh Trevor-Roper. In Moscow *Pravda* routinely compared the Warren Report to the Nazi version of the Reichstag Fire. Subsequently the Soviet Government requested that the U. S. Embassy stop distributing copies of the report, claiming that it was "slanderous to the Soviet people." In many other countries, where "palace plots" were understood as a way of life, the conspiracy theory was readily accepted, perhaps by millions who could not believe that a powerful American President could be slain single-handedly by a weak stock clerk with a $21 mail-order rifle.

In America by the end of 1966, the total sales of all books criticizing the Warren Report had exceeded those of all versions of the report itself. Some of the better-known titles included Harold Weisberg's multivolume *Whitewash*, Richard Popkin's *The Second Oswald*, Josiah Thompson's *Six Seconds in Dallas*, Leo Sauvage's *The Oswald Affair*, Gerry Wills's and Ovid Demaris' *Jack Ruby*, John Waltz's and John Kaplan's *Trial of Jack Ruby*, and Sylvia Meagher's *Accessories After the Fact*. But probably the two most commercial were *Inquest* by Edward Jay Epstein and *Rush to Judgment* by Mark Lane.

Epstein began his research as a Cornell master's thesis—a case study of the workings of an extraordinary government body. By the time it was published in book form (June 1966) as *Inquest*, it had evolved into a scathing critique of the commission's procedures in investigating and evaluating evidence. According to Epstein, the commission had been so eager to prove that Oswald had acted alone that it used only the most hurried and slipshod methods in researching any alternative theses. While Epstein conceded that Oswald probably had fired at Kennedy, he argued that there was powerful evidence of the existence of at least one more assassin.

Two months later came Mark Lane's *Rush to Judgment*. Its attack on the commission's findings was somewhat broader than Epstein's, raising more questions and more varied speculations, including the suggestion that Oswald had not fired at all. In his ecstatic review of the book, Norman Mailer went so far as to soberly predict, with considerable historical irrelevancy, that "The Work of the Warren Commission will be judged by history to be a scandal worse than Teapot Dome."

New Orleans District Attorney Jim Garrison was an even more flamboyant critic. In February 1967, the six-foot-six Garrison, known as the "Jolly Green Giant," arrested socially prominent businessman Clay Shaw, whom he accused of being a homosexual, and linked with an Oswald-Ruby-FBI-CIA plot to kill President Kennedy. Reporters rushed to New Orleans from all over the world to interview Garrison, who now boasted that the Warren Commission was definitely discredited. Meanwhile, its chairman, who was in Lima, Peru, studying its and other South American nations' judicial systems, was persuaded by the American Embassy there to hold a news conference which he smilingly observed was his biggest since leaving politics fourteen years earlier.

"I have nothing to say about Mr. Garrison's investigations," he calmly said. "I don't know him. As far as I know, he has declined to give any information that he may have. If there are any new facts they should be developed, and if anyone has violated the law, the law should take its due course. We cannot deal with what people think, feel or believe."

Two years later, a jury deliberated less than an hour and acquitted Shaw after a bizarre forty-day trial in which Garrison was accused of bribing, drugging and hypnotizing witnesses.

By May 1967, *Esquire* magazine could cite at least sixty different assassination theories that already had been published in book or magazine form, none of which agreed with the commission's findings. And the following month both the Gallup and Harris polls reported that approximately two out of three Americans queried did not believe that the report "had told the full story"—that is, they suspected that Oswald had been involved in some type of conspiracy.

There were, to be sure, some respected nonofficial defenders of the Warren Report in print. Among the critics of the critics were Charles Roberts, *Newsweek*'s White House correspondent, and Fletcher Knebel, the best-selling author. Both pointed out that writers like Epstein and Lane were guilty of the very sins they imputed to the commission: distorting facts, ignoring testimony and selecting evidence to fit their preconceived theories. *The New York Times* and several other influential dailies reaffirmed their initial favorable evaluation of the report. And John Connally, despite the fact that his own testimony had raised problems for the commission, assailed its critics en masse as mere "journalistic scavengers." Leon Jaworski charged that the anti-Warren Report books "deserve to be in the fiction category."

Expectedly, most of the authors of the report, and the Johnson

Administration in general, defended the commission's conclusions in public. Chairman Warren, however, more than ever conscious that his role in the controversy might jeopardize the Supreme Court's dignity, scrupulously did not. He declined to discuss the report or to acknowledge—let alone comment on—its critics. He even refused to be interviewed by CBS on its 1967 three-part program upholding the report. Yet he would have been less than human if he had been able to maintain complete silence. For example, at a mid-November 1966 Washington dinner party where the Lane and Epstein books were being discussed, he is reliably reported to have blurted out: "If I were still a district attorney and the Oswald case came into my jurisdiction, I could have gotten a conviction in two days and never heard about the case again. Me conspire with Dick Russell? What possible set of circumstances could ever get us two to conspire on anything? To say that the commission suppressed the truth, and no one came forward to expose this villainy, would mean that the entire United States government was corrupt from top to bottom. One group of conspiracy theorists say that Khrushchev and Castro did it. Another group say the rich Texas oilmen were responsible. Strangely, both of these groups have condemned the commission for not finding a conspiracy."

At no subsequent time did Warren give any public indication that he had ever entertained second thoughts about the commission's conclusions. "I have never found any evidence to change my mind," he said simply. Because he was absolutely convinced of the correctness of its basic finding—that Oswald had acted alone—he tended to discount any criticism of its other findings or procedures.

Yet, by Earl Warren's own standards of "fairness," these criticisms cannot be dismissed: The *way* in which the inquiry was conducted was not always ideal. There was too little time, and perhaps there was too much White House pressure. Not all the available evidence (some withheld by the FBI and CIA) could be fully assessed. The commission was perhaps too quick to give security classifications to some evidence. Several of the commissioners lacked legal or investigative experience. Unlike a jury, they were neither in continuous session nor always all present at important hearings. The legal staff, though undoubtedly competent, was plagued with rivalries and occasional dissension. Above all, some

257

commissioners were haunted by a sense that their political function might be at least as important as—although potentially at variance with—their legal function.

Nonetheless, the commission's shortcomings do not, by themselves, invalidate its central conclusion. Whatever the problems of the lone-assassin theory, there were even greater problems with any alternative theory. As Redlich later said, "Theory after theory, claim after claim, has been advanced, but not one important fact has been added to what we had already conclusively considered. More bluntly, counsel Leon D. Hubert, Jr., admitted, "We tried. We sure tried. Each of us said, 'If I can break this thing wide open. I'm made!' "

The report included a Speculation and Rumors Appendix (XII), some of whose theories would enrich the world of science fiction. Warren himself, when reading it, shook his head and softly said, "These people say this *could* have happened. This *might* have happened. *Maybe* that happened. Their theories are all conjecture. The real truth often sounds improbable."

In the end, the Warren Commission chose to endorse the simplest, most obvious and most plausible theory. Should subsequent revelations ever prove its conclusions wrong, no one can deny that the commission, despite all its faults, heroically tried to deal honestly with the known facts for the American people. I doubt that any other investigatory body could have totally satisfied the countless well-meaning or venal skeptics throughout the world, or that any other chairman could have performed the complex task with such dedication. Yet as historian Gerald Johnson put it, "The Commission's work brought Warren nothing but months of excessively hard labor and a still-continuing shower of dead cats. It was an extreme test of sacrificial patriotism." Suddenly, his Supreme Court chambers were bombarded with a new type of hate mail. Even some of his admirers, including some history professors who had never read a line of the Warren Report, believed that the incorruptible Chief Justice had "lied" in a patriotic act of self-sacrifice.

Later in retirement, Warren summed up the experience as "the unhappiest time of my life." His namesake son remembers, "I don't know of any period which drained and aged Dad like this one. It took him a long time to recover." Unlike fellow commissioners, Earl Warren never permitted any reference to his service on the

Warren Commission to appear in his biography in *Who's Who in America*.

Happily for the nation, the Warren Report did not become a 1964 presidential campaign issue. On November 3 Lyndon Johnson, no longer an Instant President, was elected Chief Executive in his own right for a full four-year term. Winning forty-four states and 61 percent of the vote, he trounced conservative Republican Barry Goldwater in an unprecedented landslide plurality of 15 million ballots (including Warren's).

Despite some reservations about Johnson's weaknesses for Texas cronyism and political horse trading, the Chief Justice was delighted. He perceived in LBJ not the comic "Uncle Cornpone" character scoffed at by JFK's Camelot courtiers, but a dynamic self-made man even more dedicated to social reform than Kennedy and far better equipped to translate his dreams into law. He would, Warren felt, prove a valuable ally of the Court in the months and perhaps years ahead because the skilled LBJ moved boldly, under-standing precisely how to make government wheels move.

Certainly during the early period of the new Johnson Administration, Warren's prediction seemed vindicated. The President went out of his way to applaud the Court when it unanimously upheld the Civil Rights Act of 1964 and the Voting Rights Act of 1965. On March 15, 1965, he called Congress into special session to deliver an impassioned televised address on voting rights. The President concluded by citing Martin Luther King's "We Shall Overcome" slogan. Most of LBJ's former Southern colleagues remained uncom-fortably silent. Liberal legislators cheered. Applauding thunderously with them—most unjudicially—was the Chief Justice of the United States.

Warren was equally pleased with Johnson's first new Court appointment. On July 13, 1965, Adlai Stevenson, Chief U.S. Dele-gate to the United Nations, suddenly died of a heart attack on a London street. Just three weeks earlier in San Francisco, following the twentieth-anniversary celebration of the United Nations, Stevenson had gone fishing on Sunday morning with his friend Earl Warren. Johnson briefly toyed with the idea of offering Stevenson's post to Warren but soon concluded that there was no hope of (and, really, no advantage in) Warren's accepting. Instead, a week later, he recruited Associate Justice Arthur J. Goldberg for this post. To

Goldberg's vacant seat he appointed Abe Fortas, the brilliant fifty-five-year-old Washington attorney who had successfully argued *Gideon* before the Court two years earlier.

"Abe would rework the Lord's Prayer if it came in a brief," observed a Fortas-watcher. "I don't like the S.O.B. but if I were in trouble, I'd sure want him on my side." Lyndon Johnson himself once remarked, "Abe's smart as hell. He has a heart but he's no damn knee-jerk liberal."

The enigmatic, Tennessee-born Fortas had been a trusted LBJ confidant ever since Johnson's eighty-seven-vote "victory" in a 1948 Texas senatorial primary when Johnson had won the soubriquet "Landslide Lyndon." Just prior to this election, a Federal district judge had ordered the names of Johnson and his opponent, ex-Governor Coke Stevenson, stricken from the general election ballot while voting irregularities were being investigated. Although the Supreme Court was in summer recess, Johnson's lawyer, Fortas, had persuaded Justice Black to vacate—most unusually—this lower court order as an improper interference in state elections. Result: The questionable ballots were destroyed. In a new election, Johnson won his first Senate seat and began his climb to national power. The young Fortas, in turn, won the lifelong gratitude of a future President of the United States.

After Kennedy's assassination, the first telephone call that Johnson made in Dallas was to Fortas. Back in Washington, the new President asked his friend to draft plans for what became the Warren Commission. If he had deemed it politically possible, LBJ would have fired Bobby Kennedy as attorney general and appointed Fortas, who even had to be coaxed to succeed Goldberg. Finally, Johnson summoned him to the White House and said, "Abe, I'm sending fifty thousand men to Vietnam and you to the Supreme Court." Attorney Fortas gave up an estimated annual income of $150,000 for an Associate Justice's $39,500 salary. "When you put a man on the Supreme Court, he ceases to be your friend," Truman once bitterly observed. This certainly was not true of the uninterrupted Johnson-Fortas friendship.

Quickly, Fortas proved to be both a Great Society liberal and a valuable voting ally to the Chief Justice, who soon assigned him the writing of significant majority opinions, even bypassing brethren with longer judicial service.

During the early Johnson years, Warren was deeply involved in several landmark decisions. In March 1964, the Warren Court broadened the right of the press (*New York Times* v. *Sullivan*) to criticize the conduct of public officials. Any false statements and intentional "actual malice" now had to be proven before a libel judgment could be secured. This decision reversed a $500,000 judgment awarded a Montgomery, Alabama, city commissioner against *The New York Times* and four black ministers.

In June, the Chief Justice wrote the significant *Reynolds* v. *Sims* opinion which extended the 1962 *Baker* v. *Carr* decision. It clearly required both houses of all fifty state legislatures to be apportioned according to population, giving city and suburban voters a greater voice. A kindred, lesser-known ruling (*Westberry* v. *Sanders*) then applied this "one-man-one-vote" principle to congressional districts which would later influence the selection of U. S. House of Representative seats. "I think the reapportionment, not only of state legislatures, but of representative government," reflected Warren in retirement, "is perhaps the most important issue we have had before the Supreme Court."

The most controversial 1964 Warren Court decision—*Escobedo* v. *Illinois* expanded *Gideon*. The tribunal ruled that a suspect's failure to request a lawyer did not waive his constitutional right to have one. ("The defendant who does not ask for counsel is the very defendant who needs counsel.") The news media widely hailed the ruling as a landmark.

Though not available to the press on decisions, the former California politician still loved to mingle with newspersons whenever he properly could. Once, when swearing in a new president of the National Press Club, the not-entirely-sober Chief Justice joked: "Raise your right elbow! Do you solemnly swear that you will uphold the Constitution and bar prices of the National Press Club and promise to run it as you doggone please?" When I encountered him in April 1965, he teased me, "Your new book about that Dutch clairvoyant—Croiset, is that his name?—does he *really* solve all those crimes you say? If so, please bring him to Washington. Maybe he could help *me* solve some crimes!" When I reminded him that the Spring 1965 District of Columbia telephone book had inadvertently omitted listing the Supreme Court, he quipped: "Well, maybe they don't think we're doing anything important!"

The school prayer ruling of two years earlier still rankled many lawmakers. In November 1964 the Chief Justice, after conferring with his brethren, wrote the Capitol architect opposing a bill of South Carolina Representative Robert T. Ashmore which proposed that "In God We Trust" be inscribed above the Supreme Court bench. The privately religious Warren urged that the Court's original decor not be changed regardless of well-meaning religious or patriotic sentiments. The Warren letter helped bury the bill.

In retaliation, the following March, House members denied Justices a $3,000 annual pay raise on their $39,500 salaries, even though they then voted $7,500 increases for themselves, Cabinet officers and all lesser Federal judges. Once again the Chief Justice was chastised for lacking prior judicial experience and—a new point of criticism—for visiting the French Riviera during his summer vacation. Congressman Morris K. Udall, who deplored the House's behavior, termed it "Kick-the-Court-in-the-Pants Day."

Miscellaneous matters concerned Warren, too, during these years. In June 1964 he flew to New York to attend a dinner for the John F. Kennedy Memorial Library, at which Jacqueline Kennedy made her first public appearance since her husband's assassination. In October Warren again visited New York to help celebrate the eightieth anniversary of Eleanor Roosevelt's birth. (She had died two years earlier.) And in late January 1965 he flew to London to attend Winston Churchill's funeral, representing President Johnson, who was hospitalized with a severe bronchial infection. Capitol eyebrows fluttered when the President bucked protocol by sending the Chief Justice instead of new Vice President Hubert Humphrey to be an official U. S. representative. Columnist Art Buchwald wisecracked that it was probably because it was impossible for the genial Humphrey ever to look sad.

On the same mission was former President Eisenhower. The two men took advantage of the long plane ride to discuss their differences more frankly than ever before. Eisenhower expressed disappointment that Warren had not been the political moderate the President had expected in many Court decisions. When asked for specifics, Eisenhower referred vaguely to "those Communist cases" on which the Supreme Court had ruled. Since Eisenhower would not elaborate, the Chief Justice privately concluded that he could not—that in fact he did not really know what decisions he was talking about.

So, to the veiled amusement of eavesdroppers on the plane, Warren proceeded to give the man who had appointed him an elementary lecture on the functions and purposes of the Supreme Court. He noted that the Court was hardly his own creature, but composed of nine Justices who reached their conclusions independently and often in disagreement. They were, however, all united in believing in the absolute primacy of principle.

When recounting this episode, critics of the late President are partisan in contrasting the two men: Eisenhower, the ill-informed, somewhat prejudiced politician *v.* Warren, the wise and uncompromising man of principle. Although this viewpoint is not without merit, the nobility of Warren's stance should not be overestimated. In some respects he was addressing himself to an abstract ideal rather than to the more complicated reality. True, the Justices were independent. Yet it would be naïve to ignore the importance of the actual influence Warren exercised over them. Certainly the Justices tried to be guided solely by principle. But who among them could honestly say that he never assessed the probable social consequences when applying a principle? More basically, are pure and fundamental principles always as self-evident as Warren seemed to suggest? Warren occasionally oversimplified. And in that oversimplification—a tendency to focus on the ideal rather than the real— perhaps lay one of the central keys to his character as Chief Justice, the source of his greatest strength and greatest weakness.

Three months after their trip, Warren again irritated Eisenhower when he presented to former President Truman the annual Freedom House award in New York—an honor which Warren himself was to receive four years later, on his retirement.

Could Dwight Eisenhower possibly have been thinking of the unpredictable man he had named to the High Court when he wrote two years later in the January 1967 *Reader's Digest*: "I propose that tenure for all Federal judges, including members of the Supreme Court, be limited to 20 years in the same Court or to the time when the judge reaches the age of 72." By then, Warren was approaching 76 and had served more than 13 years.

Increasingly, Warren was feeling closer to the Justices "in the books" than to many of his contemporaries. Holmes and Brandeis were his favorites—and he tried to honor their memories.

The Chief Justice regretted never having met Brandeis but he once faced Holmes. He twice told me about that with great relish.

263

District Attorney Warren, who was admitted to practice before the U. S. Supreme Court in 1932, journeyed to Washington to defend Alameda County in a case brought by the Central Pacific Railway which sought to affirm the right of way on an 1859 easement. Though opposed by three highly skilled attorneys, the young unaccompanied Warren won a unanimous decision the following month.

By a curious coincidence, this was the last case that Holmes heard. It was argued on Thursday, January 7, 1932, and with classic simplicity, after Court had adjourned at 4:30 P.M., the ninety-one-year-old Holmes casually remarked to his clerk, "I won't be down tomorrow morning." That evening, he wrote his formal resignation to President Herbert Hoover, which was accepted several days later.

Warren smilingly recalled that when he returned to California, lawyer friends twitted him: "Holmes sat on the United States Supreme Court for thirty years, on the Massachusetts Supreme Judicial Court for twenty years, he has educated several generations of judges and lawyers, but after hearing Earl Warren argue a case, he ups and quits! Earl, you ought to be ashamed of yourself for driving Justice Holmes off the Court!"

Nearly twenty-five years later as Chief Justice, Warren, when learning that Holmes's $300,000 bequest to the United States Government was lying idle gathering no interest, had sparked the passage of Public Law 84246, in which the Holmes bequest was used to publish a much-needed definitive 12-volume history of the Supreme Court. And now, in 1965, as an elector of New York University's Hall of Fame for Great Americans, he enthusiastically helped achieve the admission of Holmes. (Since an individual must be dead at least twenty-five years before being eligible, Warren himself probably will be nominated after 1999.)

Brandeis likewise was honored by Warren through his extra-judicial work for Brandeis University. Former Dean Clarence Berger recalls the Chief Justice's assistance at a fund-raising cocktail reception in Los Angeles in December 1965: "When the Chief Justice arrived, he asked how the fund-raising was going. When he heard far from satisfactory, he suggested we try a second round. He followed us around the room as we approached each prospect. He didn't say a word, just joined each little group we formed, smiled encouragingly at each 'victim' as we closed in on one generous donor after another and gave each a bear hug in succession. Within 15 minutes, we had obtained more than a quarter of a million dollars in pledges for our young university. We teased the Chief Justice at the banquet that evening, saying that his silence had been golden."

Judicial reform was another extracurricular activity of Warren's. He was particularly troubled by the growing backlog of cases which congested the calendars of Federal courts. He chose to attack the problem through the medium of the Judicial Conference. "Prior to Warren's tenure," says former Maryland Senator Joseph D. Tydings, "the Judicial Conference of the United States was largely a moribund institution, serving primarily as a social gathering, twice a year, for the ranking circuit judges. During the Warren years the Conference was made an effective policy making body to improve the Federal judicial machinery."

The High Court was extremely busy during the 1965–66 term. Some of the cases it heard attracted considerable attention as, for example, the "fair trial-free press" case of convicted wife-murderer Dr. Samuel Sheppard, successfully appealed by a then relatively unknown attorney named F. Lee Bailey. Although few of the Court's 1965 decisions involved startling new interpretations of the law, this would hardly be true of those in 1966.

In March 1966, three important obscenity decisions were handed down. Warren voted somewhat chastisingly to uphold the convictions of the flamboyant Ralph Ginzburg, publisher of *Eros* magazine, and the less artistic pornographer Edward Mishkin, but strangely exonerated Putnam's publication of *The Memoirs of Fanny Hill*. To puritanical Earl Warren, the character and conduct of the individual or publisher seemed more important than the "obscene" publication in question.

Earl Warren's seventy-fifth birthday fell on March 19, 1966. He then held one of his rare news conferences. Did he plan to retire? "No, I have not given serious thought to retirement," the robust jurist said, but maintained that he certainly favored "the infusion of new blood" into government. What did he think of all the bills in Congress setting a specific compulsory retirement age for Federal judges? Fine, grinned the Chief Justice, pointedly adding, "This should be required for *all* public officials in *all* branches of our government"—an obvious reference to the Congress.

At his family's birthday party for him that Saturday evening, Warren had a surprise visit from President Johnson, who dropped by the Chief Justice's apartment armed with presents. One was the inevitable photograph of LBJ, inscribed, "To the greatest Chief

Justice of them all." Other gifts were a copy of the *Oxford History of the American People* and a bottle of choice thirty-year-old Scotch.

Four nights later President Johnson entertained the Warrens and four of their children and spouses at the annual White House reception for the Federal judiciary. Before the reception, the Warren tribe had cocktails in the Johnson family living quarters on the second floor. Later in the evening, the President reminded his guests that when Speaker Sam Rayburn was alive, wherever Mr. Sam sat at any social event, *that* was the head of the table. "Now wherever Warren sits is the head of the table," the President declared.

Three weeks later, on April 27, Warren was wryly amused at having to confront private citizen Richard Nixon in a new role, when Nixon appeared before the U. S. Supreme Court for the first and only time pleading a case. It was against *Life* magazine, and Nixon's task was to uphold an appealed $30,000 invasion of privacy judgment which his client, James J. Hill, had won in a lower court against the periodical. In 1955, *Life* had published a review of a fictionalized play, *The Desperate Hours*, concerning a family that had been held hostage by escaped convicts and which it had compared to Hill's. Nixon argued that the magazine had "fictionalized for the purposes of trade" and had published "in reckless disregard of the facts."

Thirty-one times Nixon was interrupted by the Justices during the two-hour hearing. Only once did he lose control. That was when the Chief Justice gently needled him about misunderstanding a California privacy law passed during Governor Warren's own administration.

Nixon lost the case by a slim 5–4 decision, but *Life* subsequently settled out of court. Ironically, dissenting Justice Fortas urged Nixon's client to seek a new trial against the "reckless and irresponsible assault" by *Life*—which three years later, in an exposé article, was largely responsible for Fortas being forced to resign from the Supreme Court.

Two infinitely more important cases were *Escobedo* v. *Illinois* and *Miranda* v. *Arizona*, still considered perhaps the most controversial ruling ever handed down by the Warren Court. It has long troubled not only law-enforcement officers but many Americans worried about rising crime rates. The antecedents of *Miranda* may be traced to the so-called "Communist cases" of the late 1950s and *Gideon*, all of which illustrated Warren's growing preoccupation with the subject of criminal justice.

This concern had been sharply expanded in 1964, in the *Escobedo* case. Danny Escobedo, a Chicagoan of Mexican descent, had been arrested on suspicion of murdering his brother-in-law. A confession had been extracted from him before he could consult his lawyer, who was standing outside the room where he was being held, but denied permission to speak to his client. On the strength of this confession he was indicted, convicted and sentenced to life imprisonment.

The Supreme Court was divided on the question of whether Escobedo had been denied due process, but a narrow 5–4 Warrenite majority held that the confession obtained under such circumstances was inadmissible. Police and prosecutors nationwide were outraged, not only because of what the decision said but because of what it implied. *Gideon* had established the right of the accused to be represented by counsel. *Escobedo* suggested that certain kinds of testimony given by the accused person before he had conferred with his attorney could not be used in court. Now lawmen waited apprehensively for further clarification of what the High Court would define as the rights of the accused and the duties of the police. *Miranda* v. *Arizona* was the answer.

Ernesto Miranda, an indigent Mexican-American, had been convicted by a Phoenix court in 1963 of kidnapping and rape. Although at the time of his arrest Miranda had signed a compromising statement containing a typed-in clause to the effect that he had full knowledge of his legal rights, his attorney claimed he had not done so "voluntarily, knowingly or intelligently" and that, in fact, he had never been advised of his right to remain silent under police questioning. Thus, it was argued, the signed statement, the principal evidence against Miranda, was inadmissible and his conviction should be reversed.

The Court was even more sharply divided over *Miranda* than it had been over *Escobedo*. Once again the vote was 5–4. Merits apart, if the Court ruled in favor of the plaintiff, it would be breaking new constitutional ground after nearly two centuries in defining precisely what the Fifth Amendment meant in saying that "No person . . . shall be compelled in a criminal case to be a witness against himself."

Warren delivered the hard-hitting majority opinion on June 13, 1966. Citing several proven instances of police brutality in obtaining confessions, he warned that when law-enforcement officers neglect to use fair methods, "they can become as great a menace to society as any criminal we have." The former California prosecutor added, "This Court has recognized that coercion can be mental as well as physical and that the blood of the accused is not the only hallmark of unconstitutional inquisition." The correct rule of procedure, he explained, is that the police must clearly inform any suspect of his right to remain silent *immediately* upon apprehension, and the suspect must have his lawyer present *before* he can be questioned. If the suspect indicates that he wishes to remain silent, all interrogation must stop. Since these conditions had not been fulfilled in Miranda's case, his conviction was overturned.

Warren was saying, in effect, that few criminal cases are really tried in court. The real "trial" often takes place in a police station. Therefore, the Constitution had to be interpreted to mean that a suspect's rights have to be protected from the minute he is taken into custody. That is the law of the land, ruled the man who did not always adhere to this philosophy when prosecuting crime in California or even when he first ascended to the Court.

The dissenting opinions from the conservative Justices were bitter. Harlan flushed visibly when he denounced Warren's opinion as "dangerous experimentation . . . don't be fooled by it." White warned, "In some unknown number of cases, the Court rule will return a killer, a rapist or other criminal to the streets . . . to repeat his crime whenever it pleases him." And Clark insisted that the Court had pulled the rug from under the law-enforcement agencies by changing the traditional rules of interrogation at, as he put it, "one fell sweep."

Shocked law-enforcement officers swiftly pointed out that the *Miranda* ruling might result in countless thousands of imprisoned criminals having to be released because they had been convicted on the basis of now-illegal confessions. Dismayed by this prospect Warren ruled several days later that the practical effects of *Miranda* would not be retroactive and would only apply to criminal cases begun *after* June 13, 1966. The legal basis for this pronouncement was, to say the least, shaky, but certainly no one wanted to challenge it.

But with regard to *Miranda* itself, there were challenges aplenty. The decision was denounced regularly and ringingly in the halls of Congress. (Oddly, one of Warren's most vocal defenders in the House was the man he had so overwhelmingly defeated in the 1950 gubernatorial race, James Roosevelt.) Eventually, much of this congressional criticism found its way into the Crime Control and Safe Streets Act of 1968, which, among other things, specified that confessions are admissible in Federal courts if given voluntarily. In state prosecutions, however, the provisions of *Miranda* necessarily had to remain in full effect.

Opposition to *Miranda* soon became a campaign rallying cry to escalate political careers. It would be a major issue in Richard Nixon's presidential campaign in 1968. George Wallace never wearied of telling audiences: "If you walk out of this hotel tonight and somebody knocks you on the head, he'll be out of jail before you're out of the hospital, and on Monday they'll try the policeman instead of the criminal." Some conservative lawyers, such as William Rehnquist (now Associate Justice Rehnquist), endeared themselves to powerful right-wing political leaders with vitriolic condemnations of the Warren Court, thereby paving the way for their future advancement.

But *Miranda* also had its influential partisans. Harvard Law Professor Paul Freund said: "The decision is a sound one. If the states had been more imaginative in providing safeguards in interrogating suspects, such as providing tape recorders and limiting the time of questioning, there would have been no need for the rule." Then-Detroit Police Commissioner Roy Girardin suggested that *Miranda* might improve police work, making law enforcers "investigate more thoroughly, find more evidence and more witnesses." Former Prosecutor Burton Roberts, now a New York Supreme Court judge, pointed out: "The means used by people in a democracy are as important as the ends themselves. . . . . The Supreme Court decisions are having a healthy influence by letting people in the ghetto know that certain police procedures are frowned on." California Congressman James Corman added that "*Miranda* makes the Constitution's guarantee of due process a reality for *all* people"; and New York attorney Leon Blaufarb maintained that "*Miranda* personifies what the Bill of Rights really means, and Warren monumentally caught its spirit."

Warren himself always seemed faintly puzzled by the furor that *Miranda* had provoked. Years later, in retirement, he remarked: "The third degree was common years ago when I was district attorney and attorney general. But if, instead of beating a prisoner to get a confession, he is given a lawyer and an opportunity to talk to him and the police are enabled to talk to him, after that, it is just a question of common humanity that nobody should want to avoid. The hardened underworld types already know their rights, but the poor and illiterate need this protection. This basic constitutional safeguard is a procedure followed by the FBI for many years."

Today *Miranda* remains not only one of the most argumentative but in some ways the most typical decision of the sixteen-year Warren Court. Yet its constitutional bases are sound. It derives from a fundamental American principle that few would challenge in the abstract: protection of the rights of the accused. Despite the increasingly conservative temper of the Burger Court in the years since Warren's departure, the Court—though modifying—has thus far been unable to find a basis for overturning *Miranda*. But whenever an apparently ironclad criminal prosecution is thrown out of court because police officers have failed to follow *Miranda* requirements, critics are still quick to protest that this Warren Court ruling "coddles" criminals and "handcuffs" police.

Basically, the question comes down to defining the point at which preserving an individual right begins to conflict with the rights of society—a perennial problem in a democracy. Warren, in his untheoretical way during his maturing Chief Justiceship always tended to favor maximum protection of individual rights. Apparently he believed that however great the danger might be that an individual's rights could infringe upon community rights, the potential danger of the community's oppressing the individual was incalculably greater. And that probably still remains the best defense of *Miranda*: If it has produced some miscarriages of justice, how many far more dangerous miscarriages may it not have prevented?

On the other hand, the Warren Court ducked another sensitive subject, declining to hear any cases concerning the legality of the Vietnam War in 1967. This prompted then University of Nebraska Assistant Law Professor Leonard V. Kaplan to charge: "If the Warren Court cannot really handle Vietnam or civil disobedience issues, perhaps it is no longer relevant as an institution of justice." Other constitutional scholars, though, pointed out that no Supreme Court has ever ruled on the legality of *any* war, and that to do so might well be beyond the Court's constitutional power.

The following year, a lesser known but landmark anti-wiretapping decision was handed down. Illegally secured evidence through electronic eavesdropping of a telephone booth was outlawed by the Warren Court in *Katz* v. *United States*. Reversing a 1928 wiretapping law decision in *Olmstead* v. *United States*, the ruling attempted to educate law-enforcers on the meaning of the Constitution's search-and-seizure clause. Echoing the Brandeis dissent in the Olmstead case and what Holmes later called "dirty business," Earl Warren, their late-blooming judicial disciple, wrote: "The indiscriminate use of wiretapping is an outrageous violation of the privacy of individuals and can lead to the grossest kind of abuses." Wiretapping was thus declared unconstitutional and inadmissible as evidence unless authorized by warrant.

Yet the Chief Justice's increasingly fervent feelings did not always influence his brethren. In November 1967 he stood alone and apart from them in their 7–1 majority ruling without comment upholding the New York Stock Exchange's brokerage commissions system. The appeal had been filed on behalf of five mutual funds which argued that the setting of minimum commission rates for security transactions constituted a price-fixing conspiracy. Earlier, its suit had been dismissed without trial by Chicago's U. S. District Judge Julius N. Hoffman (of later "Chicago 7" notoriety) and had been affirmed by the U. S. Circuit Court there. Now, in an unusually bitter four-page dissent, Warren called this a "blunderbuss approach," and claimed that the U. S. Department of Justice antitrust division should have been asked to present its views. "This is no ordinary case," wrote Warren. "It is of the utmost importance to millions of investors and concerns practices which have an impact upon the economy."

The Court's composition changed again in 1967 when Thurgood Marshall was appointed to succeed Tom Clark, who resigned after his son Ramsey was named Attorney General—to avoid any possible appearance of conflict of interest. Thus, the Warren "activists" picked up another vote. Marshall was the first black justice to be appointed to the U. S. Supreme Court. A Pullman car steward's son, great-grandson of an African slave, the fifty-seven-year-old Marshall had been an NAACP attorney for twenty-five years, and was chief counsel in the 1954 school desegregation suit. He was carefully groomed for the High Court through key appointments by both Presidents Kennedy and Johnson—as Warren approvingly reminded Southern senators who were silent on the nomination. Marshall, in

1961, had been named a U.S. Court of Appeals judge for the Second Circuit in New York and, in 1965, U.S. Solicitor General.

In June, shortly after Marshall was appointed but before he was confirmed, the Chief Justice wrote to Johnson:

Dear Mr. President:

It was thoughtful of you to call me in San Francisco at the time of your appointment of Thurgood Marshall. I was pleased to hear the news. It was an excellent appointment. Few men come to the court with better experience or a sounder preparation for our work. Also it is in keeping with your policy of opening governmental policies to all without regard to race, religion or economic status. In this respect, no other President has done as much as you have.

All of us know Thurgood and will welcome him to the court in the belief that he will make a real contribution to its jurisprudence during the many years we hope he will be able to serve.

We look forward to his early confirmation and qualification.

Marshall was quietly confirmed in August.

Chief Justice and Nina Warren continued to be frequent White House guests. Lady Bird Johnson, in her later-published *White House Diary*, remarked that the Warrens "are always on hand as helpful standbys and ornaments." The Warrens attended not only the official judicial receptions, dinners for foreign dignitaries and swearing-in ceremonies of governmental appointees, but even some Johnson family functions, including the wedding of their elder daughter, Lynda Bird.

At Christmas 1967, several Johnson family culinary presents inspired this thank-you note from the Chief Justice: "We devoured the bread, which was made even more tasty by the pear preserves. It brought back memories of my days as a small boy eating bread and jam in mother's kitchen."

The Chief Justice reciprocated by congratulating the President on special occasions such as LBJ's sixtieth birthday. He thanked Warren, writing, "Even as the years mature us, time strengthens our friendship . . ."

On November 8, 1967, President Johnson sent Warren this whimsical letter:

Dear Mr. Chief Justice:

I think you should know of a rather remarkable event. A member of the press has done you a good turn.

It spoils the man-bites-dog story only slightly to reveal that your benefactor is our kind and mutual friend, Drew Pearson.

He has written me of your difficulties in finding a pool fit for winter dips. By coincidence, I happen to have one—warm, wet and absolutely snoop-proof.

I hope you will avail yourself of it. It is large enough for any friends you care to bring. You might even ask Drew—though he seems to need no pool to make splashes.

Bring your suit the first time and leave it on the peg. I will try to float free and join you from time to time.

The same day LBJ wrote Pearson, who was then feuding with Richard Nixon: "I am reassured that certain of your recent encounters with Californians have not affected your fondness for all natives of the state."

The year 1968 was climactic for Earl Warren as well as for the nation which struggled with such diverse events as the assassinations of Robert F. Kennedy and Martin Luther King, demonstrations on the streets of Chicago and at Columbia University, the My Lai massacre, Lloyd Bucher's surrender of *The Pueblo*, the storming of the U. S. Embassy in Saigon, the Russian rape of Czechoslovakia, the Kerner Commission Report, the replacing of the word "Negro" with "black" in the language and the erosion of President Lyndon Johnson's credibility gap.

Although in good health and enjoying his job, after reaching his seventy-seventh birthday on March 19 Warren began seriously to consider retiring. He remembered what Justice Black had told him that Chief Justice Charles Evans Hughes had said before retiring at seventy-nine: "Oh, I can go on for a few years but I don't want to continue under the delusion of adequacy." If Warren retired, because of his service of more than ten years he was entitled to receive his full $40,000 annual salary ($500 more than the Associate Justices). In retirement, he hoped to work at the new Federal Judicial Center in Washington to reduce Federal court congestion.

The Center had finally been created by Congress after strong White House pressure.

On March 31 President Johnson suddenly announced over nationwide evening television that he would not seek re-election. This decision was prompted by his weakness in the early primaries, his uncertain health and, above all, the unpopularity of his Vietnam policies.

In his Supreme Court chambers, Earl Warren handwrote this letter on April 2:

Dear Mr. President:

Your speech to the nation was magnificent but it ended on what to me was a sad note. I had hoped that you would decide differently, as you have earned another term of more tranquil years. However, the final note was one that will resound through history. In the past six years you have done more to make our citizenship conform to the American Dream than any of your predecessors, and if your Administration had been a century or even a generation earlier, the tragedy of our cities and other domestic problems would not be plaguing us as they are today. You have broken the back of discrimination. The foundation for the Great Society has been laid but the implementation of your vision for it must be done by others. I hope they will have your determination and courage in carrying through.

Your burden has been great but your reward will be greater. The old order of discrimination is gone, and looking at our present difficulties, we can say, "These too shall pass," and America will be in for happier days. That will be your reward.

Nina and I send our heartfelt good wishes to both you and Mrs. Johnson.

President Johnson replied on April 30 in part: "I have had many occasions in my public life to think of you as the kindest and wisest man I have ever known. Your recent letter confirms my judgment and adds to my great debt of the heart."

In the original draft of this letter, the President had called Warren merely "the kindest" man he had ever known. In the revision, he had added "the wisest."

On June 5, presidential candidate Robert Kennedy was assassinated in a Los Angeles hotel after his sweeping California Democratic primary victory over Senator Eugene McCarthy. The murder of forty-two-year-old Bobby—less than five years after his brother's death—deeply disturbed the retiring Chief Justice. He was confident that RFK would have been elected President in November, would have continued JFK's and LBJ's programs and, because of Bobby's capacity for growth, would have made an excellent President. Now, Johnson began reconsidering his decision not to run again.

For Richard Nixon, the Republican front-runner, the Bobby Kennedy assassination was an unanticipated political advantage. Earl Warren now feared the political worst: the probable election of his longtime California enemy as President of the United States in November. This unhappy prospect impelled the Chief Justice to hasten a decision which he had long been pondering.

Six days after the Bobby Kennedy tragedy, President Johnson received this memo from his aide, James R. Jones: "Justice Fortas called to say that Chief Justice Warren would like to see the President at the President's convenience. Shall I schedule Chief Justice Warren for an appointment later this week?" Emphatically, the President checked, "Yes."

Two days later, on Thursday, June 13, 1968, this aide's 3:15 P.M. Memorandum for the Record states: "Chief Justice Earl Warren met with the President at 9:25 A.M. today and departed the President's office at 9:40 A.M. He came down to say that because of age he felt that he should retire from the Court and he said he wanted President Johnson to appoint as his successor someone who felt as Justice Warren did."

The Chief Justice returned to his Supreme Court chambers and wrote two retirement letters to the President. The first was a terse, one-sentence communication closing, "Respectfully." The second was a chatty letter of explanation ending "Sincerely." Both letters (dated June 13, 1968) were hand-delivered to the White House late that afternoon by a Supreme Court messenger. In the second letter, explaining that he was retiring "solely because of age," Warren wrote: "When I entered public service, 150 million of our 200 million people were not yet born. I, therefore, conceive it my duty to give way to someone who will have more years ahead of him . . . I believe there are few people who have enjoyed serving the public or who are more grateful for the opportunity to have done so than I."

The first, more formal, letter had simply advised the President of Warren's intentions to resign "effective at your pleasure." This phrase, however, immediately raised some questions in the White House and elsewhere. Since Warren had set no date, did the letter imply that his retirement was *contingent* upon something—Johnson's appointing a successor acceptable to Warren, perhaps? Or on the Senate's confirming that appointment? Actually, as Warren soon made clear, he had not intended his words to convey anything more than a courtesy to the President. If it contained a hidden message, this was no more than a gentle reminder about a situation of which both men were acutely aware: The appointment had to be made and confirmed *before* January 20, 1969, for on that date the new President might very well be Richard Nixon.

Although Johnson did not release Warren's resignation letters for nearly two weeks, word of their existence soon leaked out. The press was alert to the political implications of the move. As the New York *Daily News* June 22 page-one headline correctly put it: "Earl Warren to Quit Court. LBJ Faces Row on Successor."

Conservative Republicans, heartened by the prospect of a GOP victory in November, were determined not to be cheated of Nixon's opportunity to appoint a conservative to replace Warren as Chief Justice. Senators Robert Griffin of Michigan and John Tower of Texas publicly warned that they would lead a fight in the upper chamber to oppose any lifetime appointments to the Court by a lame-duck President. Governor Ronald Reagan of California accused the President and Chief Justice of "playing dirty pool" and upbraided Warren for a "lack of faith in this system of ours" because he was attempting "to choose which President he thinks should dominate the Supreme Court for the next twenty years."

Evangelist Billy Graham took a somewhat less combative tack. In the course of thanking the President for a recent visit to the LBJ ranch he wrote:

> *I just heard on the news that Chief Justice Warren has resigned. If this news report proves to be correct, it is my prayer that you will give serious consideration to balancing the Court with a strong conservative as Chief Justice. I am convinced that many of the problems that have plagued America in the last few years are a direct result of some of the extreme rulings of the Court, especially*

in the field of criminology. I believe that our mutual friend, Governor John Connally, would make an ideal and popular choice. He might not be popular with the extreme liberals and radicals who are already fighting you anyway but he would make a great Chief Justice.

You may rest assured that you are in my thoughts and prayers every day.

Speculation over whom Johnson would name centered around Abe Fortas, Attorney General Ramsey Clark, Secretary of Defense Clark Clifford and Texas Federal Judges Sarah T. Hughes and Homer Thornberry. Ironically, Arthur Goldberg, now in private practice, whom Johnson had apparently promised to return to the Court, possibly as Chief Justice, was now in LBJ's disfavor after quitting his United Nations post in disagreement over White House Vietnam policies.

But there was no dearth of other proposals. Los Angeles Mayor Sam Yorty made an impassioned pitch for *his* candidate:

My dear Mr. President:

In the event that Chief Justice Earl Warren does resign, I hope that you will consider Justice Mildred Lillie as a replacement.

I believe that she would be an excellent replacement. She is popular with women everywhere and important in California where she is very popular.

Welly K. Hopkins, a former Texas state senator, recommended Henry H. Fowler, Secretary of the Treasury, citing among other qualifications: "He is a Virginian, in the prime of life, his birthday and your own being almost identical."

A telegram to the White House from a Charlie Smith in Kingsland, Georgia, suggested:

SINCE EARL WARREN HAS RESIGNED AS CHIEF JUSTICE YOU HAVE A GOOD SUBSTITUTE IN WASHINGTON, D.C. I SUGGEST MR. [RALPH] ABERNATHY WHO IS ALREADY IN YOUR CITY.

Soon the speculation ended. On June 25 at 8:30 P.M., White House private secretary Mary Rather prepared a memo for the President stating: "The Attorney General [Ramsey Clark] called and said he wanted to be sure you understood about sending over to him the draft of letter to Chief Justice Warren so he could put some technical things in it."

At his news conference the next morning, President Johnson read and released Warren's two June 13 letters as well as his own June 26 reply, which read in part:

My dear Mr. Chief Justice:

It is with the deepest regret that I learn of your desire to retire, knowing how much the nation has benefited from your service as Chief Justice. However, in deference to your wishes, I will seek a replacement to fill the vacancy in the office of Chief Justice that will be occasioned when you depart. With your agreement, I will accept your decision to retire effective at such time as a successor is qualified.

Simultaneously, the President announced that he had named Associate Justice Abe Fortas to succeed Warren.

The appointment should have come as no surprise. For thirty years the hard-driving Fortas had been one of LBJ's closest and most trusted unofficial advisors, even, inappropriately, during the past three years while sitting on the Supreme Court. He was thoroughly acceptable to Warren, whose liberal and innovative judicial philosophy Fortas could be expected to uphold. If either Warren or Johnson worried that the intense, sardonic Fortas might lack the conciliatory skills that had enabled Warren to produce so many unanimous or strong majority decisions, neither man gave any public hint of such a concern. It was going to be hard enough to get Fortas confirmed without voicing any private reservations.

To fill Fortas' vacant Associate Justice seat, Johnson appointed another old friend, Judge Homer Thornberry, a fifty-nine-year-old former Mayor of Austin, Texas, and successor to Johnson's seat in the U. S. House of Representatives. President Kennedy had named Thornberry a Federal District Judge at Vice President Johnson's recommendation in 1963. Two years later, President Johnson promoted him to the U. S. Fifth Circuit Court of Appeals—and now to the U. S. Supreme Court. Before Johnson had appointed Thurgood Marshall the previous year to the top tribunal, he had seriously considered nominating Thornberry instead. The retired Johnson claimed in his memoirs that the Thornberry appointment was suggested to him by Senator Russell as a condition for supporting the Fortas nomination. However, LBJ's irrepressible brother Sam, in his book, *My Brother Lyndon*, gleefully insists: "He [Thornberry] was one of Lyndon's oldest friends. He would always start laughing at my brother's jokes even before Lyndon got to the punch line."

Warren considered it unwise for Johnson to have named both Fortas and Thornberry simultaneously because it made the President vulnerable to the charge of double "cronyism." Still, Warren vigorously defended the right of *any* President, regardless of his lame-duck status, to appoint new members to the High Court. At an extraordinary news conference (his first in three years) held on July 5, ten days after the Fortas-Thornberry announcements, in the Supreme Court's Conference Room, the Chief Justice asserted: "As long as a man is President, he has a right to perform the duties of his office. There always ought to be a Chief Justice of the United States because the Court is a continuous body and should have the leadership it is entitled to have." This remark was widely interpreted as a veiled threat to the Senate that Warren might withdraw his resignation should Fortas not be confirmed.

The remainder of the press conference showed that Earl Warren could still play politics. He denied—apparently quite untruthfully—that he had discussed the Fortas and Thornberry appointments with Johnson, but praised both nominees unstintingly. Loftily he repudiated the suggestion that his resignation was timed to prevent another President—notably Nixon—from appointing a successor: "That is in the realm of politics. I left politics fifteen years ago and would hate to have political matters injected into stories about my retirement." No one took him seriously, of course, but then, probably no one was meant to. Plainly this was the beginning of a major political battle.

The acrimonious three-month controversy over the Fortas confirmation soon became a partisan circus, with some sideshow pantomime on the Warren Court. On July 11 the Senate Judiciary Committee opened hearings. The thrust of the initial opposition argument was that since there had been no vacancy to fill, it could not properly be said that Warren had resigned at all. This was not, of course, a vote of confidence for Warren, but merely a device for stalling the Fortas confirmation. It was apparently assumed that even if Warren were to continue to serve as Chief Justice into the next Administration, his age, health and distaste for Nixon would eventually force him to resign, thus leaving the way open for the appointment of a conservative successor. Better to suffer on for a few more years under Warren than be stuck with a decade or more of Fortas.

The defense, led by Attorney General Clark, naturally took the opposite view. It cited historical precedents in which Presidents had nominated, and the Senate had confirmed, candidates for high positions while their predecessors were still in office and even on the bench. But everyone knew that the legalistic arguments propounded by both sides were mostly hot air. In the end, it would come down to who had the votes.

If confirmed, Fortas would receive a mere $500 salary boost to $40,000 and be given the use of the Supreme Court's only chauffeured limousine. The latter would have supplemented the fashionably old late-1950 Rolls-Royce driven by him and his tax-lawyer wife, who practiced under her maiden name of Carolyn Agger.

Shortsightedly, the overconfident Fortas accepted the Judiciary Committee's invitation to testify. He was the first Chief Justice nominee in history ever to do so. Fortas could easily have declined on the grounds of judicial independence, as the unconsulted Warren had hoped he would. Warren himself had respectfully declined to testify during his own confirmation hearings, preferring to let his California record speak for him. Now, in facing the committee's onslaught, Fortas was whiplashed for his LBJ "cronyism," including his giving advice, while on the Court, to the President on the Vietman war and urban riots, and for helping the President draft State of the Union messages. Even more unfairly, Fortas now became the target of fifteen years of conservative fury against Warren Court decisions. Lawmakers could not impeach "That Man" who headed the Court, but his nominated successor was an acceptable surrogate.

"Mallory! Mallory! I want that name to ring in your ears." shouted South Carolina Republican Senator Strom Thurmond at Fortas. The learned legislator was referring to a controversial Warren Court criminal justice decision made eight years before Fortas ever sat on the bench.

During his four agonizing days of grilling, Fortas was reluctantly drawn into discussions about virtually every liberal Warren Court decision in which he had participated, from definitions of obscenity to criminal defendants' rights. Hostile senators read them aloud. Fortas' judicial propriety was also questioned as the result of a *New York Times* revelation that he had accepted a $15,000 fee for conducting a series of summer seminars at American University's law school. The issue was neither the fee nor the lectures, since the Court was then in summer recess, but the fact that these tax-deductible funds were solicited by the late Paul Porter, his former law partner, from businessmen who might be involved in future Supreme Court litigation.

Anti-Semitism, too, reared its ugly head, despite denials by Fortas opponents. One committee member was overheard to exult after a hearing: "I think we've got that Jew-boy sonofabitch in a box now."

On August 8, an American Conservative Union statement assailed Justice Fortas' "political mischief" and charged that "[he] appears to be to the left of Chief Justice Warren . . ."

Then vacationing in the West, Warren told a luncheon of the Montana Supreme Court Justices in Helena on August 23: "There seems to be some manuevering going on in Washington. I can assure you that the delay is not because they want to retain *me*. If it's a choice of taking Abe Fortas or keeping me, they'll take Abe. But it looks like I'll be back to open the Supreme Court in October."

In Washington, an infuriated President Johnson, holding a "backgrounder" interview with newsmen, bitterly predicted that if Fortas was not confirmed, Warren would serve another four years— whoever became President. ABC television newsman Bill Gill used this item until he was forcefully reminded by a White House official that LBJ's remark was off the record.

On September 13, the embattled and embarrassed Fortas reversed himself. He wrote Mississippi Senator Eastland, the anti-Warren Court Judiciary Committee chairman, that he would no longer testify.

The full Judiciary Committee finally approved the Fortas nomination 11–6, moving it to the Senate floor. There, the political gladiators sprang into even more feverish action. A coalition of Republicans and conservative Southern Democrats led by Senator Griffin (encouraged offstage by GOP candidate Nixon) staged a filibuster for six days to prevent a vote on the Fortas nomination. Two-thirds of the Senators present—59 votes—were needed to invoke cloture, a ruling which would have limited debate, ended the filibuster and permitted a vote on the nomination. On the crucial October 1 cloture vote, the tally was 45 aye, 43 nay—14 short of the needed number. Thus, the filibuster appeared to doom the nomination. With Fortas' scalp in his lap, Senator Griffin joyfully warned that should the nomination again be brought up, at least a dozen other Senators were ready to speak against it. Had Fortas' foes really been certain of victory, they would doubtless have permitted a vote and not resorted to filibuster.

The next day, Fortas wrote President Johnson requesting that his nomination be withdrawn to stop the "destructive and extreme assaults upon the Court." Immediately, Johnson complied with "deep regret," terming the Senate action "historically and constitutionally tragic."

Almost immediately, people began to besiege the President with suggestions for new nominees. They included such liberals as Michigan Senator Philip A. Hart (floor manager of the Fortas nomination) and California Senator Thomas H. Kuchel, as well as Defense Secretary Clark M. Clifford, Treasury Secretary Henry H. Fowler and Cyrus R. Vance, U. S. negotiator with the North Vietnamese in Paris. Arthur Goldberg was strongly recommended by Senator J. William Fulbright, who reasoned, "Goldberg is entitled to it. He was talked off the Court." But the hurt and bitter Johnson, whose Master Plan had gone awry, proudly refused to name a Fortas substitute. In his heart, Lyndon Baines Johnson knew that he never would have sat in the first seat in the land had it not been for the old friend whom he now reciprocally sought to elevate to the nation's first judicial chair. To the sentimental Texan, the Fortas debacle was a political Alamo.

Deploring the Senate's failure to confirm his friend, he now formally requested Chief Justice Warren to stay put "until emotion subsided, reason and fairness prevail." Immediately, the "resigned" head of the Supreme Court issued this one-sentence assent: "The President's statement speaks for itself and calls for no additional elaboration by me." Privately, he sorrowfully added, "Since they won't confirm Abe, they'll just have to take me for a while." The forgotten man in this misfired judicial power play was Judge Homer Thornberry. There was now no vacancy for him as the 1968–69 Supreme Court term opened on October 7. Associate Justice Fortas returned to his regular chair at the end of the bench and, in the stormy center seat, the seventy-seven-year-old Warren reluctantly resumed the duties which he had intended to relinquish.

Still, this did not end the episode. Although Fortas' nomination had been thwarted, Warren's status was still unclear. Under what circumstances would his resignation become effective? It had been offered to President Johnson, who, unable (and now unwilling) to appoint a successor, had in effect declined it. Could it be assumed that the offer would automatically extend to Johnson's successor?

The Republicans, led by Everett Dirksen, insisted it was clear that the Chief Justice would not have to write any new letters; his retirement request obviously would remain in effect (unless Warren formally withdrew it) and could be accepted by the new President. By contrast Democrats, headed by Senate Majority leader Mike Mansfield, did not find this obvious at all. On the contrary, they contended, unless Warren specifically renewed his offer to the new President, he could stay on the Supreme Court indefinitely.

Warren could easily have clarified this dispute either by withdrawing his resignation or by announcing his intention to resubmit it to the new President at the earliest opportunity. But he did neither. He himself was sorely perplexed. To intimates he admitted that now he wanted to retire more than ever. Yet he had promised Johnson to stay on and he meant to keep his word, even though this involved the unattractive likelihood for continuing to serve during a possible Nixon Administration.

The bleakness of this prospect was hardly lightened by the tenor of the 1968 Republican presidential campaign. More than ever before, the record of the Warren Court was now viewed by conservatives as a prime target for attack, and Richard Nixon had no intention of letting this opportunity go unexploited. He accused the Warren Court of "seriously weakening the peace forces and strengthening the criminal forces in our society." The Court was too "permissive" in its philosophy, too slapdash in its methods ("the fastest track in the nation," Nixon called it). If elected, Nixon promised to appoint only "strict constructionists," judges who would "interpret, not try to make, law." And so on.

But to the beleaguered Chief Justice, "strict construction" translated as diminution of individual rights. "During the entire campaign," the unforgiving Warren later contended "the principal issue was 'law-and-order.' It merely was an exercise in the rhetoric of accusation and recrimination which just increased divisiveness throughout the nation."

Until now, crime had never been a major presidential campaign issue. But "law-and-order" proved a better campaign issue for Nixon than Vietnam, because neither hawks nor doves were much reassured by his promises to end the war quickly. Still, Vietnam also helped Nixon, for it was a crushing liability to his Democratic opponent whom young voters shortsightedly scorned. Hubert H. Humphrey, a moderate dove, was probably more eager to bring a quick end to the American involvement in Vietnam than Nixon. But as Johnson's Vice President, he could not publicly voice his true feelings about Vietnam without appearing to be disloyal to his Chief. This insoluble dilemma ultimately proved fatal to the cheerful man's candidacy. In a spiritless election, Nixon narrowly won.

Warren had been clinging to the faint hope of a Humphrey victory as the best solution to his own problems. Now though, he had to face a stubborn, unpleasant reality. His only conceivable motive for remaining as Chief Justice in the face of an openly hostile administration would be to try to outlast Nixon. In 1972 a Democrat *might* be elected and Warren *might* be able to ensure that the Chief Justiceship would pass to a liberal. Yet it was equally possible that Nixon would win a second term, and it was not certain that Warren's health would permit him to continue for even four years, let alone for eight. And even if it did, there would inevitably be other Court vacancies which Nixon would fill with his "strict constructionist" and "law-and-order" appointees. Thus, the chances of preserving the character of the Warren Court seemed painfully remote. Moreover, the possibility that the nation might be plagued with protracted guerilla warfare between the Executive and the Judiciary appeared all too real. For his own sake and that of the country, Warren concluded, he must step down at the earliest opportunity. Yet the Chief Justice knew—better than most—that the Court's vital work would be disrupted if he resigned in mid-term.

Warren's discomfort was communicated by his son-in-law, John Daly, during a Washington golf match with William Rogers, soon to be named Nixon's Secretary of State. Rogers promptly telephoned Nixon at his pre-Inauguration headquarters in New York's Pierre Hotel, explaining Warren's concern both for the Supreme Court and himself.

The incoming President had still been unsure what Warren would do—and, for that matter, whom he wanted to succeed Warren. Should it be Thomas Dewey? Herbert Brownell? John Mitchell? Charles M. Rhyne, his Duke University classmate and former American Bar Association president? Judge Henry J. Friendly of the U. S. Court of Appeals for the Second Circuit? Chief Judge Stanley J. Fuld or Judge Charles Breitel of New York State's highest Court of Appeals? Or should he promote Associate Justice Potter Stewart, as many believed that he would? Stewart would have been the easiest to name, but the unforgiving Nixon, who remembered the Republican jurist's vote against him in the *Hill* v. *Life* case snapped to an aide: "Screw Stewart!"

The Rogers telephone call interrupted these deliberations. By affirming his intention to resign, Warren had relieved Nixon of a potentially thorny problem. In return, Nixon gracefully proposed a formula which would accommodate both their interests: Warren would continue to preside over the Court until the end of its current term in June 1969, when his resignation would become effective. Warren accepted with gratitude. "This sensible and dignified arrangement worked out between President-elect Nixon and Chief Justice Warren," wrote *The New York Times* on December 5, "ends the confusion about whether the Chief Justice is staying or leaving. He is doing both. By remaining on the bench and then retiring, the Chief Justice helps to remove the Supreme Court from the political category of a captured prize."

On January 20, 1969, the Chief Justice administered the presidential oath of office to his lifelong political enemy. The ceremony seemed to mark the twilight of Earl Warren's public career and the resurrection and apogee of Richard Nixon's.

Yet for both the fourteenth Chief Justice and the thirty-seventh President of the United States their struggle with each other was far from ended.

—————— *Chapter Eight* ——————

The Nixon Years: 1969–1974

*O*n April 22, 1969, President Nixon honored retiring Chief Justice Warren at a lavish White House dinner. The guest list of 110 included the entire Warren family, the other eight Supreme Court Justices, Vice President Agnew, ten Cabinet members and some of the men most likely to be considered for Warren's position. Conspicuously absent was Warren's close friend, Senator Thomas H. Kuchel, the assistant Republican floor leader, whom Governor Warren had named to fill Nixon's vacant Senate seat when he became Vice President. "Nixon invited [Senator] George Murphy but not me," remembers the still-unforgiving Kuchel.

The President warmly toasted Warren's fifty years of distinguished public service. Warren reciprocated with equal warmth, replying, "I approach retirement with no malice in my heart toward anyone."

Both men had been behaving with such decorous insincerity ever since their pre-Inauguration agreement about Warren's retirement. In fact, they probably still detested each other as much as they ever had in the past.

It was, after all, too much to suppose that either could erase past memories. Nixon could never forgive Warren for not supporting his House and Senate candidacies in 1946 and 1950. Moreover, the new

President suspected that Warren devotees—if not Warren himself— had been responsible for leaking the news of Nixon's secret campaign fund, thereby nearly causing Eisenhower to dump him from the GOP presidential ticket in 1952. And, of course, Warren had given Nixon a bad scare in late 1955 after Eisenhower's heart attack, when the polls had clearly shown that Chief Justice Warren was favored over Vice President Nixon as Ike's potential successor.

For his part, Warren had mistrusted Nixon ever since being outraged by the smear tactics Nixon had used in his campaigns against Voorhis and Douglas. ["I'm sorry about that (Douglas) episode," Nixon admitted to British publisher David Astor in 1957. "I was a very young man."] Warren was likewise certain that Nixon, despite his public protestations of loyalty, had betrayed him in the 1952 race for the presidential nomination by secretly switching his allegiance to Eisenhower. Governor Warren had then remarked to me in his Sacramento office, "Nixon plays for keeps, but his keeps are all for himself!" In 1960 Warren was overjoyed that Kennedy had nosed out Nixon for the presidency. In 1962, through his namesake son, Warren had helped Edmund "Pat" Brown—whom President Nixon now had charitably invited to the Warren White House dinner—crush the former Vice President for the California governor-ship. And in 1968 presidential candidate Nixon had never moderated his savage denunciations of the Warren Court—which hardly endeared him to the soon-to-retire Chief Justice.

Warren already had voted against Nixon for President *twice*, having cast absentee ballots for Kennedy in 1960 and Humphrey in 1968, and even later would vote for McGovern in 1972. This never has been a secret to Warren family members and his intimate friends. Even Democrat W. Averell Harriman, when both were speaking at the Truman Library in Independence, Missouri, teased him publicly, "I'm not at all sure that on occasions, in the privacy of the voting booth, we did not vote for the *same* candidate."

Neutral observers had long noted the mutual antipathy between the two men. During his early California years, the enterprising Nixon had vainly sought to latch onto the elusive coattails of popular Governor Warren. Even as Vice President he crudely attempted to drag Warren and the Supreme Court into partisan politics on Lincoln's Birthday, 1956 (February 12), by crowing that "a great *Republican* Chief Justice" was solely responsible for the 1954 deseg-regation decision. Nixon later "explained" that he had intended to insert a comma between "Republican" and "Chief" but Warren—and Eisenhower, too—remained unconvinced.

A year later, when the American Bar Association met in London, Warren informed bar officials that he might not attend the convention if Nixon was on the program—since that would give a political aura to the agenda. "If you let that fellow in, count me out," were his words, as reported by pro-Nixon biographer Ralph de Toledano, much to Warren's embarrassment. The Bar Association chose not to invite the man who was a heartbeat away from the presidency.

Even more embarrassing to the Chief Justice was the incident two years later in June 1959, at the twenty-fifth wedding anniversary party for his friend *Denver Post* correspondent Barnet Nover, at which Mrs. Warren was unable to accompany him. Warren then met Earl Mazo, who had just published a pro-Nixon biography. He was reported to have objected to an excerpt of the book in *Look* magazine that said he had tried to stop Nixon's political career, and quoted him as having said: "I don't like it when you use this book to step on my head—to go over my body to promote Nixon." Clark R. Mollenhoff, then a Des Moines *Register* correspondent and later a Nixon White House aide, disregarding the off-the-record aspect of the private party, published a sensational copyrighted story, claiming that Warren had called Mazo "a liar." In his memoirs, Warren denied this, saying, "It was a good commercial for the Mazo book but nothing else. I was taught better manners than that. . . ."

Both personally and politically, Warren had always sought to disassociate himself from his California rival. The Chief Justice privately joked about his own one-man "enemy list."

Once, when Warren fell overboard after a big fish toppled his small boat in Spring Lake, Virginia, in July 1955, he was embarrassed because he was reminded that the same thing had happened to Nixon off Florida's West Coast shortly before. Warren swore his fellow fishermen to secrecy. When one of them, Associate Justice Tom Clark—who did not equate this amusing mishap with a hush-hush Supreme Court conference—asked why, the Chief Justice quipped: "Because I don't want to be put in the same class with Nixon!"

Even now, while the two men hypocritically played at exchanging toasts, President Nixon was preparing to deal Warren a secret new blow through the person of another dinner guest, Abe Fortas,

Warren's close Court colleague. John Mitchell, Nixon's new Attorney General, had already instructed the Justice Department to prepare a memorandum citing the legal grounds for Fortas' impeachment and prosecution. The main charge was that Fortas, three months after ascending to the Supreme Court, had accepted a $20,000-a-year retainer from the foundation of financier Louis E. Wolfson. Although Fortas insisted that he had subsequently returned the money and severed connections with the foundation, he had, at the least, been guilty of a serious impropriety.

Two weeks after the White House dinner, Mitchell visited Warren in his Court chambers and confronted him with the evidence against Fortas. Warren knew about the charges. They had already been leaked to the press and had been published that week in *Life* magazine. On the strength of the evidence, Mitchell demanded Warren's assistance in compelling Fortas to resign.

Warren was now in a bind. According to his own well-known lofty standards of ethics, what Fortas had done was unforgivable. Yet Fortas was his friend and—at least in the popular mind—a leading exemplar of judicial liberalism. His removal would tarnish both Warren and the Court while lending credence to Nixon's campaign fulminations over the need to replace "Warrenite" justices with "law-and-order" appointees.

By the same token, Warren had every reason to suspect both the motives and methods of the "new Nixon" and the new administration. Only two months earlier, for example, it had made what Warren considered a grossly improper and stealthy attempt to influence the Court's wiretapping decisions. Mitchell had sent his young Director of Public Information, Jack C. Landau, from the Department of Justice to pay an informal call on Justice Brennan at the Court. Brennan was so shocked by this emissary's remarks that he immediately brought him into the chambers of the Chief Justice. There, the nervous young visitor repeated the administration's concern (he mentioned both Nixon and Mitchell by name) that the Court's recent antiwiretapping decisions might inhibit present and future governmental use of covert electronic surveillance on all the embassies in Washington, and that publicizing these national security measures would only embarrass the government. Landau added that Mitchell *hoped* the unpopularity of the Court's position on wiretapping would not result in congressional legislative reprisals—or even a constitutional amendment—to limit the Court's powers in this area. Since

Warren and Brennan were unaware of any such congressional sentiment, both interpreted this as a veiled threat of administration-inspired reprisals to influence their decisions of three upcoming (March 24) government wiretap cases. Outraged, they remained uninfluenced. Warren now had no illusions on how far Mitchell or Nixon were capable of going to achieve their ends. He had always deemed Nixon a politician with plastic principles, but in his sixteen years on the Supreme Court, no one had ever attempted so brazenly to influence forthcoming decisions.

Thus, Warren now could not bring himself to collaborate with Mitchell. Yet neither could he defend Fortas. He had no choice but to wait in tortured silence while the destruction of Abe Fortas followed its inevitable scenario.

On Monday, May 12, Mitchell announced—and Warren unhappily confirmed—that he had informed the Chief Justice of the charges against Fortas. On that and the following day, the House moved swiftly and noisily toward impeachment proceedings. On Wednesday, Fortas sent a one-sentence letter of resignation to Nixon and a four-page letter of explanation to Warren. Although denying any wrongdoing, he acknowledged that, in the present circumstances, resignation was the only course left open to him. Nixon, who was about to deliver a major televised address on Vietnam that evening, attempted to postpone the announcement of Fortas' resignation so that the media could report his own speech without distraction. Fortas would have none of that, however, He quickly released the story of his resignation himself through the Supreme Court press officer, Bert Whittington, whom he telephoned at home, ordering him to have the announcement on the news wires within fifteen minutes.

The path was now open for Nixon to fill not one but two Court vacancies.

Sparing Warren's feelings did not seem to be high on the President's list of priorities. Merely six days after Fortas' resignation was made public, Nixon announced over nationwide television his choice for the first of his new Supreme Court appointments. Standing at his side before the cameras was a tall, husky, distinguished-looking man whose well-combed white hair peaked in a kind of pompadour. The President introduced the sixty-one-year-old Minnesotan—then relatively unknown outside legal circles—as the new Chief Justice. Illuminatingly, at the White House dinner honoring Warren a month earlier, he had been the only sitting member of a lower Federal court present.

Warren Earl Burger had been perhaps the most conservative judge on the predominantly liberal nine-man U. S. Court of Appeals in the District of Columbia. Nixon claimed that he had known Burger for twenty-one years and said that he was a man of "unquestioned integrity" (unlike Fortas, perhaps?). Not that they were close friends; Nixon later was quick to point out that Presidents should *avoid* appointing intimates to the Supreme Court (unlike LBJ perhaps?). But Burger's long experience, his "law-and-order" approach to crime and "strict constructionist" philosophy of judicial restraint in interpreting constitutional questions made him, in Nixon's opinion, "superbly qualified" to succeed Earl Warren.

The Burger appointment automatically excluded, as Nixon explained, Attorney General John Mitchell; Secretary of State William Rogers; and Charles A. Rhyne, his Duke University classmate. For other unexplained reasons, Nixon said that he had ruled out Associate Justice Potter Stewart (whom most other Justices had believed Nixon would promote), Thomas E. Dewey and Herbert Brownell. Nixon, in a surprisingly unreviewed passage in his memoirs wrote: "My first choice was former Attorney General Brownell." But Brownell would have faced a Senate confirmation battle, Nixon was warned even by Brownell himself.

Immediately after the Burger announcement, the retiring Warren, although privately pained, issued this two-sentence statement, reminiscent of a losing incumbent candidate's concession after an election: "I want to extend to Judge Burger my congratulations on his appointment and wish for him both success and happiness during his tenure as Chief Justice. I will be glad to do anything I can to facilitate his taking over the duties of the office at the end of our term." Warren, of course, had not been consulted about the Burger appointment. As a "courtesy," he had been informed of it merely a few hours earlier by Mitchell. Shortly after the announcement, one irreverent Washington restaurant proprietor—an Earl Warren admirer—now whimsically added a law-and-order "Warrenburger" to his menu, priced at two cents. It consisted of one slice of bread and one glass of water.

Nixon apparently had begun to consider Burger seriously during the 1968 campaign, when some of Burger's off-the-bench criticisms of the Warren Court were brought to his attention. Deploring the Supreme Court's tendency "to make law," Burger had said: "There is no reason why we as judges should regard ourselves as some kind of Guardian Elders ordained to revise the political judgments of elected representatives of the people." Referring to the *Miranda* decision, he disparaged the Court's "almost undignified haste to clothe detailed rules of evidence and police station procedure in the garb of constitutional doctrine." All this had gone down very well indeed with the candidate who then was campaigning his way into the White House partly by promising to change the makeup of the Supreme Court.

Burger recollects, "I first met Earl Warren in 1945 or 1946 while he was governor." But Warren remembered first meeting Burger, then a forty-one-year-old St. Paul attorney, in 1948, at the Republican National Convention in Philadelphia. Burger was then floor manager for Harold Stassen, who was seeking nomination at the convention that ultimately chose the Dewey–Warren ticket.

In 1952 the paths of the two future Chief Justices crossed again, this time at the Chicago convention. There, Burger ebulliently thumped for Eisenhower during the crucial credentials battle, and helped throw the Stassen votes which nominated Ike on the first ballot. As a reward, Attorney General Brownell the following year made Burger his assistant in charge of the Department of Justice's Claims Division, which was soon renamed the Civil Division.

Two years later, Warren and Burger met a third time, when Assistant Attorney General Burger argued the *Peters* v. *Hobby* case against then-private attorney Abe Fortas. Burger lost in a majority opinion written by Chief Justice Warren, who ruled that a public employee could confront his accusers if denied security clearance.

Now, as expected, Burger's nomination moved through the Senate like a hot knife through butter, aided probably by Senator Dirksen's assurance that "he looks like a Chief Justice, he speaks like a Chief Justice, and he acts like a Chief Justice." On June 9, 1969, just nineteen days after he had been named, he was overwhelmingly confirmed with but three nay votes. By comparison, Warren had been compelled to wait five uncomfortable months before the Upper Chamber had approved his nomination. "Like Fortas, Burger, too, it turned out, had taken foundation money for dubiously valuable services," contended law professor Philip Kurland of the

University of Chicago, "but the Senators found no need to look into this." An optimistic Democratic senator who voted for Burger's confirmation vouchsafed, *"Anything* can happen to a man who supported Stassen and then became Chief Justice."

Curiously, just a week after Burger's confirmation, and a week before Warren left the bench, the two men had occasion to clash judicially. Burger's U.S. Court of Appeals, in an opinion written by him, had declined to restore the seat which the House of Representatives had denied New York Democrat Adam Clayton Powell. Warren, who had no liking for, or illusions about, the arrogant, flamboyant Powell, nevertheless asserted, in the majority opinion, the Court's jurisdiction over constitutional legislative disputes and added that Congress could not by a majority vote "exclude"—as differentiated from "expel"—a duly elected representative. The vote reversing the U. S. Court of Appeals decision was 7–1.

Representative Gerald Ford was one of several congressmen who publicly disagreed with the Warren Court ruling, stating, "I think the Supreme Court was wrong. It puts the Judiciary at the top and the House of Representatives and Executive below." It is unclear from Ford's statement where the Senate fitted into his equation.

In another twilight move, Warren, determined to avert any future episodes such as the Fortas imbroglio, urged his fellow Justices to adopt restrictions on their off-the-bench activities. This would have approximated the code of conduct that the Judicial Conference had recently applied to lower court Federal judges, in which it was recommended that they disclose their incomes to the Conference and refrain from accepting fees for off-the-bench activities such as lecturing, writing or serving on foundation boards.

"Ironically, Burger might also be affected by the proposed rules," reported the May 30, 1969, issue of *Time* magazine. "He receives about $2,000 a year plus expenses for serving on the Board of the Mayo Clinic in Minnesota. . . . While this connection seems innocent enough, it would probably be dissolved if Warren's proposed rules against outside activity went into effect."

Not surprisingly, Warren was rebuffed by a majority of the Justices. They delayed a vote on their retiring head's proposed reform. In October, they would have a new—and perhaps less exacting—Chief Justice.

On the sunny morning of June 23, 1969, Richard Nixon and Earl Warren acted out the final scene in the scenario of their "sensible and dignified arrangement." This was the day of Warren's retirement. For the first time in history, an American President, in eulogizing a departing Justice, would address the Supreme Court.

Clad in striped trousers and a cutaway coat, Nixon arrived early. He alighted from his Lincoln limousine and entered the Marble Palace through the basement entrance. He sat silently in the packed courtroom for eighteen minutes while the Warren Court rendered its final three decisions. Then, after being recognized by the Chief Justice, the President walked to the lawyer's lectern facing the center of the long mahogany bench. For seven minutes the President dilated on the dignity, fairness, integrity and humanity of his retiring rival. Earl Warren, he said, had "helped to keep America on the path of continuity and change which is so essential for our progress."

Warren thanked the President for his "generous and greatly appreciated words." But in a quietly chiding tone, saying "you might not have looked into the matter," he reminded the President that the Supreme Court was a "continuing body"—implying that it would survive any transitory embarrassments caused by individual members. Then, in a passage that came as close as either man wished to acknowledging the irony of the situation, he remarked:

> *I cannot escape the feeling that in one sense, at least, this Court is similar to your own great office, and that is that so many times it speaks the last word in great governmental affairs . . . it is a responsibility that is made more difficult in this Court because we have no constituency. We serve no majority. We serve no minority. We serve only the public interest as we see it, guided only by the Constitution and our own consciences. And conscience is sometimes a very severe taskmaster.*

Then the fourteenth Chief Justice of the United States beckoned his successor and administered the hundred-word oath of office to him. Everyone rose. Warren climaxed the transition by saying: "Ladies and Gentlemen, the Chief Justice of the United States." Following the ceremony, the President and two Chief Justices posed for photographers on the Supreme Court steps, flanked by the massive marble pillars. All smiled dutifully for continuity and history.

Later, at his final news conference, the retiring Chief was asked whether the Warren Court decisions would endure.

"Naturally I would hope that they would, but I would not predict."

What was his major frustration during his sixteen years on the Court?

The silver-haired patriarch pondered the question. Then he smiled broadly before replying: "I can't really think of any. It has *not* been a frustrating experience."

How would he like the Warren Court to be remembered?

"As the People's Court."

California Congressman James C. Corman threw a surprise party for Warren but, as John Ehrlichman wrote me on September 25, 1977, from his Safford, Arizona prison cell: "Nixon [avoided] holding the traditional White House dinner for the Court until after Burger was Chief. There is no doubt that Nixon felt antipathy for Warren."

Although few men in contemporary American public life had been more controversial than Earl Warren, most of his critics responded to the news of his retirement with (at least overt) benignity. An exception was the New York *Daily News*, which saw fit to grace the occasion by characterizing him as "a power grabber, a twister and stretcher of the Constitution, an appointed judge without judicial instincts. We're happy to see him retire and won't pretend otherwise."

But encomia were mostly the order of the day. Senator Edward Kennedy said: "Our nation is stronger, freer and truer to its ideals because there was a 'Warren Court.' . . . We must not forget what he stands for." Senator Alan Cranston added: "I hope that future historians will say of Earl Warren and his times that in an era of doubt and confusion, of bigness and computers, of nuclear bombs and urban tensions . . . that in such an era he returned to the sources of America's greatness." Comparing Warren to Thomas Jefferson, *The New York Times* editorialized: "He had depended upon an unblinking integrity, a firm common sense and a deep feeling for the liberal and egalitarian values which moved . . . the founders of this nation." And in an open letter to his young grandson, Drew Pearson (to whose column Governor Warren had periodically "fed" anti-Nixon material, according to syndicate manager John Osenenko) wrote, "Dear Danny, A very great man retires from the Supreme Court today. He is also very much criticized. . . . By the time you are in college, Earl Warren will be regarded as a man who molded America as much as any of our great Presidents."

So The Chief stepped down.

By rights, Earl Warren should have lived out his golden years in his cherished Golden State. When the California press reported that he was house-hunting in the San Francisco-Berkeley-Sacramento area, real estate agents deluged him with mail and telephone calls. But the traditional "Potomac Fever" overcame him. Unable to forsake the nation's capital, he decided to remain in his hotel apartment, and he moved into a relatively small office in the Supreme Court building which looked out toward the Capitol. He was as entitled to these quarters as he was to his full $40,500 annual retirement salary.

One morning when strolling around the building, Warren noticed Chief Justice Burger inspecting with the gardener a colorful new flower bed outside his window. The thoughtful Burger told me, "He loved flowers and I enjoyed putting some outside his window."

The former Chief asked the new Chief how on earth he had time to worry about flowers.

"When I reminded him," recollects Burger, "that I walked around the building almost daily to relax and relieve my frustrations, just as he went to football games and duck hunting, he laughed heartily and said: 'You'd better find a bigger place to walk—this place is not large enough to work off the frustrations of a Chief Justice!' "

During the months following his retirement, Warren found much to fill his time. Suddenly he felt free to do what he had been unable to while on the Court. There were many ceremonial duties to perform, honors to be accepted and speeches to be delivered at many colleges, Freedom House and elsewhere. There was a trip to Bangkok for the Conference on World Peace Through Law. And, of course, there was the World Series between the Mets and the Orioles to be eyewitnessed with intense concentration. (The Baseball Hall of Fame in Cooperstown, New York, still preserves the methodically filled-in scorecard Warren kept at Shea Stadium during the third game.)

Equally absorbing, if less edifying, was the spectacle of the Nixon Administration's efforts to fill the vacant Fortas seat. In keeping with the successful "Southern Strategy" Nixon had espoused in his 1968 campaign, the President in August nominated Clement F. Haynsworth, Jr., of Greenville, South Carolina, the conservative Chief Judge of the Fourth Circuit Court of Appeals. By ordinary standards this was a reasonable enough choice. The fifty-six-year-old Haynsworth, a Harvard Law School graduate with considerable judicial experience, was a Southern Democrat-turned-Republican who could be expected to be a respectable law-and-order, strict-constructionist Justice. But an alliance of the AFL-CIO and some civil rights groups, still enraged over the Fortas ouster, perceived the nomination as a determined administration assault upon High Court liberalism. They decided to gun for Haynsworth.

Accordingly, Haynsworth's opponents unearthed a story that he had once ruled on a case in which he had a financial interest. Although the accusation fell short of suggesting that Haynsworth was guilty of an illegality or even of being self-serving, the hint of impropriety was enough for the now-sensitized Senate. It rejected Haynsworth by a 55–45 vote on November 21. This was the first time in nearly forty years that the Senate had flatly rejected a Supreme Court nomination. Seventeen members of the President's own party voted with the opposition. The pleased Warren was advised of the anti-Haynsworth strategy, although there is no evidence that he contributed to it.

On January 19, 1970, President Nixon tried again. This time his nominee was G. Harold Carswell, a Southern conservative judge on the U. S. Court of Appeals for the Fifth Circuit in Tallahassee, Florida. He was, if anything, an easier target than Haynsworth. Warren was appalled by the Carswell nomination, while that of Haynsworth had merely depressed him.

Carswell was immediately accused by civil rights groups of having a background of racial bias and of having publicly advocated segregation and white supremacy. Legal scholars gave his judicial record generally low marks. Louis H. Pollak, then Dean of the Yale Law School, (now a U. S. District Judge), and William Van Alstyne, Professor of Law at Duke University, both told the Senate Judiciary Committee that Carswell's abilities were at best "mediocre." This characterization prompted Republican Senator Roman Hruska of Nebraska to defend Carswell in one of the more extraordinary rebuttals in Senate history: "Even if he is mediocre, there are a lot of mediocre judges and people and lawyers and they are entitled to a little representation, aren't they? We can't have all Brandeises and Cardozos and Frankfurters and stuff like that."

Nor was the nominee's case strengthened when it became known that a member of Carswell's court, with the tacit approval of a "high official in the Justice Department," had undertaken an intensive telephone campaign to persuade Federal District judges to endorse the nomination. By now, many affronted senators began to feel that the nomination itself was another example of administration high-handedness. Not even a belated American Bar Association rating of Carswell as "qualified" could save him. On April 8 the Senate rejected him 51–45. Spectators in the galleries noisily applauded. President Nixon promptly accused the Senate of anti-Southern prejudice. New York University law professor Norman Redlich, who lunched with Warren on the day the Senate voted, recalls Warren's extreme pleasure at the outcome.

Humiliated, Richard Nixon now chose to vent his fury on one of the liberal giants still on the Court, Warren's intimate friend William O. Douglas. John Mitchell was assigned the task of uncovering evidence against Douglas, and House Republican Leader Gerald Ford was designated to present it in the most inflammatory way possible.

On April 15, a mere week after the Carswell rejection, Ford rose on the House floor to demand that Justice Douglas be impeached. He charged that Douglas had accepted an annual $12,000 retainer from a foundation with gambling connections; that Douglas had failed to disqualify himself from hearing cases in which he had a personal interest; that he had been paid to give legal advice in violation of Federal law; that he had contributed an article to a "pornographic" magazine; and that he had written a book advocating "hippie-yippie style revolution." Ford charged further that Douglas personally had "defied the conventions and convictions of decent Americans" by behaving like a "dirty old man by consorting with all those women, even if he did marry them." He even hinted that Douglas might have underworld ties. He closed his remarks by proposing to the House an arresting moral precept. "An impeachable offense," he said, "is whatever a majority of the House of Representatives considers it to be at a given moment in history."

This intemperate—even scurrilous—speech from an ordinarily genial lawmaker sparked a seven-month investigation by a House Judiciary subcommittee. It was agonizingly protracted, probably to bring maximum embarrassment to Douglas and all his supporters including his unhappy former Chief. In the end, the subcommittee voted 3–1 that it found no evidence to support Ford's charges and that there were no grounds for impeachment.

Three years later, at his 1973 confirmation hearings for the Vice Presidency, Ford admitted that his anti-Douglas evidence had come primarily from raw (that is, unevaluated) FBI files supplied by Mitchell's Justice Department. "Looking back," he admitted, "what I did was perhaps too strong." Privately, he was said to have wondered aloud if he hadn't been "had." After Douglas' retirement following a severe stroke, he wrote me this tight-lipped sentence on May 6, 1977: "I have no information on Ford's attitude towards his efforts to impeach me."

All this, of course, was intensely painful to Warren. In the eighteen months since his resignation, he had seen his beloved Court subjected to the most callous—and now, finally, the cruelest—kind of political manipulation. The Court's honor and dignity had been severely impugned, and despite the subcommittee's belated findings, considerable damage had been done. Warren was realist enough to concede that Douglas was at least partly to blame. Like Fortas, the unconventional Douglas had probably conducted himself imprudently—not much of a defect in an ordinary man but potentially lethal to a Justice of the United States Supreme Court. Without rancor, but with genuine sorrow, Warren privately felt that Douglas, like Fortas, had let down the Court, especially the Warren Court.

But if Warren was prey to such thoughts, he never betrayed them in public. His personal affection for Douglas remained undiminished. Three years later, at a 1973 law dinner honoring Douglas in New York City, his former Chief genially toasted him:

> *On New Year's Day this year, I made two bets. One was that Hank Aaron would break Babe Ruth's home run record, and the other one was that Bill Douglas would beat Stephen Fields's record for longevity on the Court. Hank Aaron didn't quite make it; he missed by one home run. That was because so many pitchers walked him he couldn't hit the ball. But they couldn't walk Bill. One of them tried to in the House of Representatives. But the only credit he got was for a wild pitch. So I won one of my bets. I got a 500 batting average, which isn't bad for a retired Chief Justice!*

In mid-1970, President Nixon, continuing to protest that the Senate would never confirm any Southerner for the Supreme Court, named a Northern strict constructionist for the Fortas seat: Minnesotan Harry Andrew Blackmun, sixty-one, a judge for eleven years on the U. S. Court of Appeals for the Eighth Circuit. The quiet, conservative, noncontroversial Blackmun had been a boyhood friend, ideological ally and best man at the wedding of Warren Burger, who obviously had recommended him to Nixon. Although no trailblazing jurist, Blackmun was deemed competent and meticulous. After a perfunctory probe, he was swiftly confirmed by the Senate 94–0 on June 22.

Burger and Blackmun were soon irreverently dubbed "The Minnesota Twins." One Court-watcher brought smiles to Warren and others by quipping that it would be cheaper to give Chief Justice Burger two votes and have only eight Justices.

The Blackmun appointment was another step in the undoing of the old Warren Court. Burger was now firmly in command of a conservative majority which could, at its strongest, include Blackmun, Harlan, Stewart, White and sometimes even the increasingly erratic Black. The liberal bloc had dwindled to a minority of three: Douglas, Brennan and Marshall.

Inevitably, the new Court, to Nixon's delight, soon began chipping away at the old Warren tribunal decisions, especially those pertaining to criminal justice, civil liberties and Federal dominion over state jurisdiction. It was a frustrating time for the holdover Warren Court liberals. As Brennan angrily wrote in an April 1971 dissent: "Since the Court this term has already downgraded citizens receiving public welfare and citizens having the misfortune to be illegitimate, I suppose today's decision downgrading citizens born outside the United States should have been expected."

Meanwhile, the Nixon Administration continued its steady drumfire on the old Court. The American Bar Association convention in London in July 1971 rang with denunciations of Warren Court decisions. This was, as one eyewitness observer wrote, "not so much a project of the ABA as the work of Chief Justice Burger and Attorney General Mitchell." Both worked closely with the ABA and were featured convention speakers.

It was no surprise to the retired Chief Justice that the ABA had been chosen as a vehicle for assailing the Warren Court. It had lent itself to such activity since 1957, when an ABA committee had charged that no less than fifteen Warren Court rulings had "aided the Communist cause." So flimsy had been the rationale for these charges, and so transparently political their motive, that Warren swiftly resigned his ABA membership. Until the end of his life, he persisted in viewing the ABA as predominantly a glorified political lobby for conservative commercial and industrial interests.

Despite the savage assaults by the Nixon Administration on him, his Court and his friends, the first two years of the Chief Justice's retirement were not altogether unhappy. Earl Warren was too much an activist to sit idle while a hostile President and administration sought to besmirch his record, if not his name.

Now, he spoke out energetically and often on matters that he deemed important. In April 1970, in a speech to the Bar Association of New York City he scolded the ABA: "Throughout the McCarthy era and for years following that shameful period, while the Federal Courts were struggling to make the Bill of Rights and the Civil War Amendments meaningful in our society, the organized Bar of the Nation did little to assist." On May 9 he warned an NAACP Legal Defense and Educational Fund audience of 1,500 that failure to enforce the 1954 desegregation decision had brought the nation to a state of crisis and to a society "more divided than any time in the past hundred years." The following day he told the B'nai B'rith Anti-Defamation League that no less than twenty million Americans, mostly black, still must be considered chronic victims of defamation. When Warren was later given this organization's 1970 Profiles in Courage Award, Senator Edward Kennedy saluted him: "We have seen his courage not just in profile but in full face . . ."

The retired Chief Justice jabbed at the Nixon Administration and the New Left in other speeches, such as one in June at the University of Santa Clara commencement exercises. "Some would supplant a part of our freedoms with policies of repression in an effort to establish what they would euphemistically call 'Law and Order,' " he said. "Others would destroy all our institutions in the name of reform and still greater freedoms. But the four most meaningful words in the Constitution for the disadvantaged are 'due process' and 'equal protection.' . . ."

In the fall of 1970 he accepted the chairmanship of the American Civil Liberties Union's 50th Anniversary Committee. Founder Roger Baldwin recollects, "He had been stung by the 'Impeach Earl Warren' campaign and felt that he belonged with our crowd." At the ACLU's hundred-dollar-a-plate dinner in New York on December 8, he again obliquely assailed the Nixon Administration: "The atmosphere is again becoming repression-laden and we may be in for another wave of hysteria in the name of safety. . . ."

Warren's admirers—which included many book publishers—urged him to put down his ideas more explicitly and at length in book form. They particularly wanted a hard-hitting, human interest autobiography which would name names, anecdotally tell the inside stories about the great and controversial Court decisions, the Justices' personalities (including the Burger Court), the Warren Commission trauma, his personal relationships with six Presidents, and giving the undeserving, in his half-century career, their comeuppance.

Nothing, of course, could have been farther from Earl Warren's style. He had never considered writing his memoirs, as he had informed me and many others over the years. He never kept a diary, made notes or tapes of great events, or in any systematic way saved important documents. Why? Primarily because he had a compassionate, deeply ingrained reluctance to commit to paper unkind thoughts about even such longtime enemies as Nixon. "If I ever wrote an autobiography, I'd have to tell a lot of things about some people and that wouldn't be fair," he once remarked to me. A gentleman of the old school, Warren was the despair of frustrated would-be editors who even offered to furnish him ghostwriters, at least two of whom made fruitless trips to Washington. So did several eminent law professors who had vainly sought the Chief Justice's cooperation in a proposed "legal biography" of him.

Because of his concern, however, at how the Nixon Administration was eroding the Bill of Rights, he did accede to a request from Quadrangle Books (a *New York Times* subsidiary) to write a short book on the meaning and responsibilities of citizenship. As he explained in a *New Yorker* magazine interview, "The *Times* Book Division asked me to do a book on citizenship and I accepted. Do you know what seems strange? I discovered that practically no one has ever written a book on citizenship. You can look through library catalogues and find almost nothing on the subject. . . ."

Finally, in July 1970, he succumbed to the blandishments of Doubleday's persuasive senior editor, Kenneth McCormick, to write his memoirs. But plainly Warren had not relented in his refusal to indulge in *ad hominem* of any sort. The proposed book, McCormick then said, would be "anecdotal, warm and vital" and would be completed in eighteen months. It was, regrettably, never completed.

Fortunately, future biographers and historians need not depend solely upon Warren's incomplete memoirs for unpublished material about him. Late in 1969 the University of California's Regional Oral History Office launched an Earl Warren Oral History Project. Its goal was to tape-record the recollections of key persons—friends, foes and family—who had been intimately involved with Warren's early life and thirty-three-year career in California up until his appointment as Chief Justice in 1953. The project was funded by an initial grant from the National Endowment for the Humanities. It was soon matched by private donations from Warren's friends and former law clerks.

"When I first went to Washington to discuss it with retired Chief Justice Warren," recollects Amelia Fry, the project's capable director, "frankly, I was somewhat worried. I knew how other public figures had tried to control the research centers recording memoirs about themselves."

But Warren immediately put her at ease, assuring her, "You must have a completely free hand to do an independent study."

"I took a deep breath and was completely relieved," admits Oral Historian Fry. "After that, he never asked us who we were interviewing or interfered with our work in any way. He had a great sense of what is proper and appropriate, even when retired."

Retirement also enabled Warren to indulge both his passion for foreign travel, developed in maturity, and his commitment to internationalism, which he said "recharged my batteries." As governor of California, he had had relatively little time or opportunity to study foreign affairs except when playing host at the opening of the United Nations in San Francisco in 1945. But after 1953, whenever the Supreme Court was in recess, he enthusiastically traveled overseas, usually to attend international judicial conferences. He was elected the first president of the World Association of Judges, a voluntary organization of jurists and lawyers from 117 nations dedicated to establishing the legal bases for world peace. In 1959 he helped found the International World Peace Through Law Conference and never missed its biennial meetings thereafter. In 1971, when the retired Chief Justice and his Court were being excoriated at the American Bar Association Convention in London, Warren was telling delegates at the Fifth International World Peace Through Law Conference in Belgrade that it was high time mainland China, North Korea and

North Vietnam be admitted to the United Nations. "The world peace movement," he said, "is the biggest legal issue of our time." Ironically, the ABA did not learn of these remarks until later.

Few Americans realize that by the time of his retirement, Warren already was a figure of enormous stature and prestige to hundreds of millions overseas. "I have yet to go anywhere in Africa," Justice Marshall reported in 1969, "that I don't find a good word for our Supreme Court. In fact, I have yet to go to *any* country in the world where I don't find somebody . . . who will say: 'Give my best to your Chief Justice.' " Ireland's late President Cearbhall O'Dalleigh remembered Warren as ". . . calm, clear, Olympian. His authority was unforced but all-pervading." In Israel and even the U. S. S. R. people queued up for his autograph. When he addressed the West German Supreme Court he was given an unusual standing ovation. In Peru, farm workers who could not understand a word of English walked miles to hear him speak. In India he required a police escort to prevent him from being mobbed by his admirers. In Albania, Bulgaria, Rumania and Yugoslavia, he shared person-to-person fellowship with top judges as well as with obscure gypsies by the river in the moonlight. "The people in all these countries are very important for world peace and I want to know more about them," he explained.

In view of his international eminence, he was named chairman of the United Nations Association of the USA. On October 29, 1971, he spiritedly presided over a convocation on the China Question before three thousand delegates in New York. This conference laid the groundwork for the entrance of China into the United Nations before President Nixon's historic 1972 trip there.

"Adlai Stevenson once commented," remarked Warren in his astonishingly unreported speech, "that man seemed to be a rare animal who was able to read the handwriting on the wall only when his back was up against it! The handwriting is there now. Do we dare to read it? We can endow our international institutions with peace-keeping powers sufficient to restrain not only the small but also the great states."

"That last sentence was tantamount to World Government— but not quite," observes Thomas Liggett, *World Peace News* editor-publisher. "I felt that the United Nations Association kept Warren from going 'all the way' on World Government. I must say that the man certainly grew amazingly from the time I first met Governor Warren in 1949 as city editor of a California newspaper."

"I thought his enthusiasm for world law via United Nations covenants a bit premature considering that they have no enforcement powers," recollects Roger Baldwin, who was associated with him in these projects. "But he had a vision I share. Our timetables were different. He was on the road to the future of law, and sure of it."

Domestic law likewise occupied the retired jurist. In 1971 the Earl Warren Legal Training Program was founded by the NAACP Legal Defense Fund to increase both the number and location of black and civil rights lawyers, especially in the South. Each year it awards scholarships to several hundred black law students, enabling them to attend fifty-three predominantly white law schools. "The Warren program has contributed very substantially to the desegregation of Southern law schools," concluded a 1973 report by the Carnegie Foundation, the prime funder. This project also grants four-year fellowships to train black civil rights lawyers in the LDF's New York and San Francisco offices. "Earl Warren Scholars" have often become community leaders, too: One served as mayor of Prichard, Alabama; another became a municipal judge in Houston, Texas; others were elected to the Arkansas state legislature and North Carolina Board of Governors. Warren himself hoped that the program would "dignify the rights of not just blacks but American Indians, Chicanos, Asians and other disadvantaged minority groups."

Yet he still managed to keep a fatherly eye on his beloved, changing Court.

The retired Chief was dismayed when two of the Warren Court's legal luminaries were suddenly hospitalized for critical illnesses in August 1971. Hugo Black, the liberal senior member in age (eighty-five) and service, developed a serious blood vessel inflammation after suffering a stroke. John Marshall Harlan, near blind at seventy-two, was stricken with bone cancer in the lower spine. The gentle, erudite Harlan had been the Warren Court's conservative conscience—"Frankfurter without the mustard," as he was characterized. Both resigned in September, a week apart, shortly before their respective deaths.

This gave President Nixon his third and fourth Supreme Court seats to fill in less than three years.

Speculation on successors included Virginia Republican Congressman Richard Poff, a Nixon friend, who withdrew when his record was scored by civil rights and labor leaders; West Virginia Senator Robert Byrd, a onetime Ku Klux Klan organizer who possessed a night-school law degree but had never passed a bar examination or practiced law; Herschel Friday, an Arkansas municipal bond lawyer who had vigorously resisted the Little Rock School Board desegregation; and similarly undistinguished Judge Mildred Lillie, of California's State Court of Appeals. When the American Bar Association, now sensitive to criticism for having endorsed Haynsworth and Carswell, was cool to Poff and Byrd, President Nixon decided to appoint Friday and Lillie. The now cautious ABA, however, refused to approve either.

Nixon was infuriated. At Attorney General Mitchell's prodding, he suddenly decided to appoint two dark horses. That same evening, October 21, 1971, the President went on nationwide television to announce his unballyhooed nominations, neither of whom had had "prior judicial experience."

The first appointee was Lewis F. Powell, Jr., a conservative Richmond, Virginia, corporation lawyer and former American Bar Association president. The quiet, intellectual Powell modestly protested that he was too old (sixty-four) for the Court, but Nixon telephoned him saying, "Ten years of Powell is worth thirty years of anyone else." Although critical of Warren Court criminal-law decisions, Powell seemed a humane, moderate, open-minded man who had even been praised by the Virginia NAACP branch. While Warren deemed Powell no scholarly Black or Harlan, he considered him certainly the best of the Nixon nominees. Powell's quick confirmation, 89–1, demonstrated that the Senate could approve a qualified Southerner, despite Nixon's petulant protests after the Haynsworth and Carswell fiascos.

Nixon's second appointment, however, was different. William H. Rehnquist was a gifted forty-seven-year-old right-wing lawyer, a rabid Warren Court critic and an assistant attorney general in Mitchell's Justice Department. He appeared to be a thoroughgoing Nixon devotee: a Vietnam hawk; a champion of covert surveillance, "no-knock" police entries and preventive detention in the name of national security; and even an articulate defender of the Carswell nomination. Nixon described him as "the President's lawyer's lawyer." But others termed him "Nixon's hired gunslinger." He was the first Supreme Court nominee opposed by the American Civil Liberties Union in its fifty-two-year history. Despite opposition by Senate liberals, Rehnquist was confirmed in December by a comfortable 68–26 margin.

Warren had, of course, sworn in Burger and had willingly attended Blackmun's induction. In other circumstances, he probably would have also attended Powell's induction. But Rehnquist was too much for him. When Powell and Rehnquist were simultaneously administered oaths of office on January 7, 1972, Warren was absent. He was, according to his office, in California fulfilling "a long-standing engagement." The corpulent Californian was in fact taking the opportunity to sojourn at a "fat camp" where he hoped to lose a dozen pounds, and perhaps forget the Nixonian scales of justice.

The replacement of Black and Harlan by Powell and Rehnquist was swiftly interpreted by Warrenite liberals as a Court setback. Most conservatives, however, saw it as progress and Nixonites considered it a political triumph. The Committee to Re-elect the President gleefully boasted about this Supreme Court turnaround in a fund-raising letter signed by finance chairman Maurice H. Stans, later of Watergate fame: "He [the President] has appointed four members to the Supreme Court who can be expected to give strict interpretation to the Constitution."

Whether or not "strict," at first it was like-minded. The "Nixon Four" voted as a bloc in fifty-four out of sixty-six cases heard by the Court during the 1972 spring term. Actually, no Warren Court decisions were overturned, but many were redefined in ways that limited their scope (former interpretations were now sometimes referred to as "harmless error"). Police powers, especially with respect to search and seizure, were broadened: *Harris* vs. *New York*, for example, gave law enforcers the right to use a previous arrest for *any* crime as a warrant to search for evidence that an arrested person might have committed another, different, crime. And whereas the Warren Court had always sought to interpret the Fourteenth ("equal protection" and "due process") Amendment as broadly as possible, the new Nixonized Court seemed preoccupied with discovering limitations to its extent. "If the Burger Court trend continues," quipped *The New York Times'* Herbert Mitgang, "the day may come when the phrase over the Supreme Court would have to be rechiseled symbolically to read: Equal Justice under Law and Order."

The remaining three liberal Justices became increasingly

restive. Douglas was frankly insubordinate. Well before the term had ended, he packed his bags and prematurely departed for his hideaway home in Gooseprairie, Washington. "One of our brethren leaves town early and tries to conduct his business back and forth four thousand miles away, or however far it is out there," sneered Chief Justice Burger. There had been tensions on the Warren Court, naturally, but nothing like this. As one Federal judge—no admirer of Warren—remarked, "With all his faults, Warren at least held the Court together, something Burger can't seem to do."

Liberals on and off the Court complained not only of the philosophy of the "Nixon Four," but even of some of their methods. Justice Rehnquist was accused not only of failing to disqualify himself but of actually casting the deciding vote in several cases in which he had earlier been involved as assistant attorney general. Chief Justice Burger was rebuked for playing favorites in assigning the writing of opinions; for wanting to change the shape of the bench; make uniform the varying size of the Justices' black leather chairs; substitute British red robes for the traditional black ones; and bring his own desk into the sacrosanct Conference Room. Some snipers even berated Burger, an efficient no-nonsense administrator, for what they called his excessive preoccupation with the minutiae of Court management, alleging that he left behind him a trail of handwritten notes such as "check inkwell" or "fill water pitcher," often adding the phrase "This is an order." Blackmun was criticized for being too slow in producing his few opinions.

Such personal attacks on the new Justices were understandable, if not always pardonable. They were the inevitable detritus of mounting liberal dismay at the Court's new orientation. Although it was alien to Warren's nature ever to stoop to public attacks upon individuals, or to engage in backstage intrigue, he was increasingly urged by liberals to speak out against the Burger Court's direction. But, as always, he declined with that old-fashioned fastidiousness that his more zealous partisans often found so frustrating. "When you're on the Court," he would calmly answer, "you try to be responsible. Off it, the same should be true."

This concept of responsibility seems to have been largely a matter of personal style. If Warren believed that it would be irresponsible of him to criticize the Burger Court publicly, he simultaneously felt that it would be equally irresponsible to refrain from reaffirming, whenever possible, general principles of justice which he thought the Court was neglecting during the Nixon era.

He had several opportunities to do so in the spring of 1972, when he delivered a series of lectures at three major universities. At Notre Dame, he spoke about civil rights. Deploring the fact that the Warren Court desegregation decisions were not being uniformly obeyed throughout the nation, he conceded: "Racial discrimination is never settled until it is settled right. It is not yet rightly settled."

Reverend Theodore M. Hesburgh, Notre Dame's president, who had chaired President Johnson's Civil Rights Commission, recollects, "I was enormously impressed by Earl Warren's dedication to the law and to young students of the law. He spent long hours with them after his brilliant lectures."

At one informal session, several hundred students and faculty crowded into a basement lounge. A barely audible question came from the back of the room.

"Many have suggested," began the question, "that you were the greatest Chief Justice since John Marshall . . ."

The young questioner paused. The elderly Warren smiled broadly. With a wink, he joked: "Could you say that again—just a little louder, please?"

At Berkeley that same April, as a Regents Lecturer he conducted informal discussions with both graduate and undergraduate students who planned legal careers. Although Berkeley then was notorious for student unrest, the retired Justice reminded his listeners:

> *The greatest advances have been preceded by periods of extreme social disorder. . . . We may find hope in the disenchantment of youth. . . . They are searching, as we should have done long ago, for a synthesis that will improve life not just for a few . . . but for all mankind.*

While there, Warren, who as a youth had nearly flunked out of law school, received two honors: the Clark Kerr Award for contributions to higher education, and membership in the scholarly society, Phi Beta Kappa.

The following month at Brandeis University, where the Earl Warren Chair in Constitutional History and Law had been established sixteen years earlier, he was awarded the first Samuel C. and Minna Dretzin Prize for a major constructive impact on education. This prize included a $5,000 cash award, which Warren declined in accordance with his lifelong policy of refusing monetary honorariums. Instead, the retired Justice planted a willow tree near Brandeis' famed interfaith chapel, consecrated for worship by Catholic, Protestant and Jew alike.

Warren's short citizenship book was published in June 1972—ironically the month when the Watergate break-in occurred. The title, *A Republic, If You Can Keep It*, stemmed from a response made by eighty-one-year-old Benjamin Franklin, whose age Warren now had reached. At the close of the 1787 Constitutional Convention, an anxious woman standing outside Independence Hall had asked the astute Franklin, "Well, doctor, what have we got—a republic or a monarchy?"

"A republic, if you can keep it, "Franklin had answered.

Like so many of Warren's public utterances, this well-intentioned book was couched in generalities, and most readers and reviewers found it boring. As the Philadelphia *Bulletin*'s reviewer put it, "The prose is dull, the tone is overly didactic, and at times the book reads as if Warren were aiming his message at not terribly-bright junior high school students." Only a few thousand copies were sold and the book is now out of print.

Yet despite its defects—and, in another sense, because of them—this sober little patriotic primer commands an interest. It is a typical unghosted Warren product. Everything that Warren wrote was obviously important; all his observations were balanced and fair; all his conclusions were unexceptionable. Therefore, the book reads like second-rate campaign oratory—a congeries of political and legal homilies which succeeds neither as explication nor as exhortation. At the same time, this forgotten book has a curiously appealing quality, especially in such lines as "Public offices were never meant to be sold like soap or cereal." Warren was not only at home with platitudes, he valued them. A basic truth, no matter how simple or obvious, was for him something to be cherished and deeply felt. Perhaps he could not imagine that his readers might not share his single-minded concern for first principles. He made no artful concessions to their desire to be entertained with novelties or provoked with personalities and specifics. Thus, his book was a kind of honorable failure as well as the unremunerative opposite of Nixon's shriller but more lucrative opuses.

While bookstores were returning unsold copies of *A Republic, If You Can Keep It* to the publisher, Richard Nixon was moving triumphantly toward re-election. Senator George McGovern, the Democratic nominee, conducted a campaign of such appalling ineptitude that Nixon—had he been a man of different temperament —need not have worried about his own re-election. Unhappily for himself and the nation, he *did* worry. But in the fall of 1972 only a handful of administration insiders perceived how far his concerns had prompted him to go. He was overwhelmingly re-elected, carrying 60.7 percent of the popular vote and forty-nine of the fifty states.

Nixon now reveals that he entertained some doubts about being reelected after his April 30, 1970, Cambodia speech. At 10:30 that evening, he was informed that Chief Justice Burger was at the White House gate with a letter for him. He instructed the Secret Service agent to usher him up immediately. Burger, congratulating him on his speech, said that it had a sense of destiny. In his memoirs, Nixon writes somewhat indelicately, ". . . if this operation doesn't succeed—or if anything else happens that forces my public support below a point where I feel I can't be re-elected—I would like you to be ready to be in the running for the nomination in 1972."

President Nixon's re-election, though hardly unexpected, was disheartening enough for Warren, but another matter was now beginning to trouble him nearly as much. So much, in fact, that it finally led him to break his self-imposed silence about the Burger Court.

Hardworking Chief Justice Burger had become increasingly troubled over the Supreme Court's mounting case load. In mid-1971, as chairman of the Federal Judicial Center, he had appointed an eminent seven-member committee to study this vexing problem and to recommend ways to reduce the burden upon the nine Justices. Harvard Law professor Paul A. Freund, Brandeis' one-time law clerk, was named chairman in December 1972. This committee recommended that Congress create a new National Court of Appeals to "screen all petitions for review now filed in the Supreme Court." It was to be composed of seven judges then on the U.S. Court of

Appeals, who would be assigned to rotating three-year terms and need not be headquartered at any specific place. This proposed court—which was soon irreverently dubbed the Mini Court—would have the absolute power (previously exercised only by the U.S. Supreme Court) to deny any application seeking the High Court's *certiorari* jurisdiction. It would, for example, have transmitted to the Supreme Court approximately 400 of the 3,643 cases filed in 1971. In turn, the Supreme Court would presumably have reviewed about 150 of these 400. For the overwhelming remainder of the cases, the suggested National Court of Appeals would in effect have been a Court of Last Resort.

The violence of the retired Warren's immediate reaction to the Freund Committee's recommendation was startling. He had, after all, silently endured personal insults, the steady erosion of his judicial legacy and ruthless political attacks upon his friends. Was this simply a last straw? That assumption undervalues (as people too often did) the depth of Earl Warren's commitment to first principles. He swiftly judged the Mini-Court proposal as sacrilege—a violation of the Constitution and repudiation of the most elementary equity. The man who had sparked some of the greatest changes in American judicial history now was determined to battle what he deemed an attempted desecration with all of his bodily and intellectual strength.

To mobilize sentiment against the Mini-Court, the retired Chief Justice immediately wrote to his sixty former law clerks, many of whom now were leaders in America's academic and legal circles. Warren's letter to his 1961 clerk, Peter Ehrenhaft, a member of the Freund Committee, was reportedly "less than polite." In Warren's view, this Mini-Court was a political gimmick (Nixonian?) to keep the Supreme Court from performing its constitutional duty. "The assault is both cynical and formidable," he insisted.

Publicly, the ordinarily calm Warren denounced the Mini-Court in his strongest judicial blast since his retirement four years earlier. He assailed the "highly secretive" report, pointing out that the committee had not sought the opinion of any judge on any court, including the six living former Supreme Court Justices.

Warren's wrath was voiced in a Law Day address before the Association of the Bar of New York on the evening of May 1, 1973. Earlier that day, Mayor John Lindsay had presented him with the Gold Medal of the City, thanks to the enterprising footwork of then New York City corporation counsel Norman Redlich.

"If the doors of the Supreme Court were to be shut to fully ninety percent of the citizen's complaints," charged the retired Chief Justice, "and if the complainants were forced to accept the final judgment of a chance group of unknown and temporary subordinate judges, its public stature as a 'palladium of justice' and 'citadel of justice' would soon begin to fade."

Warren amplified these charges in an *American Bar Association Journal* (July 1973) article. He deplored that "The Supreme Court would have no power to review or second guess the denial of a petition by any of the rotating panel of judges. . . ." Under a Mini-Court, he contended, there never could have been a *Gideon* case. Bitterly, he added that the recommendations

> *spring solely from a study group appointed by my successor, consisting of seven lawyers and law school professors. No past or present member of any court was included . . . none of the learned legal societies and no bar association was officially represented. . . . The study group was kept highly secret. . . . Only after its report was formally released, following the traditional leak to the press, were we apprised of the nature of this study group. . . . The result, released through a televised press conference, by seven individuals speakng only for themselves. . . .*

Replying to Chief Justice Burger's claim that the Supreme Court workload had tripled since 1951 and quadrupled since 1935, he sarcastically continued:

> *Such a facile and unevaluated use of numbers, reminiscent of the McCarthy days, leaves the public with a false impression of the workload of the Court and the ability of the Justices to manage that work load. . . . In my sixteen years of service on the Court . . . I never saw the slightest evidence that any member of the Court was distracted from full devotion to the decisional processes. . . . The study group has simply misunderstood and misdiagnosed the capacity of the Supreme Court to manage its own internal decisional processes. . . . This assessment can only be characterized as naïve. . . . The proposal . . . is fraught with practical, jurisdictional and constitutional problems of the first magnitude. . . . The Court would lose its symbolic but vitally important status as the ultimate tribunal to which all citizens, poor and rich, may submit their claims. . . .*

Warren's concluding words contained the heart of his message. Every Justice, he insisted, had an instinctive "feel" for which cases were important and it took years to acquire such confidence:

> *Most of the time, the new court would not be acting as a court; it would . . . be acting essentially as a National Court of Glorified Law Clerks. . . . When the jurisdiction of the Supreme Court is exercised by two courts, have we not created two Supreme Courts in contravention of the Constitutional limitation? [Article III of the Constitution says there shall be but "one Supreme Court."] The study group . . . has inadvertently condemned its own proposal on both constitutional and practical grounds. . . . We must reject the cynical approach of those who would destroy or invade the functions of the Supreme Court merely to solve passing problems. . . .*

The articulate Douglas threw in a fast right hook for his former Chief. "We are, if anything, underworked not overworked," he insisted. Stewart, more temperately, told the *Harvard Law Record*: "The heavy case load is neither intolerable nor impossible to handle."

Warren's crusade against the Mini-Court proposal demonstrated how much power he could still command. Although the ABA, at the prompting of Burger and Mitchell, managed to keep the issue alive, numerous judges and lawyers who otherwise might have been reluctant to offend Burger and Mitchell's Justice Department now rallied behind the former Chief Justice. Earl Warren had bested Warren Earl. Thus, there was little hope that any action would be taken on the proposal while an angry retired Chief Justice lived.

Unfortunately, that was not to be too long.

The final year of Earl Warren's life was played out against the lurid backdrop of the Nixon Administration collapse amid the nation's gravest constitutional crisis since the Civil War. Warren witnessed all but the final acts in the downfall of Richard Nixon, the man with whom his own life had been so curiously entwined for nearly three decades.

Although the Watergate break-in had occurred a year earlier, it was not until the summer of 1973 that its full impact began to be felt publicly. In January the trial of the Watergate burglars ended; seven men were convicted, two of them officers of the Committee to Re-elect the President when John Mitchell headed it. Even before the verdict, thanks largely to the investigative efforts of *Washington Post* reporters, it became apparent that the Watergate "affair" had reached high into the Nixon Administration. As a result, in February the Senate created a Watergate Investigating Committee, chaired by North Carolina's colorful seventy-six-year-old Sam Ervin. The dismaying chain of revelations that followed dominated the headlines and national consciousness for most of 1973.

In April, Warren warmly eulogized former President Truman, who had died four months earlier, in a speech at the Truman Library (of which he was a director) in Independence, Missouri. Perhaps remembering Truman's characterization of Nixon as that "shifty-eyed goddam liar not fit to lace Earl Warren's shoes," Warren took the occasion to assail the Nixon Administration in his strongest words until then. He claimed that it had produced "more divisiveness in the nation ... than there has been in my lifetime." Contrasting the spitefulness that the present administration continued to show toward its political opponents with the more forgiving conciliatory policy of President Truman, the retired Chief Justice said sadly, "I sometimes wonder if that wholesome approach has departed permanently from the American scene."

That summer, while much of the nation sat glued to television sets watching the unfolding drama of the Senate Watergate hearings, Warren eagerly departed the nation's capital. In July he went to California, where he administered the oath of office to Tom Bradley, the first black mayor of Los Angeles—a ceremony he enjoyed infinitely more than swearing in Nixon as President four years earlier. In August he flew to Abidjan, the Ivory Coast capital, to attend the sixth World Peace Through Law convention. There, as president of the World Association of Judges, he scolded 2,600 lawyers and jurists representing 123 nations for not having compelled their governments to implement the twenty-five-year-old United Nations Universal Declaration of Human Rights. He did not except himself or the United States from this dereliction, admitting this nation's (meaning the Nixon Administration's) growing willingness to invade privacy through government-sponsored electronic surveillance. For having "made the cause of human liberty the great cause of his life" and for his "contributions to human rights which will live and be praised forever," he was given the convention's first Human Rights Award.

By the time he returned to Washington in September, the Watergate scandal had reached the Oval Office. Testimony presented at the Senate hearings had revealed the existence of the Nixon tapes. Although U.S. District Court Judge John Sirica had ordered the President to produce them as evidence, Nixon seemed determined to defy this court order on the grounds of "executive privilege." Warren's private comment on this was characteristic: "A man can lie and cheat and steal and there might be some reason for his behavior. But no one—*no one*—can defy the law."

By the end of September, the Nixon Administration sorrows were coming in battalions. In another scandal, unrelated to Watergate, Spiro Agnew was accused of having engaged in corrupt practices both while governor of Maryland and even after becoming Vice President. On October 10 he resigned, pleading "no contest" to a charge of income-tax evasion rather than be tried on charge of having accepted bribes. He was convicted, fined $10,000 and placed on unsupervised probation. His successor, named by Nixon in December, was Representative Gerald Ford.

Meanwhile the President, who had indeed elected to defy Judge Sirica's order to produce the tapes, met resistance from Archibald Cox, the man he had appointed as the Justice Department's Special Prosecutor to investigate the Watergate affair for the administration. Nixon, who earlier had promised that he would not interfere with Cox's investigation, suddenly fired him. Elliott Richardson, the new attorney general, immediately resigned in protest. The result of this (October 21) "Saturday Night Massacre" was a public outcry so loud that the House of Representatives began seriously to explore grounds for impeaching the President.

At least one prominent lawmaker and one *Washington Post* official tried to consult with Warren about impeachment strategy. But he chose to hold himself aloof from such discussions or from joining in the mounting public clamor against the beleaguered President. Nixon was obviously done for. Now Warren was far more concerned with the damage that Nixon's inevitable disgrace might do to the country.

In an October National Press Club tribute to his friend the late Drew Pearson, Warren warned: ". . . we should strike at secrecy in government wherever it exists because it is the incubator of corruption." He went on to deplore that "the Cambodian bombing was deliberately concealed from the American people for two years after the fact."

The retired judge, who had always found any deception in high office offensive, voiced similar concern in a speech at the University of Georgia law school in November. Commenting on the cynical remarks made by one witness who had testified before Senator Ervin's committee, the former politician said:

I lose patience when I hear of young people staying out of politics because it is dirty. Of course there are people who betray their trust in public life, as some do in every walk of life. The news almost daily tells about scandals in business, industry and the professions. But we do not hear anyone advising young people to shun those fields because they are dirty. Nor would it be right to do so.

And regarding suggestions that the improper conduct of the President and Vice President indicated that the power of the Executive should be limited by constitutional amendment, he maintained: "We should not destroy good buildings because they have bad tenants."

The students found the retired Chief Justice's comments reassuring—infinitely more so than the Warren Commission findings on the JFK assassination. Always intensely concerned with the problems of the young, he was extraordinarily effective in dealing with them, Warren watchers had long noted. For example, his academic host at the University of Georgia speech, former Secretary of State Dean Rusk, recalls, "He proved himself a genius at communicating with young people. He said many things which we will never forget down here in Georgia."

In early December at the DePaul University College of Law in Chicago, he made some anti-Nixon Administration remarks which one of the listeners, William H. Perkins, Jr., now says "I still refer to with great interest":

We have been able to preserve our freedoms because our people, remembering the lessons of history, have enshrined the Bill of Rights in their hearts as well as in our Constitution, and until recently have believed that their high public officials were honestly committed to the preservation of those rights. . . . In modern history, more freedom has been lost through erosion from within than from outside aggression. . . . Wouldn't it be reassuring if we come out of Watergate with a new commitment to the rights of man through a modern Magna Charta for governmental conduct supplementing that which grew out of the abuses of King John more than 750 years ago?

In San Francisco later that month, the mood was lighter when he presented the first Earl Warren Civil Liberties Award to Anthony G. Amsterdam, Stanford law professor. The function, attended by more than 1,500 persons in a downtown theater, was sponsored by the American Civil Liberties Foundation of Northern California. A group of San Francisco street musicians called the Bourbon Street Irregulars played Dixieland tunes which Earl Warren, a youthful musician himself, enormously enjoyed.

"His foot was tapping and he had that happy sparkle in his eye," recollects Professor Amsterdam. "I told him that these musicians were ACLU clients and that we represented them in protecting their freedom to play on city streets without harassment by authorities."

"They're wonderful clients to have," laughed Warren. "They make good music and they make good law. What more could any lawyer want?"

The guest speaker, maverick journalist I. F. Stone, declared that the Watergate evidence thus far proved that President Nixon *must* be impeached. Along with nearly everyone present, Earl Warren enthusiastically applauded.

Although Warren was trying to rise intellectually above the sordid revelations of Watergate, he could not do so emotionally. More than most, he grieved for his country and feared for its future. And perhaps more than most, he endured the added frustration of having to suppress outward expression of his most bitter private thoughts about a man who he had always believed was never fit to be President, even when reluctantly swearing him into the office on January 20, 1969. The years had not enlarged his admiration of Richard Nixon. It is unprovable, but all too possible, that this inner turmoil contributed to his physical decline and even death.

Not only the nation but also the aging Earl Warren was in poor health. He had for some time suffered from angina pectoris complicated by coronary artery disease, although neither condition had been considered severe. On January 26, 1974, while in California, he was suddenly admitted to Daniel Freedman Hospital in Inglewood for observation of what was described as "a minor coronary problem." A week later he was released "in satisfactory condition." The problem, however, had not been minor.

For a time he followed medical orders by convalescing at the Beverly Hills home of his youngest daughter, Honeybear, and her husband, Dr. Stuart Brien. But soon he became restless, worrying about the heavy schedule of speaking engagements to which he had committed himself in the spring. He returned to Washington in time to celebrate his eighty-third birthday quietly with his wife, daughter Virginia and son-in-law John Daly on March 19. That evening, he telephoned his friend Merrell F. ("Pop") Small in Sacramento to thank him for his birthday tribute in the Sacramento *Bee*. He asked about the political situation in California and was told that it was "a mess."

"Yes," sadly remarked the former governor, "politics in California and everywhere else in the United States has been a mess ever since that fellow Nixon got into the act."

Warren's former law clerks had sought to arrange a reunion luncheon for him, but he discouraged the idea. With the specter of Watergate haunting nearly every American home, the time was not propitious for such social gatherings, he reasoned. Instead, he prepared to embark on his fatal spring speaking tour.

It began on April 17 in Washington at a press conference for the NAACP Legal Defense and Education Fund. Heartily thanking the Carnegie Corporation and Rockefeller Foundation for donating nearly $1.3 million to the Earl Warren Legal Training Program, he observed: "When I joined the bar sixty years ago, a black lawyer was a rarity. In 1965, there were only seven hundred black law students in the entire country. Today, there are about four thousand." Although insisting that many more were needed, the pleased jurist noted that the increased number of black students—whose attrition rate had sharply declined—had now made it easier to appoint the first black law professors at six state-university law schools.

Ten days later, he flew to New Orleans to receive an honorary doctor of law degree and speak at the dedication of Loyola University's new law school. Under a hot Saturday afternoon sun, he scathingly condemned the Nixon Administration, including its attorneys who had dishonored his and his audience's profession:

> *The Vice President, after a plea of guilty to a charge of felony, has resigned in disgrace. An attorney general and another cabinet member have been indicted, as have two official counsels to the President and two of his personal attorneys. Altogether twenty-one people in and around the White House have been indicted, and*

sixteen of these were lawyers. Others are under criminal investiga-
tion. Their alleged criminal offenses pertain to serious violations of
our system of justice and to the performance of the basic functions of
government. The inner sanctum of the White House has been
tarnished, and the end of the debacle is not yet in sight.

The inevitable "destructive cynicism," he vehemently claimed, had resulted in "half-baked proposals," such as abolition of the Vice Presidency and removal of the Department of Justice from the Executive branch. These suggestions, he implied, were too silly to be taken seriously. But other recommendations, likewise related to public cynicism and "the transitory emotions of their proponents"—which were linked to notions pre-dating Watergate—might even be more dangerous because their folly was less obvious. Foremost among these was the proposal confected to streamline Supreme Court procedures. Thus, the Mini-Court proposal, detested by Warren, was really an outgrowth of a pernicious long-term trend toward abolishing oral arguments in courts. But oral arguments, insisted the retired Chief Justice, were a basic part of the judicial system because only through questions and answers could the true merits of a case be uncovered. Any proposal that resulted in a lessening of the number of courts—and particularly the Supreme Court, which permitted oral arguments—therefore must be resisted.

Because Warren's health was declining, his doctor now strongly counseled that the remainder of his speaking tour be canceled. But the elder statesman ignored the advice. It was difficult for him to leave obligations unfulfilled at the best of times, and these were indeed the worst of times. Genuinely alarmed by the downbeat mood of the nation, he felt duty bound to seize every opportunity of preaching a message of hope to fellow citizens. This message was simply that Watergate must not be viewed as a failure of the American system, but rather, as its vindication—a triumphant demonstration that good institutions could not be undone by bad men, no matter how highly situated. Along with reiterations of several other precepts dear to Earl Warren's heart, this theme constituted the basis of all his remaining public utterances.

On April 30 he spoke to the Stanford University Law Forum, and on May 11 delivered the commencement address at the University of Santa Clara in California. He was too ill to attend the

NAACP's May 17 dinner in New York honoring the twentieth anniversary of the *Brown* decision, but his speech was read for him by black Judge William S. Thompson of the District of Columbia Superior Court. ("We are only part way up the mountain we have essayed to climb.")

On May 21 he considered himself well enough to deliver the commencement address at Morehouse College in Atlanta. Speaking to an overflow audience in the college gymnasium, Warren for the last time reaffirmed his faith in the vitality of the nation's institutions and values. Again he denounced the American Bar Association for endorsing the Mini-Court when "not one lawyer in a hundred has even heard of it." Using as a touchstone for his thesis the fact that a single conscientious American citizen—"a humble night watchman who was not susceptible to bribery"—had precipitated the entire chain of Watergate disclosures, the jurist who had championed the "one-man-one-vote" philosophy concluded:

> *The great virtue of our government is that people can do something about it. They elect our representatives on all levels of government, our mayors, our legislators, our governors and our President. When they have made a mistake, they can rectify it.*

Even the New York *Daily News*, which not long ago had characterized Warren as "a power grabber . . . without judicial instincts," found his words "filled with sound, solid, common sense." This was Earl Warren's final public address.

He had underestimated his failing strength and, exhausted, he returned to Washington. Two days later on May 23, he was again hospitalized. He had wanted to be treated at Bethesda Naval Hospital. As a sitting Justice, he could have been admitted there or at any Federal military hospital, but as a retired Justice, his admission required Executive approval. President Nixon was requested to sign such an order, but he refused to do so, Warren later told hospital visitor Arthur Goldberg. After Warren was admitted to the Georgetown University Hospital, tormented Richard Nixon had second thoughts. Dr. William Lukash, the White House physician, then offered to transfer the judicial patient to Bethesda, but the proud Warren declined the offer.

Now, of course, there was no question of his fulfilling any

more speaking engagements. However, characteristically, the ever-dutiful Warren wrote Dean E. McHenry, Chancellor of the University of California at Santa Cruz, a long letter on May 30, 1974, explaining in detail what he *would* have said had he been able to speak at the commencement exercises. Because it is a typical compassion-filled Warren letter, because it succinctly summarizes the "message" he then was so eager for the American people to hear and because it is his last "letter to the world," it is quoted in full:

Dear Dean:

It is very embarrassing for me to be "grounded" here on the seventh floor of the Georgetown University Hospital, looking down on Watergate, instead of being out in the Santa Cruz Redwoods on our newest campus, where I had promised to be. You were good enough to invite me so many times to speak on the campus, and I have always regretted because conflicting engagements or trans-continental travel prevented me from accepting at that particular time.

I did want so much to visit with you before your retirement at the Campus of the University, the construction of which you planned and supervised in addition to breaking new ground in the field of higher education. I remember when I first dropped off to see you. You were just leaving for some other part of the State, and your office, as I recall it, was in one of the temporary buildings of the contractor. At that time, very little had been done toward actual construction, but I was thrilled in trying to envision what would develop there on that beautiful plateau from which one could survey the great Pacific Ocean and conjure what it would mean to our Nation in the years to come.

Until last Friday, I thought that I would be able to be with you as I had spoken just two days before at Morehouse College in Atlanta, Georgia, but some angina which I have had on occasion for some time acted up, and the doctor insisted on putting me here in the hospital, where I must remain for a few days longer. I have not been ill or suffering any pain since coming here, and my doctors tell me they will have me in very good shape in a few days.

I did want to say to the people of Santa Cruz, whom I knew very well in my political years in California, that I appreciate, as I am sure they do, the tremendous job you have done at the Santa

Cruz Campus. I also wanted to tell them of our friendship, which has extended back through many years, and that when two of my daughters were at UCLA one of them was a political science student of yours. She related to me what was transpiring at the time you ran for Congress, and how you were being abused by your opponent because you did not conform to the Joe McCarthy principles of government. I sympathized with you at that time because I knew your opponent. He had been building fires under me for several years while I was in Sacramento. As I look back on it now, I am pleased that you did not win that election, because had you done so I am sure that the people would have soon recognized your worth, and would have retained you to the great loss of the University of California, which I believe has done more good for our State than any other organization in its history.

I also wanted to talk to your students, as we had agreed upon, because I would like to plead with them not to become involved in the current cynicism resulting from the Watergate scandals. In addition, I wanted to impress upon them that they not only should but could be an important factor in solving many of the problems of our day.

Too many people, in frustration because of the disclosures, have proposed measures to change even the structure of our government. Some want to take the Justice Department and the FBI out of the Executive Branch, others advocate the abolition of the Vice Presidency merely because one man has disgraced the office. Also, because crime is so rampant, they would even change the jurisdiction of the Supreme Court of the United States.

All of these things involve questions of constitutional dimension, and I wanted to point out to the students that as we approach the Bicentennial of our Nation the thing which has brought us to our present great stature has been adherence to the Constitution of the United States. I have never known anything bad happening to our Nation through adherence to the Constitution as it now stands. We are only in great national trouble when people violate or circumvent the Constitution. The atmosphere of today will permit neither proper evaluation of any constitutional change nor the consequences of doing so in such unsettled times. I believe we should remember the truism that we do not tear down good buildings merely because they have been occupied by bad tenants. Our country will survive this tragedy and will do so if an enlightened citizenry will give its attention to the affairs of government on all its levels.

I wish, Dean, that you would extend my best wishes to the people of Santa Cruz and to the students at the University as well as to your designated successor, Dr. Mark Christensen, who has already proved his devotion to the University in other capacities.

With affectionate regards to you and with best wishes for your continued success and happiness, and looking forward to the possibility of seeing you in the Bohemian Grove of Redwoods in Sonoma County later in the Summer, I am

> *Sincerely,*
> *(Signed) Earl*

Three days later, on June 2, Warren was discharged from the hospital. Although permitted to convalesce at home, he was advised to remain away from his Supreme Court office. Instead, his secretary, Mrs. Margaret McHugh, came to his apartment daily. He tried working on his autobiography but had difficulty concentrating. Justice Douglas urged him to speed up his memoirs by dictating them into a tape-recorder. Methias Warren's old-fashioned son, however, insisted upon writing his thoughts painstakingly on his yellow-lined legal pad.

On July 2, he was rushed back to the Georgetown Hospital. His physician, Dr. Oscar Mann, diagnosed his condition as coronary insufficiency and congestive heart failure. The day before, three thousand miles away in Sacramento, Governor Ronald Reagan had vetoed, in a $10 billion budget, a modest $45,000 legislative appropriation to complete the four-year-old Earl Warren Oral History project in Berkeley, despite an estimated $400 million state surplus. The National Endowment for the Humanities, which had contributed $185,000 thus far (matched by $60,000 in private donations) had its budget sliced by President Nixon. This, together with White House pressure had compelled it to cancel a planned $45,000 grant to continue the Warren project, even though it had been hailed as a notable contribution to American history.

The news of Reagan's veto was disheartening, but Warren was too preoccupied with America to worry much about this California setback. He continued to tell everyone that Watergate must be understood as a vindication of the American system of governmental checks and balances. A runaway Executive had been effectively halted by the Judicial and Legislative branches.

But had it?

The first steps had been taken responsibly enough: The Senate investigation had disclosed the facts to the electorate and Judge Sirica's lower court had ruled against "executive privilege" on the issue of the Presidential tapes. But suppose the system were to falter in the succeeding steps? The House still had to face the question of impeachment proceedings and the Burger Court still had to rule on whether or not to uphold Judge Sirica's decision.

Warren well knew that it was not enough that Richard Nixon, trapped in a White House bunker, had been destroyed politically. That had been accomplished extralegally, by the power of public opinion. The true test of the American constitutional system would be determined by what the Congress and the Supreme Court did next. If they contrived to *avoid* their responsibilities, or if they discharged them with less than courage, objectivity and complete independence, the resulting damage could be drastic.

In his final days, how deep were Earl Warren's private fears about the outcome of Watergate? Outwardly, he steadfastly maintained that the Court and the Congress would do their duty. Yet a sense of his underlying concern is implicit in certain conversations reported by several hospital visitors. For example, a former clerk who visited Warren in his hospital room recalls asking if the impeachment of a President might not be "unthinkable" in view of the damage it would do to public confidence in the government. "No," snapped Warren, "only the alternative is unthinkable." Stirring in his bed, the former Chief Justice animatedly dilated on the crucial importance of the fundamental right to impeach. At every level—from the President down to the humblest voter—the strength of the American governmental system, he argued, consisted in its capacity to rectify mistakes through elections, impeachment and the dominion of law over men. As to what the threat of impeachment meant to public officials,—well, during his sixteen years as Chief Justice he had had some experience with that himself, he said with a faint smile.

Another reported conversation may have come closer to revealing Warren's most immediate worry. A visitor told him of a rumor that President Nixon had boasted: "I'll win in the Supreme Court. I've got four votes there already. Burger thinks the whole thing is a disgrace." This hearsay upset Warren visibly. The Court, the former judge dissented, *had* to rule against the President's claim of "executive privilege." That the Judiciary, not the Executive, was the final arbiter of the law had been a basic principle of American government since John Marshall's ruling in *Marbury* v. *Madison* in 1803. To concede the President's claim in the present crisis would be tantamount to saying that an American President was *above* the law.

Still, Warren's unrelenting profession of faith that the Burger Court would uphold the Sirica decision never betrayed what may have been his inner doubt. The Supreme Court of the United States is no place to cash in political I.O.U.s, he insisted. On July 8, the day the Court began its historic deliberations in the *United States* v. *Nixon*, Warren told a hospital visitor, former Justice Arthur Goldberg, "No man, not even a King, can put himself above the law. I am confident the Court will do its duty—and so will the nation." But such words suggest a complacency that Warren almost certainly could not have felt. Perhaps they are better understood as incantations than as prophecies.

On the following morning, Tuesday, July 9, Warren's physician considered his patient's condition satisfactory. "Justice Warren was fairly cheerful under the circumstances," recollects Dr. Mann. Downtown, Judge Sirica was denying motions to delay or dismiss the trial, or move it out of Washington.

Late that afternoon the restless patient was visited for a half-hour by his closest Warren Court associates, Brennan and Douglas. They remained until 5:30 P.M. The lonely Warren asked them to stay, but both felt that he appeared too weary and weak.

"He was full of good spirits, though," remembers Douglas. "He talked about the Court, what decisions were coming up and whether the old Warren Court decisions were in jeopardy, such as the school integration and reapportionment cases. He had closely followed the Nixon case, which we had heard the day before, but of course we couldn't talk to him about that. But we listened. He sure made a good oral argument in fifteen minutes!"

Two hours later, the patient's condition took a sudden turn for the worse. Emergency medical measures were attempted. But at 8:10 P.M. on the warm Washington evening of July 9, 1974, Earl

Warren, eighty-three, died of cardiac arrest. Nina, his devoted wife of forty-nine years, and their youngest daughter, Mrs. Stuart Brien, who was visiting from California, were at his bedside.

"Death cancels everything but truth," William Hazlitt wrote in 1821. "It is a sort of natural canonization."

Earl Warren was dead but his convictions—and the controversies they had provoked—about the country and Court were to remain very much alive.

The tributes came swiftly from old friends and old enemies. President Nixon, fast approaching his personal Armageddon, took the time to eulogize his fallen rival. The Warren legacy, said the man who had fought it with such single-minded ferocity, "will reflect the highest purposes of America forever." And of Warren himself, Nixon accurately and generously said, "In all things he was never a partisan of political advantage but always a partisan for America." Curiously, many newspapers and other media chose not to include these words of the President in their July 10 obituaries of Warren.

Chief Justice Burger's praise was more guarded. On July 11 he remarked on a CBS "Special Report":

> *In his sixteen years on the Supreme Court, controversial though it was at times, it was nevertheless a very dynamic period. People will disagree about some of the results. Taken as a whole, any fair-minded person must recognize that this was a great period in American history. One of the most significant things probably— and it was one of the most controversial—was that the Court exhibited a willingness to take a new look at the problems of criminal law administration. It brought a great deal of problems on the Court, but it opened up new vistas in the entire field. And taken as a whole, the country is the better for it.*

A supplementary assessment by the Fifteenth Chief Justice about the Fourteenth Chief Justice remains sealed until 1990 in the Earl Warren History Archives in Berkeley's Bancroft Library which now houses 54 bound volumes of 154 other transcripts.

All the other present and former Justices added their tributes:
Douglas: "Earl Warren . . . knew how the other half lived. . . . high above the crowd, a man of great integrity, a fearless man who stood up and was counted on the great issues of his era." *Brennan:* ". . . one of the greatest figures of American history . . . People were

his concern, especially ordinary people. . . . To me he was a Super Chief." *Stewart:* ". . . an indispensable maker of the history of . . . our time . . . a man of firm and sometimes stubborn principle . . . his greatness lay most truly in the fact that his virtues were the simple virtues. . . ." *White:* ". . . a remarkable man in every respect . . . I enjoyed him immensely . . . a great American." *Marshall:* "I think he is irreplaceable . . . a true brother in every sense of the word. . . . Viewing him from both sides of the Bench, one could not but be impressed by his devotion to 'The Law of the Land.' " *Blackmun:* "The Court and the nation have greatly benefitted by his presence here . . . A stalwart friend and guide." *Powell:* "I [knew] and admired him as a remarkable American for many years. . . . Not . . . well known but perhaps of historical significance . . . was his unpublicized leadership in trying to extend adherence to the rule of law world-wide." *Rehnquist:* "The qualitites of personal warmth and friendliness which he possessed in such large measure could not help but make an impression . . . an inspiration for all Americans." *Clark:* "He stood high among his peers because they knew his word was his bond. . . . In his private life he was . . . delightfully entreating and totally open-hearted . . . enjoying his friends, putting up with his enemies . . . the epitome of a Great Chief. . . ." *Reed:* ". . . a gentleman whose constitutional philosophy was an inevitable extension of his personal rectitude." *Goldberg* hailed him as a "great emancipator . . . the flame burned bright while the torch was in his keeping." Fortas called him a "giant."

His wife of forty-nine years said simply to Dorothy (Mrs. Arthur) Goldberg: "Every moment was beautiful. Young people who don't know what a real marriage is miss so much!" Eric Sevareid, a swimming companion, observed, "Baseball, football and fly fishing lost a friend but America gained a legacy." Lady Bird Johnson wrote to me: "How could a man of such benevolence, fair play and justice have been the object of such ugly 'Impeach Earl Warren' signs? Our country is forever in his debt."

In the white-marbled Great Hall foyer of the United States Supreme Court, the body of Earl Warren lay in state on Thursday, July 11, and on the morning of Friday, July 12, in a flag-draped bronze coffin. It was the first time in American history that a deceased Justice had been so honored. The black velvet-covered catafalque included a section used for Abraham Lincoln. To permit loan of this stand, both houses of Congress had passed special resolutions within ninety minutes.

At the head of the casket stood the black leather highback armchair that Warren had used during his sixteen years on the Court. It bore a small bronze plaque saying "The Chief Justice."

Nine thousand persons, from the eminent elderly to obscure teenagers in blue jeans, filed past to say farewell. Four thousand of them signed the commemoration book. Outside in the blazing sun, the flags fluttered at half-mast.

Nine present Justices and four former ones lined up on the descending marble steps as honorary pallbearers. They received the casket before it was transported in a ceremonial procession to Washington's National Cathedral for an hour-long funeral service beginning at 1 P.M. on Friday, July 12.

More than one thousand persons crowded the Gothic-style Episcopal Cathedral. The funeral service brought together President Nixon and all the Justices who four days earlier had heard the Watergate tape case which would determine his Presidency. Others included many Federal judges, congressional leaders and thirty-nine members of Earl Warren's family. Two of his longtime religious friends extolled the man who belonged to no organized church.

Rabbi Alvin I. Fine, professor of humanities at San Francisco State University, eulogized him as a "classic American who would have signed the Declaration of Independence":

Human decency and kindness were so instinctive, honor and dignity so natural in him, that there could be no unguarded moments of indiscretion when he was anyone but the true Earl Warren. Neither criticism nor disagreement nor vilification caused him to lose his head . . . One of the giants of our generation has fallen and a part of every man has fallen with him.

The Most Reverend Phillip M. Hannan, Roman Catholic Archbishop of New Orleans, called him a humanist who related principles to persons, not to legal abstractions. Because he believed that "law floats in a sea of ethical principles," he judged the Constitution by his conscience, his set of ethical principles.

When the service concluded, President Nixon escorted the black-veiled widow from the quiet Cathedral before returning to his own unquiet White House.

Earl Warren's body was then borne across Washington's Potomac River to Virginia for burial on a grassy knoll in Arlington National Cemetery. Black comedian Dick Gregory, jogging there on a path, was chased away by Secret Service agents. This intemperate Warren Commission critic later indelicately wrote: "It was really weird. Either I should have been at the funeral, or else I had chased Earl Warren all the way to his grave." One-time First Lieutenant Warren was buried with full military honors. A six-horse caisson carried the casket to the hilly grave site surrounded by evergreens, a few feet from the grave of John Foster Dulles, whom Dwight Eisenhower had wanted to appoint Chief Justice instead of Earl Warren. A U. S. Army detail fired three volleys. A bugler sounded taps. The Army band played "America the Beautiful." Military escorts clad in blue punctiliously folded the American flag which draped the casket and handed it to Chief Justice Burger, who in turn handed it to Mrs. Warren.

Twelve days later, Chief Justice Burger opened the July 24 session of the Supreme Court with a eulogy to his predecessor. It was a peculiarly fitting moment for such a tribute, for on this day the Court showed the nation that it had indeed "done its duty." The vote on *United States* v. *Nixon* was unanimous: 8–0. (Rehnquist had properly disqualified himself on the grounds that he had previously been associated with the case during his Justice Department days). The President could not withhold the controversial tapes on the grounds of "executive privilege," the Court ruled, and must surrender them forthwith. The opinion was written by Chief Justice Burger himself.

Burger's critics have suggested that early in the Court's deliberations he had attempted to persuade his reluctant colleagues to support the President's position. This, however, does not appear to have been the fact. According to Barrett McGurn, the Court's capable information officer, Burger worked extremely hard on the case, exhaustively researching all the applicable law for forty-one consecutive days prior to the beginning of the oral arguments. When he finally indicated what his own conclusion was, it proved contrary to that of the man who had appointed him. The President, after hearing the decision, reportedly blazed with unprintable fury at his San Clemente retreat, shouting that Burger was no better than Warren.

Three days later, on July 27, the House Judiciary Committee recommended to the full House of Representatives three articles of impeachment against the President. The vote was 27–11. It voted 38–0 that he had obstructed justice. On August 5, the President reluctantly surrendered the disputed tapes: They indicated that, notwithstanding his assertions, he had had knowledge of the Watergate burglary six days after it had occurred. Four days after the release of these tapes, on August 9, President Nixon resigned rather than endure certain impeachment by the House and probable conviction by the Senate. His resignation followed Chief Justice Warren's death by precisely one month. That the activist jurist would have greeted this resolution of a constitutional crisis and national nightmare with the profoundest relief is beyond doubt.

In one sense, the long antagonism between Warren and Nixon ended with the death of one and the disgrace of the other. In another sense, it persists to this day, for both men left rival legacies as well as opposing philosophies and deeds. Contrasted with the landmark decisions and judicial reforms which survive Warren's Chief Justiceship are the law-and-order judicial appointments that Nixon made so lavishly during his Presidency. Not only did Nixon select four of the current Justices of the Supreme Court, he also named more Federal judges (220) than any President in history to date. Most still hold office. Few, one may assume, would have felt at home in the Warren Court atmosphere.

Today an ex-President in San Clemente limbo through his Chief Justice and three appointees remains a kind of Ghost at the Judicial Banquet. Some diehard Warrenites have even bitterly termed the Burger Court "Nixon's Revenge." But happily for America, Justices have exhibited remarkable independence of the Presidents who appointed them. Warren emancipated himself from Eisenhower. And Burger some day may fully break the Nixonian knot. The late Harvard Law Dean Roscoe Pound once reminded, "Justice is an alloy of men and mechanisms in which men count more than machinery."

Nixon in his memoirs attempts to latch on to Warren's respectability and reputation for integrity. In deploring the open hearings of Senator Ervin's committee, he writes: "Earl Warren had once called it 'frontier justice' to haul prospective defendants up before public hearings." Nixon neglects to document when and where Warren said this and undoubtedly quotes it out of context, because Warren both as governor and Chief Justice *never* opposed fair, legitimate open public hearings. Similarly, Nixon writes: ". . . investigation of the secret multimillion-dollar Bahamian bank account supposedly maintained for me by Rebozo turned out to be a 'con man with a criminal record' who made an identical allegation years earlier against Earl Warren." Here, again, Nixon fails to document when this charge was made about Warren and by whom.

On the other hand, Warren in his incomplete memoirs, in keeping with his habitual reticence, avoided publishing any but the most perfunctory observations about Nixon. Direct references to Nixon are conspicuous by their dearth and impersonality (and doubtless would have been even had the book been completed).

But a curious sidelight to the Warren-Nixon feud persists—a mystery which may never be solved. Warren is known to have kept at least one early "Nixon file." When he resigned as governor of California to become Chief Justice, he turned over to the California State Archives in Sacramento 420 sealed brown cardboard boxes containing an estimated 800,000 copies of official and personal correspondence, memoranda, campaign records and assorted memorabilia. They are housed in a basement vault and, according to Warren's stipulation, were to be unsealed only after his death. When the files were opened on July 10, 1974, reporters rushed to consult the material in the folder labeled "Nixon." It was empty, its contents removed by "persons unknown." *Who* cheated history? Warren himself? A Warren aide? Or a Watergate type burglar?

Thus, unless this or some other "Nixon file" ever surfaces much of what Warren thought about Richard Nixon from Whittier to Watergate and vice versa, remains in limbo. Not even The Earl Warren Oral History Project is of much help in this regard, even though many Warren intimates recorded such statements as "Earl never trusted Nixon," "Warren didn't think Nixon was an honest man," and "The Chief hated Nixon's guts."

But the retired Warren himself specifically declined to discuss Nixon in his interviews for the Berkeley Oral History Project— which is an unfortunate loss for American history. Director Amelia Fry, says, "The one thing he became annoyed with me about was whenever I asked him about Nixon. I pressed, I probed, but he refused ever to discuss the subject."

Warren's reluctance to give oral or written public expression to his innermost thoughts about individuals whom he truly disliked —such as Nixon—however admirable, can burden a biographer. To learn what was really in the Chief Justice's heart and mind, occasional reliance must be made upon the insubstantial medium of private conversations reported at second hand. A hitherto unrevealed one—which confirms my own periodic observations about the Warren-Nixon relationship over three decades—was told to me at press time by a highly respected journalist who never published the conversation himself. I offer it as a final comment of the long, antagonistic relationship between Earl Warren and Richard Nixon.

Four months before Warren died, Alden Whitman, then the Boswell of *The New York Times* obituary pages, was preparing a pre-obituary interview of the retired Chief Justice. The dying Warren well understood that in this interview he could speak frankly about matters which the trusted journalist would not publish during Warren's lifetime. The interview took place in the retired Justice's Supreme Court office. It began at 2:30 P.M. and unexpectedly stretched out for more than three hours. Warren spoke at length, with uncharacteristic candor and choler, about a wide range of topics including his personal motives for resigning, the Burger Court, Nixon, Watergate and his hopes and fears for the future of the Republic. He spoke on matters which he never would have discussed with a journalist, in retirement or while on the High Court. His most unjudicial words were prompted by his growing fury at the revelations of the White House-planned wiretaps, mail openings, break-ins and now attempted cover-ups.

"Nixon's not important," affirmed the old man. "*The country, the country* is important. But it's going to rot under Tricky." He sighed and then added that his twenty-eight-year political adversary was the most reprehensible President in American history, who had abused not only the office but, perhaps even worse, the American people.

As the session was drawing to a close, Earl Warren walked over to the curtainless window which overlooked the majestic Capitol. He stood silent. Dusk was gathering in the sky. A distant church bell sounded.

Finally, he said softly, "It's difficult to conceive of anyone living to be eighty-three and having no regrets." Then he turned to his visitor and, in a voice choking with emotion, said: "If I had ever known what was going to happen to this country—and this Court—I *never* would have resigned. They would have had to carry me out of here on a plank!"

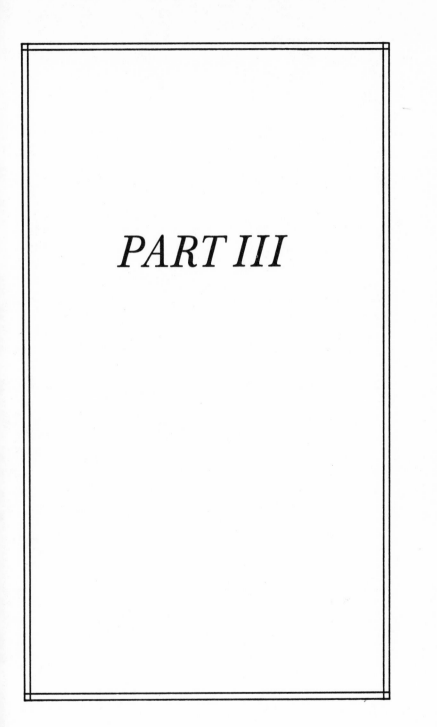

PART III

Chapter Nine

The Warren Legacy

*E*arl Warren left America a legacy of radical change and enduring controversy. To some, such as a middle-aged Chicago public relations executive, "He was the man who got your grandmother raped, and made the streets unsafe with his civil liberties bullshit." To Theodore M. Hesburgh, president of the University of Notre Dame, "He was a giant in an age of midgets." To William F. Buckley, Warren was "a disaster to the Constitution of the United States, to the highest standards of jurisprudence and to the Federal system, which is a lot for one Justice to be." But according to Arthur Goldberg, "The flame burned bright while the torch was in his keeping."

So it goes, and so it is likely to continue for a long time to come.

No thoughtful person can be indifferent to the legacy of Earl Warren: Controversy, Contrast, Courage, Compassion and Conquest. Yet it is a legacy that is not always easy to define, even though it was a monument to social justice. Generally, it takes years to assess the full implications of any important Supreme Court decision. The practical results are often slow to materialize and sometimes rather unexpected. It was, for example, not at all clear when the *Brown* desegregation decision was handed down in 1954 that two decades later the issue's storm center would be school busing.

Nor is the effect of a Supreme Court decision always *caused* by the decision itself. Very often a "majoritorian" Court simply makes a legal pronouncement of some conclusion already reached by American society through an evolving consensus. Thus, America may have been *ready* for the legal, social and ethical revolution which characterized the Warren era.

Warren's opinions may lack the philosophic majesty of a Marshall, the intellectual ardor of a Brandeis, the free speech passion of a Black or the individual liberty fervor of a Douglas. Yet some approach a kind of low gear greatness in their own down-to-earth way. "He wrote simply like Lincoln," insists Lee Rankin.

"What the hell difference does it make how well an opinion is constructed or whose language was actually used," observes a Court insider. "The test is whether the opinion solved great problems at the time and stood up as a monument in the history of the country. Few of Frankfurter's obfuscated opinions, or those of the other great legal scholars, meet this test. Warren's opinions do."

The Warren legacy has both objective and subjective aspects. The objective, or institutionalized, part consists of the judicial decisions, legal reforms and subsequent administrative acts that have become formal government rules which regulate our daily behavior. By contrast, the more elusive subjective phase seeks to comprehend the mysterious quality of the man himself and the way he affected our minds and hearts—either because we think that Earl Warren personified the true spirit of justice or because we feel he affronted it.

Let us begin with the landmark Warren opinions in the objective aspect.

The epic legislative reapportionment decisions—which Earl Warren himself considered the Court's most important rulings during his sixteen-year tenure—have become routinely accepted without any of the *Sturm und Drang* associated with him. Hardly anyone now seriously challenges the equity of the "one-man-one-vote"rulings. Because the difficult political readjustments have been made, the once-violent opposition has largely faded away. Few reapportionment complaints have been brought into Federal courts, even though the Warren tribunal specifically established the machinery for this purpose.

The effects nonetheless have been profound. Political doors formerly shut have been quietly opened to countless city and

suburban voters in choosing members of state legislatures and of
Congress. Everywhere women, blacks and members of other
minorities, in areas once dominated by rural interests, now have a
vastly better chance of being elected to public office. Even Chief
Justice Burger conceded in a May 1975 tribute: "The reapportionment cases brought into focus his [Warren's] vast understanding of
the American political process and his passion for fairness."

Jimmy Carter, whose election as governor of Georgia in 1971
was in part due to a 1963 Warren Court reapportionment ruling
which outlawed Georgia's ancient county-unit method of choosing
legislators, later as President daringly urged this "one-man-one-
vote" doctrine for Rhodesia. Prime Minister Ian Smith, who had
once protested that "never in a thousand years" would he accept this
principle, did an about-face on his objection in November 1977.

Warren always maintained that the reapportionment decisions were "more important" than the desegregation ones because,
he argued, if the nation had followed a "one-man-one-vote" philosophy, then segregation *never* could have survived. Perhaps this is an
Olympian view. America, however, should be grateful that Earl
Warren addressed himself to *both* problems.

In the field of desegregation, much of the thunder, lightning
and philosophic objections against it has evaporated, simmered
down or gone underground. Legal equality—and even compensating inequalities weighted in favor of racial minorities such as in
the 1978 *Bakke* v. *University of California* ruling—is now professed
public policy and is accepted, even if often grudgingly. Indeed, so
much has occurred since the 1954 *Brown* decision that its issues at
present appear almost antediluvian. Even the Warren Court's "with
all deliberate speed" formula now seems overcautious.

The *Brown* decision wrought a revolution of awesome proportions. Today the old stereotype of a segregated South and an
integrated North no longer is true. Southern public classrooms in
primary and secondary schools are more integrated today than
those in the North and West. Once-embattled Little Rock now
boasts that it has "the most totally integrated school system in the
country." The University of Alabama, where Governor George
Wallace attempted to prevent integration by standing in the door-
way, now has more enrolled black students than Harvard, Yale,
Princeton and Dartmouth combined. Thus, most Southern states
are now in virtual full compliance with the 1954 *Brown* decision.

Ironically, since Warren's death the desegregation drama has been played mainly on Yankee stages.

Busing was introduced as an unpopular but well-meaning method of enforcing the Warren Court decision to end Jim Crow schools. Designed to achieve "racial balance," it has proceeded smoothly for many years in numerous school districts throughout the South. As North Carolina Senator Robert B. Morgan, who originally opposed busing, says, "It's not desirable, but we're doing it all over the South—and it's working."

But today, unfortunately, countless white and black parents are in explosive conflict over the busing of their children, especially at great distances, in major Northern and Western cities, including Los Angeles, Cleveland and Chicago. Busing has hastened a "white flight" to the suburbs or into private or parochial schools, leaving many big city schools predominantly black, with the statistical truth and effects being heatedly debated in scholarly journals.

Federal and state judges, seeking to implement the Warren Court decrees, increasingly have ordered school districts to bus pupils. In Dallas; Milwaukee; Omaha; Kansas City, Missouri; Columbus, Ohio; Wilmington, Delaware and elsewhere this has been achieved peacefully. By contrast, in Boston, Louisville and other communities, violence had erupted before court-ordered busing began. Seattle in 1977 and Berkeley, California, in 1968 chose voluntarily to desegregate their schools without court or Washington pressure.

President Ford injected court-ordered busing into the 1976 political campaign when he urged that antibusing legislation be introduced in Congress—as it has been. But the Carter Administration now seems to be somewhat reversing eight years of Nixon–Ford policy on school integration by having HEW withhold education funds from schools that refuse to desegregate or comply with court-ordered busing—which most agree is far from an ideal solution.

Unfortunately, the only alternatives presently suggested have not been widely adopted: 1) building new schools at the edges of white and black neighborhoods; 2) establishing more "magnet schools" in black areas to lure white students who would voluntarily transfer to them.

The present Supreme Court has had a mixed record in school desegregation. Though it has left the Warren Court decisions largely intact, it has struck down large-scale integration and busing orders in Detroit; Austin, Texas; Indianapolis, Indiana; and Dayton, Ohio; ruling that lower courts had not proven clear "intent" to discriminate, something which may be a task for a telepathist rather than a jurist. Translated, this in effect means that you can discriminate racially—as long as you don't legally admit it!

Granted, the busing controversy is a peculiarly unpleasant manifestation of a still-unsolved problem. Yet is is also true that since 1954 the progress made toward the goal of racial equality has been impressive. Problems remain, but the advances have been remarkable. Blacks have achieved an unprecedented number of positions of power in government, the law, business and the professions. More than a hundred blacks now serve in Congress or in Southern state legislatures, whereas a mere dozen years ago there were no black lawmakers south of the Mason-Dixon line. As of July 1977, 4,311 blacks were holding elective office, the most in once racially repressive Mississippi, which James Meredith, the first black student to be admitted to the University of Mississippi in 1962, now calls "the most integrated state in the Union." Who could have imagined in 1954 that at the 1976 Democratic National Convention, delegates chanting "We Shall Overcome" would observe the spectacle of Rev. Martin Luther King, Sr., and George Wallace praying together? Who, for that matter, could have imagined elected black mayors of Atlanta and New Orleans, and of Andrew Young in his United Nations post? Or once-diehard segregationist Senator Strom Thurmond escorting his six-year-old daughter to an integrated Columbia, South Carolina, school where she has a black teacher and a black principal?

The long struggle for racial equality neither began nor ended with *Brown*, but it will always be remembered as a milestone—an exemplary moment when the Chief Justice and his eight similarly courageous brethren decided that the time had come to put an end to hedging, trimming and postponing—and move to crumble bigotry's barriers. If Earl Warren had resigned or died right after the 1954 desegregation ruling, that decision alone would have assured his name in the history books forever.

Not so with the controversial school prayer rulings of 1962 and 1963, which flared up during the third Ford–Carter debate on October 21, 1976. Regional challenges are now emerging in many states.

New Hampshire in 1975 passed a law permitting local school

boards to decide whether to require that the Lord's Prayer be recited in public schools. Although a Federal District Court in Concord declared this law unconstitutional in 1976, a new law was passed in 1977. In 1978 Governor Meldrim Thomson failed to secure Supreme Court permission to lower flags on state buildings on Good Friday. A Connecticut law now requires "silent meditation" in all public schools. Maine is considering a similar statute. Both houses in New Jersey passed such a bill in 1978. Similarly, school prayer adherents are lobbying for new laws in Alabama, Pennsylvania and elsewhere. A 1978 Kentucky law requires that the Ten Commandments be posted in every public school classroom. In North Carolina school prayers precipitated bitter civic and court battles in early 1978. That state's Senator Jesse Helms has introduced a bill which would enable state legislatures to negate the 1962 and 1963 Warren Court rulings separating church and state. The Roman Catholic hierarchy, which had supported these rulings, reversed its stand in 1973, urging a constitutional amendment authorizing public school prayers.

Perhaps the reason for this upsurge in behalf of school prayer is a hope that the current Burger Court will one day reverse its predecessor's decisions. The present Justices seem nearly evenly divided over the church-state issue.

In criminal justice, the Burger Court has not flatly overturned the Warren Court decisions that expanded the rights of the accused and the indigent. More frequently it has chipped away at them, interpreted them narrowly, limited their scope, found them in "harmless error," dismissed appeals without explanation and even restricted its own jurisdiction. But the spirit that animated the Warren rulings has been sharply restricted. What the Warren Court gave, the Burger Court has been trying to take away in the area of criminal justice, the most significant category of disagreement between the fourteenth and the fifteenth Chief Justice.

In a series of decisions since 1970, the Burger Court has clearly curtailed the rights of persons suspected of having committed crimes. Today, police are permitted to make warrantless arrests; to stop and frisk motorists at will; to accuse people publicly of being active criminals, even if they have never been convicted of a crime. Prosecutors now have infinitely greater power in plea-bargaining with defendants. The Court also has curbed Federal judges who seek to prevent state and local police from violating the constitutional rights of suspects. Moreover, it has severely limited the number of legal remedies available to suspects who claim their rights have been violated. It has also questioned the extent of the right of privacy by ruling that states may imprison individuals for committing homosexual acts, even when these occurred in private between consenting adults. Although the Warren Court had decreed that "unreasonable search and seizure" evidence was illegal and inadmissible ("the exclusionary rule"), the Burger Court has ruled that this is not a constitutional guarantee, but only a judge-made tradition. Thus, persons who believe that they have been convicted in state and local courts on the basis of "tainted evidence" are now denied the remedy of appealing their cases in Federal courts. For many behind bars, this had clamped the prison doors tighter. Access to Federal courts generally has been far more limited than in the Warren years.

Similarly, the Burger Court in 1976 denied lower-court Federal judges the right to intervene in state convictions—no matter how improper—until the appellant has exhausted all state remedies. This was a direct reversal of a 1963 Warren Court decision in *Fay* v. *Noia*. Observes Michigan law professor Yale Kamisar, "It seems like I'm seeing an old movie run backwards."

Many of the Burger Court's majority opinions have been written by Rehnquist; most have drawn sharp dissents from Brennan and Marshall. Duke University law professor William Van Alstyne characterizes these decisions in general as "a drift towards protecting the government, protecting the police, instead of the individual." Thus, in a Pickwickian sense, the Burger Court may also be accused of being "activist."

Still, the anguished complaints of law-enforcement officers over *Miranda* have subsided considerably. As Albert A. Seedman, retired Chief of Detectives of the New York City Police Department, puts it: "I was a policeman for twenty years before *Miranda* was handed down. It was tough for old-timers like myself who used to kick doors down and never had to get a search warrant before the *Mapp* case. But, okay, under our system of jurisprudence everyone is entitled to legal protection, and law enforcers are better off with witnesses whose credibility can't be impeached."

Today, understandably, *Miranda* and other Warren Court

criminal justice decisions will never inspire wide popular enthusiasm. But, then, they never did. Majorities are never enthusiastic about permitting their rights to be infringed upon by those of minorities, let alone by those of suspected criminals. Defenders of these rights always risk unpopularity. Yet in retrospect, most Americans probably salute the courage of such defenders as Earl Warren and are grateful for whatever they have accomplished in protecting people against law enforcement abuses.

Curiously, Warren's so-called procommunist and civil liberty rulings, such as in *Peters*, *Watkins*, *Sweezy* and *Kent*, are no longer lambasted. Always alert to the danger of tyranny by any majority, Warren would have denied that communism ever was the central issue in the first place. Today, *detente* has replaced the Cold War and the McCarthy Red-baiting hysteria of the 1950s is remembered with considerable shame.

Less well-known than Warren's milestone opinions are his other contributions to the law and legal profession—yet their effects are still very much with us today. Throughout his tenure as Chief Justice, he toiled hard to achieve greater involvement by Federal courts into the actions of local and state courts, as well as by higher Federal courts in lower Federal ones. This hardly popular move was, understandably, resisted by lower court judges as an unwarranted attempt to centralize the American judiciary, and it has been sharply slowed down by the Burger Court. Warren, however, always maintained that only by dovetailing the efforts of the courts at every level could uniform justice be attained.

The main medium through which he attempted to expand the jurisdiction of Federal courts, set uniform policies, codes of personal conduct and the like, was the United States Judicial Conference, a rather sleepy institution until he revived it. Warren enlarged its functions, attracted nearly two hundred judges to work on advisory committees and farsightedly devised the blueprint for the Federal Judicial Center, which has helped enormously in improving court work since 1968. Although the Judicial Conference is not now as dynamic as in Warren's day, it is certainly far more influential than when he activated it. Since then, however, it has often been used in ways that Warren would have disapproved. Four months after his death, for example, the Conference vigorously fought a proposed congressional measure that would have prohibited all Federal judges from sitting on cases involving companies in which they owned even a single share of stock. Speaking for the Conference, Chief Justice Burger said that the law was unnecessary because the judiciary already had cleaned its own house voluntarily. Congress passed the law anyway, perhaps in part because Earl Warren had so strongly advocated it before he died.

The emergence of a public-interest bar is another Warren legacy. A large number of activist lawyers view the law as a basic tool for seeking social change in poverty and environmental law and other areas where the impoverished and minorities are least able to defend themselves. Unfortunately, they now must face a Federal bench that, under Burger Court influence, has shown noticeable hostility toward civil rights defendants and class action suits. Organizations such as the American Civil Liberties Union now consider many state supreme courts to be far more liberal than the U. S. Supreme Court. The ACLU claims that it won about 90 percent of the cases it brought before the Warren Court, but now loses about two out of three. "I'm not going to give Rehnquist and those other Nixon Justices a chance to knock out my teeth again," vows a Washington civil rights attorney. "I'd rather take my chances in any good state court these days. The Warren honeymoon is over but at least he helped to improve many state courts."

This was the conclusion of a major recent study of a random sample of 5,904 cases in sixteen state supreme courts published in the spring 1978 *Stanford Law Review* by Berkeley's Robert A. Kagen, the University of Virginia's Bliss Cartwright, Stanford's Lawrence M. Friedman and Yale's Stanton Wheeler. These four legal scholars found that state supreme court judges have become less concerned with the protection of property rights, more concerned with the individual and downtrodden, and more willing to consider rulings that promote social change. The study found:

> . . . *the vast upsurge in state supreme court criminal cases is undoubtedly attributable to changes in legal doctrine and practice as well, particularly the "due process" revolution of the late 1950s and 1960s. The Warren Court's extension of criminal defendants' constitutional rights, including the right to free counsel, facilitated and encouraged criminal appeals and postconviction*

345

relief applications. In fact, criminal cases with constitutional issues account for 73.5 percent of the increase in state supreme court criminal cases between 1960 and 1965–70. . . .

In another ironic twist, today the Warren Court influence is reflected in the way some leading state judges are invoking their own state constitutions to negate conservative Burger Court rulings, as the New York Court of Appeals did in a 1978 case. A top state court generally has the final word in interpreting its own state constitution. Though U. S. Supreme Court Justices rarely discuss in public state appellate actions, Justice William Brennan did so in the January 1977 *Harvard Law Review*, urging public interest lawyers to utilize state courts more instead of attempting to secure a review by the High Court in Washington.

In other judicial areas, the Warren legacy is less easy to gauge. His opposition to the proposed Mini-Court succeeded during his lifetime, but since Burger still appears to support the proposal, it may be revived.

In cases involving the First and Fourth Amendments, the contrast between the two Chiefs has become increasingly apparent. Today the press has become an endangered species. Chief Justice Burger frequently has led the assault in both majority and gratuitous opinions as well as in some reported off-the-bench remarks which indicated an astonishingly unjudicial attitude toward the press which he has sought to explain in these words: "We must not confuse the role of the media with that of the government."

During the Warren tenure, the June 1978 *Stanford Daily* right-to-rummage ruling—which enables police to secure warrants for unannounced newsroom searches for notes, photographs and what-have-you—probably never would have been upheld. Warren most likely would have mustered a majority consisting of himself, Black, Douglas, Brennan and Goldberg to oppose such First and Fourth Amendment press restrictions. I likewise doubt that the New Jersey Superior Court's punitive actions throughout 1978 against *The New York Times* and its reporter, Myron Farber, who was jailed for 40 days, would have been sustained when Earl Warren sat on the High Court center seat. The Warren Court's 1954 *New York Times* v. *Sullivan* decision, which broadened media rights to criticize public officials providing there was no "actual malice" was no accident. Typically, Warren himself in a January 1955 National Press Club talk saluted journalism's practitioners saying: "They are the greatest friends that the public has . . . they are not public officials but they are public servants. . . ."

Though difficult to assess, Warren's influence is still significantly felt through countless former associates in Washington, California and elsewhere. They include former law clerks, law students, gubernatorial assistants and Warren Commission aides. Many now hold prominent positions in government, universities, law schools and on Federal and state benches. Most now cherish the memory of their onetime Chief and are attempting to remain faithful to his philosophy, as I keep learning even at press time.

On the other hand, if a man is remembered by his enemies, Earl Warren's list includes Richard Nixon, the late Senator Joseph McCarthy, and two of President Carter's recent targets: the American Medical Association and American Bar Association.

Warren's passionate, long-time interest in world law thus far probably has accomplished little more concrete than to create a large reservoir of international good will and to keep bright an ancient hope. Yet the World Conference on World Peace through Law, which he helped launch with Charles R. Rhyne, an eminent Washington attorney who strangely enough was both his friend and Nixon's, still meets biannually and its delegates never cease lauding Earl Warren, the unexpected statesman, as a symbol of the United States being a humane nation.

It is ironic and somewhat sad that so many millions remember Earl Warren only for the chairmanship of the commission that investigated President Kennedy's murder. Some of them still excoriate him in the grave for this. Many have forgotten his incomparably greater achievements as Chief Justice and nearly eleven-year-governorship of California. But in years to come, his assassination commission work will fade and his Supreme Court influence will grow, predict numerous historians.

But, alas, the Warren Report controversy is part of his legacy, too. Despite the countless hostile words about the report, after more than fifteen years there is little hard fact to dispute its findings and central conclusions. Only largely unsubstantiated allegations, inferences and speculations remain. Too much of the "new evidence" and bizarre theories approximate science fiction. William T. Coleman, a commission lawyer (later Secretary of Transportation in the Ford Administration), pointing out that the Watergate cover-up lasted less than six months before it was exposed, asks how in a free society any cover-up of the Kennedy assassination could have been concealed fifteen years—especially with so many investigators uninterruptedly studying it? "Over the years, one set of conspiracy theories had only to be cut down for a new set to crop up with the inevitability of mushrooms after rain," observes Priscilla Johnson McMillan, author of *Marina and Lee.*

Yet a conspiracy industry continues to thrive, pouring forth a seemingly endless river of lectures, books, articles, movies, radio and TV programs more concerned with commerce than truth, and having little to do with good taste—with some notable exceptions, such as the CBS-TV programs. *Reader's Digest* reportedly spent more than a half-million dollars on research trying to prove that Oswald was a Soviet spy for what the *Washington Post* calls an "essentially dishonest book." University of Wisconsin history professor David Wrone has enumerated approximately 500 book titles alone on the JFK assassination. Brandeis University professor Jacob Cohen forecasts: "There will come a time when many of the writers and lecturers who have gained celebrity by raising doubts about the assassination will be known for what they occasionally were: conscious liars."

Since Warren's death, the U. S. Government revelations have been more illuminating, even during an era of collapsing credibility. The 1976 Senate Intelligence Committee investigation disclosed evidence of plots to murder Cuban Premier Fidel Castro and that the FBI had destroyed a letter in its Dallas Bureau received from Oswald about ten days before the murder. Whatever these disclosures may suggest about CIA and FBI practices, thus far they have failed to shed any indisputable new light on the assassination itself. The nearly 100,000 pages of FBI files released in December 1977 and January 1978 under Freedom of Information pressure corroborate the Warren Commission conclusions. Similarly, hundreds of pages of Secret Service documents made public in December 1977 show that this agency was likewise unable to link Oswald with a Cuban conspiracy.

The House Select Committee on Assassinations spent $5.8 million in 1977 and 1978—the most in congressional investigative history—to re-probe the JFK and Martin Luther King murders. At first, because of its publicity mania and savage rivalries, the committee almost disbanded. Reorganized in mid-1977, it proceeded more responsibly until its final days in late December 1978 when it desperately tried to justify its existence. Although indicating earlier that it would support the Warren Report conclusion that Oswald was the lone assassin (based upon the bulk of its testimony), now the committee did an about-face, saying that JFK "probably" was the victim of a "conspiracy." This confected assertion echoed the last-minute suggestion by two acoustic experts of a dictabelt recording of sounds on the motorcycle radio of a Dallas policeman, who later denied that the open microphone could possibly have been his. The committee could not identify who the alleged conspirators were; could not link Oswald with any second assassin; could produce no shells from the grassy knoll which hit the limousine or its occupants; and had no proof of any missile ever having been fired from the imagined rifle. Despite what Chairman Louis Stokes called these "loose ends," he urged the FBI to locate the alleged mystery gunman. However, Director William Webster, a former Federal judge, was unconvinced by the committee's "evidence" of any conspiracy—something Earl Warren himself had concluded fifteen years earlier.

The subjective part of the Warren legacy may be the more important. The effect that the memory of a great man produces on our imaginations often outweighs his actual achievements.

To better understand this subjective aspect, one must harken back to the "Warren Paradox"—that is, those elements of his life which even today many find baffling, if not contradictory. How could a man whose early public career had shown him to be little more than a conventional conservative suddenly—within less than a year—have emerged as a trailblazing liberal? How could a man who had never been a sitting judge have shepherded a flock of Supreme Court decisions that helped change the face of America—for good or ill? Finally, how could a man with such commonplace personal characteristics have come to play such an heroic (or, if you prefer, demonic) role in the nation's annals?

All these questions are, of course, variations of one premise: that there was something fundamentally incongruous about Earl Warren; and that somehow he was greater than the sum of his parts.

The American West has produced many notable liberal figures, such as Senators Hiram Johnson and Burton K. Wheeler, who began their careers battling the vested interests but wound up bitter old men defending the Establishment. The happier, late-blooming Earl Warren *reversed* this process. Although starting as a conservative, in maturity he became predominantly an apostle for the underprivileged. Dr. Isadore Rossman, a leading New York gerontologist, reports: "Most individuals, as they age, tend to show a constriction of mental capacity and perspective, but some, like Earl Warren, exhibit a phenomenon of broad continuous intellectual growth." Louis Brandeis once wrote: "If we are to be guided by the light of reason, we must let our minds be bold." Earl Warren must have taken this advice literally—even if subconsciously—possibly for a long time, but surely after getting his bearings on the Supreme Court.

Yet how does one square the plainness of Warren's personality with his Man of History role? Certainly it is not unusual for glad-handing American public figures to adopt (or retain) man-in-the-street mannerisms for wholly political reasons. Few exceptional men, though, have ever successfully projected an image as unexceptional as Warren's. Throughout his adult life, his public persona was that of a typical simple, hearty, honest, unintellectual, upright, middle-class American who was a convivial companion and worked diligently at whatever job he held. He liked nothing better than to return at the end of a busy day to his adored American-as-apple-pie family. He had no pronounced aesthetic interests. Once when he saw a Louise Nevelson sculpture, he said, "I don't understand it." Nor did he seem overburdened by an excess of imagination. The opinions and attitudes he voiced and wrote about most subjects would have seemed commonplace even to readers of the *Reader's Digest*. Even his face was bland—big, open, benign, innocent of any hint of fire or tension. He was free of cynicism and sophistication, a home-grown "conservative-progressive" without a trace of Marxism, a stolid problem-solver who was more pragmatic than ideological.

But the moment one attempts to apply to Earl Warren the equation of *orthodoxy-predictability-conformity*, the computer comes up with the wrong answers. On the Supreme Court, the name of Warren's game was nonconformity on a grandiose—even historic—scale.

Some may—and did—argue that this conventional image Warren projected might have been merely a façade masking another, hidden, inner man of more Promethean proportions. This stereotype suggestion, however, not only misrepresents the man but misses his essential character. Mostly, he was exactly what he *seemed* to be. If his character has little-understood dimensions, it was not because he concealed them. "The public man *was* the man, which is a great deal more than the rest of us can ever hope to be," wisely observes Harvard law professor John Hart Ely, a Warren Commission staff member.

Once, in the spring of 1957, in an effort to fathom the "mystery" of Warren's character, I took advantage of an opportunity to make a list of the books in the bedroom-study of his six-room, ground-floor apartment in Washington's Sheraton-Park Hotel. The results were more disappointing than surprising. Warren's books, by and large, were those of a serious, thoughtful man; but to me, at least, they indicated no dazzling insights into his thinking.

In front of the bookcases on a high red leather-topped table rested a one-volume *Columbia Encyclopedia*. Lining the bookshelves were the Chief Justice's basic law reference tools, a colorful cavalcade of bound green, red, brown and blue books. They then included 125 volumes of the *U. S. Supreme Court Reports*, 20 volumes of the *U. S. Supreme Court Digest*, 60 volumes of *American Jurisprudence*, over 200 volumes of the *U. S. Code Annotated*, 125 volumes of *Corpus Juris Secondum* as well as many other legal reference books including *Federal Tax Regulations* and, of course, the *Constitution of the United States of America*.

On other shelves nestled books about and by U. S. Supreme Court Justices, presumably used by the conscientious Warren to further familiarize himself with judicial thinking. These included biographies of Holmes and Cardozo; books by Hughes, and Brandeis, and Douglas' *Almanac of Liberty* and, interestingly, a small old volume entitled *Early Days in California: Attempted Assassination of Justice Field*.

In the center of the room on a round mahogany table next to his twin bed rested a new large-size, color-illustrated Bible given to the Chief Justice by his youngest son, Bobby, on his last birthday. Following a lifetime habit, Warren tried to make it a practice of reading the Bible a few minutes daily, when rising and retiring.

Other books reflected the man's broad general interests, mostly in current nonfiction and contemporary problems. "Novels are too exciting to read before bedtime," he explained. On his night table was a copy, with favorite pages turned down, of Mary Laswell's humorous *One on the House*. Because he had enormously enjoyed the author's previous book, *Suds In Your Eye*, his eldest daughter, Virginia, had affectionately inscribed it: "Here's suds in your eye, Dad!"

In addition, these books also were neatly piled up on his night table: Sandburg's *Abraham Lincoln: The Prairie Years*, lawyer Lloyd Paul Stryker's *The Art of Advocacy*, *Washington Post* editor Alan Barth's *Government by Investigation*, sports autobiographer Grantland Rice's *The Tumult and The Shouting* and *Our Spiritual Recovery* by Edward R. Elston, President Eisenhower's Washington pastor. Sandwiched in between were *Conservatism in America*, *The Faulkner Reader*, *Constitutional Law Principles*, *A Long Line of Ships*, *The Supreme Court in U. S. History*, *The Nuremberg Case*, *The Olympics*, *Legal Aid in the U.S.*, *Everyday Life in Ancient Times*, and various nature books about fish and wildlife. One can only guess how many he actually read or merely skimmed.

But a barometer of his increasingly more specialized interests since that time is the collection, 600 books in all, of the books from his chambers which he bequeathed to the Supreme Court library. They included many well-thumbed, pencilled volumes on U. S. civil liberties, minorities, the Constitution and individual Justices; the laws of England, India, Pakistan, Thailand, Israel, Korea, Bolivia and the Somali Republic; religious and philosophic treatises; and a 1776 book of bibliophilic value by Englishman Richard Price succinctly titled *Observations on the Nature of Civil Liberty, the Principles of Government and the Justice and Policy of the War with America*.

Probably more revealing than his reading habits, was Warren's well-known addiction to spectator sports. Much has been made of this amiable weakness. He frequently dragged not only his clerks but several of his anti-sport fellow Justices (some of whom had never attended a ball game in their lives) to witness the local Redskins and Senators games. But often he went unaccompanied. "I remember seeing him plow his way alone and unrecognized up to the top seats of some night games in Washington," recalls Brandeis biographer A. L. Todd.

Roy Campanella, the star black Brooklyn Dodger catcher, was his favorite player. "I really hate to see Leo Durocher win," Warren once said, "because I don't like his 'Nice Guys Finish Last' philosophy." During the October World Series, he arranged for a messenger to bring in the inning-by-inning score to the sitting Justices. Observing protocol, each would have it passed up the ascending ladder of seniority to the Chief. Few attorneys, then presenting their erudite arguments, ever knew what Warren and the other Solomons on the bench were engrossed in reading. Although the Chief never publicly admitted it, an important reason that the weekly Conference was switched in 1955 from Saturday to Friday was to enable the Chief and his brethren to watch the Saturday games on television!

Whenever attending a ball game, Warren's concentration was all but absolute. Former New York Governor W. Averell Harriman recalls:

> *One November we drove out to the stadium together and my wife sat next to him during the game. She was about to undergo an examination for her naturalization and had been told that she must know all about the Constitution, so she asked the Chief Justice what she ought to know. He didn't bother very much about that, but he took the trouble to educate her about American football in such skillful detail that she has enjoyed the game ever since.*

Both as governor and Chief Justice, he seldom missed a Rose Bowl game or the East-West Shrine contest in San Francisco, where he could be observed wearing his Shriner's fez between the halves. In Washington, he often threw out the first ball at the annual congressional baseball game. "He was probably America's number-one baseball fan," said the late Paul Porter, a former Fortas law partner, with whom Warren often discussed sports but not law.

One afternoon I overstayed my visit at the Warren's Washington apartment and I was still there when he arrived home at 6:30 P.M. from the Court. After greeting Mrs. Warren and me, he said with mock ferocity, "Good Lord, are you two still talking while a seventeen-inning ball game is going on?" I laughed and asked if that was the only news he had heard on the car radio while being driven home. "Oh," said the Chief Justice only half in jest, "That's just like the newspaper where I always turn to the sport pages first to read about men's achievements. Then I turn to the front page to read about their failures."

I have occasionally wondered—without wanting to push the thought too far—whether Warren's passion for sport may not have had *deeper* implications. Did he, perhaps, find in sport—in contests governed by set rules and animated by the spirit of fair play—which was basic to him—a satisfying model of some ideal society ruled by law and universal good will?

But in at least one area, he was not always fair. When donning his judicial robe to hear an obscenity case, Warren was unable to shed his conventional Middle-American attitudes. His puritanism then superseded his civil libertarianism. He could never satisfactorily adjust his longtime prejudice against pornography to the principle of free speech, or accept the Douglas-Black certainty that *any* censorship of "obscenity" is a clear violation of the First Amendment. To Earl Warren, peddlers of smut had no rights under the First Amendment. Not only did certain types of pornography offend his basic personal morality, but they were, he was convinced, a significant peril to America's moral fiber. Thus, he expended considerable effort in an unsuccessful pursuit of a legal definition of "obscenity," as have other Justices equally fruitlessly ever since.

Revealingly, in a separate but concurring 1957 opinion in *Roth* v. *United States*, which brought into the language the phrases "prurient interest," "patently offensive" and "redeeming social value," Warren opened another Pandora's box by writing: "It is not the book that is on trial, it is the person. The conduct of the defendant is the central issue, not the obscenity of the book or picture. A wholly different result might be reached in a different setting." This suggested that Warren's definition of obscenity might be conditional on a court's interpretation of the private motives of its author or purveyor—something virtually beyond the power of most courts to determine equitably. Indeed, when the Supreme Court itself attempted to apply this criterion nine years later in the *Ginzburg* v. *United States* decision, it provoked a storm of justifiable criticism.

Between *Roth* and *Ginzburg*, Warren's legal position on obscenity grew increasingly muddled. In 1961, in *Times Film* v. *Chicago*, he voted with the minority *against* the right of a local board to require that its permission be obtained before the film *Don Juan* could be publicly exhibited. In 1964, in *Jacobellis* v. *Ohio* again he voted with the minority, saying that a theater manager (who had shown a critically praised erotic French art film) *could* be convicted of obscenity by a local court because "there is no provable national standard [regarding obscenity] and perhaps there should be none." By contrast, in another 1964 case, *A Quantity of Copies of Books* v. *Kansas,* he voted with the majority *in favor* of a newsstand dealer whose entire stock of books had been seized by the police, who claimed that some of them were pornographic.

It is not surprising, therefore, that by the time of the *Ginzburg* case, Warren and his Court were hopelessly confused on the obscenity issue. Actually, these related decisions concerned three unrelated cases, only one of which involved the publisher of *Eros* magazine, an artistic magazine which is fairly tame by 1979 standards. In one case, Ginzburg was appealing a conviction for having used the mails to advertise, promote, distribute and sell *Eros* and *The Housewife's Handbook on Selective Promiscuity*, both of which a Pennsylvania court had found obscene. In a second case, the Warren Court was asked to review a New York conviction of one Edward Mishkin for distributing a large number of books with such titles as *Screaming Flesh, The Whipping Chorus Girls* and *Cult of the Spankers*. The third case concerned a Massachusetts ban on the sale of *Fanny Hill*, recently published by the old established house of G.P. Putnam's.

In *Ginzburg* Warren voted with the 5–4 majority in affirming the state court's harsh five-year prison sentence and $28,000 fine. Warren and the majority of six had less trouble in upholding the conviction of Mishkin. But on *Fanny Hill* Warren and a majority held for Putnam's.

None of this, of course, made any legal sense. As Stewart reminded in his dissent: "The First Amendment protects us all with an even hand. It applies to Ralph Ginzburg with no less completeness and force than to G. P. Putnam's. . . . This Court has no power to pick and choose." It was, in the words of *Library Journal*, "an incredibly jumbled decision," and one in which, as *Publishers Weekly* said, "the Bill of Rights lost a measure of its greatness. . . . The Supreme Court has taken a giant step backward."

Warren's position, if such it can be called, on obscenity was his greatest judicial aberration. The stands he took on most issues were based upon well-defined principles and an acute understanding of what the law can and cannot do. But on this subject the judge in him fell victim to the man. "I'd punch any man in the face who would show that [an erotic book] to one of my daughters," he shouted at fellow Justices. He found most of the sexual sales material that was sent through the mails to his home "unspeakable."

But on at least one occasion, sex amused more than angered the Chief Justice. The incident was related to me in confidence by a Warren intimate:

> *My favorite Earl Warren story shows that he was as much a male as any other man. We were once talking about a pretty woman*

*who seemed to be enamored with the law, and as a consequence,
with Federal judges. She had earned a reputation as a woman who
would do anything, at any time, for a Federal judge and she
showed up wherever Federal judges gathered. The Chief Justice
said that she once came to see him in his Chambers and that she
put on one of her greatest shows, dressed as sexily as she could get.
"There she sat, her dress half-way up her body, her legs cocked up
and her floozy staring me right in the face," the Chief Justice
chuckled. He said that he concluded the meeting as quickly as
possible, shook hands with the woman, and had her escorted out.*

Be what may, Earl Warren's strong feelings about overt or implied
indecency made it impossible for him to be objective about the
obscenity issue. Thus, he fell into the—for him—untenable position
of trying to justify censorship. It was "his one blind spot," Douglas
said sorrowfully.

There may have been other, if less legally significant, ones.
Warren always seemed ill at ease when ruling on other "consentual
crimes" such as narcotics, bribery and gambling. He was especially
hard on gambling, an attitude which may have stemmed from his
boyhood memories of the trickery in Bakersfield's gambling houses.
Although capable of defending gamblers whose right he believed
had been violated by the police or the courts, he judged gambling
itself to be a repulsive social blight. He even went so far as to write in
a 1968 case, *Marchetti* v. *United States*, that he did not deem that
gamblers should be protected by the Fifth Amendment. Fortunately,
on this issue he spoke for a minority of one.

Nor did he always— as his critics insist—vote automatically
against the government whenever it was assailed under the Bill of
Rights. For example, in upholding the conviction of a draft card
burner in 1966, he wrote: "We cannot accept the view that an
apparently limitless variety of conduct can be labeled 'speech'
whenever the person engaging in the conduct intends thereby to
express an idea." Was patriot Warren's distaste for the "idea"
behind draft card burning then dominating his subconscious mind?
Another time, when a twenty-one-year-old Army private requested
Warren to prevent the Pentagon from shipping him to Vietnam
pending his appeal before the U. S. Court of Appeals, the Chief
Justice declined without comment to intervene. Was the patriot
jurist then reluctant to rock the boat against President Johnson's
controversial war?

Even if Warren's "Middle-Americanism" imposed a few liabilities upon his judicial performance, it simultaneously conferred some important assets. It may, for example, have nurtured his gift for understanding and relating to many different types of people. Because he honestly thought of himself as an ordinary man, he was without intellectual pretense or class arrogance. Always at ease with others, he was an attentive listener who radiated simple humility and a benign desire to do and say the right thing. He had a talent for being both affable and dignified in a way that most persons found comfortable and reassuring.

These natural gifts had been considerably developed by his experience as a California joiner of fraternal organizations and as a quintessential lone-wolf politician. Similarly, his "nonpartisan" background as an elected officeholder likewise proved an administrative asset in the Supreme Court's center seat. He had well learned how to convert his amiability into gentle manipulation; how to express himself in words and actions that were, if not stylish, readily comprehensible to everyone; and how to derive from his compassionate understanding of diverse individuals useful insights into their concerns and desires. All this was to stand him in good stead as Chief Justice of the United States.

Unlike most other recent Chief Justices, who considered it a waste of valuable judicial time, the affable onetime California politician actually enjoyed welcoming attorneys newly admitted to the Supreme Court practice. In Warren's admission to the bar, which was the first order of business in open court after the cries "Oyez! Oyez! Oyez!", the gracious Chief Justice's unfailing courtesy, friendly smile and warm words made the occasion memorable for newly inducted attorneys, generally for the rest of their lives. The Chief Justice often took the time to converse not only with them but with their spouses and children. In his sixteen years on the top tribunal, Earl Warren admitted approximately twenty-five thousand new lawyers. Yet the ceremony was never a perfunctory repetition of those that had preceded it.

Former U.S. Senator Ralph W. Yarborough of Texas remembers:

> Numerous times I went to the Supreme Court to introduce lawyers generally from my state. I was always impressed with both the decorum of the Warren Court and the kindly, friendly, individual welcome of the Chief Justice. There was no brush-off in his manner.

It was a "Come-in-and-be-welcome" greeting. It was a minor function but Warren elevated it to the dignity of other Court proceedings. Since then, the situation has changed. Lawyers can now be admitted to practice in the Supreme Court by mail without ever even appearing before it. If they appear, they sit in a bunch over at one side and do not come before the podium to be welcomed personally, one by one, as in Warren's day.

During oral arguments, Warren was attentive, courteous and even-handed. Occasionally, he jabbed at an attorney who was pleading what he deemed an unfair argument. When a lawyer defending segregation mentioned "the People," Warren demanded, "What people are you talking about?" But if a lawyer's allotted time had been consumed by an unusually large number of questions from the bench, the Chief Justice would often grant him a few extra minutes (unlike the imperious Charles Evans Hughes, who was famed for cutting off lawyers in midsentence). The questions Warren himself asked frequently astonished attorneys who were deeply involved in technical legal points: "Is that fair?" "But is it right to treat somebody that way?" and even "Is that what America really stands for?" Such questions were, of course, rhetorical, since it was the responsibility of the Court, not the attorneys, to answer them. Yet they served to set a humanitarian tone in the Courtroom, to remind everyone present *why* they really were there. Warren believed, as Columbia law professor Curtis Berger put it, "The heart of the law is the heart of the lawyer."

If most attorneys liked and admired Warren, his law clerks almost worshiped him. He hired three or four bright young law school graduates each year. Although traditionally they served only a year on the Court, that was usually more than enough time for them to develop highly emotional bonds with their Chief. He spent hours talking with them at their frequent Saturday luncheons at the University Club, always encouraging them to speak frankly in disagreeing with him. He defended them against right-wing attackers such as then attorney Rehnquist and Lloyd Wright (chairman of an Eisenhower-appointed antisubversion commission). But he never asked them to draft opinions on controversial issues for which he thought that he alone should assume responsibility. If his relationship to his clerks seemed old-fashioned paternalism, so it was. "I came to know all of them intimately," he said. "Whenever they left me, I felt like I did when one of my own boys left home to go off to college."

Warren's easygoing charm served him well in his dealings with most Presidents, lawmakers, members of the press and men in the street, but its greatest effect was upon his Supreme Court brethren. One of them, Justice Burton (whom I had known as a U. S. senator from Ohio) then told me about the young Latin American lawyer whom Burton had asked whether he had noticed anything different between the new Warren Court and its predecessor tribunal. "Yes, indeed," the visitor said, "some of the Justices smiled!" When Warren came to the Court, the Associate Justices, even in the happiest circumstances, behaved toward one another with ceremonious reserve. Because several of them were privately at war with each other, this reserve was often interpreted to convey disdain. It was assumed that an effective Chief Justice, as first among equals, must be a benevolent autocrat, after the fashion of Hughes.

But such behavior was completely inconsistent with Earl Warren's relaxed democratic character. He swiftly brought to the Court a refreshing atmosphere of informality, and greater congeniality among the Justices. It was so delicately tuned, however, that it never in any way lessened the dignity of the Court or its sensitive members. Warren called all his colleagues by their first names although they always continued to address him respectfully as Chief (Douglas and Brennan affectionately referred to him as Super-Chief). Warren made a point of casually dropping in on them in their chambers unannounced. He socialized with them whenever possible and had Mrs. Warren bake cakes for them on their birthdays. Although pleasantly firm, he never pulled rank, never bullied, never—even under the extreme later provocation of Frankfurter—permitted himself to lose his temper, never allowed anyone to imagine that his disagreement betokened disrespect. When assigning opinions the Chief never played favorites. "There is no more intimate association, other than man and wife," he once remarked, "than what we have on the Supreme Court. It can be very pleasant and stimulating, or it can be bedlam and almost hell."

But it was seldom either bedlam or hell under Warren. He was as warm, tactful and skilled a Chief as he was a husband and father. Before long, he was presiding over a kind of Fun Court, where the Justices began to enjoy their intellectual discussions at the weekly Conferences in a constructive instead of sniping spirit. It would be too much to say that the extraordinary admiration he eventually elicited from his colleagues was based solely on their personal affection for him. But, as the success of the *Brown* deliberations suggests, it certainly helped.

At the outset, both Reed and Clark had indicated that they planned to vote for the continued application of the "separate-but-equal" rule. Even Black, though favoring the reversal of *Plessy*, was leery of too forceful implementation. Jackson wanted to write a separate concurring opinion. So did Frankfurter, who fretfully argued for "judicial restraint."

At that time, Warren, with his lack of judicial background and short period on the Court, could hardly have overawed his brethren with the sophistication of his legal argument. That he finally persuaded all fellow Justices to agree with him (and, equally astonishing, with one another) on *Brown* was a major triumph of personal diplomacy. If the Justices were not yet prepared to give him their fullest measure of respect as a judge, they obviously had already come to regard him highly as a man. The Chief was exceedingly solicitous of his brethren in ill health, such as in reducing the reading matter of the near-blind Harlan, and the workload of the incompetent Whittaker.

The warm personal feelings that the Justices had for their Chief was undoubtedly one of the key factors in his ability to lead until his retirement, and in the performance of the Warren Court. Although his judicial skills steadily improved, they were never the primary source of Warren's influence. His judicial strength sprang from his humanity, which even Frankfurter acknowledged in saluting his Chief's "heart" in the early years. Brennan has suggested that highly developed judicial skill may have very little to do with greatness in a Chief Justice. Men like John Marshall and Earl Warren, he points out, could easily have made poor state or lower Federal judges; yet they possessed precisely the qualities of personality, vision and political sensitivity needed to give character and leadership to the Supreme Court. As Clark once said of Warren, "His was an example that not only endeared him to each of us but stimulated greater achievements in all of us." If the Warren Court was more intellectual than the present Supreme Court, it was blessed with such judicial giants as Black, Douglas and Frankfurter, though today Powell is making independent overtures in that direction. If Burger is a commanding leonine figure reminiscent of

MGM's Leo the Lion, his predecessor was a friendlier shaggy bear whom Justices, strangers and children could cuddle.

Still, Warren's influence over his brethren went far beyond mere personal charm. They were impressed by his integrity, independence and activist sense of the Court's social responsibility. New York University Law Dean Norman Redlich composed a delightful fantasy in the April 1975 *NYU Law Review* . He pictures a quiet country lane in Heaven where two departed Supreme Court Justices were strolling, carrying their dog-eared copies of the Constitution.

"I hear that there are some new proposals, "to lighten the workload," observed Justice Harlan.

"Now that Earl Warren is on his way up here, one of these plans might get through," retorted Justice Black.

Traditionally, the Supreme Court often has been the most inactive, weakest, remotest and "least dangerous" branch of the United States Government, a brake on, rather than a spur to, public policy. When Warren came to the Court, however, both the President and the Congress seemed unwilling or unable to cope effectively with the broad domestic issues then confronting the nation. The new Chief Justice chose to step in to fill this void—to be decisive where the other two branches of the government were indecisive, and to provide leadership where it was lacking. This dynamic concept of the Court's role was denounced by many critics as "political," and in a sense it was. But whatever one calls it, most of the Associate Justices found it both lofty and exhilarating. Even the conservative Burton could exult: "Our new Chief doesn't go for fine legal points but he has something more important—a fine political sense." And the Court's long-time public information officer, Bert Whittington, now speaks on Warren's "uncanny ability to recognize those cases out of the hundreds filed each term that were important to the law and the country and which would make history."

Although criticism privately hurt the sensitive Warren, it stiffened the resolve of the man whom California detractors had called a "Stubborn Swede." The Chief Justice was both hurt and horrified by the proposed Council of State Governments' constitutional amendment to create a "Court of the Union" composed of the Chief Justices of the fifty state supreme courts, who would be given power to reverse *any* (translated "political") decision of the United States Supreme Court. The Nixon-sparked 1968 Omnibus

Crime Control Act likewise pained the former prosecutor. Warren's "political" decisions, his naysayers conceded, were not motivated by partisan politics. Rather, they protested, Warren's sin was that he could never tell the difference between *interpreting* and *making* law. Frankfurter and Harlan never failed to cite this alleged fault whenever disagreeing with their Chief. Thus, for example, in his dissent on the far-reaching reapportionment case, *Reynolds* v. *Sims*, Harlan petulantly wrote: "This [majority] view, in a nutshell, is that any major social ill in this country can find its cure in some constitutional principle, and that this Court should 'take the lead' in promoting reform when other branches of government fail to act. . . . The Constitution is not a panacea for every blot upon the public welfare, nor should this Court, ordained as a judicial body, be thought of as a general haven for reform movement."

Yet these critics were disingenuous or at least confused in their insistence upon distinguishing between interpreting and making law. As Warren himself, with homely logic, put it:

> *The Court doesn't [make law] consciously. It doesn't do it by trying to usurp the role of the Congress, but only because of the very nature of our job. When two litigants come into Court, one may say: "An act of Congress means this." The other says it means the opposite. We then say it means one of the two or something else in between. In that way we are making the law, aren't we?*

In this illustration of how the Court works, Warren himself may have been somewhat disingenuous. Naturally, if the Court meets an important constitutional issue head on, his point is valid. But the High Court is neither obliged to hear, nor to make definite rulings on any case. Actually, it often *avoids* controversial issues as a matter of policy, thus endorsing the legal status quo. Whatever the Court proceeds to do—or not do—inevitably has significant legal and frequently social consequences. In that sense, it does "make" law and is often "political." So-called judicial restraint can only be fully achieved through a policy of avoidance. The alternative must be some type of "activism" which label-users then call "liberal" or "conservative."

Thus, much of Warren's "activism" consisted merely in a readiness to face important issues directly unlike the Burger Court which avoids confrontation wherever possible. By refusing to permit his Court to avoid difficult, even "dangerous" cases, the mild-mannered Warren made it inevitable that it would constantly be embroiled in controversy and that its rulings would often produce far-reaching results. This inspired the "Impeach Earl Warren" cries, even though there never were any specific impeachable offenses. "It is particularly ironic that a man as warm, gentle and soft-spoken as Earl Warren became a lightning rod for such bitter and intense attacks," noted then-Senator Walter F. Mondale at Warren's death. The retired Warren himself once casually remarked to a friend, "You know, everything that I ever did in my life that was worthwhile, I caught hell for."

But, of course, there was more to it than that. The Warren Court decisions had a distinctive character. And however much those who championed judicial restraint couched their attacks in the language of legal principle, what they probably objected to most was the character of the decisions. Warren, the fourteenth Chief Justice, helped to forge a legal revolution, just as Burger, the fifteenth, seemingly is presiding over a counter revolution.

Both Warren's admirers and detractors describe his key decisions as "liberal." But this inexact politically-burdened word is more distracting than illuminating. Actually, the entire pattern of Warren's celebrated "change" from conservatism to liberalism is easier to understand without any conventional labels.

Moreover, the "change" may be less in a man than in society's revised attitude toward him. Once at the Bohemian Grove retreat in California, Governor Warren remarked to former President Herbert Hoover, "Years ago you were the most cursed man in America but now the attitude toward you is very favorable. How do you explain the change?" Hoover replied, "I just outlived the bastards!"

Warren's comments about the "change" in his own attitudes and outlook sometimes sounded inconsistent. Two observations of a former Chief Justice judging himself are illuminating. In retirement, he said: "I don't see how any man could sit on the Supreme Court and not change his views substantially over a period of years. Change, if you are to do your duty . . . I saw things in a different light." Yet in a preliminary draft of some pages intended to be included in his unfinished memoirs (but never inserted before his death), he wrote: "It is not reasonable to expect that, at the age of 62, one who had lived and acted in government with certain principles for a third of a century would without reason reverse his way of life and endeavor to uproot things he had long believed in."

These two statements are not as contradictory as they may seem. Warren undoubtedly changed his views about several significant issues during his lifetime. The legislative apportionment system he favored as governor of California he later struck down when he was Chief Justice. In California he had advocated compulsory flag salutes for schoolchildren, but opposed them in Washington. Some of his prosecutions while a district attorney and attorney general, he later admitted, never could have met the criteria of *Escobedo* or *Miranda*. On the so-called communist cases, his evolution from *Barsky* to *Sweezy* was so extreme as to represent a reversal of position. And the harsh actions he had championed in the internment of Japanese in California during World War II troubled him deeply in later years (he had begun to express regret as early as 1947) and were completely at variance with his Court record as a civil libertarian.

But it is one thing for a man to change his opinions and another for him to change his principles. In his California days and during his early months on the Court, Warren occasionally found it expedient not to measure his actions against his principles too carefully. Yet that is not the same as saying that his principles were lacking or that he had changed them. When Black heard in 1954 that his Chief's "new liberalism" was influenced by him and Douglas, he protested, "Why, Warren came to the Court with the same ideas I had. He got them in California—I in Alabama." Before becoming a judicial ombudsman, Warren had unquestionably enlarged and altered his horizons through experience. He sometimes changed his attitudes, but not necessarily his basic beliefs. People can change their outlooks but still remain essentially the same. Churchill once said: "The only guide to a man is his conscience; the only shield to his memory is the rectitude and sincerity of his actions."

There is probably nothing like service on the Supreme Court for making a man reassess his most cherished assumptions; as Dr. Johnson said about the threat of hanging, it concentrates a man's mind wonderfully. The difference between District Attorney Warren and Chief Justice Warren may have been less that the man changed as he grew older than that during his Court years he became increasingly true to himself. If he was a yokel, as some naysayers contemptuously claim, he emerged a highly knowledgeable, responsible and creative yokel. Morton Sontheimer, a former San Francisco city editor and now a New York public relations advisor, quips: "Warren was a bit of a jerk as a district attorney. But his magnificent decisions as Chief Justice proves there is hope for jerks!"

More soberly, Abe Fortas once perceptively observed:

> When a man is on the Court, after a while the kind of man he is, and the kind of mind he has, and the kind of heart he has, really emerge. It's a test of the essential quality of the man. That's one of the reasons so many men appear to change after they go on the Court. Their roles in life prior to this incumbency may have caused them to behave one way, but then on the Court they have to face up to what they really believe. In this they are assisted by their colleagues and by study and by what they hear in argument.

Among those who hold that Warren never fundamentally "changed" is U.S. District Judge Albert C. Wollenberg of San Francisco: "The man who fought the Ku Klux Klan in the 30's was no different from the man who decided that black children should no longer be ghettoized by their government." Roger Baldwin agrees: "I first met him in California when I called on him as Attorney General in 1939 and found him, contrary to reports, very sympathetic to what we in the American Civil Liberties Union wanted. I am not surprised he turned out such a liberal; the basis was there."

Was Earl Warren, then, simply a lifelong "closet liberal"? I think not. Of course, his nearly eleven-year governorship in many ways foreshadowed the activist, libertarian Chief Justice. But his deepest fundamental beliefs were always anterior to what we ordinarily mean by liberalism or conservatism. He believed in equal justice before the law; the Constitution; in protecting the rights of the individual; in patriotic duty; in mercy, honor, decency and fair dealing; and in the elementary Judeo-Christian canons of personal morality. There was hardly anything he believed in that could not, in theory, have been endorsed by virtually any honest American— black or white, Republican or Democrat, conservative or liberal. If his value system had a single ideological basis, it was probably not much more complicated than simply trying to live by the Golden Rule.

Warren's own plain almost Biblical words, written in retirement and now engraved on his tombstone, sum up his philosophy:

> ... *Where there is injustice, we should correct it; where there is poverty, we should eliminate it; where there is corruption, we should stamp it out; where there is violence, we should punish it; where there is neglect, we should provide care; where there is war, we should restore peace; and wherever corrections are achieved, we should add them permanently to our storehouse of treasures.*

What became so controversial about Warren, what made his behavior sometimes seem philosophically radical, was not that his principles were novel or unpopular, but that he was so disconcertingly determined to put them into practice. In this sense, he might be compared to that familiar figure in literature, the "wise fool," who causes consternation in society because he insists upon literally practicing basic moral precepts to which others merely give lip service.

Whenever Earl Warren strolled around the Marble Palace, I remember, he never tired of glancing up at the four words chiseled in stone above the pillars: "Equal Justice Under Law." He grew to believe in them almost as a religious commandment. To a Scandinavian immigrant's son who became an embattled judge, these were not empty words, a tired platitude or an abstract dream of the Founding Fathers. Others—including perhaps the majority of today's Supreme Court—tend to emphasize the word "Law." Earl Warren stressed "Equal Justice."

Like the Supreme Court structure itself, the fourteenth Chief Justice was a symbol of national integrity. One of the greatest satisfactions of his half-century of public service was that not one of his appointees was ever accused of dishonesty or violating an oath of office. Moreover, Warren himself never personally profited from any speech, article or type of commercial activity while on a public payroll. That, in itself, is a unique legacy, especially in the light of Watergate and assorted recent U. S. Government, state, municipal and corporate corruption. Even when writing the will for his modest estate, which was given outright to his wife (and his Court papers ultimately to the Library of Congress), Judge Earl Warren leaned over backward to avoid the appearance of impropriety. In 1975 *Trusts and Estates* magazine reported: "Mr. Warren did not try to reap the full tax benefit by dividing the estate into two separate trusts and giving his widow a life interest in both."

Earl Warren, indeed, was a paradox in twentieth-century American government, bridging the best of the nineteenth-century with the hopes and promises of the twenty-first. To me, the true "Warren Paradox" is that the man was both less complex and more consistent than those who have found him so puzzling. That his actions surprised others invariably seemed to surprise him. The more one tries to characterize him as a "crusading liberal," "coddler of criminals," "socialist," "procommunist" or "judicial dictator," the more one blurs the portrait. He was both less and more than any of these things. He was an old-fashioned American humanist who happened to believe with all his heart that "law floats in a sea of ethics." With Walt Whitman he would have agreed: "Underneath all, I swear nothing is good that ignores individuals."

Once again, it was the now wiser Fortas who put the matter most plainly. In a CBS–TV interview after Warren's death, he told Eric Severeid:

> *The Constitution is a statement of ethical principles, particularly the Bill of Rights. . . . To me the most glorious thing about Earl Warren was that he never lost sight of that. . . . He had a clear conception of what's right and wrong in terms of the Constitution, of the law, of social behavior and social ethics. And with a man of his force, his simplicity, his clarity and purity of mind, it was very difficult to argue a point because he was on the side of right, because his values were so pure, so clear, so simple. . . .*

Should a Chief Justice—or any judge—ever, no matter how pure his motives, assume the role of a moralist? There are powerful arguments to the contrary. Judicial purists repeatedly have cautioned against what Justice Robert Jackson once termed "the treacherous ground we tread when we undertake to translate ethical concepts into legal ones." Among the legal criticism leveled against Warren was that he often permitted—even encouraged—lawyers to make evidentiary disclosures which technically were extraneous to formal record. He did not do this through ignorance or inadvertence. (His colleagues conceded that, as Douglas said, "He was well trained as a lawyer and definitely not over his head when it came to the work coming to his desk as Chief Justice.") Rather, he was consciously prepared to bend strict legal procedures if he thought that it would help him to discover "the right thing to do."

Posterity will judge Warren for what he did less for its effect on the letter of the law than for his contributions to the quality of life in America. That is his prime judicial legacy.

It is perhaps the same with Presidents: We do not necessarily consider them great in direct proportion to the strictness with which they observed the doctrine of separation of powers. In our constitutional system of government, the law is more concerned with providing safeguards against potential abuses than with offering scope for conceivably dangerous leadership. Under both aspects, Presidents and Chief Justices who are determined to lead, sometimes must risk bending the rules a little—or even a lot. If they succeed in benefiting the nation and moving it forward, in time they will be not only forgiven but even honored. Should they fail, they will be condemned for having transgressed, as had Lyndon Johnson in the Vietnam enterprise.

Earl Warren took such a risk. Did he succeed? During his lifetime many people thought that he had not. Yet with each passing year, their numbers are dwindling. If he took occasional liberties with his judicial prerogatives, as some detractors contend, this criticism will fade in time. He looms not only as a great Chief Justice but as one of the century's greatest Americans.

Archibald Cox foresightedly encapsulated this emerging perception of Earl Warren in a tribute in the November 1969 *Harvard Law Review*:

> *One may criticize the craftsmanship of some [of his] opinions, doubt whether the lines of distinction were always meaningfully drawn between borderline cases, and argue that sometimes the Court pressed its enthusiasms beyond their proper limits. Yet it is infinitely more important that on the great occasions and in the consistent thrust of lesser rulings the decisions of the Warren Court brought the law more nearly into accord with the best and truest aspirations of the American people. . . . Indeed the decisions of the Warren Court seem to me always to have had deeper and stronger support in the country than the volume of professional criticism and vocal public resentment might seem to indicate. The reapportionment cases are the clearest example . . . [and] I cannot believe that when forced to face up to the question . . . [of segregation] many*

Americans would want their courts to hold that their Constitution sanctioned apartheid. Similarly, I suspect that in the face of deep concern for law and order, the sober second thought of the community approves the essential thrust of the constitutional reforms in criminal procedure.

Cox's words could be amplified by similar encomia from the writings and remarks of hundreds—perhaps thousands—of impartial thoughtful men and women who have come to share this emerging vision of Warren.

But there is one quotation above all others with which I think it fitting to end this book. The words are Warren's own. They are not about himself—he was far too modest ever to have presumed to have composed his own valedictory. And yet—irony of ironies—they happen to apply perfectly to him.

On August 24, 1955, less than two years after being appointed to the Supreme Court, Earl Warren spoke these unconsciously prophetic words in Independence Hall in Philadelphia on the occasion of the John Marshall Bicentennial Ceremonies:

The controversy which raged around Marshall during his long career quickly subsided at his death and he soon became judged by the rule of reason rather than the rule of perfection. Today we appraise him as we do a lofty mountain peak—not by the crevices, jagged rocks and slides that are so apparent at close view, but by the height, the symmetry and grandeur it acquires in the perspective of the distance. Thus viewed, John Marshall stands out as a colossus among the giants of his time.

Was mountain-climbing Earl Warren then unwittingly penning his own portrait for history?

Selected Bibliography

Books

Abell, Tyler, ed. *Drew Pearson Diaries* 1949–59. New York: Holt, Rinehart and Winston, 1974.

Abraham, Henry J. *Justices and Presidents: A Political History of Appointments to the Supreme Court.* New York: Oxford University Press, 1974.

Adams, Sherman. *First Hand Report.* New York: Harper & Brothers, 1961.

Ashman, Charles R. *The Finest Judges Money Can Buy.* Los Angeles: Nash Publishing, 1973.

Belin, David W. *November 22, 1963.* New York: Quadrangle, 1973.

Bell, Jack. *The Splendid Misery.* Garden City, N. Y.: Doubleday & Co., 1960.

Bland, Randall W. *Private Pressure on Public Law: The Legal Career of Justice Thurgood Marshall.* Port Washington, N. Y.: Kennikat Press, 1973.

Childs, Marquis. *Eisenhower, Captive Hero.* New York: Harcourt, Brace and Co., 1958.

Christman, Henry M., ed. *The Public Papers of Chief Justice Earl Warren.* New York: Capricorn Books, 1966.

Clayton, James E. *The Making of Justice: The Supreme Court in Action.* New York: E. P. Dutton, 1964.

Costello, William. *The Facts About Nixon: An Unauthorized Biography.* New York: Viking Press, 1960.

De Toledano, Ralph. *One Man Alone: Richard Nixon.* New York: Funk & Wagnalls, 1969.

Dorman, Michael. *The Second Man.* New York: Delacorte Press, 1968.

Douglas, Paul. *In the Fullness of Time: The Memoirs of Paul H. Douglas.* New York: Harcourt Brace Jovanovich, 1972.

Douglas, William O. *Go East, Young Man, The Early Years: The Autobiography of William O. Douglas.* New York: Random House, 1974.

Eisenhower, Dwight D. *Mandate for Change: The White House Years.* Garden City, N. Y.: Doubleday & Co., 1963.

Eisenhower, Milton S. *The President Is Calling.* Garden City, N. Y.: Doubleday & Co., 1974.

Epstein, Edward Jay. *Inquest.* New York: Viking Press, 1966.

Ford, Gerald, and John Stiles. *Portrait of the Assassin.* New York: Simon and Schuster, 1965.

Frank, John P. *The Warren Court.* New York: The Macmillan Company, 1964.

Friedman, Leon, and Fred L. Israel. *The Justices of the United States Supreme Court, 1789–1969: Their Lives and Major Opinions*, 4. vols. New York: Chelsea House/R.R. Bowker, 1969

Goldberg, Arthur J. *The Warren Era of the Supreme Court.* Chicago: Northwestern University Press, 1971

Goulden, Joseph C. *The Superlawyers: The Small and Powerful World of the Great Washington Law Firms.* New York: Weybright and Talley, 1972.

Graham, Fred P. *The Self-Inflicted Wound.* New York: The Macmillan Company, 1970.

Gunther, John. *Inside U. S. A.* New York: Harper & Brothers, 1947.

Harbaugh, William H. *Lawyer's Lawyer: The Life of John W. Davis.* New York: Oxford University Press, 1973.

Harvey, Richard B. *Earl Warren: Governor of California.* New York: Exposition Press, 1969.

Hill, Gladwin. *Dancing Bear: An Inside Look at California Politics.* Cleveland: World Publishing Co., 1968.

Hughes, Emmet John. *The Living Presidency.* New York: Coward, McCann and Geoghegan, 1973.

Huston, Luther A. *Pathway to Judgment.* Philadelphia: Chilton Books, 1966.

Jackson, Donald Dale. *Judges.* New York: Atheneum, 1974.

Johnson, Lady Bird. *A White House Diary.* New York: Holt, Rinehart and Winston, 1970.

Johnson, Lyndon Baines. *The Vantage Point.* New York: Holt, Rinehart and Winston, 1971.

Katcher, Leo. *Earl Warren: A Political Biography.* New York: McGraw-Hill, 1967.

Kohlmeier, Louis M., Jr. *God Save This Honorable Court.* New York: Charles Scribner's Sons, 1972.

Lash, Joseph P. *Eleanor: The Years Alone.* New York: W. W. Norton & Co., 1972.

———. *From the Diaries of Felix Frankfurter.* New York: W. W. Norton & Co., 1975.

Levy, Leonard W. *Against the Law: The Nixon Court and Criminal Justice.* New York: Harper & Row, 1974.

Lewis, Anthony. *Gideon's Trumpet.* New York: Random House, 1964.

Liston, Robert A. *Tides of Justice.* New York: Delacorte Press, 1966.

Lurie, Leonard. *The Running of Richard Nixon.* New York: Coward, McCann & Geoghegan, 1972.

Lyon, Peter. *Eisenhower: Portrait of the Hero.* Boston-Toronto: Little, Brown and Company, 1974.

MacKenzie, John P. *The Appearance of Justice*. New York: Charles Scribner's Sons, 1974.

Manchester, William. *The Glory and the Dream*. Boston-Toronto: Little, Brown and Company, 1973, 1974.

————. *The Death of a President*. New York: Harper & Row, 1967.

Mason, Alpheus Thomas. *The Supreme Court from Taft to Warren*. Baton Rouge: Louisiana State University Press, 1958.

Mayer, George H. *The Republican Party 1854–1964*. New York: Oxford University Press, 1964.

Mazlish, Bruce. *In Search of Nixon: A Psychohistorical Inquiry*. New York: Basic Books, Inc., 1972.

Mazo, Earl. *Richard Nixon: A Personal and Political Portrait*. New York: Harper & Brothers, 1959.

McMillan, Priscilla Johnson. *Marina and Lee*. New York: Harper & Row, 1977.

Meyer, Howard N. *The Amendment that Refused to Die* (revised). Boston: Beacon Press, 1973.

Mitau, G. Theodore. *Decade of Decision: The Supreme Court and the Constitutional Revolution*. New York: Charles Scribner's Sons, 1967.

Nixon, Richard M. *Six Crises*. Garden City, N. Y.: Doubleday & Company, 1962.

Political Profiles, *The Kennedy Years* and *The Johnson Years*, editor, Nelson Lichtenstein, Ph. D., University of California, Berkeley; and *The Eisenhower Years*, editor, Eleanora W. Schoenbaum, Columbia University. New York: Facts on File, 1976–77.

Report of the President's Commission on the Assassination of President Kennedy. Government Printing Office, Washington, D. C., 1964.

Sayler, Richard H., Barry B. Boyer, and Robert Gooding, Jr. *The Warren Court: A Critical Analysis*. New York: Chelsea House, 1969.

Schell, Jonathan. *The Time of Illusion*. New York: Alfred A. Knopf, 1976.

Schwartz, Bernard. *The Law in America: A History*. New York: McGraw-Hill, 1974.

Scigliano, Robert. *The Supreme Court and the Presidency*. New York: The Free Press, 1971.

Shogan, Robert. *A Question of Judgment*. New York: Bobbs-Merrill, 1972.

Simon, James F. *In His Own Image: The Supreme Court in Richard Nixon's America*. New York: David McKay Company, 1973.

Steamer, Robert J. *The Supreme Court in Crisis*. Amherst: University of Massachusetts Press, 1971.

Stone, Irving. *Earl Warren: A Great American Story*. New York: Prentice-Hall, 1948.

The Witnesses: The Highlights of Hearings Before the Warren Commission on the Assassination of President Kennedy. New York: Bantam Books, 1964.

Tributes to the Honorable Earl Warren to Commemorate the Occasion of His Retirement from the Supreme Court June 23, 1969, Delivered in the U. S. House of Representatives and the U. S. Senate. Washington: United States Government Printing Office, 1970.

Warren, Earl. *A Republic, If You Can Keep It*. New York: Quadrangle Books, 1972.

——. *The Memoirs of Chief Justice Earl Warren*. New York: Doubleday and Co., 1977.

Weaver, John D. *Warren: The Man The Court The Era*. Boston-Toronto: Little, Brown and Company, 1967.

West, J. B. with Mary Lynn Kotz. *Upstairs at the White House*. New York: Coward, McCann & Geoghegan, 1973.

White, Theodore H. *The Making of the President 1964*. New York: Atheneum, 1965.

Wilkinson, J. Harvie, III. *Serving Justice: A Supreme Court Clerk's View*. New York: Charterhouse, 1974.

Periodicals

American Bar Association Journal vol. 60, October 1974 pp. 1228–36. *The World of Earl Warren* by Eugene Gressman, Justice William O. Douglas and Judge William S. Thompson.

California Law Review vol. 58, no. 1, January 1970. *Earl Warren—A Tribute*. Contributions by Harry S. Truman, Arthur J. Goldberg, Albert C. Wollenberg, Thomas H. Kuchel, Edmund G. Brown, James H. Oakley, Horace M. Albright, Joseph W. Bartlett, David E. Feller, Jack Greenberg, Adrian A. Kragen, Helen R. MacGregor, Arthur H. Sherry.

Hastings Constitutional Law Quarterly vol. 2, no. 1, Winter 1975. *Chief Justice Earl Warren: A Tribute*. Contributions by his former law clerks: Graham B. Moody, Jr. (1955 Term); Robert J. Hoerner (1958 Term); Arthur Rosett (1959 Term); Ralph J. Moore (1959 Term); Peter D. Ehrenhaft (1961 Term); Stuart R. Pollak (1962 Term); James K. Hoenig (1963 Term); Scott H. Bice (1968 Term).

Nebraska Law Review vol. 48, no 1, November 1968. An issue dedicated to Earl Warren. Contributions by Lyndon B. Johnson, William O. Douglas, Tom C. Clark, Charles Morgan, Jr., Articles on aspects of the Warren Court by Alfred Avins, Clarence Mitchell, Leo Konowitz and a book review of an Archibald Cox volume, *The Supreme Court: A Question of Relevance* by Leonard V. Kaplan.

Notre Dame Lawyer vol. 48, no. 1, October 1972. *Notre Dame Law School Civil Rights Lectures*. Foreword by Thomas L. Shaffer. Introductory remarks by Rev. Theodore M. Hesburgh, C.S.C., and Francis X. Beytagh. Lecture by Earl Warren.

Acknowledgments

My debts are many: to those who helped when the pages were blank, to others who proffered aid even when this overdue book was on press.

The exhilarating dividend of this demanding adventure was my privilege to encounter in person, by telephone and by mail scores of the keenest judicial, legal and political minds in America, thanks to the lofty regard for the subject's significance rather than to the author's limited credentials. Some sources, regrettably, through propriety or innate modesty, requested anonymity. To these phantom benefactors, I acknowledge my appreciation however inarticulate.

To others, I happily record my indebtedness.

Many judges on Federal and state benches generously refreshed their memories and insights for this undertaking. I am particularly grateful to retired Supreme Court Justice William O. Douglas and to Judge Charles E. Wyzanski, Jr., Senior District Judge, U. S. District Court in Boston, for detailed, illuminating, first-hand communications. Other helpful Federal jurists included Judge Walter E. Craig, Chief Judge, U.S. District Court, Phoenix; Judge David N. Edelstein, Chief Judge, U.S. District Court, New York; and Judge Charles W. Joiner, U.S. District Court, Detroit. Among the state judges to whom I am likewise thankful are Judge Louis H. Burke, Supreme Court of California in San Francisco and Justice Walter V. Schaefer, Illinois Supreme Court, Chicago.

Busy law professors, too, graciously gave of their time and talents. Here, my lasting thanks is to Mr. Norman Redlich, Dean of the New York University Law School and a former Warren Commission counsel. Among the private attorneys to whom I am grateful is Mr. Edward Ross of New York City. The late Mr. Joseph Frank, a New York attorney friend, inadvertently permitted me to eyewitness some unWarren-like perversions of justice.

In academia, I am especially obligated to Dr. A. L. Sacher, chancellor, Brandeis University; Dr. Milton S. Eisenhower, president-emeritus, The Johns Hopkins University; and Professor Dallin H. Oaks, president, Brigham Young University, a Warren law clerk.

Other Warren law clerks who furnished revealing observations about their Chief were Mr. Martin F. Richman, New York, Mr. Peter D. Ehrenhaft, Washington, D.C., and Mr. Graham B. Moody, Jr., San Francisco.

Mr. Banning E. (Bert) Whittington, the Supreme Court information officer during Warren's sixteen-year tenure, was of inestimable aid. Mr. Barrett McGurn, his successor on the Burger Court, was likewise extremely cooperative.

A gifted historical researcher was immeasurably supportive. Ms. Amelia R. Fry, who directed the Earl Warren project in the Regional Oral History Office in the University of California's Bancroft Library, was invariably available for endless counsel and documentation. Mr. David L. Snyder, of the California State Archives in Sacramento, also rendered invaluable assistance, including furnishing some photographs.

Three former First Ladies—Bess Truman, Mamie Eisenhower and Lady Bird Johnson—furnished helpful contributions.

In five Presidential libraries, these staff members steered me to obscure documents concerning the relationship between Governor and Chief Justice Warren and their respective Presidents: Mr. William R. Emerson, director, Franklin D. Roosevelt Library, Hyde Park, New York; Dr. Philip D. Lagerquist, archivist, Harry S. Truman Library, Independence, Missouri; Mr. Don W. Wilson, acting director, Dwight D. Eisenhower Library, Abilene, Kansas; Ms. Ann L. Travis, John F. Kennedy Library, Waltham, Massachusetts; Ms. Claudia Anderson, Lyndon Baines Johnson Library, Austin, Texas.

Other librarians who lightened my research load include Mrs. Lynn Ashe, formerly of Westhampton Beach, N. Y.; Mrs. Nina

Caspari, Kern County, California; Mrs. Nancy Bressler, Princeton University Library, and many others. Highly useful target research was cheerfully provided by Mrs. Lillian Guide, Ms. Teresa Allen, Mr. Richard Rodda, Mr. Alden Whitman, Mr. Richard Gillman, Mrs. Priscilla Johnson McMillan, Mr. Ted Betts, Mr. Jose Schorr, Mr. Harry Starfield, Mr. Zachary Sklar, Mr. Tom Mahoney, Mr. Louis J. Slovinsky, and Mr. Julian Bach, my literary agent.

Among those who shed light for me on some hazier aspects of the Warren Commission were Commissioner John J. McCloy, New York; Mr. David W. Belin, Des Moines attorney; Law Professor Leon Hubert, Tulane University, New Orleans; attorney Leon Jaworski, Houston; and Mr. Waggoner Carr, Austin, Texas.

For their devoted editing during the several drafts of the original thousand-page-plus manuscript, I thank Mrs. Queena Pollack Fineman, my biographer sister (who furtively inveigled me into the world of print some decades ago); Mr. John Grayson Kirk, Prentice-Hall's editor-in-chief, Trade Book Division; and Mrs. Shirley Stein, editor, Trade Production.

Two members of the Warren family were exceptionally helpful over an intermittent two-decade period: Mrs. Earl (Nina) Warren, the Chief Justice's lovable wife, and Judge Earl Warren, Jr., of the Municipal Court in Sacramento.

Many longtime Warren aides also helped enormously. They include Mr. J. Lee Rankin, former U.S. Senator Thomas H. Kuchel, retired Los Angeles Superior Court Judge Victor R. Hansen, Mr. Oscar Jahnsen, Miss Margaret Bryan, the late Miss Helene R. MacGregor, and Mr. Merrell F. Small.

Personal assistance in my own family was rendered by my two daughters, Miss Susan Pollack, an *East Hampton* (N. Y.) *Star* reporter, Miss Deborah Pollack, a California college student, and my brother Mr. Albert L. Pollack of Philadelphia.

Above all, my deepest debt is reserved for Margit Chanin, my closest comrade, who typed the manuscript (along with Mrs. Evelyn Viesz and Mrs. Muriel Allard). A leading New York art dealer, she has tried to teach me the art of living while simultaneously enabling me, in many locales, to complete "The Book."

If I have failed to commend other deserving individuals for their help, here or elsewhere, I trust that they will compassionately understand my unintentional neglect. As courteous Earl Warren himself might have said, to have thanked them would only have been fair.

Index

Warren, Earl (*continued*)
  "humorless and prudish," 46
  left-handed, 21
  never planned to write memoirs, 302–3
  no middle initial, 17
  personality changes, 94–95
  "pick it up by the four corners," 48
  plainness, 350
  puritanism, 350
  Shriner, 353
  smoking, 28
  spoils system rejected, 86
  as presidential aspirant, 4–14
    1944 campaign, 5, 92–93
    1952 campaign, 6, 130–37, 287
    1956 campaign, 8–10, 183–84
  solicitor-generalship offered to, 146–47, 149, 155, 156
  speeches of, 45, 132, 179, 301, 309, 317, 319–21, 369
    1938 campaign, 64–65
    1948 acceptance, 112
    1949 Los Angeles, 4–5
    1954 Columbia, 170
    1955 on Bill of Rights, 30–31, 180–81, 346–47
    1963 Kennedy assassination, 224
  U.S. Attorney Generalship sought by, 72
  will of, 366–67
  in World War I, 33–35
  See also Warren Commission
Warren Earl, Jr. (son), 51, 124, 145–46, 212, 214, 258
Warren, Erik Methias (Matt; father), 17–22, 24–27, 29, 35, 41, 148
  correspondence courses of, 26, 63
  murder of, 61–63
  original name of, 17
  Warren's wife and, 41, 453
Warren, Ethel, *see* Plank, Ethel
Warren, James (son), 85, 124
Warren, Nina (wife), 38–41, 45, 51–53, 63, 122–23, 133, 157, 221, 327, 359
  broken foot of, 139
  children of, 51–52
  first marriage of, 40
  foreign trips of, 145–46, 148, 181
  marriage to Warren of, 42–43
  in 1948 campaign, 112, 115, 116
  pronunciation of first name of, 39
  refurnishing of Executive Mansion by, 87–88
  at Supreme Court sessions, 162, 164, 175, 181

  threats to, 52–53, 57
Warren, Nina Elizabeth ("Honeybear"; Mrs. Brian; daughter), 51, 100, 115, 133, 145–46, 148, 319
  illness of, 122–23, 327
Warren, Robert (son), 51, 111
Warren, Virginia (daughter), 51, 106, 115, 123, 145–46, 148, 175
Warren Act (California), 75
Warren Commission, 11, 228–59, 260
  photographs and X-rays from, 63, 245–46
  reactions to report, 253–58, 347–49
Watkins, Arthur V., 171
Watkins v. *United States*, 187–88
Webb, Ulysses S., 60
Weissman, Bernard, 241, 247
Welfare, 106
Wenzell, Adolph, 199
Werdel, Thomas H., 131, 134, 135
Westberry v. *Sanders*, 261
Wheeler, Burton K., 349
Wheeler, Stanton, 345
Whitaker-Baxter public relations advisors, 81
White, Byron, 213, 300, 328
Whitman, Alden, 333
Whitney v. *California,* 48
Whittaker, Charles E., 194, 212, 360
Whittington, Banning E. (Bert), 11, 165, 290, 361
Willens, Howard P., 232
Willey, Harold B., 162, 163
Willkie, Wendell, 74, 92–93
Wilson, Charles, 179
Wilson, Woodrow, 72
Wiretapping, 47–48, 169, 270–71, 289–90
Wisconsin Idea, 30
Wolfson, Louis E., 289
Wollenberg, Albert C., 81–82, 365
Workmen's compensation, 169
World Association of Judges, 303
World Bar Association, 213
World Peace Through Law Conference, 296, 303, 315, 347
World War I, Warren in, 33–35
World War II, 73–76, 85, 90–92, 126
Wright, Lloyd, 358
Wyzanski, Charles E., Jr., 151–52, 174–75, 197

Yarborough, Ralph W., 221, 357–58
Yates v. *United States,* 188–89
Yorty, Sam, 277

Zapruder, Abraham, 244, 246